THE POLI
LEO STRAUSS, UPDATED EDITION

Regards,
Shadia

The Political Ideas of Leo Strauss, Updated Edition

With a New Introduction By the Author

Shadia B. Drury

First St. Martin's Press paperback edition: 1988
PALGRAVE MACMILLAN™ updated edition: June 2005
175 Fifth Avenue, New York, N.Y. 10010 and
Houndmills, Basingstoke, Hampshire, England RG21 6XS
Companies and representatives throughout the world.

PALGRAVE MACMILLAN is the global academic imprint of the Palgrave Macmillan division of St. Martin's Press, LLC and of Palgrave Macmillan Ltd. Macmillan® is a registered trademark in the United States, United Kingdom and other countries. Palgrave is a registered trademark in the European Union and other countries.

ISBN 1–4039–6954–X

Library of Congress Cataloging-in-Publication Data

Drury, Shadia B., 1950–
    The political ideas of Leo Strauss.
    Bibliography: p.
    Includes index.
    1. Strauss, Leo—Contributions in political
science. I. Title.

JC251.S8D78   1987   320'.01   87–4778
ISBN 1–4039–6954–X

A catalogue record for this book is available from the British Library.

PALGRAVE MACMILLAN updated edition: June 2005

10 9 8 7 6 5 4 3 2 1

Printed in the United States of America.

To Dennis

Contents

Straussians in Power: Secrecy, Lies, and Endless War

When *The Political Ideas of Leo Strauss* was published in 1988, it astonished the academic community (including many of Strauss's students) because the analysis it presented of Strauss's political ideas was radically at odds with his reputation in the academy. The book painted a clear but disturbing picture of Strauss's political thought, which was based exclusively on an analysis of his published works. It provided extensive textual evidence to show that, contrary to received opinion, Strauss was not a traditional conservative nor a quiet interpreter of old texts, but a representative of a new brand of rabid, radical, nihilistic, and postmodern conservatism. Instead of being a defender of religion and a critic of moral relativism, the book revealed Strauss as an atheist and a moral nihilist who advocated the use of religion, morality, and family values as useful political tools by which to placate and manipulate the masses. Instead of being the self proclaimed protégé of Plato, the book revealed Strauss's political thought as a dark brew of ideas borrowed form Machiavelli, Freud, and Nietzsche. In short, the book showed that Strauss was a sworn enemy of freedom and democracy who believed that the best form of government is the absolute but covert rule of a 'wise' elite independent of law. And while some of Strauss's students quibbled with particular details of his view on this or that, the general picture has been quite undeniable.[1] And despite their staggering numbers within the academy, the Straussians have not managed to produce a comprehensive account of Strauss's work that could displace the critical analysis provided here.

In writing the book, I was primarily motivated by the desire to expose the purposeful deception and studied obscurantism of a school of thought that had become so prevalent that it threatened the meaningful exchange of ideas in the academy. My initial desire was to smoke the Straussians out of their caves and force them to defend their ideas openly before their peers. With the exception of a few candid exchanges, mostly in private, the exercise was rather futile. But the book was also intended as a warning that the tendency of Strauss's students to gravitate toward positions of political power is disconcerting because those who believe the things that Strauss believed are bound to behave badly when they are in positions of power and influence.[2]

The drift of Straussians from the academy into the highest levels of government has reached its zenith in the administration of George W. Bush. This has made Strauss a subject of great interest outside the academy. Highly publicized Straussians were among the most prominent neoconservatives who engineered the aggressive foreign policy of the Bush administration. There is no denying that Strauss shaped the minds of the men who embarked on a foreign policy that has had monumental ramifications for America and for the world. There is a clear link between theory and practice: there is a definite connection between the political ideas of Leo Strauss and the ruinous state of American democracy and its tragic foreign policy. These recent developments are the reason that the book is being republished (exactly as it appeared in 1988) with a new introduction.

No one represents the daunting political power of the Straussians in the Bush administration more than Paul Wolfowitz, Deputy Minister of Defense and assistant to Vice President Dick Cheney. Wolfowitz was one of the key architects of the war on Iraq and a self-proclaimed follower of Strauss. Wolfowitz was a student of Strauss in Chicago and then a student of Allan Bloom at Cornell. Bloom's *Closing of the American Mind* popularized the ideas of Strauss and used them to criticize American culture. Bloom denounced American liberal society for being empty, nihilistic, and meaningless. He compared his American students to 'naked animals' without the 'trappings of civilization', with nothing to live or die for.[3] He lamented that, unlike their parents, they did not have faith in God to fill the void, or a war effort to give their life meaning. In planning the war against Iraq, was Wolfowitz providing the cure to the malaise diagnosed by his teacher? Was he providing the antidote to modern nihilism? I do not pretend to know. What I do know is that enthusiasm for war is integral to Straussianism.

Wolfowitz is believed to be the Washington operative portrayed in Saul Bellow's novel *Ravelstein* who calls his aging professor for strategic political advice. And even though Bellow's portrait of Bloom misses the mark, Bellow gets one thing right – many of Strauss's students have been animated by a sense of mission – a mission of great political urgency to save America from her liberal decadence.[4] But, can a senseless war be a remedy for decadence?

Abram Shulsky, the Director of the Office of Special Plans, which was created by Secretary of Defense Donald Rumsfeld, was a student of Strauss. Shulsky was responsible for finding intelligence that would help to make the case for the war on Iraq. We know now that the intelligence was misleading, exaggerated, and even false. Shulsky has publicly declared that Strauss shaped his approach to politics in general and intelligence in particular. He tells us that he learned from Strauss that 'deception is the norm in political life'.[5] Shulsky no doubt imbibed Strauss's sense of crisis; and in the context of the perils at hand, what are a few big lies for those who have a grand and noble mission to save Western civilization from the dangers of liberal modernity? Nevertheless, Strauss would have been distressed at Shulsky's injudicious openness.

William Kristol, editor of the *Weekly Standard*, and chairman of 'The Project for the New American Century', in which the neoconservative foreign policy is clearly outlined, was a student of Harvey Mansfield at Harvard, who is another well-known follower of Strauss. Kristol wrote his doctoral thesis on Machiavelli – a topic that was as dear to Strauss as it was to Mansfield.[6] As I show in this book, Strauss denounced Machiavelli as a teacher of evil – but only because he made the mistake of stating the truth about politics in his own name, rather than putting it in the mouths of Sophists, madmen, women – or anyone who would not be believed.[7] Strauss endorsed Machiavellian tactics in politics – not just lies and the manipulation of public opinion, but every manner of unscrupulous conduct necessary to keep the masses in a state of heightened alert, afraid for their lives and their families, and therefore willing to sacrifice themselves for the nation. For Strauss as for Machiavelli, only the constant threat of a common enemy can save a people from becoming soft, pampered, and depraved. And if no enemy can be found, one must be invented.

It is worth noting that the best Straussians, those who fully understand Strauss, are the most dangerous and most strident of the neoconservatives; but not all neoconservatives are Straussians.

Even though Irving Kristol, the father of neoconservatism, acknowledges Strauss as the greatest influence on his thought,[8] most neoconservatives have not read Strauss, and those who have read him are not likely to have understood him. The relation of Strauss and the neoconservatives is complex, and I have dealt with it extensively elsewhere.[9] But there is no doubt that Strauss has bequeathed to the American neoconservatives a heady concoction of ideas that explains their penchant for secrecy, lies, and deception, their confidence in the almost limitless manipulation of public opinion, their aggressive foreign policy, their virulent nationalism, and their madly theological approach to politics.

There is clearly something in Strauss's thought that resonates with those who are disenchanted with liberalism. Whether they understand Strauss or not, all neoconservatives share his profound antipathy to secular liberal society (what Strauss referred to as 'modernity'). Like Strauss, neoconservatives are convinced that secular liberal society constitutes a 'crisis' that threatens Western civilization. This shared aversion to liberal society leads them to converge on the same policies – policies that are intended to 'turn back the clock' on the triumph of liberalism. Nothing short of the complete overhauling of liberal values will suffice; instead of freedom – virtue; instead of individuality – community and family values; instead of self-confidence – self-contempt; instead of leisure – self-immolation and self-sacrifice; instead of peace and order – perpetual war and struggle against the enemies of the nation; instead of skepticism and critical thinking – religion, mindless faith, and unswerving devotion to the nation and its God.

Strauss is the key to understanding the political vision that has inspired the most powerful men in America under George W. Bush.[10] In my view, men who are in the grip of Straussian political ideas cannot be trusted with political power in any society, let alone a liberal democracy. This book explains why this is the case.

When I wrote this book in the mid-1980s, I never dreamed that the tyranny of the 'wise' would ever come so close to being realized in the political life of a great nation like the United States. But fear has gripped Americans since the attacks of September 11, 2001, and fear is the greatest ally of tyranny. In my view, what is most troublesome about the neoconservatives is that in looking to Strauss for guidance, they are flirting with an ominous form of tyranny – a tyranny with an endless appetite for war, death, and sacrifice.

THE COVERT RULE OF THE WISE

I have never criticized Strauss for being elitist or anti-democratic. In *The Political Ideas of Leo Strauss*, I criticize Strauss for cultivating an arrogant, unscrupulous, and mendacious elite – an elite that has a profound contempt for the rule of law, for morality, for ordinary people, and for veracity. It is not his elitism, but the kind of elite that he has cultivated that I set out to criticize.

In my view, elitism is quite compatible with democracy. Every society, even the most democratic, is elitist. Liberal democracy is profoundly elitist. It differs from traditional aristocratic society in the way it justifies its inequalities. In liberal society, inequality is supposedly based on merit, not birth. Careers are open to talents – all talents regardless of birth. That is the liberal dream; but it is a half-truth at best. Democracy keeps liberalism honest; it keeps it striving for equality of opportunity, even if it sometimes forces liberalism to employ dubious methods in quest of that ideal. Democracy also allows people to choose the elites that govern them. And their choices may be wise or foolish. But if there are laws in place that set limits on what those in power can do, then those who rule are likely to cause less harm.

I am not under the democratic illusion that people actually govern themselves in a democracy. The best that any society can deliver is an *honest* ruling elite that respects the law, is grateful for its opportunities and privileges, mindful of the trust of its fellow citizens, and has ample regard for ordinary people – their common sense, their natural decency, and their right to equal protection under the law. But Strauss has taught his students a profound contempt for ordinary people. The latter must be ruled by the superior few – not honestly or with candid veracity, as Pericles ruled over democratic Athens, but by duping, deceiving, and manipulating them. In fact, Strauss states categorically that 'it is impossible for a wise man to benefit his city except by deceiving it'.[11] Strauss made this comment in the context of his defense of the treasonous and unscrupulous Athenian general, Alcibiades. Alcibiades was a student of Socrates, and his moral depravity is one of the reasons that Socrates was accused of corrupting the young. The statement is a measure of Strauss's contempt for democracy and for ordinary people – they cannot be persuaded; they must be duped.

Like Plato, Aristotle, and other aristocratic thinkers, Strauss thought that the rule of the wise is in theory the best regime. I am certainly inclined to agree. In theory, why would anyone be opposed to the rule of the wise? If the wise are good and care about truth and justice, there would be no objection to their rule – *in theory*. But there's the rub – there is no evidence that Strauss's wise elite is either good or just, even in theory. The evidence presented in this book reveals that Strauss's wise elite is duplicitous, double-crossing, and morally unscrupulous.

In this book, I document the gloomy nature of Strauss's elitism. Following what he supposedly regards as the wisdom of the ancients, Strauss denies that there is any natural right to liberty. Human beings are born neither free nor equal. The natural human condition is not one of freedom, but of subordination. And in Strauss's estimation, the ancients knew that there is in truth only one natural right – the right of the superior to rule over the inferior – the master over the slave, the husband over the wife, and the wise few over the vulgar many.[12]

The crux of the matter is that those who are destined for subordination have no rights in Strauss's scheme of things. Strauss's scholarship is profoundly deceptive. Even though his book, *Natural Right and History*, sports the Declaration of Independence, the book is intended to undermine the whole idea of natural rights. Notice that the term 'natural right' in the title is singular, not plural. The book starts with a criticism of relativism, in order to pave the way for the celebration of nature – not the natural rights of the Declaration (as the cover of the book would lead one to believe), but the natural order of domination and subordination.

In *On Tyranny*, Strauss refers to this classic natural right as the 'tyrannical teaching'. It was tyrannical in the classic sense of being rule above law or rule in the absence of law.[13] This is how Strauss interpreted the rule of the philosopher kings in Plato's *Republic*. But for Plato, the rule of the philosophers is unachievable. According to conventional wisdom, Plato settled for the rule of law as the best attainable regime. But Strauss does not endorse this solution entirely. Nor does he think that it is Plato's *real* solution – the real solution is for the wise to rule behind the scene.[14] They must draft laws; and they must pose as prophets so that people will believe that their laws are divinely inspired.[15] But the wise must also be free to ignore the laws whenever they find it advantageous to do so. Classic natural right is characterized by its 'flexibility' and its unwillingness to recognize any categorical imperatives.[16] In short, the real Platonic solution as understood by Strauss is the *covert tyranny of the wise.*

According to Strauss's esoteric teaching, the covert tyranny of the wise is made possible only by the *rule of gentlemen.* In this book, I document Strauss's understanding of the three types of men: the wise, the gentlemen, and the vulgar. The wise are the lovers of the harsh unadulterated truth. They are capable of looking into the abyss without fear and trembling; for they recognize neither God nor moral imperatives. They are devoted above all else to their own pursuit of the 'higher' pleasures, which amount to consorting with their 'puppies' or young initiates.[17] The second type is the gentlemen, who are lovers of honour and glory. They are the biggest dupes for the conventions of their society, or the 'illusions of the cave', in Straussian lingo. Gentlemen are the true believers in God, honour, and moral imperatives; as a result, they are ready and willing to embark on acts of great courage and self-sacrifice on a moment's notice. The third type is the vulgar many who are lovers of wealth and pleasure. They are selfish, slothful, and indolent. They can be inspired to rise above their brutish existence only by fear of impending death or catastrophe.

The covert rule of the philosophers is facilitated by the overwhelming credulity of the gentlemen. For all his nobility, the gentleman is gullible and unworldly. And the more gullible and unperceptive he is, the easier it is for the wise to control and manipulate him. The philosopher must impart to him the harsh truths about the world and about his inferiors without destroying his ideals. The message is this. You are noble and honest; and the world is bound to be a better place if noble men such as yourself reign supreme. But virtue is bound to be defeated if she is naïve enough to play by the rules. If you want political power and success, you have to rely on deception, guile, and fraud. Besides, you know what the ordinary masses are like; they are content to live and die like beasts – eating, drinking, gambling, and fornicating. If you wish to move them to acts of courage and self-sacrifice, you must make them believe that their very existence is under threat. Anyone who thinks that politics is possible without guile and fraud is a fool. In this way, the wise provide the gentlemen with a brutalizing education. George W. Bush may well have been the perfect gentleman.

Strauss maintained that the wise are also just. But in this book, I document Strauss's dual use of key words such as justice, piety, nobility, and the like. Strauss's insistence on the separation of moral from intellectual virtue is another way of saying that the wise are not morally trustworthy. In fact, deception and dissembling are intrinsic to the justice of the wise. The result is that Strauss has created a whole class of compulsive and self-righteous deceivers inside and outside the academy. And when they find their way into the corridors of power, they are likely to be treacherous and tyrannical.[18] And when they are found out and chastised, they will complain of persecution. And this will only confirm their belief in the necessity of proceeding more cautiously and with greater circumspection. But they never stop to think that maybe there is a connection between esotericism and persecution after all; but it is not what Strauss assumed it was. Maybe the philosophers are *not* persecuted because of their superiority; maybe they are persecuted because their secrecy rightly arouses suspicion. Maybe they are persecuted because people hate liars; they hate to live a lie; and they love truth, even if it is harsh.

For all his gloom when discussing the realities of political life, Strauss is bright and gay when it comes to the superior type. In fact, he regards comedy as the most appropriate medium for presenting the philosopher. This explains his admiration for Aristophanes. In Strauss's estimation, Aristophanes provides the most accurate picture of Socrates when he compares him to a dung beetle. Apparently, 'this small and contemptible beast' soars 'higher than the eagle of Zeus', enters the world of the gods, and 'sees with his own eyes the truth about the gods'.[19] As a result, this 'manly hero' manages to liberate himself from the fear of the gods that grips ordinary mortals. The philosopher does not weep, but laughs – at death, mortality, and even the gods. Strauss makes a point of telling us that Jesus weeps, but Socrates laughs.[20] Strauss thinks that the same view was subtly affirmed by Plato in the *Euthyphro*. According to Strauss, the dialogue is intended to show that Socrates is not pious in the ordinary sense of weeping, worshipping, and sacrificing. But if piety is redefined to mean imitating the gods, then the wise can be said to have their own brand of piety – just as they have their own brand of justice.[21]

Without mincing words, we can conclude that the piety of the wise consists in the imitation of the gods. And anyone who has the slightest familiarity with pagan gods knows that they are not in the least mournful or grim. They are intoxicated, erotic, and gay. And they are certainly not too concerned with the happiness of mere mortals. They have no pity or compassion for them. On the contrary, the pain, suffering, and tragedy of mortals provide them with entertainment. As Nietzsche explained, suffering is objectionable and senseless unless it is witnessed. Accordingly, mankind has invented gods to witness their suffering and give it meaning.[22] Only then, does suffering become heroic and significant. The gods witness the tragic fate of humanity without partaking in it. The Trojan wars and similar tragic atrocities were festivals for the gods, intended for their pleasure and amusement. In other words, the earth is a stage; and as human beings, we were obliged to keep it interesting. But Strauss knew that the gods are a fiction – the only real gods are the wise few who live secretly in the midst of ordinary mortals.

Strauss draws our attention to the similarity between the pagan gods and the philosopher when he points out that the philosopher is not a benefactor who is concerned with human affairs. On the contrary, the philosopher will be detached from human affairs and 'firmly settled' in the 'Islands of the Blessed', where the gods reside.[23] His attitude toward his inferiors is one of indifference or neglect.[24] It comes closest to Nietzsche's 'pathos of nobility and distance'.[25] It is difficult not to conclude that Strauss educates an elite of callous ruffians unfit for political power. So, when Strauss tells us that it is necessary to 'found an aristocracy within democratic mass society', we have every reason to expect the worst.[26]

SUBVERTING DEMOCRACY

There is an important difference between criticizing democracy and subverting it from within. I think that democracy deserves criticism because there is no evidence that democracy is a good form of government, let alone the best form of government. Why should the will of the majority be superior to the judgment of an educated, thoughtful elite of goodwill and decency? Is the will of the majority anything more than the collective might of the most numerous? Is democracy rooted in anything more than the principle that might is right?

We live in a democratic age that takes the goodness of democracy for granted. But as democracy becomes more and more corrupted, we must return to the roots of our democratic tradition and ask the fundamental question: On what ground has democracy been defended as a form of government?

Aristotle, who was no great friend of democracy, admitted that democratic forms of government have at least two claims to legitimacy. First, two heads are better than one. The process of public debate and deliberation is itself of value. Not only does it satisfy human gregariousness, it brings to light the advantages and disadvantages of alternative policies. In so doing, it enhances the rational and deliberative powers necessary to make wise choices. Only those who think that their wisdom is unassailable and cannot possibly be enhanced by listening to other points of view, are likely to reject the contribution that democracy can make. Second, even those who do not themselves have practical wisdom are capable of judging if others are fit to rule – just as someone who has no expertise in house-building can judge if a house is well built by living in it.

Despite these advantages, democracy is nevertheless a form of government that has serious shortcomings. It is vulnerable to the tyranny of the majority over individuals and minorities. And the tyranny of the majority is just as bad as any other tyranny. Like other forms of government, democracy is good only when the power of the people is limited by laws and constitutions. The liberal tradition – with its emphasis on the rule of law and the protection of individual rights – prevents democracy from collapsing into mob rule.

Nevertheless, liberal democracy is still vulnerable to the rise of demagogues who are skilled at the manipulation of the people through a combination of deceit, chicanery, and great rhetorical skill. In times of crisis and despair, it is easy for demagogues to convince the people that they have the solutions to all their ills, if only they could act without hindrance or constraint. In such times, the people come to see the checks on power as unnecessary obstacles to their safety and security. Eventually, the rule of law itself becomes an impediment to the rule of the superior – a nuisance that prevents the elite from providing the needed salvation. Demagogues are not critics of democracy; they are intent on sabotaging it from within. There is absolutely nothing wrong with being a critic of democracy, especially in a liberal democratic age. Only by being cognizant of its shortcomings can we avoid the pitfalls of tyranny to which all regimes are liable. But criticizing democracy and being cognizant of its shortcomings is one thing, and subverting it from within is another. Criticizing it can potentially make it better or guard against it being worse than it has to be. But sabotaging it from within exploits its vulnerabilities by destroying the rule of law, the checks on executive power, and the like. All this is likely to be done by an elite in the misguided belief that it has special access to truth, unrivaled wisdom, unassailable insight, and no need for any limitations on its power whatsoever. This is precisely the sort of tyrannical elite that is intellectually disposed to sabotage democracy. This is precisely the sort of elite that Strauss cultivated. Strauss thought that he was following Plato's idea of the philosopher king; but as I show in this book, his vision comes much closer to Nietzsche's superman – but without the latter's softer side.[27]

When the treacherous and unscrupulous Alcibiades was accused by the Athenians of plotting to subvert their democracy and establish a tyranny, Strauss came to his defense, saying that the Athenian distrust of Alcibiades is typical of the democratic distrust of the superior few, and that if Alcibiades was really plotting a tyranny, it would have been the best thing for Athens.[28] The fact that Alcibiades, an Athenian general in the Peloponnesian Wars, betrayed Athens by offering his services to her Spartan enemy, is also excused by Strauss, who claimed that it was the fault of the *demos* – Alcibiades had 'practically no choice but to escape to Sparta, to become a traitor to his fatherland, . . . and to embark on a policy of amazing versatility'.[29] But surely, this nonsense reveals Strauss's partiality. Alcibiades had a choice. He did not have to escape to Sparta. He could have defended himself against the charges. And if he could not defend himself because he was guilty, or because he was not confident that he would get a fair trial, then he could have sought refuge in some obscure city state. Instead, he went to Sparta and offered her his military expertise.

When Strauss is criticized for his anti-liberal and anti-democratic views, his disciples come to his defense by steadfastly maintaining that he is a champion of liberal democracy. On one level this is a bold-faced lie, which has made it (and continues to make it) impossible to have any meaningful discourse about Strauss. But on another level, there is a sense in which Strauss was not opposed to democracy any more than he was opposed to the brute reality of life. He believed that political affairs mirror nature, where the strong will always rule over the weak. So, even though the superior are *entitled* to rule over the inferior many, no one can ignore the sheer force of numbers. And this is why Strauss cannot object to democracy without also objecting to the brutal reality of existence. But to say this is not to say that he is a democrat, let alone a *liberal* democrat.

Strauss had a special dread of *liberal* democracy because he associated it with the Weimar Republic in Germany – the regime in which Hitler emerged supreme. The ghosts of Weimar inform all of Strauss's work.[30] He feared that what happened in Germany could happen in the United States, and he wanted his students to learn from his experience. Strauss assumed that liberal democracy is a spineless regime without any firm beliefs – a regime ruled by the rabble as represented by Hitler. Strauss confused the principle of equal rights and equal dignity before the law with a nightmarish egalitarianism.[31] And he surmised that when the rabble reigns supreme, the superior few will inevitably be persecuted. For Strauss, the plight of the Jews in Germany and the plight of Socrates and Alcibiades in Athens represented the fate of the superior at the hands of the inferior. Strauss therefore surmised that liberal democracy poses the greatest threat to the superior type.

Surely, one moment's reflection reveals that this analysis is seriously flawed. Athens was the embodiment of democracy as mob rule or tyranny of the majority. It was not a *liberal* democracy with a constitution protecting the rights of individuals and minorities. Nor were there any checks and balances on the power of the mob. Besides, everything we know about Alcibiades indicates that he was a scoundrel, and the jury is still out on Socrates.

There is no doubt that we live in a democratic age; but it can hardly be described as an age in which excellence, superiority, and human greatness are persecuted. We live in an age in which athletic, scientific, and artistic achievements are worshipped; we live in an age of super-athletes, super-heroes, and supermodels.

Moreover, the principle of equality before the law is no threat to excellence and superiority. Justice requires it. Far from being subversive of excellence, this principle is necessary for the rule of law, without which no society can claim to be excellent.

Strauss is right about one thing. Democracies are always vulnerable to the rise of demagogues. Hitler did come to power in a democracy. But he quickly amassed power to himself, subverted the rule of law, and ran roughshod over civil rights. Anyone who hopes to avoid the horrors of the Nazi past should not decry the *liberal* restraints on democracy – rule of law, protection of civil rights, limitations on executive power, and the like. In other words, anyone who hopes to avoid the horrors of the Nazi past had better not rely on the inspiration of Nietzsche, Heidegger, and Carl Schmitt – as Strauss did.

It is not liberalism, but Strauss's philosophy that invites the horrors of the Nazi past. Strauss's conviction that there is no disagreement among the wise, who instinctively recognize the truth and know what is to be done, mirrors Hitler's celebration of the genius who can learn nothing from the discussions and deliberations of others. Strauss's contempt for ordinary people, and for philosophical debate, mirrors Hitler's contempt for Parliament as a useless debating society.[32] Strauss's insistence on lies, myths, and illusions as necessary for the vulgar many, echoes Mussolini's paean to myths and illusions and Hitler's reliance on propaganda as a means for controlling and manipulating the masses. The centrality of the enemy (including the internal enemy) reveals the close alliance of Strauss's politics with the politics of the Nazi jurist, Carl Schmitt.[33] Finally, Strauss's 'tyrannical teaching' betrays a disregard for law and due process that is characteristic of tyrants of every stripe.

Strauss and his followers talk incessantly about the 'crisis of liberal democracy'. They believe that they have diagnosed the source of the malaise and know just how to alleviate the symptoms. Straussians and neoconservatives believe that the liberal elite is the problem. Liberals, especially those in positions of power and influence, are the internal enemy. If America is to be saved, the liberal elite must be replaced with the neoconservative or 'Leo-conservative' elite. And this has indeed come to pass. But far from 'ennobling democracy', Strauss and his neoconservative admirers have contributed to the 'crisis' of liberal democracy that they fulminated about so endlessly.

The administration of George W. Bush can be understood as a historical manifestation of the Straussian subversion of liberal democracy with secrecy and lies.[34] The catastrophe of September 11, 2001, created the perfect conditions in which the liberal elements of the regime were undermined. Exaggerating and exploiting the threat to the nation, the Bush administration managed to increase its executive power. It convinced Congress to surrender its right to declare war. It persuaded Congress to pass the Patriot Act, which gave police and the executive branch of government unprecedented powers. It is now possible for people to be arrested and held indefinitely without charge, without legal council, and without a trial. And if Daniel Ellsberg is right, there is a more radical and far-reaching version of the Patriot Act waiting for another perfect opportunity – another terrorist attack and a heightened climate of fear – to facilitate its approval by Congress. The American people were asked by their president to get used to their lack of freedom as the 'new normal', as if their compliance with this state of affairs was a patriotic act. Meanwhile, foreigners – especially those who have been critical of the administration in print – are afraid to travel to America.

Led by the neoconservatives, the administration of George W. Bush used lies to manipulate public opinion in order to justify a costly and needless war – the invasion of Iraq in 2003. It misled the American people into thinking that the tyrannical Saddam Hussein of Iraq had stockpiles of the most lethal weapons of mass destruction known to man and that he was connected to al-Qaeda, the militant Islamic terrorist organization led by Osama bin Laden that attacked the World Trade Center in New York on September 11, 2001. During the invasion of Iraq, over one thousand young Americans lost their lives and over one hundred thousand Iraqis were slaughtered by a bombing campaign of 'shock and awe'. But interestingly, the Iraqis were not intimidated by the superior firepower of the Americans, who were faced with a vicious insurgency, and as I write, they are still mired in what seems to be a war without end. Meanwhile, the lies that led the country into war have been exposed. There were no weapons of mass destruction and no connection between the secular dictatorship of Saddam Hussein and the militant Islamic terrorists. In its own defense, the administration and its neoconservative elite have claimed that they were misled by faulty intelligence. But that too has been exposed as a lie. The intelligence was not faulty – it was cooked up by an administration with an appetite for war and conquest.[35] The only reason for the war was 'regime change' or the desire to remake the world according to the whims of the administration. But that would have been a hard sell.

The purposeful misleading of the populace tramples on the most fundamental principle of democratic politics – trust. In a democracy the people entrust the ruling elite with power and they trust that the power will not be abused; they trust that their sons and daughters will not be needlessly sacrificed. A government that elicits the ultimate sacrifice from its people under false pretences forfeits their trust. Many of the people who marched in the streets protesting the war before it started were rightly suspicious that their government was involved in deception – that Saddam Hussein had no nuclear weapons and no capacity to make them.[36]

The neoconservatives have inherited from Strauss an unduly extravagant confidence in the ability of the elite to manipulate the 'images in the cave' or to shape the perception of reality among the populace – and that includes Congress. And even a free media is often willing to go along with the filtering of information, selective reporting, and the like – for love of country, of course. During the war on Iraq, only dead enemy soldiers were seen on television, but not dead American soldiers. And when the American casualties took a sharp rise after the President declared 'major combat operations' over, the White House banned cameras from portraying the body bags of American soldiers being loaded onto aircrafts. Nor was the control of public opinion limited to the media. It extended to the Universities with the creation of the infamous Campus Watch project by Daniel Pipes to monitor and intimidate University professors who were critical of Israeli or American foreign policy. Students were encouraged to inform on their professors. The American Council of Trustees and Alumni, which was established by Lynne Cheney (wife of Vice President Dick Cheney) and Senator Joseph Lieberman, accused the academy of being unpatriotic and anti-American. Dissent became treasonous.

The neoconservative efforts to shape reality were not limited to the home front. They made every effort to shape the opinions of their enemies. So much so that the Bush administration conducted what it called 'Perception Management Operations'.

These were intended to win the hearts and minds of the people of Iraq, Afghanistan, and the Muslim world. A report from the 'Advisory Group on Diplomacy for the Arab and Muslim World' tried to explain why they have not been successful in improving the American image in the Muslim world. They surmised it was lack of funds, and lack of research into the vagaries of the Muslim mind. The report sounds as postmodern and Nietzschean as Strauss. It reads as if reality is irrelevant.[37] It reads as if the world is made of primordial stuff on which the strongest, the most ingenious, or the most galling can impose their own order, their own truth, and their own justice.

The neoconservatives have learned a great deal from Strauss's postmodern conception of 'noble lies'. And it must be admitted that postmodernity has removed the stigma that was once associated with lying. In the absence of any reality independent of power, the creative art rules supreme. In such a world, truth is construction. Lying is simple creativity. Politics is no longer the domain of judicious lying, or lying to the enemy to ensure survival or avert annihilation. Lying has become synonymous with politics, and politics has become ubiquitous. In such a world, what could be more creative than lying? After all, a great lie, one that is believed, gives form to the void, imposes order on chaos, and creates the world out of nothing. But not everyone is equal in the art of creative lying. Those who excel will no doubt subvert the truths of the defeated. In the end, the superior few will triumph and truth will be simply the interest of the stronger – that is, the most skilled and most creative liars.

The neoconservative justification of lying and deception has its source in the Straussian conviction that the people cannot be trusted. They must be led by worldly statesmen who are cognizant of the dangers – not the usual ineffectual liberal elites. Nor can the people be persuaded. They are inclined to cling doggedly to their civil liberties, unmindful of the risks. They cannot be expected to understand the urgent need for the expansion of government surveillance and detention powers. Nor can the people be expected to appreciate the necessity of lavish spending on the military. Even less are they likely to comprehend the efficacy of pre-emptive strikes, arbitrary arrests, secret detentions, indefinite incarcerations, military tribunals, and summary executions. In short, a free people cannot be expected to endorse the activities of the Bush administration – at least not without a well-orchestrated campaign of deceit and duplicity intended to manufacture an ominous sense of foreboding.

THE *CON* IN NEOCONSERVATISM

Neoconservatism is Straussian not only in its content, but also in its form; like Strauss, it is a master of double-speak. The only aspect of neoconservatism that is not indebted to Strauss is its economics – Strauss had a European contempt for commerce and no interest in economics. But even the economic policies of the neoconservatives are highly duplicitous. In other words, there is a great deal of *con* in neo*con* ideology.

Let's start with the economic con. The economic rhetoric of the neoconservatives is liberal and individualistic: we will cut the government down to size; we will get the government out of your pocketbook; we will cut taxes and put the money in your pocket; we trust individuals to create jobs, to look after their own affairs, and to pull themselves up by their own bootstraps. All this is good liberal talk that resonates well in an individualistic liberal culture. But in truth, the neoconservative enthusiasm for capitalism is not a concession to liberal individualism, but quite the contrary. It is corporate capitalism that the neoconservatives champion – and corporate capitalism is compatible with a conservative and Straussian vision of society because it requires authority, discipline, conformity, and hierarchy.

Then there is the conservative con. Neoconservatism is too radical to be conservative in any meaningful sense of the term. Classic conservatism is appealing precisely because it has modest expectations of politics; it eschews all utopian projects as dangerous dreams. Classic conservatism is moderate and wary of radical change because it understands that society cannot be built like a brick house. Classic conservatism values order and stability above all else. In contrast, neoconservatism is bent on radical change; for there is nothing in the liberal present that it cares to conserve – except the exploitative excesses of corporate capitalism.

The radical and immoderate character of neoconservatism has been vividly illustrated by President George W. Bush. In an interview with *Christianity Today*, Bush gave classic expression to the neoconservative commitment to the dramatic transformation of *both America and the world.* He claimed that his job as president is to 'change cultures'.[38] He explained that his intention is not only to transform Iraq and the whole of the Middle East, but also the United States. Describing his presidency, he said: 'it is a historic opportunity to change the world and change the country'.[39] He described the cultural shift as a shift from a 'feel good society' to 'the responsibility era'. The 'feel good society' is a clear reference to American liberal society – it is an accurate description of liberalism, which tells us that we should be free to do whatever feels good as long as we do not harm others. In contrast, the 'responsibility era' emphasizes virtue, community, discipline, and self-sacrifice. To herald the coming of this new era, the president told his audience that he will rely on his military abroad and his 'army of compassion' and their 'faith-based initiatives' at home. On his part, he promised to pass a constitutional amendment called 'The Marriage Act' that would save America from the onslaught of same-sex marriages and other liberal follies. He also promised to create a 'culture of life' that would eventually outlaw abortion. What he did not say is that the restrictions on abortion are integral to the grand plan because a ban might keep women busy having babies – lots of babies. In this way, women will become useful once again; they will return to their vocation as factories for soldiers – after all, America will need lots of soldiers in her endless struggle to conquer and transform the world.

A genuinely conservative and reasonable president would not regard his job as an opportunity to transform the world. A genuinely conservative and modest president would consider his job to be maintaining order, guaranteeing respect for the Constitution, and defending America's long-term interests around the world. No president with conservative or sensible instincts would embark on world transformation. But the Evangelical audience was not in the least perturbed by President Bush's apocalyptic vision – they were familiar with the apocalypse and comfortable with a jihadist mentality of global proportions.

So, how will America be transformed? Here is where the political con comes into play. Irving Kristol came up with the solution that has become the cornerstone of neoconservative politics: use democracy to defeat liberty. Turn the people against their own liberty. Convince them that liberty is licentiousness; that liberty leads to crime, drugs, rampant homosexuality, children out of wedlock, and family breakdown. And worst of all, liberal society is soft on communism or terrorism – or whatever happens to be the enemy of the moment. And if you can convince people that liberty undermines their security, then you will not have to take away their liberty; they will gladly renounce it.

In an essay entitled 'The New Populism: Not to Worry', Irving Kristol argued that Americans should embrace populism, or the rule of the majority, despite the reservations of the Founding Fathers.[40] This is what I have called the 'populist ploy', in which radical democracy or populism is used to undermine the liberal elements that moderate and set limits to the tyranny of the majority.[41] The result is not a more democratic society, as the rhetoric of the neoconservatives would have us believe – the result is an oligarchic society led by an elite of 'gentlemen' and CEOs. Far from being democratic and populist, neoconservatism uses populism as a ploy for anti-liberal as well as anti-populist ends.

In the election of 2004, the populist ploy succeeded. Democracy was successfully used to defeat liberty and social justice. The majority of Americans voted for a government that eroded civil rights while undermining the traditional liberal limitations on executive power. Frightened Americans voted for a government that declared a permanent state of emergency as an excuse for suspending the rule of law. Devout Christians voted for a government that promised to defeat evil. Working-class Americans voted for a government that was antithetical to their material interests – a government whose fiscal policies consisted in massive tax cuts for the rich, at a time when a costly war drove government deficits to record highs. Ordinary people voted for a government that sacrificed their children in a senseless war, while giving its corporate friends the spoils of war in the form of oil revenues and reconstruction contracts in Iraq.

Neoconservative ideology is laced with deception. Far from being conservative and moderate, neoconservatism is radical. Far from being populist, neoconservatism is elitist and oligarchic. Far from being democratic, neoconservatism subverts democracy with its lies and deceptions. There is perhaps one thing that neoconservatism is honest about – its visceral hatred of liberalism. But even *that* is concealed by a blurring of the distinction between freedom and democracy, both at home and abroad.

The neoconservatives have the gall to conquer the world in the name of liberty and democratic evangelism. But on careful examination, it turns out that what they mean by liberty is free trade, córporate capitalism, and global economic hegemony of their corporate friends and allies. And what they mean by democracy is rule of the manipulated majority.

FOREIGN POLICY FIASCO

In a famous document, known as the 'Project for the New American Century', written in June of 1997, a group of powerful neoconservatives set out to 'rally support for American Global leadership'.[42] The Project is intended to inspire a 'foreign policy that boldly and purposefully promotes American principles abroad' and 'shapes a new century' favorable to American interests and American 'global leadership'. The policy consists of four recommendations: (1) increase defense spending, including the development and deployment of Global missile defenses to defend the American homeland; create a new military – U.S. Space Forces for the control of space and cyberspace; (2) strengthen ties to democratic allies to help America defeat her enemies; (3) find leaders willing to accept America's 'global responsibility', which is defined as creating an 'international order friendly to our security, our prosperity, and our principles'.[43] The document was signed by Dick Cheney, Donald Rumsfeld, Paul Wolfowitz, William J. Bennett, Jeb Bush, Norman Podhoretz, Midge Decter, Donald Kagan, Dan Quayle, Francis Fukuyama, and others. William Kristol, the son of Irving Kristol, was the 'chairman of the Project'.

The document is clear and urgent. America's military pre-eminence provides an unprecedented opportunity – this 'unipolar moment' must be seized to create a global order favorable to American interests, principles, and values. There is no hesitation or doubt that America's interests may come into conflict with her values and principles – at which point there might be difficult choices to make. The fallacious assumption is that American interests, narrowly understood, will never have to be sacrificed for the sake of American values and principles.

There is no bashfulness or secrecy associated with this document. It is posted on the World Wide Web for all to see. This is not intended as a clandestine plot for world tyranny. It is an opportunity – not only for America, but for the world; an opportunity for the world to get rid of all the dictators and exchange them for American democracy and its attendant prosperity. It is a candid expression of the commitment to 'regime change' or world transformation.

The Project provides a chilling vision of America's global dominance, which is referred to as the 'Pax Americana'. It proposes several 'theater wars' fought simultaneously in different parts of the globe away from the American homeland. Theater wars are defined as 'small wars' that are limited to particular locales and do not involve the entire world in a nuclear conflagration.[44] This is not to say that theater wars will not resort to nuclear weapons if that proves to be necessary. It also recommends the use of space as a new 'theater' of war, the development of unmanned aerial vehicles, and a global monopoly over weapons of mass destruction. The aim is to remove all adversarial, unfriendly, or undemocratic regimes from power and replace them with 'constabulary operations' or 'post-combat stability operations'.[45] With the Soviet Union out of the way, war is possible again (what a relief!). The fallacious assumption is that all unfriendly or anti-American regimes are bound to be undemocratic. In other words, the assumption is that all democratic regimes will accept American values and principles, and by implication, will serve American interests.

The document is intoxicated with power and the glorification of war as a means to political ends. Bold, daring, decisive, quick, global, combat-readiness – these are the watchwords. The spirit of the document is the antithesis of the modesty and cautious reserve that are the hallmarks of conservative politics. Like all radical political projects, it reduces politics to craftsmanship. It reads as if the world were clay or putty to be shaped according to American desire and design.

This conception of politics is devoid of all plurality – which is the very condition that makes politics necessary. As Hannah Arendt has rightly pointed out, this rejection of plurality, this insistence on shaping the world according to a single vision, is the hallmark of totalitarianism.

The goal is clear: every corner of the globe, every recalcitrant regime, every unbending knee, will bow to American power, serve her interests, and acknowledge her 'principles'. The only thing that is missing is the will to take on the task. And in an ominous prediction, the authors anticipate that some dreadful catastrophe, comparable to Pearl Harbor, will be necessary to awaken

America from her military slumber.[46] The opportunity material-
ized with the attacks of September 11, 2001. In what follows, I will
examine the intellectual roots of what I believe is a foreign policy
fiasco.

HYPER REALISM

Neoconservative foreign policy is a melange of three distinct
elements that I will call: hyper realism, sugar-coated realism, and
an enlightenment dream. Hyper realism is a hard-headed but
simple-minded brand of political realism, which I will distinguish from a more sophisticated or classic realism. Sugar-coated
realism is a political realism that is sweetened with a feverish
nationalism and a zealously militant religiosity. Hyper realism
has its source in Donald Kagan and sugar-coated realism has
its source in Leo Strauss. The enlightenment dream belongs to
Kant – but is filtered through the pessimistic lens of Strauss. I will
discuss each of these elements in turn.

Irving Kristol tells us that thanks to Kagan and Strauss, the
neoconservatives consider the most important text in foreign
affairs to be the work of Thucydides on the Peloponnesian Wars
(431–404 B.C.).[47] Both Kagan and Strauss consider Thucydides to
be the father of political realism.

Simply stated, political realism is the view that war will always
be part of the human condition, since there will always be a competition for power, because the desire for power is integral to
human nature and therefore unavoidable. Modern realists tend
to regard power as the ability to impose one's will on others –
usually by force. As a result they tend to think of power as
something akin to original sin. Kagan thinks that Thucydides
anticipated the modern doctrine of realism in the famous dialogue between the Athenians and the Melians. (This is the dialogue in which the Athenians try to persuade the Melians to
submit to the superior power of Athens for no reason other than
that the quest for power is natural and that the weak must yield
to the strong – because that is the way the world is.)[48] But Kagan
is critical of the modern doctrine of political realism because it
takes a very narrow and negative view of power. Inspired
by Thucydides, Kagan argues that power is 'neutral', and he
defines it as the 'capacity to resist the demands and compulsions

of others', which is to say that power is 'essential for the achievement and preservation of freedom'.[49]

Kagan shares the realist view that the quest for power is natural. But he thinks that Thucydides understood power more profoundly and more elegantly because he explained that people are
motivated to seek power as a result of 'honor, fear, and interest'.
Interest is a fairly clear motivation, but in Kagan's view, it is not
the decisive one. Fear is another motive, which is rooted in the
apprehension that we might live in a world defined by our enemies, where we might be compelled to do things we do not wish
to do, and so lose our freedom and autonomy. But in Kagan's
view, honor is the most important motivator of all. Kagan rightly
defines honor as regard, respect, or prestige in the world. Kagan
thinks that power and honor are reciprocal:

> When a state's power grows, the deference and respect in
> which it is held are likely to grow as well. But the opposite is
> also true: even when its material power appears to remain the
> same, it really declines if in some manner these attitudes
> toward it change. This happens most frequently when a state is
> seen to lack the will to use its material power.[50]

For Kagan, military might gives the state honor and respect; but
to maintain this respect, a state must be willing to use the power
at its disposal; otherwise, it will not be respected and will lose its
prestige and then its power.

The story of the Peloponnesian Wars can be read as a caution-
ary tale in which a prosperous democratic city (Athens) was
defeated and destroyed by an inferior city (Sparta) because of her
over-reaching ambitions, her bellicosity, her hunger for power,
and her quest for empire. But Kagan read the story as a caution-
ary tale in which a great city lost her power and prestige because
she failed to use all the military might at her disposal. In other
words, it was not that she was too imperial, but that she was not
imperial enough. And this is the lesson that Kagan applied to
modern-day America. For example, Kagan criticized President
John F. Kennedy's failure to wholeheartedly support the Bay of
Pigs invasion of Cuba by expatriates trained by the CIA. (The
invasion led the Soviets to establish nuclear installations in Cuba.
When the invasion failed, Kennedy threatened the Soviets with
retaliation if they did not withdraw their installations; and they

withdrew in exchange for America's assurance that she will allow the Castro regime to survive.) Kagan thinks that Kennedy's failure to use all the military power at his disposal to make sure that the invasion succeeded led to American loss of prestige and power in the world.[51] Kagan does not credit Kennedy's restraint with averting nuclear annihilation. The Cuban Missile Crisis is a complex affair, and I don't propose to do it justice here, but I wonder if any of us would be alive to discuss it had President Kennedy relied on Kagan as his trusted advisor.

The American defeat in Vietnam is a particular source of shame and humiliation for the neoconservatives. Irving Kristol and other neoconservatives believe that the defeat in Vietnam was due to American reluctance to use the full force of the military power at her disposal. And this led to loss of respect and loss of power. And like Kagan, they have been eager to restore American honor through the display of military might. They saw Iraq as an opportunity; and after the humiliation of September 11, 2001, the opportunity became irresistible.[52]

The weakness of the neoconservative approach to international affairs has its source in Kagan's fallacious view of honor, deference, and respect. It seems to me that there is deference that comes from fear and deference that comes from respect; and these are not the same. Deference that comes from fear will give you power, but only as long as you are able to coerce. But as soon as your back is turned, as soon as you let your guard down, your enemies will vent their hatred and contempt with whatever they have at their disposal. But perpetual vigilance is impossible. No amount of military power and coercion can succeed in ruling others, let alone the whole world. You can coerce only a minority. To rule over a population you need the voluntary compliance of the majority; and you can't expect that compliance without the deference that comes from respect, not fear. We live at a time when America surpasses all other nations in military power. And under the influence of the neoconservatives, she has been flaunting her military power. Shock and awe will not bring respect – it can only inspire fear and contempt, which diminish power. The neoconservative fixation on the display of military might has diminished American power and security. Despite their unsurpassed military might, Americans are perhaps more vulnerable than any other people – both at home and abroad.

It is important to distinguish the hyper realism of Kagan from the classic realism of Thomas Hobbes. Far from being profound and sophisticated, Kagan's hyper realism is simple-minded and naïve. Hobbes compared international affairs to a lawless state of nature in which there is an endless struggle for power after power ending only in death. In Hobbes's state of nature, no one, no matter how powerful, is secure. The most powerful individuals need to sleep or relax, at which point they are vulnerable to the machinations of the weak. The weakest person in the state of nature can kill the strongest. This is why Hobbes did not endorse the view that justice is the invention of the weak – the view of the Sophists, which is subtly endorsed by Strauss and loudly articulated by the Kagan realists.[53] Hobbes's state of nature is not just a fiction but an accurate description of international affairs. What is true for individuals in Hobbes's state of nature is true for nations. The attacks of September 11, 2001, revealed the truth of Hobbes's claim – namely, that the weakest has enough power to kill the strongest. And needless to say, the military control of space would have done nothing to secure America against the terrorist attack.

There is no doubt that being struck so forcefully and so terribly by a few terrorists acting independently of state power, was a huge blow to America's military ego. It came as a shock: how could we suffer such a lethal blow despite our unrivalled military power? In response to this question, the Bush administration started thinking like Kagan: maybe we lost our power and prestige because we have been reluctant to use the military might at our disposal. So, let's display our power and show the world what we can do. The war on Afghanistan and the occupation of Iraq were the result. 'Shock and awe' was the motto of the minister of defense. And taunting the terrorists, President Bush said: 'bring it on'. But all this display of military might was just an expression of rage that the hyper realism of the neoconservative foreign policy has turned out to be inadequate. Military might alone cannot guarantee security. Even the most powerful nation needs allies. Even the most powerful nation needs to deal more equitably with the powerless and disenfranchised to avoid the manifestations of their rage.

I think that it is instructive to compare American military might in the world to the strength and power of Gulliver among the Lilliputians, in Jonathan Swift's tale. According to Swift, the Lilliputians were so tiny that when they were a nuisance to

Gulliver, he was tempted to grab the first fifty that came within his reach and smash them against the ground. American neoconservatives are so intoxicated with American military might that they are inclined to treat the world as Gulliver was tempted to treat the Lilliputians. And they assume that America's unparalleled strength allows her to do whatever she pleases with impunity. But Gulliver had more sense. He resisted the temptation to underestimate the 'intrepidity of these diminutive mortals'. He realized that the enmity of the Lilliputians can be dangerous because they are so numerous. Their arrows were like little needles, but there were so many of them that they could easily have blinded Gulliver. So, he did not underestimate their collective power; he understood that they could hurt him. Besides, Gulliver realized that he needed sleep and could not remain forever vigilant against the schemes of all these hostile little people. He realized that in his sleepy moments, he would be vulnerable to their machinations.

Gulliver could easily have eaten five of the Lilliputians in a mouthful, but he decided to impress them by his clemency instead. He made a point of walking with the utmost circumspection in order to avoid treading on any of them. He was careful to observe the laws recognized by the Lilliputians, and did not make himself an exception to the rules that applied to others.

In contrast, American neoconservatives think that America's strength makes her an exception to the laws that are recognized by the community of nations. They think that the strong can do as they please with no regard to justice or to international law. Echoing his father Donald Kagan, Robert Kagan expressed this view in his book *Of Paradise and Power*. He stated bluntly that the concern with justice and international law is relevant only for the weak. It is a strategy by which the weak 'try to get their way in the world'.[54] The strong will do as they please. Europe is concerned with justice and multilateral action only because she is weak; but since America is strong, she can act unilaterally with no regard to either international law or world opinion.

This attitude explains America's flippant indifference to the community of nations. She has snubbed the Kyoto Accord to reduce greenhouse gases; she has refused to accept any limits on her power that the World Court might conceivably entail; and she has blithely ignored the Geneva Convention in the treatment at Guantánamo Bay of her prisoners of war, whom she has dubbed 'terrorists' and 'unlawful combatants'. Far from enhancing her power and prestige, America's conduct has made her an outlaw in the community of nations. In short, Kagan's hyper realism has been a failure.

SUGAR-COATED REALISM

Most neoconservatives are not satisfied with the hard-headed realism of Donald Kagan. They prefer a brand of political realism that was bequeathed to them by Leo Strauss. The Straussian brand of political realism is sugar-coated with a potent elixir of religious faith and nationalism – but it is hyper realism nevertheless.

Strauss expressed this brand of political realism in his commentaries on Thucydides, Plato, Machiavelli, Hobbes, and Carl Schmitt. At first blush, Strauss's political realism appears classic: appeals to justice are irrelevant in international affairs, unless the parties are equal in strength or power. Where the parties are unequal, the strong will dominate the weak.[55] The 'justice' of the state consists in doing good to friends (i.e., fellow citizens) and evil to enemies or outsiders. You will recall that this was the definition of justice suggested by Polemarchus that Socrates rejects in Plato's *Republic*. But in commenting on Plato's text, Strauss writes:

> Polemarchus's opinion properly understood is the only one among the generally known views of justice discussed in the first book of the *Republic* which is *entirely* preserved in the positive or constructive part of the work.[56]

As I show at greater length in the book, Strauss endorses a crude political realism. But that is not the whole story. Strauss makes his realism more potent by appealing to Thucydides.

Strauss tells us that Thucydides was much more than just an advocate of 'power politics' (i.e., political realism).[57] He recognized that military might was not the real secret of military success. When the Athenians saved all of Greece by defeating the Persians at Salamis, Sparta was militarily superior to Athens. But the Athenians were 'singularly public spirited', and there was no sacrifice that they were unwilling to bear for their city.[58] What made Athens 'worthy of Empire is not the large navy but the zeal and intelligence shown at Salamis'.[59] The 'virile qualities' and 'daring zeal' of the Athenians explain their success. Strauss asserts that this zeal is rooted in love of their city, belief that it is the best, and that it is the one most cherished by the gods. By the same token, Strauss is convinced that the Spartans fared badly in the first part of the war 'because they *believed* that their injustice had caused their adversity'.[60] The Spartans doubted that the gods were on their side. In other words, military success requires more than just military might – it requires a combination of nationalism and religious faith. Strauss makes the same point in his commentary on the political realism of Carl Schmitt.[61] Unlike Schmitt, Strauss insisted on upping the ante and adding to politics a moral and religious sanction. He believed that religious faith in the cosmic destiny of the nation is a useful myth – a noble lie or pious fraud that is necessary to inspire fervent zeal, self-sacrifice, and a willingness to fight to the death to exterminate the foe.

Strauss rejected the open declaration of political realism, such as the one Thucydides attributed to the Athenians in their dialogue with the Melians. The Athenians did not mince words; they made no effort to conceal their injustice. They told the Melians that if they did not cooperate, they would be wiped out. The Melians did not cooperate and were wiped out. It was not the brutality of Athens to which Strauss objected; it was her candid veracity that he could not bear. Strauss preferred Spartan brutality over Athenian brutality because the former was dressed in sacred myths.[62]

Like most conservatives, including Thucydides and Plato, Strauss admired Sparta, not Athens. Notwithstanding the proliferation of slaves in Athens, the city was relatively free, democratic, and prosperous. She was open to new ideas and innovations; she welcomed philosophers, sophists, and scientists. No doubt she reminded Strauss of America. In contrast, Sparta was oligarchic, conservative, and closed; she did not allow her citizens to listen to the newfangled ideas of sophists or philosophers, who were not allowed to travel or teach in Sparta. Sparta understood, as Strauss did, that the philosophical quest for truth is dangerous to the city – any city – because it undermines the resolute, unconditional, and unquestioning faith in the ancestral gods and institutions. And it was that undaunted faith in the divine foundation of her ancient constitution that explains the greatness and success of Sparta in the eyes of Strauss. After all, Sparta won the Peloponnesian Wars even though Athens was militarily superior. Strauss attributes Spartan success to the closed quality of her society and the uncompromising nature of her religious militarism – as if the misfortunes of Athens, such as the plague, the death of Pericles, and the rise to prominence of foolish and treacherous generals, had nothing to do with the outcome.

We should not lose sight of the fact that Sparta was a harsh and repressive society that relied on a population of brutally subjugated serfs – the helots – who vastly outnumbered the Spartans. Sparta had to become a well-oiled military machine just to maintain internal order. And she had to inculcate her citizens with myths and pious lies about the divine foundation of her constitution. No wonder she could not tolerate sophists or philosophers who might question the justice of her 'venerable' traditions.

Strauss assumed that a city needs noble lies about the divine foundations of her institutions in order to be strong. But Strauss was wrong. The lies don't work; reality is too strong. The lies were readily transparent to Sparta's oppressed population. Moreover, relying on mindless obedience, conformity, and indoctrination can only produce drones; it cannot produce culture, which requires freedom and creativity. It was Athens not Sparta that left the world a cultural legacy. There is no doubt that Pericles exaggerated the virtues of Athens in his Funeral Oration, but no one can imagine making a comparable eulogy to Sparta. Admiration for Sparta among conservatives of every stripe has its source in aristocratic mean-spiritedness. It is fuelled by the irrational feeling that freedom ceases to be valuable if it is democratized or widely disseminated.

The root of Strauss's antipathy to Athens was her philosophical love of truth, which freedom promotes. This love of truth manifested itself in her candid veracity about her foreign policy. The Athenian dialogue with the Melians and the Athenian discussion about the policy regarding Mytilene were deeply troubling to Strauss. They revealed a city in which faith in the gods has been undermined in favor of a philosophical embrace of the world as it is – without myths or illusions. Athens adopted a *realpolitik* approach to foreign policy. She justified her actions by appeals to reason, prudence, self-interest, and expediency, not to the divine laws. But Strauss insisted on sugar-coating political realism with religious zeal and a sense of cosmic entitlement.

Sadly, America was vulnerable to Strauss's not so noble lies. American exceptionalism, coupled with the American piety, made her very receptive to Strauss's message.[63] In an essay entitled 'The Coming Conservative Century', Irving Kristol declared that the three pillars of modern conservatism are religion, nationalism, and economic growth. He explained bluntly that religion and nationalism are important in providing incentives for people who are not by nature moral or political animals. Kristol endorsed a radical nationalism, as opposed to the more conservative patriotism. He explained the difference as follows:

> patriotism springs from love of the nation's past; nationalism arises out of hope for the nation's future, distinctive greatness. . . . Neoconservatives believe . . . that the goals of American foreign policy must go well beyond a narrow, too literal definition of 'national security'. It is the national interest of a world power, as this is defined by a sense of national destiny . . . not a myopic national security.[64]

It is easy to see how this sort of thinking can get out of hand. The same sentiment was echoed by Harry Jaffa when he said that America is the Zion that will light up the world.

The speeches of President George W. Bush radiate with the exceptionalism and religious self-righteousness of the neoconservatives. His language is filled with references to God, Satan, and the axis of evil. America is God's country; God is on her side; and her enemies are on the side of Satan. By conquering all her enemies, she will conquer evil. And those who are not willing to support her are 'complicit in a war against civilization'.[65]

It is worth pointing out that a Zion, properly understood, conquers the world by her example and inspiration, not by violent military conquest. Nothing has damaged the self-image of America as a Zion, a city on a hill, and a beacon to the world, than the policies of the neoconservatives. America cannot be a global bully and a world beacon at the same time.

In fairness to the neoconservatives it must be pointed out that not all of the neoconservatives believe this nonsense about America's divinely ordained mission – like Strauss, some peddled these ideas for their political effectiveness. But most of them are like the sorcerer's apprentice – victims of their own tricks. The neoconservatives are a diverse but compatible lot – there are hyper realists, sugar-coated realists (or noble liars), and true believers. The latter see the world as a macrocosm of the lawless Wild West; and they think that it is America's destiny to be the sheriff of the world. They consider it their duty to kill the outlaws or bring them to justice. As a result, they think that America is free to invade countries at will and topple governments that displease her because she is on the side of law and justice, while her enemies are unlawful combatants and outlaws. She is good and her enemies are evil. To defeat her enemies is to defeat evil itself. In Straussian terms, this mix of nationalism and religious militancy is the recipe for success. But for cooler heads, it is a recipe for disaster.

By insisting on the blind identity of American interests with the good of the world – what Strauss calls the identity of the good and one's own – American neoconservatives leave no room for self-criticism. They leave America totally bereft of moderation in her efforts to impose the yoke of her culture on others; they leave her bewildered when others resist her gift of 'freedom' and 'democracy'.

The flaw in this logic can be illustrated by returning to the story of Gulliver. One day, a fire broke out in the apartments of the Empress in the palace at Lilliput. When Gulliver realized that fire could destroy the whole palace, and maybe even all of Lilliput, and that all the efforts of the Lilliputians to quench the fire were futile, he acted quickly by putting out the fire with a stream of his urine. The dreadful noise and violence of this torrential downpour was rude, impertinent, and disrespectful in the extreme. And such disrespectful conduct was strictly prohibited by the laws of Lilliput. Nevertheless, Gulliver managed to save the palace from being totally destroyed. But despite his good intentions, Gulliver got himself into trouble for his transgression. Her Imperial Majesty was not amused. She was not even grateful. She vowed revenge. And Gulliver was forced to flee for his safety. Gulliver's success in putting out the fire was not relevant. The moral of the story is that the end does not justify the means; the means are as important as the end. Using unlawful means to achieve good ends destroys the magnificence and grandeur of the ends in view.

Leo Strauss and Allan Bloom were fascinated with the story of Gulliver – not just because sheepish intellectuals tend to have machismo fantasies, but also because the story seemed conducive

to their radical elitism. They imagined that the differences
between the superior few and the inferior many resembled
the differences between Gulliver and the Lilliputians.[66] And they
believed that those who are so different could not possibly live
by the same rules. What was appropriate for Gulliver was
not appropriate for the Lilliputians. They thought that Jonathan
Swift's tale was a justification of differential standards that
exempt the superior from the rules that apply to others. There is
one standard for the superior and another for the inferior. And
this is not just the way things are, but the way they are meant to
be for the good of the world. In his article on Swift, reprinted in
Giants and Dwarfs, Bloom argued that the benefit bestowed on the
Lilliputians due to Gulliver's immoral conduct is proof that
the superior are exempt from the rules that apply to all others.
On the Straussian reading, Swift's tale is a justification of the
immoralist point of view. But nothing could be further from the
truth.

It seems to me that the neoconservatives have applied the
Straussian interpretation of Gulliver to American foreign policy.
Accordingly, they imagine that the rules that apply to other
nations do not apply to the Unites States. America is entitled to
flout the rules of the international community not just because
she is strong, but for love of the world. As Robert Kagan claims,
America is 'a behemoth with a conscience'.[67] She does not justify
her actions with *raison d'état*, which is to say that she is not willing to say to the world what the Athenians said to the Melians
when they maintained that the strong will do whatever they please
and the weak must suffer the consequences. This Machiavellian
perspective is not congenial to America's self-image. Instead,
American realists prefer to believe, as Robert Kagan seems to
believe, that American power, 'employed under a double standard, may be the best means for advancing human progress –
and perhaps the only means'.[68] This is why Kagan maintained
that America should support arms control, but not for herself.[69]
This Straussian position rejects the minimal test of morality –
namely, that it must be universalizable (i.e., whatever is right for
us to do must also be right for others).

Straussian immoralism in international affairs differs from the
candid immoralism of *realpolitik*. The new immoralism is concealed and sugar-coated with love. It is for love of the world that
America must blithely ignore the principles of law and justice

that apply to other nations. Her transgressions will supposedly benefit the world.

A political realism embellished with national exceptionalism, a large dose of religious self-righteousness, and a demonization of the enemy, is distinctively Straussian and neoconservative. Some of the neoconservatives may believe in the myth of American exceptionalism, but the rest of the world balks at its hypocrisy.

George W. Bush gave voice to the Straussian mixture of nationalism and religiosity when he declared that 'the hand of God is guiding the affairs of this nation'.[70] He portrayed the struggle between America and her enemies as a struggle between good and evil, civilization and terrorism, democracy and tyranny, freedom and oppression. And he proclaimed that this is not a struggle about which God is indifferent. The effect was to present the policies of his administration as unassailable – and this is yet another lie. It implies that America's enemies are the enemies of truth, justice, freedom, and democracy. It portrays the enemy as Satanic, irrational, and incomprehensible – thugs, criminals, and dead-enders, as Bush and his Secretary of Defense never tired of repeating. The strategy is intended to silence debate by giving the impression that our enemies have no legitimate claims against us. By pretending that our enemies are opposed to all our wholesome values, it deflects attention from our actions and policies. As Noam Chomsky has rightly pointed out, most people in the Arab world are not opposed to American values – they are not opposed to justice, freedom, or democracy – they are opposed to American foreign policy and they have legitimate claims to make against the American proclivity for supporting corrupt and brutal regimes.[71]

A few more criticisms of Strauss's sugar-coated realism are in order. First, sugar-coated realism is much worse than honest, open, and unpretentious realism; because, when political realism assumes a religious façade, it becomes impervious to debate. It becomes difficult to convince those in the grip of sugar-coated realism that it is not in their interest to act unilaterally and in violation of the law of nations. When realism appears in the guise of a sacred doctrine, it defies any appeals to reason, justice, prudence, or expediency – the sorts of arguments that deterred the Athenian assault on Mytilene. When killing the enemy becomes a sacred duty, killing becomes a matter of course not open to dispute. This is how it was with Sparta, and it is the reason that

Strauss admired her 'piety', her 'ancient constitution', and her dedication to 'divine law'.[72]

Second, sugar-coated realism conceals the conflict between American interests and American ideals. It conceals the fact that there are hard choices and that we must often choose between our interests on one hand, and our ideals, values, and principles on the other. For example, in pursuit of her interests, the United States removed the democratically elected leader of Iran who wanted to nationalize the oil companies; instead, the United States installed the brutal puppet regime of the Shah Pahlavi.[73] Similar tales can be told in Guatemala, Congo, and Algeria. Crude realists have no objections, because they are willing to support whoever serves the interests of the nation. But the sugar-coated realists want the interests of the nation to coincide with her ideals and values. As President Bush expressed it in his Second Inaugural Address of January 20, 2005, 'America's vital interests and our deepest beliefs are now one'. But this is not always possible. For example, the overwhelming majority of Pakistanis believe that Osama bin Laden is a hero and George W. Bush is a villain. As long as this sentiment prevails, America's democratic principles are bound to come into conflict with her interests. It is certainly *not* in America's interest to topple the military dictatorship of President Pervez Musharraf and insist on free elections in Pakistan.

The conflict between American interests and ideals has manifested itself in the invasion of Iraq. The Americans portrayed their invasion as a gift of freedom and democracy. What they had in mind was elections limited to an elite group of pro-American governing councils, whose endorsement would give the appearance of legitimacy to the soft dictatorship of the American puppet regime. But the powerful Shiite cleric, the Grand Ayatollah Ali al-Sistani, denounced the American plan with a fatwa and insisted on popular elections. Thousands of Shiites demonstrated in the streets in January of 2004 demanding free elections by the people. Washington had no choice but to comply, because the alternative was having the Shiite majority join the Sunni insurgency. Nevertheless, the Americans took credit for the popular election as if it were their idea. The Shiite majority came out to vote in large numbers, and the United Iraqi Alliance, backed by Sistani, won by far the largest block of seats in the assembly, and as I write is determined to draft a constitution based on Islamic Law.

And despite all the advantages of the American backed party of Iyad Allawi – millions of dollars in campaign contributions, television appearances, advertising, and body guards – the party came in a distant third, and as a result, Allawi could not remain prime minister. This was a terrible defeat for the Americans. It meant that the new government may bring neither freedom nor a regime friendly to American interests or values. However, the neoconservatives are not in a position (logically speaking) to oppose an Islamic state which has been democratically elected. After all, the neoconservatives are enthusiastic supporters of the Jewish state, and they rely heavily on the support of the Christian Coalition in the US for political support. The conflict between principles and interests will continue to plague the administration. They will be forced to betray their principles, but they will be reluctant to admit it. The result will be an ever greater need for lies, propaganda, and spin to conceal the inevitable conflicts between their vital interests and their deepest beliefs.

Third, by adopting the Straussian blending of religion and politics, the neoconservatives make it hard to distinguish America from her Islamic fundamentalist enemies. As I have argued elsewhere, the neoconservative relation to Islamic societies is one of envy.[74] Taking their cue from Strauss, the neoconservatives envy the fervent zeal that animates their less powerful enemy. Nothing represents the Straussian ideal of political health more than the crazed Islamic youths we see on television – young men ready to immolate themselves on a moment's notice. Strauss admired a society that can cultivate young men willing to die for a hopeless cause.[75] And there seems to be no shortage of such youth in Iraq as in Palestine. To the neoconservatives, the Islamic foe seems formidable in its resolve, conviction, fervor, and tenacity. The suicide bombers are for them a vivid symbol of the strength of the enemy. In contrast, the American troops have criticized the judgment of their commander-in-chief, suffered from post-traumatic syndrome, sought asylum in Canada, and complained about the length of their stay in Iraq. All this has convinced the neoconservatives that American liberal society has made Americans soft, pampered, and without conviction.

The trouble is that the neoconservatives see America through the eyes of her ascetic and militant Islamic enemies who believe that America has lost her soul and surrendered to pleasure. And neoconservatives are convinced that the fanatical values of their

Islamic foes are the right values: the values of Sparta, the values
that are necessary for military success.

Bernard Lewis, a revered historian among the neoconservatives, admired one thing about Osama bin Laden – he was born to
wealth but abandoned it in favor of a hard and ascetic style of life.
George W. Bush echoed the fears of Bernard Lewis: he blamed
the attacks on American troops in Iraq on the perception by the
enemy that Americans are soft, weak, and unwilling to sustain
casualties; and he feared that the enemy was right. And as if to
compensate for the half-heartedness of his troops, George W.
Bush resolved to be determined, steadfast, and unwavering.
Needless to say this is not the most advantageous posture for a
commander in chief. Success in battle requires a certain flexibility –
a willingness to change tactics, to surprise the enemy, and to cut
one's losses when necessary. Osama bin Laden is a poor model
for political success – he has no state, no subjects, and no hope.
He is a man willing to die and kill for nothing more than a
delusion and a dream. Instead of trying to imitate Osama bin
Laden, it would be more reasonable to question the validity of a
war launched in the name of democratic evangelism. It would be
more reasonable to decry Islamic fanaticism instead of envying it
and wishing to emulate it. And it would be wiser to search for a
source of strength that is not mindless, fanatical religious zealotry.

In short, by following Strauss in repudiating liberalism and
longing for the closed society, the neoconservatives rob America
of her modernity, which is the source of her appeal. And it is
precisely her modern qualities – openness, freedom, individuality, plurality, innovation, experimentation, and playfulness – that
have made America so alluring to the old world – a world
engulfed in dogma, negativity, and everlasting gloom. It is her
seductive appeal, and not her military might, that has made
America a formidable enemy to the Islamic world.

ENLIGHTENMENT DREAM

Political realism, even when it is sugar-coated, cannot make sense
of 'The Project for the New American Century'. Contributing to
the sheer hubris and blindness of the Project is a dash of modern
idealism, which has its roots in the Enlightenment philosophy
of Immanuel Kant and serves as a noble delusion to inspire a
foreign policy that is self-righteous and aggressive.

Political realism is static. It tells us that this is the way the world is, and this is how it will always be: it will always be characterized by groups pitted against one another in hatred and enmity. In contrast, the idealism of Kant is historical and progressive. It tells us that the spread of enlightenment will result in a triumph of the Western ideals of reason, freedom, science, commerce, law, and republican government. This spread of Western values will in turn lead to the homogenization of the world and the end of the state of war of all against all. In the *Idea of Universal History with a Cosmopolitan Purpose*, Kant anticipated the progress of mankind toward a universal world order based on the true principles of right – an order in which man's full potentialities will be fully realized.[76] In the course of man's progress toward his final destiny, Kant imagined an earlier stage in which a league of republican states will come to dominate international affairs. In *Perpetual Peace*, he described these republican states as constitutional in their internal administration, governed by the rule of law, and having a system of internal checks on those who rule.

Kant surmised that a coalition of such states will have a peaceful influence on international affairs in the way that absolutist states could not. Republican states will be rational enough to realize that cooperation is more advantageous than war, and that commerce is a much easier and cheaper means to amass wealth. Kant imagined that the dominance of republican states in world politics will happen naturally, gradually, and through enlightenment; and belligerent states will eventually see the light and join the commercial republics. Kant believed that commerce played an important role in the process because 'the spirit of commerce' has a tendency to soften manners, and to extinguish those 'inflammable humours' that kindle wars.[77]

Kant's Enlightenment dream betrays a troublesome chauvinism. He assumed that in the march toward the cosmopolitan goal, 'our continent' will 'probably legislate eventually for all other continents'.[78] When you believe that history is progressively moving toward a goal that is nothing short of the completion of human potentialities, and you are persuaded that your own culture is at the forefront of this development, it becomes difficult to resist the temptation to impose the yoke of your culture on others. The proclivity to identify one's own values and culture with truth and justice makes it easy to condone domination as a benevolent act. This is precisely the temptation to which the neoconservatives have succumbed. In a recent essay in the *Weekly Standard*, Irving Kristol gave voice to this Kantian 'idealism':

> for a great power, the 'national interest' is not a geographical term, ... larger nations whose identity is ideological, like the Soviet Union of yesteryear and the United States of today, inevitably have ideological interests. ... Barring extraordinary events, the United States will always feel obliged to defend, if possible, a democratic nation under attack from non-democratic forces, external or internal. That is why it was in our national interest to come to the defence of France and Britain in World War II. That is why we feel it necessary to defend Israel today, when its survival is threatened. No complicated geopolitical calculations of national interest are necessary.[79]

There is nothing wrong with defending beleaguered democratic nations from their aggressive enemies (assuming Israel is the victim and not the aggressor, which is highly questionable). But the neoconservative foreign policy goes much further. It assumes that only democratic governments are legitimate, and that all other forms of government must be toppled and replaced with democratic governments if the world is to be liberated from aggression and injustice.[80] But this reasoning is seriously flawed.

First, democracy is not necessarily the best form of government, the most rational, or the most suitable, under all circumstances. Nations with illiterate populations would be far better off living under constitutional monarchies. Besides, to give foreign nations the gift of democracy is not to give them *liberal* democracy. Democracy is not a guarantee of liberty. Iraq is a case in point – just because the Iraqis can vote does not mean that they are free. The defeat of Saddam Hussein has brought the influence of Shiite clerics to bear on Iraqi society. Iraqi women have less freedom under the American occupation than they had under the secular dictatorship of Saddam Hussein. In Basra, one of the largest cities in Iraq, women are not free to walk on the street without the black hijab covering them from head to toe, for fear of being beaten up. Men are not free to shave their beards or wear jeans. The liquor stores, the video stores, and the satellite dishes have been smashed. The bars, discos, and nightclubs, have been forced to shut down. Aqila Hashimi, one of the few women on the governing council who tried to resist these developments was gunned down in the fall of 2003.[81] So, far from making the society more liberal, the Americans have made it less free by their gift of democracy.

Second, democratic governments are not necessarily more pacific than other forms of government. Kant assumed that monarchs are more inclined to declare war because they do not bear the brunt of it, while republican governments, in which the people who bear the burden also make the decision to take up arms, are not likely to favor war.[82] But clearly, Kant was wrong. Democratic governments are just as vulnerable to human passions such as revenge, hate, anger, humiliation, or pride. And these passions fuel the desire for war. The bellicosity of democratic Athens was arguably as great as that of oligarchic Sparta. The World Wars of the twentieth century had broad public support; so did the Crimean War. Surely, democratic governments can be as belligerent as tyrannies. Witness Israeli and American foreign policy. These countries are not only aggressive, they are also self-righteous, because they are convinced that they are the custodians of civilization and their enemies have no rights.

It must be pointed out that this sort of belligerence in the name of progress is the antithesis of what Kant espoused – he was convinced that progress would happen naturally and gradually; and he insisted on respect for international law. It is irrational to think that you can force a people to be free or that you can get them to agree with your principles by aerial bombardment. Universal despotism may create peace, but as Kant realized, it would be 'a graveyard of freedom'.[83]

Third, the neoconservatives share Kant's faith in the pacific effects of commerce. But unlike Kant, they find this 'fact' very troubling. The reason is this. If commerce has a softening effect on human personality, then it is an obstacle to the war and conquest in which a world empire must engage.[84] But the neoconservatives need not worry. Commerce is not the pacific elixir they imagine. Alexander Hamilton rightly mocked this view of commerce:

> Has commerce hitherto done anything more than change the objects of war? Is not the love of wealth, as domineering and enterprising a passion as that of power or glory? Have there not been as many wars founded upon commercial motives, since that has become the prevailing system of nations, as were before occasioned by the cupidity of territory or dominion?

Has not the spirit of commerce, in many instances, administered new incentives to the appetite both for one and for the other?[85]

Hamilton's words regarding commerce are particularly salient in our time. The rules of global capitalism that the Western powers, led by the United States, have imposed on the world are clearly intended to serve their interests at the expense of the poorer countries. The exploitative character of capitalism has been globalized; and this means that the frustrations of the poor and disenfranchised will be directed at those who make the rules. The spirit of commerce has so far proven to be quite unpacific. The United States has led in the creation of institutions such as the International Monetary Fund and the World Trade Organization to implement and adjudicate the rules of trade. By the same token, the United States has been unwilling to abide by the rules whenever they are not to her advantage. Unless these institutions are estranged from the very power that engendered them, international relations are bound to continue to deteriorate.

Fourth, Kantian idealism is singular and autocratic; it is profoundly antithetical to the pluralistic reality of the world. Those in its grip confuse their own model of government with reason, progress, truth, and justice. This is precisely the sort of thinking that has sanctified aggression against Iraq, Palestine, and Kashmir, by the world's democratic republics.

The upshot of the matter is that no homogeneous or universal world order, no matter how 'idealistic', can be accomplished without global tyranny. Not everyone will be willing to affirm American values and bow down to American 'principles'. This is not because they are evil and obtuse, but because these values and principles are not the only ones that are worthy of being affirmed. There is a plurality of goods, including good regimes that are not liberal democracies. To identify our form of government with truth, goodness, and justice, is a myopic combination of naiveté and arrogance. And when this provincialism is endowed with super-power, it becomes tyrannical. And that tyranny is bound to tarnish the most beloved 'ideals' and 'principles'. Far from softening the realist policies of the neoconservatives, Kant's enlightenment dream inaugurates a reign of perpetual war. What is troublesome is that the prospect of perpetual war is one that the Straussian neoconservatives are more than willing to embrace.

ENDLESS WAR

Just as the hyper realism of the neoconservatives is filtered through the sugar-coated lens of Leo Strauss, so is their idealism. Two books written by leading neoconservatives exemplify the inner struggle between the realism and the idealism of the neo-conservatives respectively – Samuel Huntington's *The Clash of Civilizations* and Francis Fukuyama's *The End of History and the Last Man*. The two books are not as diametrically opposed as is generally believed. They share some very fundamental assumptions that reinforce one another – they both glamorize war, death, and struggle, as I will explain.

My objections to Kantian foreign policy are not the sort of objections that are of concern to European pessimists such as Martin Heidegger, Carl Schmitt, Alexandre Kojève, or Leo Strauss. These writers regarded the Kantian dream of a progressive march of history toward political homogeneity, global peace, and commerce to be a very likely scenario. And they were genuinely apprehensive about the prospect of a homogeneous global order modeled on American values.[86] The real worry in the minds of these Europeans was that America might succeed. Supposedly they feared that the universal spread of the spirit of commerce will soften manners and emasculate men. Then all is lost. Nietzsche's terrifying spectre of the 'last man' would become a reality. Man would be reduced to a contented animal – well-fed and well-medicated, but without spirit or heart, devoid of great dreams, great hopes, and great wars. The last man is a pitiful emasculated creature with nothing to live or die for. His life is reduced to entertainment, consumption, and animal sexuality. Alas, virile boldness and daring zeal will be forever extinguished. Man will cease to be interesting. He will no longer be willing to rush naked into battle and headlong to his death. The 'night of the world' would be at hand (Heidegger). The 'animalization of man' would be complete (Kojève). And the trivialization of life would be accomplished (Schmitt). *That* is what the success of America's global aspirations meant to the likes of Heidegger, Kojève, Schmitt, and Strauss.[87]

In *The End of History and the Last Man*, Francis Fukuyama popularized this view of the world with all its fascistic resonances.[88] He declared that history understood as the domain of war and ideological struggle was over. America has won; the whole world has bowed down to her way of life. The end of history and the last man were already here. Commerce has softened and emasculated man. Fukuyama described a world in which all the colorful warriors around the world were giving up their body paint, and, with a gesture of resignation to the inexorable march of history, they were hanging up their swords and assuming their place behind the computer terminals.[89] How dreadful. Everything wild, unpredictable, untamed, and virile was destined to disappear from the face of the earth. The world has become predictable and humdrum. Worst of all, there are no real men left – men who are willing to die just for honor, glory, or prestige – except gangsters such as the Bloods and Crips.[90] But being all-American, and not disposed to European melancholy, Fukuyama tried to make the best of a bad situation. His advice: let's not wallow in despair; let's use commerce as the new instrument of domination.

Only a superficial reading would conclude that Fukuyama was celebrating the end of the Cold War and the triumph of American capitalism over Soviet socialism. Fukuyama had inherited from Strauss and Bloom this deadly view of the world according to which only war and struggle gives meaning to the lives of ordinary people. The logic of this way of thinking leads one to conclude that if America fails to achieve her 'national destiny', and is mired in perpetual war, then all is well. Man's humanity has been rescued from extinction. The prospect of perpetual war, struggle, death, and tragedy is sure to make life serious and keep animality at bay.[91]

In this noxious view of the world, man's humanity is defined in terms of struggle and death. Only endless war can overturn the dangerous laxity of the modern project. War is the antidote to modernity. For those in the grip of this monstrous view of the world, the suggestion that the end of the Cold War is the end of history – the end of war and struggle – is not unmitigated good news.[92]

In *The Clash of Civilizations*, Samuel Huntington brought some much needed bad news – we have a lot more enemies than we realize. The Islamic world is a particular menace. Other neoconservatives agreed: we still have enemies (thank God!). We can now get busy being real men and crush all our enemies and rule the globe. Needless to say, this is an endless task. But Huntington and the neoconservatives are not deterred, because endless war is the solution to the conflict at the heart of capitalism – the conflict between the Protestant ethic on one hand, and wealth and leisure on the other. Perpetual war may save America from the depravity and decay to which wealth makes her vulnerable. The war effort will consume the wealth that supposedly threatens America's soul.

There is a colossal failure of the imagination in this fear of wealth, happiness, and prosperity. The fear is based on the misguided belief that all that mankind can do with wealth and leisure is become debauched. But what civilization has ever been created without wealth? What civilization can leave a cultural legacy without freedom, wealth, and leisure? Wealth, leisure, and freedom are necessary to make the world a beautiful place – they provide the opportunity to create great art, architecture, literature, and music. And those who create none of these things can still enjoy them; they can dance and sing, make love and raise children. But life itself seems abhorrent to those with a jihadist mentality who long for endless struggle and the constant threat of death.

There is a secular asceticism at the heart of the neoconservative project that dovetails with the Islamist vision of life. Both sides in the struggle prefer life when it is a fight to the death. In the absence of jihad, they find life meaningless and insipid. The triumph of this jihadist mentality would no doubt please Strauss and his misanthropic philosophers. For it seems that man is destined to make the world interesting – full of catastrophe and carnage. Strauss's monstrous elite of self-anointed pagan gods (i.e., his dung beetle heroes) will not lack for entertainment. There will be more than enough bloodshed and slaughter to satisfy their taste.[93]

In conclusion, the objectives of American foreign policy under the neoconservatives are multifaceted, but equally deadly – like the neoconservatives themselves. If American foreign policy continues its belligerence, the hyper realists will imagine that American honor has been restored and world respect has been achieved. If America continues to justify all the horror of her military campaigns as a necessary means for the realization of universal democracy and future bliss, the idealists (or true believers) will be ready to pay the price. If America is mired in endless wars in the name of God and nation, the Straussians (or noble liars) will exult in the delusion that they have saved America from her animality – they will imagine that they are gods entertaining themselves with the mutual slaughter of the mortals on their television screens.

NOTES

1. See for example a collection of essays mostly by Straussians presented at a conference on my book in Quebec City (1989) and published in *The Vital Nexus*, Vol. 1, No. 1 (May 1990); see also Harry V. Jaffa, 'Dear Professor Drury', *Political Theory*, Vol. 15, No. 3 (August 1987), pp. 316–325; Fred Dallmayr, 'Politics Against Philosophy: Strauss and Drury', *Political Theory*, Vol. 15, No. 3 (August 1987), pp. 326–337; David Schaefer, 'Shadia Drury's Critique of Leo Strauss', presented at the International Society for the Study of European Ideas, held in Aalborg, Denmark, August 1992 and published in *The Political Science Reviewer*, Vol. 23 (1994), pp. 80–127; Gordon Tolle, 'Leo Strauss: Unmasked or Distorted?' *Review of Politics*, Vol. 50, No. 3 (Summer 1988), pp. 467–470; Leon Craig, review in *Canadian Philosophical Reviews*, Vol. 10, No. 3 (March 1990), pp. 104–109; Harro Hopfl, 'Covert Guardians', *The Times Higher Education Supplement*, No. 821 (July 29, 1988), p. 23; Laurence Lampert, *Leo Strauss and Nietzsche*, (Chicago: University of Chicago Press, 1996).
2. See my essay on the progress of an imaginary Straussian from the academy to the halls of power in Washington, 'The Making of a Straussian', *Philosopher's Magazine*, Issue 25, First Quarter, 2004.
3. Allan Bloom, *The Closing of the American Mind* (New York: Simon & Schuster, 1987), p. 88.
4. See my review of Saul Bellow's *Ravelstein*, 'Gurus of the Right', *Literary Review of Canada*, Vol. 8, No. 10 (Winter 2000/01), pp. 19–22.
5. Gary J. Schmitt and Abram N. Shulsky, 'Leo Strauss and the World of Intelligence (By Which We Do Not Mean *Nous*)', in Kenneth L. Deutsch and John A. Murley (eds.) *Leo Strauss, the Straussians, and the American Regime* (New York: Rowman & Littlefield Publishers, 1999), p. 410.
6. See Harvey Mansfield, *Machiavelli's New Modes and Orders: A Study of the Discourses of Livy* (Ithaca, NY: Cornell University Press, 1979).
7. See chapter 6.
8. For the influence of Strauss on Kristol, see Irving Kristol, *Neoconservatism: The Autobiography of an Idea* (New York: The Free Press, 1994), pp. 7–9, 404. For a detailed critical analysis of the work of Irving Kristol, see Shadia Drury, *Leo Strauss and the American Right* (New York: St. Martin's Press, 1997), ch. 5.
9. Drury, *Leo Strauss and the American Right*. Several articles in the popular press have rightly linked Strauss with the foreign policy of the neoconservatives, but they have not understood the complex nature of the connection. James Atlas, 'A Classicist's Legacy: New Empire Builders', *The New York Times*, May 4, 2003; Seymour M. Hersh, 'Selective Intelligence', *The New Yorker*, May 6, 2003; Paul Knox, 'The Strauss Effect', *The Globe and Mail*, July 12, 2003; Jeet Heer, 'The Philosopher', and 'Straussians Abroad', *The Boston Globe*, May 11, 2003; Christopher Hitchens, 'Machiavelli in Mesopotamia', *Slate*, November 7, 2002.
10. Aware of the fact that the Bush doctrine has become intimately connected to the ideas of Leo Strauss, Straussians in the academy have made an

effort to distance themselves and Strauss from the activist Straussians in the Pentagon and other branches of government. They have attempted to revive the old view of Strauss as a quiet little man who was interested in the study of old books. See for example Anne Norton, *Leo Strauss and the Politics of American Empire* (New Haven, CT: Yale University Press, 2004). The title of the book is rather misleading because Strauss is mentioned only in passing throughout the book, which is full of gossip about Strauss and the Straussians, but no analysis or philosophical engagement with Strauss's work. The whole point of the book is to distance Strauss from the belligerent political Straussians in the Bush administration, whom she claims were trained by Allan Bloom – the real villain in her story. The book contains no notes, references, or bibliography to back up any of her claims. Despite its implausible thesis and its lack of scholarly rigor, the book contains a few interesting chapters, especially chapter 10, which describes the stark contrast between traditional conservative sensibilities and those of the neoconservatives. See also two essays by Mark Lilla in *The New York Review of Books*, 'Leo Strauss: The European', and 'The Closing of the Straussian Mind', Vol. 51, No. 16 (October 21, 2004) and Vol. 51, No. 17 (November 4, 2004). Lilla is also eager to distance Strauss from the vulgarities of American neoconservatism – the political Straussians, the evangelical Christians, the Likudniks, and the right-wing radio personalities. Lilla seems to have utter contempt for the political Straussians whose proud American hearts apparently beat 'arhythmically' to Wagner (a veiled reference to the Nazis). Lilla claims that the Europeans rightly understood Strauss as a politically non-partisan scholar interested in the study of old books for their own sake. But when they start to tells us what Strauss found in the old books, Lilla and his fellow Europeans echo the same old themes – the conflict between philosophy and the city, the need for secrecy or esotericism, the importance of religion, the rejection of the Enlightenment, and so on. But Lilla and his European cohorts are either unable or unwilling to put these ideas into a coherent and meaningful whole. Anyone with ears to hear will recognize these as the ideas that have fuelled the rise of the radical right in America. Lilla's apology for Strauss, like Norton's, is a failure that is symptomatic of the last gasp of a retreating academic Straussianism. But Lilla is also sensitive enough to be ashamed of Straussian scholarship; he admits that the scholarship produced by the Straussians is either 'impenetrable' or totally 'unoriginal' because Strauss's teaching keeps his students intellectually in a 'well-tailored straitjacket'. One is led to the absurd conclusion that Strauss had absolutely nothing to do with all the dreadful scholarship and the equally dreadful policies he has inspired in America.

11. CM, p. 235. See guide to abbreviations of books by Strauss, p. 203.
12. See chapter 5.
13. *OT*, pp. 70, 74, 75.
14. Strauss points to the 'nocturnal council' in Plato's *Laws* and to Xenophon's discussion of 'gentlemen'. See *AAPL*, pp. 177–178: the Council is to the city what intellect is to the body of man. Strauss

suggests that in comparison to the Council, the citizens are hardly distinguishable from animals. For the discussion of the rule of gentleman see 'The Mature Socrates' in ch. 4.

15. Leo Strauss, *Philosophy and Law: Essays Toward the Understanding of Maimonides and His Predecessors*, 1935, Fred Baumann, trans. (New York: Jewish Publication Society, 1987), p. 103.
16. *NRH*, p. 192.
17. *PAW*, p. 36.
18. Shadia Drury, 'The Making of a Straussian', *Philosopher's Magazine*, Issue 25, First Quarter, 2004.
19. Leo Strauss, *The Rebirth of Classical Political Rationalism: Essays and Lectures*, Thomas L. Pangle, ed. (Chicago: University of Chicago Press, 1989), pp. 107–108. See my review of this collection in *Political Theory*, Vol. 19, No. 4 (November 1991), pp. 671–675.
20. Strauss, *The Rebirth of Classical Political Rationalism*, p. 206.
21. Ibid., 'On the Euthyphron', p. 201.
22. Friedrich Nietzsche. *Genealogy of Morals*, Francis Golffing, trans. (New York: Doubleday Anchor, 1957), Essay II, pp. 200–201.
23. *CM*, p. 125.
24. Anyone who has observed how the Straussians operate in the academy would find this hard to believe.
25. *Genealogy of Morals*, Essay I, p. 160.
26. *LAM*, p. 4. Strauss tells us that this is to be accomplished by 'liberal education', which is intended to remind 'those members of a mass democracy who have ears to hear, of human greatness'. What a grotesque conception of greatness.
27. On the noble lies of Nietzsche, Plato, and Strauss, see, 'Strauss's Bogus Authorities', in *Leo Strauss and the American Right*, ch. 3.
28. *CM*, pp. 199, 205.
29. Ibid., p. 199.
30. See 'The Ghosts of Weimar', in ch. 1 of *Leo Strauss and the American Right*.
31. This is particularly evident in the exchange with Kojève. See my analysis of this debate in *Alexandre Kojève: The Roots of Postmodern Politics* (New York: St. Martin's Press, 1994), ch. 10.
32. Interestingly, George W. Bush used the same terms to describe the United Nations.
33. In my view, Strauss radicalizes the ideas of Schmitt. See my discussion of Strauss and Schmitt in *Leo Strauss and the American Right*, ch. 3.
34. The administration's culture of secrecy is well documented in Richard A. Clarke, *Against All Enemies: Inside America's War on Terror* (New York: Free Press, 2004). See also David Corn, *The Lies of George W. Bush* (New York: Three Rivers Press, 2003).
35. See the documentary film, *Hijacking Catastrophe: 9/11, Fear, and the Selling of American Empire*, by the Media Education Foundation, www.medied.org.
36. Americans knew that Saddam had chemical and biological weapons because they sold them to him when he was launching his murderous campaign against the Kurds and the war against Iran in the 1980s. But according to experts, such weapons have a short shelf-life and were no longer viable. The people who protested against the war rightly suspected that it was an aggressive war launched for spurious military

or economic interests. America's traditional allies – Canada, France, and Germany – sided with the protesters; but most Americans trusted their government.

37. The fact that the United States is invading Muslim countries and killing countless innocent civilians seems irrelevant. The fact that the United States is giving unqualified support to Israel despite the latter's violation of dozens of United Nations resolutions – violations blessed by the United States – are no obstacle. The fact that the United States supplies Israel with billions of dollars worth of military aid, which the Israelis use to terrorize and bomb at will their Palestinian neighbors, who have no army and no air force, is no problem. More money to spend on propaganda will do the trick.

38. Sheryl Henderson Blunt, 'Bush Calls for "Culture Change",' *Christianity Today*, May 28, 2004, posted on www.christianity today.com/ct/2004/121/51.0.html

39. Ibid., p. 3.

40. Irving Kristol, *Neoconservatism: The Autobiography of an Idea*, ch. 30.

41. See 'Populist Ploy' in chapter 5 of *Leo Strauss and the American Right*.

42. 'Project for the New American Century', Statement of Principles, p. 1. Available at www.newamericancentury.org.

43. Ibid., pp. 2, V.

44. Thomas Donnelly (principle author), Donald Kagan and Gary Schmitt (Project co-chairmen), 'Rebuilding America's Defences', pp. ii, 8, available in 'Project for the New American Century', op. cit.

45. Ibid., p. 10.

46. 'Project for the New American Century', p. 51.

47. Irving Kristol, 'The Neoconservative Persuasion', *Weekly Standard*, Vol. 008, no. 37 (August 25, 2003). Irving Kristol explains that what neoconservatives have learned from Thucydides (via Strauss and Kagan) is that (1) patriotism is good; (2) world government is a bad idea; (3) statesmen should, 'above all', have the ability to distinguish between friends and foes; and (4) the national interest of a great nation transcends its borders.

48. It is important to point out that this is one of many speeches that Thucydides invents for the characters in his historical narrative. And it is not clear if any of these speeches represent Thucydides's view. See Thucydides, *On Justice, Power, and Human Nature: Selections form the History of the Peloponnesian Wars*, edited by Paul Woodruff (Indianapolis, IN: Hackett Publishing Co., 1993), ch. 6, c.

49. Donald Kagan, *On the Origins of War and the Preservation of Peace* (New York: Doubleday, 1995), p. 6.

50. Ibid., p. 8.

51. Donald Kagan, 'The Cuban Missile Crisis', in *On the Origins of War and the Preservation of Peace*.

52. See James Mann, *The Rise of the Vulcans: The History of Bush's War Cabinet* (New York: Viking Press, 2004). Mann emphasises the obsession with Vietnam and the belief that military might is the key to honor.

53. This is the sort of political realism that is defended by Robert Kagan in *Of Paradise and Power* (New York: Alfred A. Knopf, 2003).

54. Robert Kagan, *Of Paradise and Power*, p. 10.

55. See for example, *CM*, p. 183.

56. *CM*, p. 73, my italics.

57. *CM*, p. 145.

58. *CM*, p. 170.

59. *CM*, p. 171.

60. *CM*, 182, my italics.

61. See discussion and substantiation of this view in *Leo Strauss and the American Right*, ch. 3.

62. *CM*, pp. 214, 217.

63. On American exceptionalism see Seymour Martin Lipset, *American Exceptionalism* (New York: W. W. Norton & Co., 1996). On American exceptionalism and the war on terror, see Benjamin Barber, *Fear's Empire: War, Terrorism, and Democracy* (New York: W. W. Norton & Co., 2003).

64. Irving Kristol, *Reflections of a Neoconservative* (New York: Basic Books, 1983), p. xiii.

65. Speech delivered in the Philippines, October 19, 2003.

66. Allan Bloom, *Giants and Dwarfs: Essays 1960–1990* (New York: Simon & Schuster, 1990).

67. Kagan, *Of Paradise and Power*, p. 41.

68. Ibid., p. 100.

69. Ibid., p. 99.

70. CNN documentary, 'The Mission of George W. Bush', Sunday, October 11, 2004.

71. See Osama bin Laden's 'Letter to America', *The Observer*, Sunday, November 24, 2002. See also Noam Chomsky, *9–11* (New York: Seven Stories Press, 2001).

72. *CM*, p. 214.

73. See Stephen Kinzer, *All the Shah's Men: An American Coup and the Roots of Middle East Terror* (New York: John Wiley & Sons, 2003).

74. Shadia B. Drury, *Terror and Civilization: Christianity, Politics, and the Western Psyche* (New York: Palgrave Macmillan, 2004), Part V.

75. Leo Strauss, *Natural Right and History* (Chicago: University of Chicago Press, 1953), p. 318.

76. Immanuel Kant, *Idea of Universal History with a Cosmopolitan Purpose*, in *Political Writings*, edited by Hans Reiss and translated by H. B. Nisbet (New York: Cambridge University Press, 1991).

77. Kant, 'Perpetual Peace', in *Political Writings*, p. 114.

78. Kant, *Idea of Universal History with a Cosmopolitan Purpose*, in *Political Writings*, p. 52.

79. Irving Kristol, 'The Neoconservative Persuasion', *The Weekly Standard*, Vol. 008, No. 47 (August 25, 2003).

80. It is important to point out that Kant did not identify republican government with democracy. In fact, he thought that democracy is closer to despotism than either monarchy or aristocracy, and is least likely to develop into genuine republican government. See 'Perpetual Peace', in *Political Writings*, p. 101.

81. 'Iraq: Veil of Anxiety Over Women's Right', *Los Angeles Times*, March 7, 2004.

82. Kant, 'On the Common Saying: "This May be True in Theory, but it does not Apply in Practice",' *Political Writings*, p. 91, and 'Perpetual Peace', *Political Writings*, p. 100.
83. Kant, 'Perpetual Peace', *Political Writings*, p. 114.
84. Irving Kristol was delighted by the popularity of the movie *Rambo* because he thought it proved that the people still loved war. See Irving Kristol, *Neoconservatism*, pp. 360–361.
85. Alexander Hamilton, *Federalist*, No. VI.
86. See the exchange between Strauss and Kojève in *OT*, See also my discussion of Kojève, Strauss, Bloom, and other postmoderns in *Alexandre Kojève: The Roots of Postmodern Politics*. See also my discussion of Strauss and Schmitt in *Leo Strauss and the American Right*, ch. 3.
87. Straussians such as Harvey Mansfield and Carnes Lord never tire of complaining of the feminization of politics and the emasculation of statesmanship. See for example, Carnes Lord, *The Modern Prince: What Leaders Need to Know Now* (New Haven, CT: Yale University Press, 2004).
88. See 'Francis Fukuyama's Unhappy Consciousness', in Part III of my *Alexandre Kojève*.
89. Francis Fukuyama, *The End of History and the Last Man* (New York: Free Press, 1992), p. 186.
90. Ibid., p. 148.
91. See 'Allan Bloom's Last Men', in Part III of my *Alexandre Kojève*.
92. Fukuyama has had a change of heart. The war against Iraq has seriously assaulted his 'idealism' and inspired him to deliver a brilliant and blistering attack of the foreign policy of the Bush administration. See 'The Neoconservative Moment', in *The National Interest*, No. 76 (Summer 2004), pp. 57–68.
93. I am grateful to my colleague Philip Hansen for reading and discussing this introduction with me at length. I would also like to thank Ken Reshaur, Jack Gunnell, Gordon Schochet, Michael Jensen, and Brian Caterino for their helpful comments on earlier drafts. Thanks also to historian and colleague Ken Leyton-Brown for many inspiring discussions over lunch.

Preface to the 1988 Edition

Leo Strauss is generally regarded as an historian of ideas, albeit a very unusual one. He has written many commentaries on the major figures in the history of political thought; among these are books on Socrates, Plato, Aristotle, Xenophon, Machiavelli, Spinoza and Hobbes. What is unusual about these works is that their author insists that all great political philosophers conceal their true thoughts or leave them unsaid. What the philosophers wrote clearly and explicitly was their exoteric philosophy, hiding behind which is their real and more complete esoteric philosophy. Strauss therefore introduced a hermeneutic (i.e. a method of interpretation) intended to unearth the hidden thoughts of the philosophers. The method he used seemed unusual: he attributed great significance to the numbers of chapters or paragraphs in a work, he focused on what was literally in the middle of a book to shed light on the heart of the matter, and he drew important conclusions from the silences of philosophers. It is not surprising that he has come to be regarded as a most enigmatic figure among scholars. What is most baffling of all is the number of young scholars eager to follow in his footsteps.

In this book I shall ignore altogether Strauss's contribution to the study of the history of ideas. I shall argue that Strauss is a philosopher with a unique and disturbing set of ideas that he is reluctant to state clearly and unambiguously. Instead, he hides his views behind a veil of scholarship. I believe that Strauss himself wrote esoterically. The intention of this work is to uncover his esoteric philosophy.

In my attempt to uncover the hidden philosophy, I will *not* apply Strauss's method to his work. I will not attribute great significance to his silences. I will not draw any conclusions from the number of chapters in a book, or from the number of paragraphs in a chapter. Nor will I assume that what is in the center of a work is necessarily the heart of the matter. I will under no circumstances reverse what Strauss actually says or maintain that he believes the opposite of what he has actually written. I will not look behind the surface. Everything I will attribute to Strauss is directly there, not between the lines or behind the lines, but *in the lines*.

The reader is entitled to wonder: if Strauss's own political ideas can be found 'in the lines', how can they be said to be hidden or esoteric? I believe that Strauss's philosophy is esoteric in the following senses. First, it is hidden behind a veil of scholarship or dispersed in the course of detailed and sometimes tedious commentaries. It is expressed in the most unsystematic fashion – reflections on religious matters appearing in the context of discussions of social science methodology, insights about the crisis of modern times in the midst of interpretations of the plays of Aristophanes, and criticism of Aquinas in the context of an exposition on Marsilius of Padua. It is therefore important for one who would understand Strauss to study all of his work as a unity and not as isolated texts. Reviewers of his books who have tried to make sense of one book in isolation from the others have generally admitted to being puzzled and perplexed.

The second sense in which Strauss's writing is esoteric is that his intention does not readily disclose itself. What Strauss appears to say clearly, explicitly and repeatedly is not the whole truth: it hides the full complexity of what he really thinks. I am not suggesting that Strauss believes the opposite of what he writes explicitly. I have no intention of dismissing what he says repeatedly and in the most obvious places as expressions of salutary myths that have no bearing on his real thought. I intend to take seriously everything that Strauss says. I do not regard, nor do I think that Strauss ever believed, that those who write esoterically are liars. Strauss says a great deal about noble lies and pious frauds, and he certainly regards these to be the essence of every genuine political philosophy. But these noble lies contain part of the truth and sometimes the whole truth. Strauss himself illustrates how the truth is contained in the lie by the story of the pious ascetic which Al Farabi uses to illustrate the secretive nature of Plato's writings (Strauss, *What Is Political Philosophy?*, p. 135). The pious ascetic was well known in his city for his abstinence, abasement and mortification, for his probity, propriety and devotion. But for some reason he aroused the hostility of the ruler of his city. The latter ordered his arrest, and to make sure he did not flee, he placed the guards of the city gates on alert. In spite of this, the ascetic managed to escape from the city. Dressed as a drunk and singing a tune to cymbals, he approached the city gates. When the guard asked him who he was, he replied that he was the pious ascetic that everyone was looking for. The guard did not believe him, and let him go.

The pious ascetic is the symbol of the esoteric writer. He lies in *deed* or manner or style of expression, but does not lie in *speech*. It is my contention that Strauss is like the pious ascetic: if we are to understand him, we must learn to take him literally. Strauss's own noble lies, like the lie of the pious ascetic, are not simple falsehoods. They are misleading not so much because of what they say, but because of the pious manner that Strauss generally adopts when he makes his most radical statements. Moreover, what Strauss actually says seems so contrary to his reputation that we are inclined not to believe him.

The third sense in which Strauss's thought is esoteric has to do with the fact that Strauss's ideas are camouflaged by his dual use of key words like virtue, justice, nobility and gentlemanliness. The dual meanings assigned to these words is explicitly revealed only in certain contexts, but taken for granted throughout his writings. We cannot read him literally unless we understand the meanings of the words he uses. What Strauss means by virtue, justice, nobility and gentlemanliness depends on *whose* virtue, justice and nobility or gentlemanliness is at issue. Strauss does not believe that the same standards are applicable to all people. Many an apparent contradiction in Strauss's writings can be resolved simply by paying attention to the meanings of words.

Strauss often avails himself of imagery and metaphors borrowed from Plato, Xenophon, Heraclitus, Aristophanes, the Sophists and others. For those unfamiliar with such imagery, his language may seem peculiar, but on the whole the use of such imagery generally gives his writing more color than it might otherwise possess. For example, Strauss borrows the images of 'The Just' and 'The Unjust Speech' from Aristophanes's *Clouds*. The 'Just' and 'Unjust Speech' are personifications of Justice and Injustice, or Right and Wrong who are depicted on stage in a competition to possess the soul of a certain young man by their speeches. Strauss often uses the expression the 'Just Speech' even when Aristophanes is not part of the context. It will become apparent in the course of this study that this image is appealing to Strauss because justice and injustice are for him primarily a matter of speech or a way of thinking that is unsupported by any universal reality independent of man.

Strauss borrows the idea of the 'real man' from Callicles in Plato's *Gorgias* and contrasts it to the concept of the 'gentleman' drawn from Xenophon. As we shall see, the difference between the 'gentleman' and the 'real man' is the key to understanding what Strauss means by insisting that the political solution *par excellence* is the rule of 'gentlemen'.

Another example of a borrowed metaphor is that of the 'wave'. Strauss's essay 'The Three Waves of Modernity' is a play on the 'wave' metaphor in Book v of Plato's *Republic*. Plato refers to the three 'waves' which prevent the actualization of the ideal rule of the philosophers. The 'waves' are obstacles to the realization of the 'city in speech' as well as waves of laughter that Socrates expects to encounter when he suggests that philosophers should be kings or that the family should be abolished or that women should exercise in the nude with men. In the same spirit, Strauss's three 'waves' of modernity are obstacles to the realization of the regime according to nature, since modernity is a conscious revolt against nature. The waves could also be waves of laughter from those wise enough to realize the impossibility of the 'modern project'.

Strauss uses other metaphors such as the 'stargazer', which he borrows from Plato's parable of the ship where the drunken sailors are said to throw the helmsman overboard because he is a stargazer; apparently they did not know that he relied on the stars for navigation. The result is that the ship flounders aimlessly or is lost at sea.

Strauss often uses the metaphor of the cave and of darkness to refer to political society and its beliefs and opinions, whereas light and sunshine refer to the truth, knowledge and the philosophical quest. In contrast to the free flight of the philosopher, the citizen is the captive of the beliefs and opinions of his society. Closely related to the symbols of light and darkness are Heraclitus's imagery of sleep and wakefulness to which Strauss sometimes resorts. According to Heraclitus, most men live their lives in a drunken stupor, they are like sleepers oblivious to the truth. To know and to see the truth is to be awake. I suspect that Heraclitus wants to deliver mankind from their habitual oblivion. But as I will show, Strauss believes that men must be kept in the darkness of the cave, for nothing is to be gained by liberating them from their chains.

By way of abuse, Strauss's work is sometimes described as

kabbalistic. This is meant to emphasize its mysterious and obscurantist nature. But there is to my mind a more profound similarity between Strauss and the Kabbalists. The latter were Jewish mystics who sought to uncover the truth about the Godhead that is hidden in the Torah. The Kabbalists believed that the Torah was a perfect edifice, that every word, every letter was there for a purpose. Even the white around the letters was believed to contain symbols for those who could read them. The Torah was compared to a hard shell protecting a soft inner kernel of truth. It was also compared to a beautiful damsel hiding herself in a secret chamber of her palace, but revealing herself ever so slightly to her lover who haunted the palace. The lover was the student of the Torah who studied her every present and absent letter with monastic dedication. But his efforts alone could not secure his success. The damsel revealed herself to him only whenever she chose. Her beauty was not for all to see, nor was it equally harmless to all. The famous story in the Talmud about the four great rabbis illustrates just how dangerous the truth is to all but the very few. The rabbis engaged in esoteric studies and were said to have 'entered paradise'. There, on beholding the truth, the first died instantly, the second lost his reason, the third became an apostate and seduced the young; only the fourth entered and emerged in peace. Although not religious, Strauss's own conception of the truth bears striking similarities to the Kabbalists, for he also believed that the truth is dangerous: this is why it must be hidden.

As I understand him, Strauss regards political philosophy as the hard outer shell that hides a soft kernel at its center. The soft kernel is philosophy, for which only the few are fit, whereas the many are harmed by it. Political philosophy is the public face of philosophy that hides the truth, not so much to avoid persecution, but in order not to wreak havoc on society, any society.

The title of this book is the *political ideas* and not the *political philosophy* of Leo Strauss because it is an attempt to uncover the inner kernel hidden by the hard outer shell; it is not another shell. My purpose is to reveal the truth that is hidden in the midst of Strauss's commentaries. This means that I will disregard his desire for secrecy, not because I wish to threaten society, but because I believe that the *raison d'être* of esotericism will disappear if the truth does not turn out to be as terrible or as devastating as Strauss claims. Moreover, 'truths' that are taken for granted and silently transmitted from one generation to the next are far more dangerous than 'truths' which are exposed and made the subject of philosophical debate. It is time to bring Strauss's truths to the test, for only then can they become the subjects of philosophical debate, rather than articles of faith for the initiated.

In the course of this study, I propose to show that Strauss's writings contain a philosophy that is clear, consistent and comprehensive. My intention is not to heap abuse on Strauss, but to uncover the fact that he is a thinker with a set of ideas that is novel, unexpected and imaginative, even if they are somewhat perverse. Those who harbor contempt for Strauss will no doubt think that he does not deserve to be regarded as a serious thinker. But it seems to me that this judgement can only be made after the fact. Besides, the fact that his ideas have become so fashionable is sufficient reason to acknowledge that it is about time to study him carefully and take him seriously. Moreover, unless we understand Strauss, we will be unable to explain why so many have found his ideas compelling.

The first chapter is about Strauss's influence, his esoteric style of writing, his method and the method I will use to study his work. Chapter 2 deals with the philosophical assumptions underlying the esoteric style of writing, the influence of Al Farabi on Strauss's thought, and the meaning of political philosophy. I argue that, for Strauss, political philosophy is practical and that the ideal city or 'the city in speech' is not out of reach. Chapter 3 reveals the extent to which philosophy emerges as a revolt against God; it deals with Strauss's interpretation of Genesis. It also includes a dialogue between Strauss and Freud on the theologico-political problem. Parts of this chapter and the previous one form the basis of 'The Esoteric Philosophy of Leo Strauss', published in *Political Theory* (August 1985). Chapter 4 shows the extent to which Strauss shares the ideas of the Epicurians. It also exposes the radically unorthodox nature of Strauss's understanding of Socrates as revealed in the works of Aristophanes, Plato and Xenophon. Chapter 5 analyzes Strauss's conception of classic natural right and explains why it is quite antithetical to the traditions of natural law and natural rights. Chapter 6 deals with Strauss's interpretation of Machiavelli. I argue that Strauss's most significant complaint about Machiavelli is that he says in his own name the terrible but irrevocable truths that the ancients only dared to put in the mouths of madmen, slaves and sophists. A shorter version of this chapter was previously published as 'The Hidden Meaning of Strauss's Thoughts on Machiavelli', in *History of Political Thought* (Winter 1985). Chapter 7 describes Strauss's vision of modernity. Hobbes is at the center of this narrative, since Strauss regards him as *the* quintessentially modern philosopher. Chapter 8 is an account of the 'crisis' of modernity, and the role of historicism, relativism and nihilism in the process of the decline of Western civilization. Strauss has some sobering insights into the limits of politics which are intended to moderate our expectations. If we find him excessively pessimistic, we should remember that the specter of Nazi Germany is always in the back of his mind. In Chapter 9 I argue that, having understood Strauss, we cannot but conclude that his greatest intellectual debt is to Nietzsche. Strauss and Nietzsche are not strictly speaking modern, but post-modern. Chapter 10 explains the status of my interpretation of Strauss in the light of the debates among his students, and the final chapter includes the beginnings of a critique of Strauss's philosopher–superman.

I am indebted to several people: first and foremost, John W. Yolton, who has been a constant source of encouragement and inspiration. I owe a great deal to Harry V. Jaffa's long and untiring but always fascinating and open-minded correspondence. I should particularly like to thank my colleague Shiraz Dossa for carefully reading the whole manuscript, and for his impeccable literary taste that saved me from many infelicities of style, and for numerous discussions. I should also like to thank Lori Williams for proof-reading, and David Bershad for his advice on the cover. My greatest debt is to Dennis Drury for his unfailing support without which I would not have had the leisure necessary to write this book, and for his keen sense of humor which always serves to remind me that scholars ought not to take themselves or their work too seriously. Finally, I am very grateful for the assistance of the Resident Killam Fellowship of the University of Calgary for relieving me of my usual teaching duties and thus enabling me to complete the manuscript much sooner than would have been otherwise possible.

S.B.D.

1

Leo Strauss: Teacher and Philosopher

It is no exaggeration to say that the impact of Leo Strauss on the academic community in North America is a phenomenon. He is the founder of a movement, a school of thought and even a cult.[1] Leo Strauss wrote some 15 books and 80 articles.[2] However, his notoriety is due not so much to the evident superiority of his work,[3] but to the fervent devotion of his unusually arduous and zealous followers. Universities in Canada and the United States now abound with these disputatious, dogmatic and vehemently defensive disciples known as Straussians. They occupy high positions in almost all the universities in North America,[4] and have, without a shadow of a doubt, become a 'force' to be reckoned with.[5]

Leo Strauss was born in Kirchhain, Hessen, Germany, on 20 September 1899. He studied at the Universities of Marburg[6] and Hamburg where he came in contact with Husserl and the young Heidegger. In 1921 he received the degree of Doctor of Philosophy at Hamburg. From 1925 to 1932 he held a position at the Academy of Jewish Research in Berlin.[7] In 1932 he left Germany for France and England, and he went to the United States in 1938 where he joined the Graduate Faculty of the New School for Social Research in New York.[8] In 1949 he became a Professor of Political Science at the University of Chicago, where he made his mark. He taught briefly at Claremont Men's College after leaving Chicago in 1968, then retired to the life of a scholar-in-residence at St John's College in Annapolis, Maryland, in 1969.[9] When he died on 18 October 1973, eulogies poured forth from his students and disciples praising him lavishly and without restraint.[10]

He was described as 'the greatest teacher of political science since Machiavelli'.[11] He was the 'best, and the wisest, and the most just'.[12] He was a man of 'a different order'.[13] He was even compared to Socrates; and his life was believed to mirror that of Socrates in very significant ways. Like Socrates, he was a man the

1

like of which is rarely if ever experienced; and like Socrates, 'he was despised, ridiculed, misrepresented, envied, and sometimes even ignored'.[14] Like Socrates, he lived in a civilization in decline. Like Socrates, he was a gadfly who tried to awaken us from our moral and intellectual slumber. When Strauss came to Chicago in 1949, the Political Science profession 'radiated confidence in the capacity of the scientific study of politics'. But when Strauss died, it was 'far less confident'; its science seemed 'pedestrian and its mastery of political life further away than ever'. He did not change political science any more than Socrates changed Athens, but like the latter he 'administered a resounding jolt'.[15] He uncovered ignorance where previously knowledge was believed to reside. And his 'Herculean revival of the ancients' in political science was described as a 'light in the dark'.[16] Of course, all this may be a testimony not to the greatness of Strauss, but to the poverty of political science.

Those who were fortunate enough to experience the captivating art of Strauss fell prey to his spell. His students describe how they were 'captured',[17] enchanted and delighted by him. Those who wandered into his seminars at the University of Chicago were 'awestruck'.[18] He left them 'confused, excited, mildly stunned'.[19] He was, to say the least, so 'unprepossessing' that some confessed that they 'soon grew dizzy'.[20] Not only his students, but his students' students invariably describe their experience as an awakening, a 'conversion', a 'turning to light'.[21]

What was and continues to be the source of Strauss's appeal? Why did so many flock to him? Why did he have such an impact upon them? And what did he teach them? The answers to these questions are by no means clear, but his students give us some clues that lead me to come to the following conclusions. First, it is clear that there is a cult that revolves around his personality; he certainly seems to have 'permitted' the sort of discipleship that developed around him. We see his students emulating him, some with greater success than others. They too attempt to establish 'intimate ties' with their students by socializing with them, spending a great deal of time eating, drinking and talking together.[22] This practice allows the professor to enter the lives of the students and to shape their character in its most minute details. At the same time, the students are flattered to be among those chosen to be members of the charmed circle. It gives them a degree of self-esteem and a sense of belonging to a community that naturally satisfies their gregariousness.[23] It is not like belonging to any group of drop-outs or 'drones'.[24] There is a special pride in belonging to an intellectual elite. However, there is more involved in the fascination with Strauss and the Straussians, and that is the inestimable appeal of secrecy. The group is possessed of a secret wisdom; members share common insights that are not readily apparent to ordinary folk. They belong not just because they were chosen by the guru at hand, but because nature herself has singled them out.

Cynics have suggested that the real appeal of the Straussians is the material benefits they bestow on their members; they allow them to navigate through the academic labyrinth successfully because they function as a placement agency. This explanation, however, is not only uncharitable, it misses the mark. There are other ways to navigate through the academic labyrinth; becoming a Straussian is surely not the easiest among them. Indeed, it would be a most difficult route for someone who did not genuinely share the insights of the group. The cost in hypocrisy, untruthfulness and the fear of being found out would be too high to make it worthwhile. It is my contention that the real appeal of Strauss and his followers lies in the enchanting, seductive, complete and comprehensive nature of their teaching.

Strauss taught his students two things that are intimately related to one another. First, that a great book is 'literally full of wonders' and 'secret rooms'.[25] But only very careful study can elicit the secrets contained in the 'great books'. These hidden treasures are not intended to be revealed to everyone. They are profound insights into the nature of reality that are guarded by 'seven seals'.[26] That this is the case, and must necessarily be the case, is apparent to anyone who has any inkling of the truths that the great books contain. This is the second thing that Strauss taught his students: *the incontrovertible truth* about the nature of things, especially the 'human things', the world of man and politics. He taught them the truths that are affirmed by all the wise men of antiquity (and intentionally denied by the modern rebels against antiquity, nay against nature herself). In short, Strauss taught them 'to see reality'![27] It is no wonder that they regarded him as a philosopher.[28] I am convinced that Strauss's students are right; Strauss is a philosopher. Therein lies both his importance and his charm.

Strauss is not generally regarded as a philosopher, but as a scholar and a historian of ideas. This is understandable, for he was a most prolific writer on the history of political thought. His most famous books include *Persecution and the Art of Writing*, *Natural Right and History*, *Thoughts on Machiavelli*, *The City and Man* and *On Tyranny*. All his books and most of his articles are commentaries on the great political philosophers of the past, even when this is not made obvious by the titles. It is therefore not surprising that those who have written critically about Strauss have taken issue with him on his interpretations of philosophers such as Plato, Machiavelli and Locke. Others have taken issue with his hermeneutics or methods of interpretation.[29] Judged solely as a historian of ideas, Strauss deserves much of the contempt that has been heaped upon him. But Strauss is not an ordinary historian.

Strauss is an important philosopher worthy of careful study and criticism. He is a philosopher in the rich and meaningful sense of having a most comprehensive view of the world: of life and death, morality and religion, politics and society, justice and injustice. In this study I hope to show the extent to which Strauss's vision is complete and compelling, formidable and frightening. He is the author of a startling political philosophy that has captured the imagination of many. Yet the ideas that have cast such a spell are nowhere explicitly stated, disclosed or argued for. Instead, they are hidden in the midst of detailed commentaries on the history of political thought. In this book, I set out to unravel this vision, to reconstruct the puzzle whose pieces have been so widely dispersed. Unless we understand the ideas that are at the bottom of his commentaries, the latter will remain elusive. Moreover, we cannot hope to understand the reasons for Strauss's mysterious appeal unless we take him seriously as a man of ideas rather than an historian of ideas.

I have not had the good fortune to experience the personal charm of Leo Strauss, nor have I ever been enchanted by any of his students, or greatly moved by any of his books. I confess that I generally found his commentaries on the classic texts arid, insipid, tedious and repetitive. I was sympathetic with those reviewers who were genuinely perplexed as to how such rubbish could have been published. But as soon as I began to regard Strauss as a philosopher, and set out to discover the political philosophy behind what appeared to be mundane commentaries, I began to find the work of Leo Strauss fascinating, captivating and even bewitching. In writing this book, I must also be laboring under his spell. But being neither his student nor a student's student, I have sufficient distance to write a book that is not meant only for the initiated. My intention is to lay bare Strauss's ideas and assumptions. Only then can they become the subject of serious debate and criticism, rather than the objects of the clandestine discipleship of the faithful.

The task of reconstructing the political philosophy of Leo Strauss is not without its difficulties. To reconstruct the political ideas of a man from his numerous commentaries on the work of others is difficult enough under the most ordinary circumstances. In Strauss's case, however, the task is rendered more complex by his esotericism. Strauss maintained that political philosophers have always hidden their true ideas. One must therefore distinguish between their esoteric and their exoteric philosophy. What they repeat most frequently and most boldly is their exoteric or political 'teaching': a teaching they espouse publicly for political reasons.[30]

Strauss almost never refers to a writer's 'thought', 'ideas' or 'philosophy'. The distinctively Straussian word is 'teaching'. Unlike words such as philosophy, ideas or theory, the word 'teaching' denotes a multifaceted work that contains more than one message. In 'teaching' there is a teacher and a pupil, therefore what is taught will depend not only on the teacher, but also on the pupil, or the one who is being taught. Philosophers do not reveal their ideas to anyone indiscriminately. There are certain things that are not appropriate to teach to certain people. Nor is the truth equally harmless to all.[31]

When in ordinary discourse we refer to someone's philosophy, we are interested in what that person thought regardless of whom he might be speaking to. We are interested in what that philosopher regards as the whole truth. In Strauss's view, the whole truth is what the philosopher in question might say to someone he trusts, to other wise men who will not be harmed by it. The whole truth must be extracted with painstaking effort from the multifaceted teaching which the philosopher bequeaths.[32]

The reason that philosophers must write esoterically is not simply to avoid persecution for their unorthodox views. The more significant reason, and the one equally applicable to all ages, is that the truth is not harmless. Indeed, when made public, it endangers the life of society, if not civilization. A commentator who, like Strauss, is convinced that the truth is harmful will also write esoterically.

Strauss held that the truth is dangerous. This idea is understandable in the light of what Strauss believed to be the content of the truth. In the course of this study I hope to show that Strauss's claim regarding the dangerous and unsalutary nature of truth is guaranteed by what he regards as the content of the latter. If Strauss is wrong about the truth, then the *raison d'être* of his esotericism collapses.

It may seem preposterous to suggest that Strauss intentionally hid his own views. What reason could he possibly have to write with caution and reserve? Was he not fortunate enough to live and write in a society whose freedom has hitherto been unsurpassed?[33] In Strauss's view, there can be no society in which complete freedom of speech is guaranteed. Society rests on faith in the intrinsic superiority of its founding principles; without this 'unqualified commitment' of the many, any society is bound to crumble.[34] Uncovering the reason that prevented Strauss from giving a clear account of his teaching is inseparable from understanding his political philosophy. To understand his alarmingly unconventional vision is to grasp immediately why it was necessary for Strauss to write with so much caution and reserve.

It has been objected that Strauss is not himself an esoteric writer on the grounds that he has never admitted to writing esoterically himself.[35] However, Strauss himself admits to being an esoteric writer. In *On Tyranny*, he explains that a book written by a wise man does not disclose itself except in the appropriate place, which is not in the beginning.[36] Then commenting on his own work, he says that commentaries on the great books must follow their example or

> [engage] in long-winded and sometimes repetitious considerations which can arrest attention only if one sees their purpose, and it is necessary that this purpose should reveal itself in its proper place, which cannot be at the beginning.[37]

Strauss therefore abandons the practice of Anglo-Saxon writers who begin by stating their purpose clearly and unambiguously. Many of his students recognize this and follow his example. In a preface to a collection of essays in honor of Leo Strauss, written largely by his former students, the following statement explains their understanding of the style they have inherited from their master:

> Wishing neither to be destroyed nor to bring destruction upon the multitude, the considerate few have imperturbably conveyed to their readers an eloquence of articulate silences and pregnant indications.[38]

That Strauss and his followers write esoteric commentaries on the history of political thought has its source not only in their conviction that their political ideas are unpalatable to *any* society, but also in their conviction that they are the sorts of ideas that are likely to wreak havoc on public order (if widely dispersed). Their style is a testimony to their prudence (in sparing themselves) and their considerateness (in sparing the world).

Allan Bloom has usefully divided the works of Leo Strauss into three stages that reveal the deepening of his esoteric style of writing.[39] The first is the pre-Straussian phase which is represented by *Spinoza's Critique of Religion* and *The Political Philosophy of Hobbes*. This phase of his work is not characteristically Straussian. Strauss's mode of studying the philosophers in question is almost conventional. The peculiarly Straussian hermeneutics is absent; there is nothing outrageous about his manner of approaching the texts. One can even venture to add that his book on Hobbes is considered almost respectable among historians. It is no wonder that of his books this was the one of which he was least proud. As Bloom puts it, Strauss does not yet know antiquity. He knows only the 'Epicurean' criticism of religion, but he has not yet discovered 'Platonic' religious criticism. Bloom's understanding of Strauss is particularly penetrating; being true to his master, he does not elaborate further. The meaning of this will, however, becomes apparent in the following.[40]

According to Bloom, the second stage of Strauss's development is the most significant. It consists of what he considered to be a momentous discovery that was to inform his work for the rest of his life. That was his discovery of 'esoteric writing'. The latter was more than a style of writing, it was the basis of a hermeneutic that Strauss used to uncover the hidden meanings of the great writers of the past. More significantly, it was the key to understanding the philosophy of the wise men of antiquity. This philosophy was to become Strauss's own and was to appear covertly behind the multiplicity of commentaries on the history of political thought. His own style of writing during this phase is described as being 'still akin to other scholars', but the interpretations seem to be 'based on a perverse attention to detail'.[41] This was the Strauss who became the subject of philosophical comedy; the interpreter who was obsessed with the idea of a secret numerology; he counted chapters and paragraphs, he added, divided and multiplied. All these he regarded as clues by which the hidden meaning of the text could be uncovered. That period of his work is represented by *Persecution and the Art of Writing*, *On Tyranny* and *Natural Right and History*. The latter is perhaps his most famous work; Bloom describes it as an 'unhistorical history of philosophy'.[42]

According to Bloom, the third stage of Strauss's intellectual development consists of a deepening of the second stage. His discovery of esoteric writing is supplemented by a conscious effort to perfect that very style in his own writings. Strauss has fully liberated himself from the constraints of modern scholarship; he has joined his kindred spirits of antiquity. The books of his 'ripeness' were 'alien' even to his closest students. Bloom describes them as 'suffused with a tension' and 'at once unprepossessing and forbidding'.[43] The books of this period include *City and Man*, *The Argument and the Action of Plato's Laws* and *Thoughts on Machiavelli*. On rereading the latter book, Bloom is struck by its complexity; he seems almost uncertain whether he understood it the first time, and even less certain that he understands it now. He finds its contents 'guarded by seven seals'.[44]

Unraveling Strauss's own philosophical views from his interpretations is therefore regarded as 'a task of almost overwhelming complexity'.[45] Strauss's own thought is so 'compressed' into the fabric of his interpretations that 'each of his interpretations would itself require lengthy interpretations in order for it to be fully understood'.[46] Even his followers regard his ideas as 'mysterious, perplexing, laconic and singularly enigmatic'.[47] And worst of all, his silences are believed to be as significant as his lengthy discussions.[48] If he has a doctrine at all, it is certainly a most 'elusive' one.[49] Even Strauss's admirers 'exhibit uncertainty and disagreement as to what his views were'.[50]

Understanding Strauss's own ideas is not a simple task, but its difficulties have surely been exaggerated by his admirers. Strauss may be mysterious, but he is not impenetrable. Strauss's teaching is available to anyone who has the archival fortitude to unearth it. Strauss writes esoterically, but esoteric writings are not elusive to the careful reader. Otherwise Strauss could not have written his commentaries on the work of writers who had even more reason to conceal their views. Strauss is esoteric, not devious.

Equally exaggerated is the claim that Strauss's teaching is so elusive that his followers disagree about its nature. This flies in the face of the overwhelming agreement that is readily witnessed among his followers. There is a division among Strauss's students between what I will call the 'political' and the 'philosophical' Straussians. The debate between Harry Jaffa and Thomas Pangle is a case in point. But as I will show below, these two positions are integral parts of Strauss's comprehensive philosophy; they are both *perfectly* compatible with the teachings of Leo Strauss as I understand them.[51]

Thus, there are two difficulties with which an interpreter of Leo Strauss must contend. The first is that he expresses his ideas in the form of commentaries. The second is that he writes these commentaries in an esoteric style. I will discuss each in turn.

First, how should one seek to understand the political ideas that illuminate Strauss's numerous commentaries on the great books? Is it possible to construct a philosophy that is comprehensive, complete and compelling from the rare occasions in which the commentator speaks in his own name? Of course not. Nor is this necessary. Strauss almost never refrains from passing judgements on the philosophers whose work he seeks to understand. Indeed, his whole account of the history of political thought is a story of doom in which the wise, glorious and noble 'ancients' are overrun by the barbarous, impudent and vulgar 'moderns'. The history of political thought is a tragedy in the sense that the noble and superior are vanquished by the ignoble and inferior. The urbane, aristocratic and profound truths of Plato and Aristotle are replaced by the ribald, plebeian and demotic ideas of Hobbes and Marx. Strauss's narrative of doom, decline and degeneration leaves little doubt that his preference is for the ancients.[52] Suggestions that despite all appearances, Strauss did not necessarily side with the ancients are preposterous attempts at obfuscation.[53]

In interpreting Strauss, it is only reasonable to attribute to him the ideas he attributes to the wise rather than to the unwise. But we must be careful not to jump to the conclusion that Strauss is a classicist in any ordinary sense. This might lead us to the erroneous conclusion that he is tame and timid, dull and predictable. Nothing could be further from the truth. The real Strauss is surprising, shocking and simply outrageous.

We cannot hope to understand Strauss unless we understand the ideas he attributes to the ancient philosophers. What he understood by the 'ancients' and the ideas he attributes to them are not those with which they are generally associated. For most of us the names of Plato and Aristotle conjure up a certain picture that we erroneously take for granted when Strauss refers to their authority. It is important to be aware of the fact that Strauss's introduction to the classical philosophers came through the writings of the Islamic and Jewish thinkers. The latter's view of Plato and Aristotle differs considerably from the Christian thinkers of the Middle Ages whose understanding of these pagan philosophers we are more likely to share. Unless we understand the nature of the authority to which Strauss appeals in his dramatic confrontation with modernity, we will fail to grasp what is at issue between ancients and moderns, his conception of modernity and his diagnosis of its ills. The first half of this book deals with the ancients, the second with the moderns. We cannot understand his critique of the latter without grasping his unique if not altogether scandalous understanding of the former.

The second difficulty encountered by one who sets out to grasp the political ideas of Leo Strauss is deciding what to make of his esoteric style, and whether it is necessary to use his special hermeneutic to dismantle it. Must we apply Strauss's method of interpretation to his own work in order to get an adequate grasp of his thought? Or is it possible to understand Strauss using only the most conventional methods of interpretation? It seems to me that both courses of action have their hazards.

In their efforts to unlock at least a few of the seven seals that guard the political philosophy of Leo Strauss, some interpreters have turned Strauss's own methods of interpretation on his own work.[54] But in doing so, they have exposed their work to the sorts of objections to which Strauss's method is vulnerable.

Strauss's method of interpretation is notoriously lacking in clarity and rigor. The method can be described as follows. Anyone who would interpret the work of a philosopher or great writer must pay careful attention to his contradictions and other intentional blunders.[55] The latter are, according to Strauss, deliberate means by which writers conceal their thoughts. Interpreters must also beware of the beginnings of texts; these are not generally the appropriate places in which careful writers disclose their true intentions, but they nevertheless providé significant clues.[56] Careful attention must be paid to the center of any work or discussion for that is likely to be the heart of the matter. True philosophers have an esoteric and an exoteric teaching. This is necessitated by the nature of philosophy on the one hand, and of politics or 'the city' on the other. Philosophy necessarily comes into conflict with the city because it endangers 'the unqualified commitment of the many to the opinions on which society rests'.[57] Philosophers must therefore employ numerous methods of misdirection to ensure that philosophy remains the preserve of the few. Moreover, they have an acute sense of their social responsibility, and when they are not busy concealing dangerous truths, they are eagerly teaching salutary myths. For according to Strauss, 'it is not wrong to teach doctrines which one regards as erroneous'.[58] On the contrary, it is praiseworthy; it manifests the philosopher's recognition of his social responsibility.

The situation appears to confront the interpreter with insurmountable difficulties. How is the interpreter to decide which of the contradictory statements accurately represent the ideas of the philosopher? How can the interpreter distinguish between the dangerous truths and the salutary myths? If the philosopher says *P*, how would the interpreter know if he means *P* or *not P*? It is no wonder that Sabine described Strauss's hermeneutic as an 'invitation to perverse ingenuity'.[59]

Sabine's conclusion seems reasonable, but it does not reflect what actually happens. It does not account for the overwhelming unanimity readily observable among Straussian interpreters.[60] Indeed, the most persistent complaint against Straussian scholars is that they are almost never surprising; they can always be relied on not to be original. Most of their work is little more than a pale imitation of Strauss's. What is the explanation for this?

I would like to suggest the reason that may explain why Straussian scholars are so incurably predictable. It is my contention that Strauss's method is a philosophy in disguise. It is neither possible nor fruitful to use the method unless one has already accepted his philosophical assumptions: assumptions about what is wise and foolish, noble and ignoble, true and false. Those who use the method share a conception of the good, the true and the useful. They know that only the few can lead the good life, the life according to nature. They know that the truth is unpalatable to 'the city'. They know what sorts of beliefs are useful to the preservation of political order. They know which philosophers are wise and which are foolish. They know that the wise conceal the truth and pay lip service to the salutary myths. In contrast, the unwise either believe the salutary myths or believe that the truth can be openly declared without causing harm. Quite understandably, the use of Strauss's method does not yield infinitely diverse results. There is really very little 'method' in Strauss's hermeneutics. What is important about Strauss's 'method' is not its form, but its *content*. The method is inseparable from Strauss's philosophy; it contains particular assumptions about the nature of the world, of philosophy, of human nature and of political life.

Strauss begins with the assumption that the conflict between philosophy and the city is irresolvable. Those who recognize this conflict are the wise ancients, whereas those who reject the wisdom of antiquity are the vulgar and unwise moderns. The story is much more complicated and much more interesting than this, as I hope to show. However, it is meant to provide the interpreter with a guiding light. When the 'method' is so understood, it makes the task of the interpreter alarmingly simple. Strauss has provided his followers with a philosophy kit. It is certainly easy to observe how the kit has provided those unfit for the rigors of scholarship with a quick recipe or an easy path. However, Strauss has many more followers than people who truly understand him. Interestingly, such misunderstandings are not as distressing to Strauss as one would be inclined to think; for he possesses a conception of truth that is at least unconventional, if not truly unusual. He is not one to be distressed at being misunderstood. On the contrary he is likely to think that much more good can result from the failure to understand him fully than would be the case if he were to be understood perfectly.

There is a tendency for commentators to focus on the bizarre methods by which Strauss illustrates that the wisest men of antiquity share the sorts of views he attributes to them. However, in fairness to Strauss, one must point out that his advice to interpreters contains elements that are sound and invaluable. These can be summarized as follows. First, one must read very carefully. Secondly, one must not ignore the political as well as the intellectual climate in which the author finds himself. I do not believe that Strauss is the anti-historicist he is sometimes believed to be. He is anti-historicist only in the sense that he refuses to begin with the assumption that great thinkers may have unconsciously inherited aspects of the 'climate of opinion' of their time. He does not believe the latter is irrelevant, he only wishes to begin with the assumption that what makes a writer great is the ability to transcend the prejudices of his time and the conventions of his society.[61] Thirdly, one must read everything that the author has written even if it does not appear to deal with the subject-matter the interpreter seeks to understand. This is an excellent suggestion even for one who is not convinced by Strauss's reason for making it. Whether a philosopher scatters his thoughts about a certain matter purposefully to hide his views, or simply as a result of oversight, or because his views on a given matter may not be fully formed at a given time, or because he assumes connections between subject-matters that he takes for granted and does not articulate, is irrelevant. It is simply sound advice to say that interpreters must read carefully and turn every stone, even those that appear least likely to yield anything of promise. Equally important for the proper understanding of a work is noting the meaning of words. One cannot simply assume that words commonly in use today have the same meanings for philosophers of other ages, or even our own age. Philosophers may use ordinary words in specialized or technical ways. In short, Strauss's 'method' includes common sense advice that no intelligent interpreter can ignore. I certainly intend to make good use of this 'method' in examining the work of Leo Strauss.

I have no intention of following the example of those interpreters who set out to 'reverse' Strauss's method on his work. I intend to use only conventional methods in interpreting the work of Leo Strauss. I have no intention of relying on his silences to reach my conclusions. Nor will I rely on counting the numbers of times he uses or fails to use a given word or name. Nor will I conclude from the fact that he says something clearly and unambiguously that he believes the opposite. But to say all this is not to say that I will altogether ignore what Strauss regarded as his singular most important 'discovery'.[62] On the contrary, I will regard the 'method' as the key to his own political thought. The 'method' is the cornerstone of Strauss's thinking. It contains his vision of man, politics, philosophy and even of 'the whole'.[63] My aim is to unveil the philosophy that lies embedded in this 'method'. What will emerge as a result of this study will not be a figment of my imagination. It will be founded on what Strauss has actually said, understood in the context in which he said it and in the context of his work as a whole.

A question still remains: is this sound approach sufficient to unearth the esoteric philosophy of Leo Strauss? After all, Strauss himself has warned that in interpreting a book, one cannot 'disregard completely what its author says about the necessity of secrecy and caution'.[64] Strauss has certainly said a great deal about the latter, and anyone who would interpret his work would be unwise to ignore the fact that he writes esoterically. However, I do not intend to ignore this fact. I do not intend to ignore the hints Strauss gives. I will make note of what he says in the center of his text, but I will not give it so much importance as to distort its place within the whole. I will note Strauss's 'silences' in the sense of stating explicitly what is *clearly* implied by the text. Any attempt to follow a bizarre trail of misdirection is likely to obscure rather than to clarify the ideas in question. I am convinced that the esoteric philosophy can be unearthed by reading very carefully, noting the meanings of words, and understanding what is said in the context in which it appears as well as in the context of the whole.

In summary, the method I will employ in my study of Strauss is as follows. First, I will not 'reverse' Strauss's method on his work. This means that I will not under any circumstances maintain that he believes the opposite of what he says explicitly. Nor will I invent or discover complicated trails of misdirection to uncover his meaning. I believe that these sorts of tactics are a caricature of his method (for which he is largely responsible) that will not yield fruit. I am not suggesting that he has not planted such complicated trails in his work, but only that they are unnecessary for a clear grasp of his political thought. As some commentators have noted, Strauss himself tended to employ more ingenuity than was necessary to support his interpretations. What is true of Strauss is true of those who have followed his example in its minute details when studying his work. The result is at best an esoteric work about an esoteric commentator on esoteric writers.

In interpreting Strauss, I do not intend to disregard his advice to interpreters. On the contrary, I will follow his sound advice by reading very carefully and noting the meanings of words or phrases. This is the most important 'technique' that I will employ in my study of Strauss. I consider it common sense for any scholar who would understand a philosopher. It is particularly important in Strauss's case because he uses key words like justice, virtue, nobility and gentlemanliness in more than one sense. He tells us that he does this, following philosophers he admires like Plato, Xenophon and Al Farabi.[65] The special meaning of these words can only be determined in the light of their particular context as well as their context within Strauss's work as a whole.

Secondly, I will attribute to Strauss the ideas he attributes to the wise ancients. I will therefore take special care in understanding the nature of the authority to which he perpetually refers. In commenting on my work, an anonymous reviewer remarked that it has the effect of turning Strauss on his head. If it is true that my work has this effect, it is not one that is achieved by abusing Strauss's method or turning it against him. It is merely the result of understanding more fully the extent to which Strauss has turned our own understanding of the ancients on its head.

Thirdly, far from disregarding Strauss's method, I will regard it as the cornerstone of his political philosophy. In short, I will set out to discover the reasons that prevented Strauss from ever giving a sufficiently clear account of his 'teaching'. Uncovering these reasons is inseparable from giving an account of his unstated political philosophy. In doing this, I will necessarily be disregarding his own desire for secrecy. I will state without caution or reserve what Strauss says with the utmost caution, reserve and 'economy of speech'.[66] I can disregard Strauss's desire for secrecy only because I do not share his conception of the truth or his own way of regarding the value of truth. In writing this book I will be adhering to the biblical principle that the 'truth will set you free'. This is a principle which Strauss must regard with contempt, both for its indiscriminate faith in the goodness of truth and its implicit glorification of freedom.

In conclusion, Strauss's ideas are important not only because they are comprehensive and original, but because they direct and nourish an intellectual elite. Nor is this all. The influence of Leo Strauss is not limited to the academic community. He has rightly been described as a 'guru of American conservatism'[67] and his influence is said to extend to the state department's policy planning staff.[68] This is not altogether surprising or unintentional. The Claremont Graduate School in California, where Strauss's influence is particularly visible, describes itself as an Institute for the Study of Statesmanship and Political Philosophy.[69] Incoming students are informed upon arrival that they will be trained to be statesmen, senators and policy-makers, not scholars and academics.[70] As we shall see, the relationship between statesmanship and political philosophy is one of the central themes of Strauss's writings.

The extent to which Strauss's understanding of political philosophy is *practical* has not been fully appreciated. Stanley Rothman was not far off in suggesting that the appeal of Strauss has (if only in the case of some of his disciples) a close resemblance to the appeal of Marx. Like Marx, Strauss gives his followers 'simple keys' by which to unlock a troublesome, complicated and absurd world. Like Marx, Strauss teaches some of his followers not only to understand the world, but to change it.[71] Joseph Cropsey was offended by this comparison: he understood it to mean that the attraction of Strauss has its source in the lust for power.[72] But far from being offensive, the comparison with Marx is a compliment: it suggests a dedication to public life and a youthful idealism fueled by the conviction that a better world is possible. Despite its severe limitations (Straussians are conservatives without exception, and many are apolitical for reasons that will become clear below), the comparison draws attention to the practical import of Strauss's political ideas.

For Strauss, the task of political philosophy in the world is to educate a special elite that will exert its influence in political life. Democracy understood as mass rule is for Strauss an absurdity simply because 'the mass cannot rule': history shows us that only elites have and can rule. Therefore it is necessary to 'found an aristocracy within democratic mass society'.[73] Strauss and his followers believe that Plato's republic in which philosophers rule over the city is the best regime. Even though Strauss referred to this republic as a 'city in speech', he did not mean that it is unattainable. He meant only that it is improbable because it requires the happy coincidence of philosophy and political power, or the existence of princes friendly to philosophy: it requires that philosophers win the ear of the powerful.

Harry Jaffa draws attention to the reality of the good regime and the practical import of Strauss's work when he writes that

> No one who has experienced the magic of Leo Strauss's teaching can doubt that the best regime not only is possible, but that it has been actual. Nor can he doubt that whatever amelioration of our condition is possible will come about by the influence upon those who exercise political power of its spirit.[74]

In other words, for love of the world, those who have experienced the magic of Leo Strauss must set out to influence the powerful, if not to gain political power themselves. Strauss's political objectives may be well on the way to being realized. Everywhere conservative politicians are happy to lend an ear to conservative intellectuals influenced by Strauss. What are they whispering in the ears of the powerful? How do they hope to change the world? What vision of a better world do they share? Unless we understand the political ideas of the man behind this fantastic project, the very meaning of the contemporary conservative movement will remain elusive.

Despite their influence and widespread appeal, Strauss's ideas have not been laid bare, let alone critically evaluated. In this work I set out to untangle Strauss's ideas from his numerous commentaries. My aim is to interpret and understand Strauss. I will refrain from criticizing him except in my concluding remarks, where I will suggest some lines along which such criticism may proceed.

This book will naturally be denounced by the many faithful, irrespective of the truth of what it has to say about the political philosophy of Strauss. There will be two different reasons for this denunciation, corresponding to the two types of Strauss's disciples. Those who understand fully the truth of my interpretation of the hidden meaning of Strauss's thought will repudiate the book only to remain true to Strauss's desire for secrecy. The rest of his students who are veritably ignorant of his real meaning will be genuinely horrified and appalled by what they will consider to be violent distortions of their master's sacred views.

2

Esoteric Philosophy and Ancient Wisdom

Strauss begins with the assumption that there exists an inevitable conflict between philosophy and the political domain, or as Strauss says, 'the city'. Understanding this conflict is the key to understanding Strauss's political ideas.

Strauss describes his *Persecution and the Art of Writing* as a 'sociology of philosophy'. He distinguishes the latter from the sociology of knowledge. The sociology of knowledge begins with the assumption that there is a harmony between thought and the world; either thought 'determines' political institutions and social relations (idealism), or political institutions and social relations 'determine' thought (materialism). In contrast to the sociology of knowledge, Strauss's sociology of philosophy begins from the assumption that there is an irreconcilable conflict or disharmony between thought, philosophy or science on the one hand, and society, the world, the city, or the political domain on the other.[1] Strauss is therefore opposed to the contemporary fashion of regarding philosophers as men of their time. In Strauss's view, the greatness of a writer lies not so much in being a man of his time, as a man against his time.[2]

Writing in his own name, Strauss declares that there is a permanent antagonism between philosophy or science and society:

> Philosophy or science, the highest activity of man, is the attempt to replace opinion about 'all things' by knowledge of 'all things'; but opinion is the element of society; philosophy or science is therefore the attempt to dissolve the element in which society breaths, and thus it *endangers* society. Hence philosophy or science must remain the preserve of a small minority, and philosophers or scientists must respect the opinions on which society rests. To respect opinions is something entirely different from accepting them as true. Philosophers or scientists who hold this view about the relation of philosophy or science and

society are driven to employ a peculiar manner of writing which would enable them to reveal what they regard as the truth to the few, without endangering the unqualified commitment of the many to the opinions on which society rests. They will distinguish between the true teaching as the esoteric teaching and the socially useful teaching as the exoteric teaching; whereas the exoteric teaching is meant to be easily accessible to every reader, the esoteric teaching discloses itself only to the very careful and well-trained readers after long and concentrated study.[3]

This is the heart of the Straussian philosophy. The passage contains several assumptions that need to be identified. First, Strauss begins with the assumption that philosophy or science is the 'highest activity' of man.[4] Secondly, he assumes that the best political order must be one that makes the 'highest activity' possible.[5] Philosophy or science is therefore the end for which political society exists. However, philosophy or science is the preserve of the few. Political society must therefore be directed to the highest activity of man which is the preserve of the few.

Philosophy *offends* the city because it questions the opinions on which the city is based. Those who offend the citizens are likely to be ridiculed, persecuted or destroyed. Socrates is a case in point. Philosophers must therefore be careful not to offend the citizens if they care for their lives. They must therefore 'respect' the ideas of the city, which Strauss tells us is 'entirely different' from thinking them true. In other words, they must cultivate an exoteric teaching that consists in paying lip service to the ideas of the city. Ironically, the *raison d'être* of the city must be hidden from it.

We would radically misunderstand Strauss if we thought that philosophy must be hidden in order to protect the philosopher from persecution. If that is all Strauss was saying, then he could not make the sort of sweeping statement that he makes about the permanence of the antipathy of philosophy and the world. For Strauss, the conflict does not apply only to those societies that cannot tolerate the freedom to dissent. Strauss is quite earnest about the permanence and universality of the conflict.

I will state more explicitly what Strauss expresses only with the utmost reserve, even in this most explicit of his statements on the matter. Esoteric writing is not necessary simply to protect the philosopher against harmful ignorance and bigotry. There is a deeper and more important reason that corresponds to a deeper and more important aspect of the conflict between philosophy and society: the esoteric art is needed equally for the protection of society. Philosophy does not only *offend* society, it *'endangers'* it.[6] There are two reasons for this. The simpler one is made explicit by Strauss, the deeper and more significant one is apparent only to one who understands the passage in the light of the corpus of Strauss's work.

The simple and obvious reason Strauss insists on the conflict between philosophy and society is that, in his view, society cannot withstand the questioning of philosophy. Society needs 'unqualified commitment' to its own opinions and beliefs.[7] Strauss's position is diametrically opposed to the reigning liberal credo according to which depriving society of free expression is tantamount to 'robbing mankind'.[8] Unlike John Stuart Mill, Strauss does not worry that the ideas on which society rests will putrefy into 'dead dogma' if they are not perpetually challenged.[9] Unlike Mill, Strauss does not believe that truth is salutary. On the contrary, for Strauss, the ideas on which society rests cannot withstand too much scrutiny without crumbling. Societies need myths and illusions if they are to survive.[10] The deeper and more significant reason that philosophy *endangers* society begins to become apparent. The deeper reason is that the truths of philosophy are profoundly at odds with the sorts of pious myths and illusions on which *any* society must necessarily rest. The truths of philosophy therefore come into conflict not only with degenerate societies, but with *all* societies. Philosophy therefore undermines ideas that it recognizes to be necessary to the continued existence of the city. In writing esoterically, philosophers seek to protect not only themselves but their city. They recognize that far from being salutary, the truth is deadly.

Is there a truth so terrible that it threatens to wreak havoc on society unless it is kept secret? What is this deadly truth? Let me come straight to the point: in the course of this work I will show that for Strauss, religion and morality are two of the biggest but most pious swindles ever perpetrated on the human race. But paradoxically, there would be no human race were it not for these swindles. It is therefore of the utmost importance that they be sustained and nurtured. If this is true, then Strauss is right, philosophical truth is as deadly and as dangerous to society as he says it is. For surely, no society could survive in the absence of religion and morality. (As we shall see, Strauss believes that morality depends on religion.)

Strauss claims little originality for his ideas; he attributes them to antiquity, especially to Socrates, Plato and Aristotle. In view of this, it would seem that the most logical place to begin our understanding of Strauss is the classical philosophers Socrates, Plato and Aristotle; but this is not so. The logical place to begin is Strauss's commentaries on Al Farabi. There are several reasons for this. First, in Strauss's view, we cannot understand the classical Greek philosophers if we rely on the Christian tradition of Neoplatonism because the latter tends to Christianize pagan philosophy.[11] Instead, Strauss relies on Al Farabi and the Islamic philosophers.[12] This may account for Strauss's radically original, if not scandalous, interpretations of classical thought. Secondly, the Islamic philosophers, Avicenna, Averroes, Avempace and in particular Al Farabi were the first to bring to the attention of Leo Strauss the discord between philosophy and the city. Farabi is regarded by Strauss as the depository of the wisdom of antiquity. Strauss's view of Al Farabi is therefore essential in understanding anything about Strauss. Indeed, the ideas Strauss attributes to Farabi are repeated like variations on a theme in all of Strauss's commentaries on the 'ancients'.

Whether Strauss actually 'recovers' the wisdom of antiquity or invents it is not of great consequence. What is important for my purposes is to understand the ideas Strauss attributes to antiquity, the ideas Strauss shares with 'his' antiquity.

The Islamic philosophers were the first to bring to the attention of Leo Strauss the precarious predicament of philosophy and of true philosophers in the world. The dangerous plight of the philosopher was particularly acute in the Islamic world where philosophy became a suspect pursuit and philosophers a suspect group of men. Indeed, the word philosophy of *falasifa* in modern Arabic still carries a derogatory connotation indicating empty talk full of false human pride setting itself up above divine wisdom. The *falasifa* were suspected of irreligion because of their praise of the pagan philosophies of Plato and Aristotle.

Strauss is reluctant to say explicitly that the suspicions of the world were true and that the *falasifa* were irreligious. He says merely that their opponents were instrumental in helping them conceal their thought because they 'feared the harm which its publication would cause to those of their fellow-believers whose faith was weak'.[13] The Islamic philosophers thought that the Islamic civilization could not sustain itself if the Islamic religion were undermined. Philosophy must remain hidden so that its irreligious nature does not threaten political order and stability.

The belief that religion is necessary for politics is not peculiar to the Islamic philosophers. The same view is expressed by Plato in the *Laws*. According to Strauss, the *Laws* is Plato's political dialogue *par excellence*.[14] He gives by way of evidence for this the fact that it is the only dialogue that begins with the word 'God'.[15] We are to understand that if *the* political dialogue must begin in this manner, then politics must be absolutely in need of a belief in God or gods and in rewards and punishments in the next life, if not in this one. Because people are 'not capable of virtue',[16] they must be made to believe that their laws have divine origin, that they were made by gods or men inspired by gods. But Strauss knows, as does his Plato, that the originators of law are not gods but human beings.[17] The best laws have their source in wisdom, not gods.

For Strauss, the philosopher *qua* philosopher cannot believe in an afterlife.[18] In his commentary on Aristotle's *Nichomachean Ethics*, Farabi declares that the only happiness is in this life, and that all divergent views are but 'ravings and old women's tales'.[19] He makes the same point in his commentary on Plato, where he denies that Plato believed in the immortality of the soul or in the life beyond. Strauss describes this as a 'flagrant' violation of the *letter* of Plato's teaching. He notes that Farabi makes this remark at the precise point where Plato maintains the very opposite. For Strauss, such flagrant violations of the text are indications that Farabi is expressing his own views. That is not to say that he misrepresents Plato, nor does Strauss think so. He is completely loyal to the intention, the aim and the spirit of Plato. Farabi sees in Plato an esoteric writer, a kindred spirit. Plato appeals to the immortality of the soul only because it is an expedient means by which to motivate the vulgar to act justly.[20]

According to Strauss, the Islamic philosophers made two fundamental assumptions. First, they assumed that philosophy by its very nature is fundamentally irreligious or that philosophical truth can never be reconciled with the truth of revealed religion, whether Islam, Judaism or Christianity. Secondly, they believed that religion is necessary for the maintenance of a civilization in a condition of health, order and stability. The best legal system needs the support of religious doctrine to sustain it and secure strict adherence to law. Recognizing this, philosophers must keep philosophy hidden not only to protect themselves, but to protect the very political order that gives them nurture and makes possible the cultivation of philosophy. They must therefore espouse an exoteric 'teaching' in contradistinction with their esoteric philosophy. As Strauss says,

> The exoteric teaching was needed for protecting philosophy. It was the armor in which philosophy had to appear. It was needed for political reasons. It was the form in which philosophy became visible to the political community. It was the political aspect of philosophy. It was 'political' philosophy.[21]

Political philosophy is therefore the garb in which true philosophy makes its appearance in the world; it is the exoteric face that philosophy uses to present itself to the world. Political philosophy is a salutary teaching that hides the true or esoteric philosophy. Strauss's famous essay 'What is Political Philosophy?' must therefore be read in the light of the preceding quotation.

Unless read very carefully, Strauss's *What Is Political Philosophy?* seems to tell us only what we expect to hear: namely, that political philosophy is a branch of philosophy devoted to acquiring knowledge of the good life and the good society which makes possible the good life. The essay appears pleasant, predictable and tame.[22] However, it begins to take form when the meanings of the words are understood. The good life is the life of the philosopher, or the life dedicated to philosophy.[23] But philosophy 'endangers' the city, therefore the good for which society must be organized is one in which only the few can partake. These few must therefore exercise utmost discretion if they hope to prevent philosophy from destroying the city. They must 'justify philosophy to non-philosophers, to ordinary citizens, to the political community'.[24] Strauss tells us that 'they must follow the example of Odysseus'.[25] He leaves us in the dark as to what the example of Odysseus entails. Should they blind Polyphemus, the one-eyed cyclops? Apparently not. In another book, Strauss tells us that Odysseus was a 'safe speaker'.[26] There, he explains that a safe speaker conceals the truth from the many while revealing it to the few.[27] This is the 'deeper meaning' of 'political philosophy':

the adjective 'political' in the expression 'political philosophy' designates not so much a subject matter as a manner of treatment; from this point of view, I say, 'political philosophy' means primarily not the philosophic treatment of politics, but the political, or popular, treatment of philosophy, or the political introduction to philosophy – the attempt to lead qualified citizens, or rather their qualified sons, from the political to the philosophic life.[28]

Political philosophy is therefore the practical or political aspect of an activity that is not itself practical or political.[29] Political philosophy serves a practical function. It protects the world from philosophy and philosophy from the world. Keeping philosophy hidden not only protects society, it secures the freedom of philosophy because 'society will always try to tyrannize over thought'.[30] Political philosophers must at the same time be careful not to bury philosophy in so much secrecy that it would never see the light of day.

Strauss is a political philosopher. That is not the same as being a liar. Political philosophy is not a bundle of lies. Like Farabi's pious ascetic, it tells the truth and nothing but the truth. This is precisely why one can interpret Strauss without perversely and arbitrarily reversing what he does say explicitly. Strauss tells the truth (or parts of the truth in different places), but he employs a great deal of 'caution or thrift in communicating'.[31] His intention is to lead to the truth those who are fit for it (i.e. potential philosophers). The process is a matter of dragging them out of the cave, or 'liberating them from the charms which obstruct the philosophic effort'.[32] These are the charms by which society attempts to 'tyrannize over thought'.

Strauss provides the best description of this process of liberation in *What Is Political Philosophy?* The example is from Plato's *Laws*. Strauss explains the meaning of the fact that *the* political dialogue *par excellence* begins with an extensive conversation about wine.[33] He notes that the interlocutors are old citizens of communities famous for their laws and for their obedience to their old laws. These men therefore are loyal citizens in the grip of the social charms that obstruct the philosophic effort. If they are to engage in a philosophical dialogue with the Athenian, they must be 'liberated' from these 'charms'. The Athenian therefore engages them in a conversation about wine-drinking, or a pleasure that is forbidden to them by their old laws. The idea is to remind the old men of 'secret and pleasurable transgressions of their own'.[34] The conversation about wine is therefore a 'vicarious enjoyment of wine'.[35] It has a similar effect to actually drinking wine, it 'loosens their tongues; it makes them young: it makes them bold, daring, willing to innovate'.[36] In short, it makes sober, old, law-abiding men like Kleinias and Megillos much more fit for philosophy than they would normally be.

For Strauss, philosophy is 'the very opposite of sobriety or moderation; thought must not be moderate, but fearless, not to say shameless'.[37] Nevertheless, all the talk about wine is not likely to make men like Kleinias and Megillos truly fit for philosophy. They could never be young potential philosophers to whom the truth should be fully revealed. It would be neither safe nor possible to 'liberate' them completely from the 'charms' with which society holds them captive. The Athenian will therefore allow them only a glimpse of the intoxication, madness, boldness, fearlessness and shamelessness that is philosophy. To give little more than a glimpse, he needs moderation, the very opposite of philosophy ('moderation is not a virtue of thought').[38] He needs something foreign to pure philosophy, he needs 'political philosophy'. Political philosophy is therefore the exercise of moderation in speech. 'Moderation is a virtue controlling the philosopher's speech.'[39] Political philosophy is the 'mating of courage and moderation'.[40] In short, political philosophy is moderate speech about immoderate, not to say shameless, intoxicated thoughts.

Al Farabi was particularly sensitive to the dangers of philosophical intoxication. He understood the conflict between philosophy and the world, and so became exceptionally adept at the esoteric art of writing. Strauss's admiration of Farabi is undeniable. He is a master of the lost art of antiquity, and Strauss sets out to be his apprentice. The art consists in a variety of techniques meant to conceal the heterodox teachings from all but the few who could read carefully and who could think. Clues to this peculiar form of writing include the following: contradictions, principles frequently stated but silently contradicted by upholding incompatible views, inexact repetitions, pseudonyms, strange expressions, a frequent use of technical language, ambiguity of expression, and other infelicities of style. All of these must be assumed to be deliberate since it is foolish to think they would escape an intelligent man. The young men with intelligence who can read between the lines will be *struck* by these literary deficiencies and will understand their meaning.[41] Writing between the lines does not, however, preclude stating important truths openly and unambiguously by using as his mouthpiece some disreputable character. Nor is this an indication that a philosopher disapproves of the ideas in question or thinks them false. It shows only, as Strauss explains, 'how much they disapproved of *pronouncing* the *truths* in question'.[42] For example, Strauss believes that Plato uses Thrasymachus as his mouthpiece.[43] (In what is to follow, I will show how Strauss uses Machiavelli as *his* mouthpiece.[44])

Strauss gives a vivid contemporary example of how a man of heterodox views would proceed to avoid persecution by writing esoterically. A philosopher from the communist block would do well to acquaint himself with this peculiar style of writing. (We should not be fooled by this example. Strauss thinks that every genuine thinker, every man against his time, had better acquaint himself with this style.) The imaginary writer from the communist block might declare that he has set out to provide a critique of liberalism when the contrary is his true aim. He would first have to state the liberal position he really wants to defend.

> He would make the statement in the quiet, unspectacular and somewhat boring manner which would seem to be but natural; he would use many technical terms, giving many quotations and attach undue importance to insignificant details; he would seem to forget the holy war of mankind in the petty squabbles of pedants.[45]

(A better description of Strauss's work could not be found.)

The bulk of the work would consist of 'virulent expansions of the most virulent utterances in the holy book or books of the ruling party'.[46] (Strauss uses this technique very skillfully in *Natural Right and History*.) Only when he reaches the heart of the argument

> would he write three or four sentences in that terse and lively style which is apt to arrest the attention of young men who love to think. That central passage would state the case of the

adversaries more clearly, compellingly and mercilessly than it had ever been stated. . . .[47]

In this way the philosopher can express himself while avoiding persecution. The only trouble is that there may be careful readers or 'clever men' who are not trustworthy, and having 'found the author out' would reveal all and denounce him to the authorities. Strauss raises this objection only to dismiss it, saying that thoughtful men are generally trustworthy and not cruel, and that the Socratic dictum that virtue is knowledge must be largely true or esoteric writing would not be possible.

One of the most powerful vehicles at the disposal of esoteric writers is to use the mantle of the history of ideas to express their own views. Not surprisingly, Farabi, a true master of the art,

> avails himself then of the specific immunity of the commentator or the historian in order to speak his mind concerning grave matters in his 'historical' works, rather than in the works in which he speaks in his own name.[48]

Farabi's commentary on Plato is therefore the clue to Farabi's own thoughts. As Strauss remarks, 'we admire the ease with which Farabi invented Platonic speeches'.[49] In other words, what Farabi tells us Plato thinks we can safely take as an indication of Farabi's own views.

It would be a mistake to conclude from the fact that philosophy is so shrouded in secrecy that it has no political function to play. For Farabi as for the other esoteric philosophers, philosophy has a most significant role to play in political life, that is, if the opportunity presents itself. Indeed, Farabi thought, following Plato, that the key to the complete happiness of nations and cities is the rule of the philosophers. But since the rule of the wise is unlikely in the real city, we have two choices. First, we can give up worldly happiness altogether. We can resign ourselves to the fact that the good political order is unrealizable. Philosophers would then forsake politics altogether, or abandon the cave in favor of the sunlight, and consorting only with one another, attain personal happiness by engaging in the supreme human activity of contemplation. But such happiness is likely to be precarious. Man is a political being who cannot realize himself except as part of a political community. Ultimately, politics makes possible the philosophical life which requires leisure. Renouncing politics altogether is therefore not a reasonable option for one who, like Farabi, rejects the belief in a happiness different from the happiness of this life.

The second option is to find a way whereby the philosopher can rule in the real city. Farabi believed that Plato found the solution and follows him in adopting it as the most viable one available. The philosopher cannot rule *openly* in the real city. Plato has given us ample reasons why that is so. Both Strauss and Farabi regard these reasons to be valid for all time.

The alternative to the open or public kingship of the philosopher is a hidden or secret kingship of the philosopher. Strauss seems to endorse what is the only reasonable solution. He describes it as follows:

> We may say that Farabi's Plato eventually replaces the philosopher–king who rules openly in the virtuous city, by the secret kingship of the philosopher who lives privately as a member of an imperfect society which he tries to humanize within the limits of the possible.[50]

The 'secret kingship' of the philosopher depends on the 'chance' that there may be princes friendly to philosophy. This is what Strauss means when he says that the best political order can be realized only by chance.[51] In other words, the best political order is not *impossible*, but only *improbable*. In Strauss's view, Marx's communist utopia is impossible; it depends on a radical change in the nature of human things. In contrast, Plato's 'city in speech' is only improbable. It depends on the chance coincidence of philosophers and princes friendly to philosophy who are willing to listen to their advice. The 'city in speech' becomes a reality when the philosophers win the ear of the powerful. In this way, philosophers can rule the city behind the scenes with no risks to themselves or to philosophy. The solution can be found in the difference between Plato's *Republic* and his *Laws*. The *Laws* fulfills rather than violates the intention of the *Republic*. When Strauss studies Plato's *Laws* for himself, he comes to the same conclusion as Farabi. The Nocturnal Council is cleverly introduced only in the twelfth book of the *Laws* where it is likely to be missed. It ensures the secret rule of the philosopher in the real city.[52]

The actualization of the 'city in speech' is therefore highly probable. In the light of this we can understand Jaffa's remark that 'No one who has experienced the magic of Strauss's teaching can doubt that the best regime not only is possible, but that it has been actual. Nor can he doubt that whatever amelioration of our condition is possible will come about by the influence of those who exercise political power by its spirit.'[53]

Strauss believed that liberal democracy is good in so far as it is a kind of aristocracy in disguise.[54] There is little doubt that many of his students understand their task as one of establishing the secret kingship.[55]

Farabi compares the secret kingship of the philosopher in the real city with the role of the prophet. Like the prophet, the philosopher does not and ought not rule the city openly by holding political office. He can rule only vicariously by the influence he is able to exert on the powerful. That wisdom is, however, not to be confused with the religious knowledge of the prophet. The similarity between the philosopher and the prophet is much more superficial than either Farabi or Strauss would have us believe. The philosopher's wisdom does not consist in religious knowledge, for the latter is according to Farabi 'the lowest step on the ladder of cognitive pursuits'.[56] Neither Farabi nor Strauss makes clear what the wisdom of the philosopher is, but there is sufficient evidence here (and throughout the corpus of Strauss's work) to indicate that it dispenses with the sorts of limitations that the Sacred Law tends to impose on the affairs of men. The point of the secret rule of the philosopher is to replace the Sacred Law with his own wisdom. Strauss understands Farabi as a man who lays the foundation for the 'secular alliance' between philosophers and princes friendly to philosophy. In so doing, he 'initiates the tradition whose most famous representatives in the west are Marsilius of Padua and Machiavelli'.[57] Strauss silently omits Plato. The implication is that the tradition that Strauss describes belongs equally to Plato as to Machiavelli.

In the following chapters, I will argue that Strauss's moral philosophy fails to recognize any absolute limits on human conduct; and this to my mind explains Strauss's rejection of the tradition of natural law: a fact that is very ill-understood, if at all, and one that is obfuscated by all his polemics against the atheism and relativism of modernity. In what is to follow, it will become apparent that the philosopher who has the ear of the powerful will give advice that is not unlike the sort that Machiavelli gives his prince. Suffice it to say here that the irreligious character of philosophy facilitates the sort of moral ruthlessness that the esoteric philosophers believe is required by politics.

Strauss describes Farabi's view of morality as 'shocking'.[58] However, he commends him for expressing this shocking 'truth' with the utmost caution and restraint. By carefully unpacking the meaning of his terms, Strauss reveals to us part of his meaning. He notes that each of the words 'virtue', 'nobility' and 'happiness' has two meanings. There is true or real virtue, nobility and happiness, and apparent virtue, nobility and happiness.[59] The morally virtuous life is *not* the life of *true* virtue, nobility and happiness; it leads only to 'apparent happiness'.[60] Moral virtue leads only to things that are 'useful', 'necessary' or 'noble' in the vulgar sense. The moral life is not truly the 'desired way of life'.[61] The truly desired and desirable way of life is the life of contemplation. The highest life is therefore not the morally virtuous life. The life of contemplation (the life of the philosopher) transcends the sphere of morality, just as it transcends the sphere of politics and necessity.[62] It is a life that one might venture to describe, following Nietzsche, as beyond good and evil.

Strauss describes Farabi as a man who might have been attracted as a pupil of philosophy to what he 'abhorred as a believer'.[63] His mind must have consisted of 'two hermetically sealed compartments'.[64] It was the sort of mind that is 'conveniently attributed to the Latin Averroists'.[65] (Similarly, Jewish Straussians have been regarded as Latin Averroists and described as 'Hellenized Jews'.[66])

Let me summarize in more explicit terms what Strauss says only implicitly about Farabi's philosophy. There is no life beyond this life. There is no happiness but the happiness to be found in this life. There is no transcendent God. Philosophers are as gods among men. The only happiness accessible to us is through the rule of the philosophers. But the philosophers are neither loved nor recognized. On the contrary, they are despised and ridiculed. Instead, people wish to be ruled by the Divine Law. In their ignorance, they fail to recognize the shortcomings of law and its inability to accommodate the variable circumstances of human life. People are also ignorant of the absolutism of the Divine Law and hence of the sacrifices it will exact. If man is to be modestly happy, wisdom must replace law and philosophy must replace the dogged adherence to Sacred Law.

If the philosophers seem arrogant that should not surprise us; they are a sort of wounded aristocracy, a jilted deity. Nor should it surprise us that they are made a laughing stock by the world. They are rather awkward and their step is unsure in the darkness of the cave; *that* is not their domain. They belong to a domain outside the cave with the sun and the other heavenly bodies. If they attempt to openly take their rightful place at the helm, they will be thrown overboard as stargazers by the drunken sailors.[67] Yet despite the abuse heaped on them by a vulgar and ungrateful world, they will not take revenge. They should retreat, and consorting only with one another, live in a sort of Epicurian garden pursuing their own happiness through the activity for which they are supremely fit, namely contemplation of the intelligent heavenly bodies with whom they share a special kinship. But they do not. For love of the world, they find a way to rule in secret. If they say that there is no connection between philosophy and the world or between the 'city in speech' and the earthly city, that is only their exoteric philosophy; the means by which they protect philosophy and themselves from the ruthless persecution of the vulgar. The esoteric philosophy is about the secret kingship of the philosopher. If the philosopher is identified with the *Imam*, or the descendant of the prophet Muhammad, that is only a concession to public opinion; it is a 'noble lie', a 'pious fraud', a matter of 'considering one's social responsibilities'.[68] Nor is it altogether false, since the role that the philosopher must occupy in the real city is not unlike that of the prophet who has the ear of a god-fearing king. The difference is that the philosopher is a prophet without a god. But that is *his* secret.

Esoteric writers share in common not only a certain style of writing, but certain assumptions about man, politics, religion, morality and philosophy that necessitate the cultivation of this special style. They believe that there is in the nature of philosophical truth something dangerous to political order and the stability of civilization. Strauss is reluctant to say this explicitly, but he apparently shares the sentiment of the esoteric writers of antiquity who considered philosophy and religion to be mutually exclusive and antagonistic, yet recognized that religion is a necessary foundation for human civilization. Civilization needs religion in order to flourish; but philosophy presupposes complete freedom from the restraints which religion must necessarily impose on thought. It was their belief in the permanent discord between reason and revelation, or Athens and Jerusalem, that enabled them to accept 'persecution' with such equanimity. They believed that the irreligious truth of philosophy is not one that the 'vulgar' can withstand. Only the philosophers have the fortitude to withstand such hard truths. One even gets the impression from Strauss that the philosophers delight in what may lead others to despair – namely that there is no God, no unchanging moral law and no support in the universe for justice.

The Jewish philosophers Helevi and Maimonides inherited the 'art of Plato' from the Islamic philosophers. They took it for granted that being a Jew and being a philosopher were mutually exclusive.[69] Strauss explains that the Jewish tradition emphasized God's justice and not his wisdom. This contributes to (although it does not explain) the lack of proximity of Judaism to philosophy. As Spinoza said bluntly, the Jews despised philosophy. More explicitly, the antipathy between philosophy and Judaism or Islam is coeval with the antipathy of true philosophy or pagan philosophy to revealed religion as such. In the light of this truth we must conclude that Christianity has for some time labored under a gross illusion.

Strauss explains that the difference between Christianity on the one hand, and Islam and Judaism on the other, is that the latter consider the sacred doctrine to be a legal interpretation of Divine Law (*talmud* or *figh*), whereas for the Christian the sacred doctrine is revealed theology. This is why Maimonides's *Guide of the Perplexed*, the Jewish equivalent to St Thomas Aquinas's *Summa Theologica*, never acquired the authority or stature of the latter. But Strauss is not to be understood as praising Christianity for its open-minded and unreserved love of wisdom. On the contrary, Christianity has done a disservice to philosophy. It drew it to its bosom only to impose upon it the yoke of divine supervision, which is tantamount to its destruction, since (as I will show below) the essence of philosophy is freedom from authority, particularly divine authority. Of course, Strauss does not say all this explicitly, but he does say that,

the precarious status of philosophy in Judaism as well as in Islam was not in every respect a misfortune for philosophy. The official recognition of philosophy in the Christian world made philosophy subject to ecclesiastical supervision. The precarious position of philosophy in the Islamic–Jewish world guaranteed its private character and therewith its inner freedom from supervision.[70]

One of Strauss's current followers, whose speech is much less moderate than his master's, has expressed the matter as follows:

> No, the bishops were correct, in their instinctive condemnation of Aristotle when he first appeared in Paris in the thirteenth century. But penetration was achieved, and as the intruding body was encapsulated and neutralized, the ichor began quietly to flow. And so the little pagan child was nurtured and fed and christianized [*sic*]. A diapered and tractable baby ape . . . is much less trouble than a naked squalling human infant; so even if he's not exactly ours, they must have felt, lets keep him![71]

The message is clear. The exquisite, divine pagan philosophy was mutilated and disfigured by Christianity until finally the immortal ichor flowed out of its veins and it turned into a grotesque little ape. It is not so much charity that forced the Christian philosophers to keep the little one, they could not do otherwise; this disfigured shadow of what pagan philosophy once was, *is* their baby. Besides, who would want it?

For Strauss the antipathy between Islam or Judaism and philosophy is 'identical with the issue of Jerusalem versus Athens'.[72] (Strauss commonly uses Jerusalem and Athens as symbols of religion and philosophy respectively.) Judaism and Islam recognize the permanent conflict between philosophy and religion that is denied by Christianity. Although Strauss does not make the comparison, the belief in the harmony between philosophy and revelation in Christianity is akin to the belief in the harmony between philosophy and society characteristic of the sociology of knowledge. Just as the sociology of knowledge fails to see the permanent discord between philosophy and the world, so Christianity fails to recognize the permanent incompatibility between reason and revelation, Athens and Jerusalem. And this gives one reason to think that Strauss believes modernity to be the heir of Christianity.

In summary, I have in this chapter attempted to establish three things. First, that the esoteric–exoteric style is necessary not only to protect the philosophers from persecution in societies hostile to philosophy, but to protect society from the anti-religious and anti-moral nature of philosophical truth which endangers society. This style allows the philosopher to endorse the salutary myths necessary for the preservation of society while revealing the truth for those who are fit for it. In this way, the philosopher discharges his social duty, which is to lie nobly. The existence of God and His immutable Law is one of the most pious frauds that the philosopher can perpetuate. If the vulgar discovered, as the philosophers have always known, that God is dead, they might behave as if all is permitted.

Secondly, I have tried to establish that for Strauss, philosophy, although not itself political, has a political role to play. Nor is this role limited to the dissemination of salutary myths. The very truths that when made public endanger the city, are the city's only hope for happiness. The shameless, intoxicated ideas of the philosopher alone can deliver the city from the oppressive harshness of Sacred Law. This can be accomplished only through the secret kingship of the philosopher.

Strauss is mistakenly regarded as one who maintains that philosophy provides us only with transcendent ideas that are politically unrealizable, unattainable and impracticable.[73] Strauss has done much to perpetuate this kind of misunderstanding. He and his followers never tire of repeating that Plato's *Republic*, which they openly embrace as their political ideal, is a 'city in speech'. This must be taken literally. It means exactly what the words say: the republic in which the philosopher rules *openly* is a 'city in speech', a city that is politically unattainable. In the real city, the philosopher *can* rule, but only in secret, by having influence over the powerful. The open rule of the philosopher in the ideal city is replaced by the secret kingship of the philosopher in the real city. The philosophical ideal can only be attained by chance. It depends on the chance occurrence of princes friendly to philosophy. It is by no means beyond reach.

Thirdly, I have tried to show that Strauss shares the assumptions of the esoteric philosophers. This is clear not only from the fact that he regards them to be wise, but also from the fact that he elaborates the same themes when he writes in his own name.[74] It is therefore not surprising to find him reluctant to make his ideas public or express them openly. Strauss too writes esoterically. He too avails himself of the immunity of the commentator. None of this precludes his saying anything lucidly and clearly in that lively style that is bound to 'arrest the attention of young men who love to think'. Like his counterparts in antiquity, he is not foolish enough or cruel enough to utter dangerous truths lucidly and clearly in his own name. Like his counterparts in antiquity, he uses some disreputable character as his mouthpiece. Who could be more disreputable than the diabolical Machiavelli?

Following the example of his imaginary writer from the communist block, Strauss appears to attack that which he really intends to defend. I will show below how he does this in *Thoughts on Machiavelli* and in *Natural Right and History*.[75] What description of Strauss's work would be more apt than his own description of how his imaginary writer from the communist block would proceed? Does Strauss not frequently write in a quiet unspectacular and boring manner? Does he not give many quotations and attach undue importance to insignificant details? Has he not stated the case of Machiavelli and of Thrasymachus more compellingly and mercilessly than it has ever been stated before? Does not the bulk of *Natural Right and History* consist in the most virulent expansions of the most virulent utterances of the holy book of the ruling party? Does it not begin with the Declaration of Independence and its simple-minded belief that all men are created equal, its childish trust in God, and in the inalienable rights of individuals? And has Strauss not told us that the wise know better? And are we not entitled to think that Strauss shares the views of those he considers most wise? When Strauss attributes to Plato the thoughts of Thrasymachus, are we not entitled to attribute these same ideas to Strauss? For is he not by his own admission the guardian of the wisdom of antiquity? And was it not his unique achievement to have 'single-handedly revived an interest in the classical texts and the knowledge they contained' at a time when 'classicists no longer took seriously the content of the books entrusted to their care'?[76]

All this is not as preposterous as it may seem. For Strauss, the ills of modernity have their source in the foolish belief that there are no harmful truths, and that belief in God and in rewards and punishments is not necessary for political order. Strauss follows the esoteric writers because he is convinced that religion is necessary for the well-being of society. But to state publicly that religion is a necessary fiction would destroy any salutary effect it might have. The latter depends on its being believed to be true. The indignant tone Strauss adopts in the act of revealing the atheism of Hobbes and Locke or the anti-Christian philosophy of

Machiavelli should not blind us to the fact that he shares their 'modern' sentiments even as he criticizes them. What he abhors is their lack of 'social responsibility', or their foolishness in thinking that the public dissemination of the truth will not harm the city.

3

Philosophy's Hidden Revolt against God

The conflict between philosophy and society has its origin in the fact that philosophy cannot rationally justify the two things on which society rests: morality and religion. For Strauss these two are not separate. Morality has its source in law, and the latter cannot elicit the respect and obedience of the many if it is not believed to have divine origin. Strauss follows the Judaic and Islamic tradition in conceiving of religion in terms of Sacred Law. In this chapter I will set aside the question of morality and focus on what Strauss believes to be at issue between philosophy and religion, reason and revelation, or as he likes to say, Athens and Jerusalem.[1]

In *Natural Right and History* Strauss explains that philosophy and religion recognize two different authorities. Philosophy regards nature as the supreme authority; 'the discovery of nature is the work of philosophy'.[2] The philosopher juxtaposes the natural to the artificial, conventional, traditional or ancestral. The natural is deemed to be even older than the ancestral and hence more authoritative. So much so, that the term nature came to be used as a synonym to what is good and wholesome in contradistinction to the artificial, conventional and unwholesome.[3] But society cherishes its traditions and conventions because it believes them to have a divine origin, to have been founded by gods or sons of gods, or men to whom God has spoken directly. Strauss therefore identifies the ancestral with the divine code; so much so that he uses the two terms interchangeably.[4] Philosophy therefore presupposes doubt of authority, not only human, but divine.

According to Strauss, Socrates used reason and nature to challenge convention and religion. His intention was to replace 'the cave of Zeus' with the light of philosophy. He made reason and nature, rather than convention and religion, the ultimate standard. It therefore does not surprise Strauss that Socrates was condemned to death: he does not think that Socrates was falsely or unjustly accused.[5]

Philosophy therefore emerges as a challenge to authority, ancestral or divine. Indeed, Strauss believes that Aristophanes points to the truth when he suggests that Socrates's fundamental premise could induce a son to beat up his father or to repudiate the most natural authority.[6] In Strauss's view, this explains why the philosophical discussion in Plato's *Republic* begins only after the withdrawal of Cephalus, the aged father who departs to take care of the sacred offerings to the gods.[7] Cephalus represents the intimate link between ancestral and divine authority; Plato's subtle symbolism is intended to indicate the antithesis between philosophy and the ancestral or divine. Strauss remarks that Herodotus testifies to 'this state of things' when he tells us that 'free discussion took place in truth-loving Persia after the slaughter of the Magi'.[8] The death of God and the ascendancy of philosophy seem to go hand in hand.[9]

The opposition of philosophy to traditional or divine authority has its source in the fact that they are two competing authorities, each claiming to be the legitimate one. Strauss discusses the issue in the midst of his commentary on Max Weber's methodology in a rather long diversion that is only superficially connected with Max Weber, if at all:

> The fundamental question, therefore, is whether men can acquire that knowledge of the good without which they cannot guide their lives individually or collectively by the unaided efforts of their natural powers, or whether they are dependent for that knowledge on Divine Revelation. No alternative is more fundamental than this: human guidance or divine guidance. . . . The first possibility is characteristic of philosophy or science in the original sense of the term, the second is presented in the Bible. The dilemma cannot be evaded by any harmonization or synthesis. For both philosophy and the Bible proclaim something as the one thing needful, as the only thing that ultimately counts, and the one thing needful proclaimed by the Bible is the opposite of that proclaimed by philosophy: a life of obedient love versus a life of free insight.[10]

This is the clue to the discord between reason and revelation. It is not just that each claims to be the supreme authority or 'the one thing needful' for the good life; they each contain *conflicting* conceptions of the good life for man. On the one hand, 'man is so built that he can find his satisfaction, his bliss, in free investigation, in articulating the riddle of being'.[11] But on the other hand, man's yearning for a solution attracts him to revelation. But philosophy cannot 'grant that revelation is possible' without also granting that the philosophical quest is not necessary. One is a life of obedient love and submission that renounces reason, the other is a life of free insight and inquiry that exalts reason. Nor can the philosophical life presuppose the truth of revelation because that would mean that 'the life devoted to the quest for evident knowledge available to man as man, would itself rest on an unevident, arbitrary, or blind decision'.[12] Strauss says all this in the midst of his commentary on Max Weber's methodology, and after what seems like a very long digression, he writes, 'But let us hasten back from these awful depths to a superficiality which, while not exactly gay, promises at least a quiet sleep.'[13] Strauss's style is here at its liveliest. It is bound to arrest the attention of young men who love to think.

Philosophy and religion are not simply two aspects of the good life. They are mutually exclusive ways of life, each animated by its own 'peculiar passion'. Philosophy is a life animated by 'the philosophic desire or *eros*'.[14] Strauss complains that in the 'Christian Middle Ages' philosophy was 'deprived of its character as a way of life', and regarded only as a very important compartment.[15] What he means is that the Christian philosophers of the Middle Ages failed to understand that the philosophical *eros*, like *eros* in general, is all consuming, it leaves no room for any other love, especially not the love of an envious, demanding, possessive, jealous and vengeful lover, the God of Abraham, Isaac and Jacob.

It may be objected that Strauss's depiction of the conflict between faith and reason is highly artificial. It may seem that the conflict on which Strauss insists is one that is necessitated by his fallacious conceptions of the two antagonists. As contemporary Thomists have argued against Strauss and his followers, reason and faith need not be mutually exclusive.[16] Properly construed, faith has its foundations in reason: one must have reasons for believing. Why then must reason and faith be defined in ways that necessarily make them hostile antagonists?

Strauss does not provide very persuasive arguments to support his contention that faith and reason must necessarily be locked in an irresolvable conflict. He does, however, bring to bear an overwhelming amount of authoritative support for his position.[17] Not only do the Islamic philsophers, following Socrates, Plato and Aristotle, endorse the inevitability of the conflict, *the Bible itself recognizes it*.

Strauss has bequeathed to us two commentaries on Genesis that are intended to show that the Bible endorses his conception of faith and reason and their inevitable conflict.[18] His commentaries also shed light on his own view of the human condition and the place of philosophy in the world.

In 'Interpretation of Genesis' and in 'Jerusalem and Athens' Strauss maintains that the primary prohibition in the Bible is a prohibition against philosophy. The Bible prohibits philosophy because it understands it to be coeval with reason, and the latter is in conflict with faith. The Bible therefore endorses Strauss's view that faith is anti-reason. It understands faith to be 'meritorious' only if it is 'faith against heavy odds'.[19]

'Interpretation of Genesis' is a discussion of the biblical account of creation. The gist of it is that the biblical account is unintelligible, the biblical God is inscrutable, and biblical faith is irrational. Stated directly and to the point, Strauss's argument is as follows: on the one hand we are told that God created the world in six days but these could not be days in any ordinary sense; for days in the ordinary sense are determined by the movement of the sun, and the sun did not exist prior to the creation. We are also told that God created the vegetative world on the third day, and the sun on the fourth. But how can there be vegetation without sun? In short, it is an 'improbable' or unlikely tale.[20]

Even more difficult to understand is the nature of the creator. One cannot begin to speak of Him without contradictions. Strauss regards God's omniscience as incompatible with human freedom. Just as puzzling is the fact that God contains within himself a dualism that is fundamental to most cosmogeonies – the dualism of male and female: 'God created man in his image, in his image, in the image of God, did God create him, male and female did he create them.' Strauss comments that the biblical author had to attribute the dualism of male and female to God because the biblical account of the origin of the world rules out the possibility of generation from a god and goddess. The result is not just an unintelligible account of the origin of the world, but the emergence of a baffling, incomprehensible, mysterious and inscrutable God.[21]

Strauss does not present the impenetrable nature of the biblical God as an oversight on the part of the biblical authors – something that can be accounted for by their lack of sophistication. On the contrary, the Bible intends to reflect the 'inscrutable mystery of the ways of God which it would be impious even to attempt to comprehend'.[22] The unreasonable nature of the biblical account, of the biblical God, and of biblical faith in general, is according to Strauss 'admitted and even proclaimed by the biblical faith itself'.[23]

Any link between man and God is not through understanding or reason but 'covenant' defined as a 'free and mysterious action of love on the part of God, and the corresponding attitude on the part of man is trust, or faith . . .'[24] The Bible is not intelligible; nor does it ask us to understand, but only to believe.

Strauss believes that the biblical author sets out purposely to deprecate cosmology or philosophy ('all philosophy is cosmology', says Strauss)[25] by deprecating heaven and the heavenly bodies. In traditional cosmologies, life on earth needs heaven, the source of rain. The heavenly bodies are intelligent and alive, they are gods worthy of human worship. In contrast to heaven, earth is a lowly place, and the human is a word of deprecation. All this is true for Greek philosophy as much as for Greek cosmology. Both represent man's attempt to comprehend the whole by his own efforts. It is the sort of knowledge accessible to man as man; it is autonomous knowledge that man acquires without supernatural assistance. The Bible declares such knowledge to be impossible and prohibits its pursuit.

In the biblical account, the heavenly bodies are created things; they are lifeless, not divine. When God speaks to Israel in Deuteronomy,[26] He forbids the worship of sun, moon and stars, these do not deserve worship. The heavenly bodies, sun, moon and stars, are mere tools or instruments for giving light to the earth. This means that 'heaven is deprecated in favor of earth'.[27] Heaven needs earth, without which it is devoid of purpose and not the reverse. Moreover, heaven is the only thing which is not called good by God, and is not even blessed by God.[28] All this indicates for Strauss that the intention of the author is a demotion of heaven. Strauss supports his interpretation with an overwhelming attention to detail that might lead one to forget the point he is making.

Although it might seem like it at times, Strauss is *not* advocating the worship of the heavenly bodies. He regards the latter as a symbol of cosmology or philosophy, and hence of the knowledge man can attain by his own efforts. The deprecation of the heavenly bodies is therefore a *demotion of philosophy*. It prepares the way for the prohibition against eating of the tree of knowledge. The tree of knowledge represents the knowledge of good and evil in human affairs that man can achieve by reflection on the nature of things. What the Bible means to prohibit is 'becoming wise by the contemplation of heaven.'[29]

In Strauss's view, the Bible replaces reason by faith against all reason, against all odds. In Genesis 'there is not a trace of an argument' in support of the assertion that the world is created. This is a strange complaint for one who has declared without a trace of an argument that reason cannot establish the existence of God, and that the argument of God's existence from the manifest order of the world is 'not valid'.[30]

In 'Jerusalem and Athens' Strauss develops the same thesis even more fully. He describes the condition of man in the garden of Eden as devoid of evil, old age and death. Adam and Eve live happily knowing neither sorrow nor toil. Their life is also marked by a conspicuous absence of the arts and crafts. It is characterized simultaneously by simplicity and abundance. But it is a life lived under the tutelage of God. For Adam and Eve lived as children in the garden of Eden. They were forbidden to eat of the tree of knowledge but not of the tree of life. This means that they were to partake of eternal life as long as they were obedient to God. God's prohibition against eating of the tree of knowledge is a prohibition against the pursuit of autonomous or independent wisdom. Strauss understands it as a prohibition against philosophy, or the knowledge that man can attain independently by his own efforts. The first and most fundamental prohibition in Genesis is again declared to be a prohibition against philosophy.

Despite the innocence of man's childlike existence, Strauss does not believe that man in the garden of Eden was altogether devoid of knowledge. On the contrary, man has always been a being 'that can understand to some degree that knowledge of good and evil is evil for it'.[31] Having been created in the image of God, man could not have been entirely devoid of knowledge. If that were so, his desire for it would be incomprehensible. Furthermore, being like God, man must have found limitation and prohibition inconsistent with his nature. This means that man was so constituted that he was 'congenitally tempted' to disobey.[32] But the biblical author did not wish to leave this impression. He was therefore compelled to supplement his account of the transgression of man in the first chapter with a different account in the second. The purpose of the second account is to eradicate the impression that man was congenitally tempted. If the latter were the case, then man could not be responsible for his lowly condition. In his 'Interpretation of Genesis', Strauss explains that the purpose of the second account is to show that man did not disobey either because he was needy or because he was too much like God to withstand a prohibition against knowledge.[33] The ease and abundance of man's beginning ensures that man was not compelled to be harsh, uncharitable or unjust out of need. But the fact that man is created in the image of God presents a difficulty that is removed in the second account of the creation of man. According to the latter, man is created out of the dust of the earth and so is not tempted either by need or by his 'high estate'. Strauss remarks that all this makes disobedience 'shockingly ill founded'.[34]

The Bible intends to teach that man was meant to live in simplicity, without knowledge of good and evil.[35] Strauss believes that the Bible is right, this is the sort of life that is fitting for the many. Generally speaking, knowledge is bad for man, it threatens to destroy him. In the form of the arts, crafts and technology, knowledge threatens man with extinction – a fact of which we are painfully aware in the twentieth century. But even though knowledge (at least in the hands of the many) is a hazard to life and happiness, man is nevertheless drawn to it by a sort of inexplicable *eros*.

The choice between knowledge and eternal life is one with which man is confronted from the beginning. In choosing knowledge, man forfeits eternal life. This choice is the key to the human condition. Evil is the price man must pay for his love of knowledge. But evil is also the emancipator of man from bondage. Had they not sinned, Adam and Eve would not have earned their freedom. Only in the light of Strauss's understanding of the biblical myth can we make sense of the epigraph to the second chapter of *Persecution and the Art of Writing* from W. E. H. Lecky, which reads:

That vice has often proved an emancipator of the mind, is one of the most humiliating, but, at the same time, one of the most unquestionable, facts in history.[36]

Vice, not virtue, is therefore the true companion of philosophy. Crime is the beginning of wisdom.

Strauss's interpretation of Genesis is not unlike Hegel's. They both agree that the serpent was right after all. In Hegel's view, the serpent did not lie in telling Eve that eating of the tree of knowledge will make her like God. What he failed to tell her is that the success will not be achieved immediately. It will be preceded by a long dialectical process known as history.[37] But at the end of history, the alienation of man and God that will inevitably follow upon disobedience, will be overcome in a new synthesis that will establish the identity of man and God. For Strauss, the serpent was only telling part of the truth. Crime and suffering are the price man must pay for love of knowledge. But there will be no respite, there will be no reconciliation at the end of history. As a seeker after wisdom, man sets himself up in permanent opposition to God; an opposition that is identical with the conflict between the love of knowledge and the love of God, or between Athens and Jerusalem.

We must not imagine that Strauss means to castigate knowledge any more than a romantic means to castigate romantic love just because it necessarily ends in death and tragedy. On the contrary, like the romantic, Strauss means to tell us that knowledge, like love, is worth the highest price. Like the object of the lover's quest, knowledge may be fleetingly embraced, but it can never be possessed any more than romantic love can be consummated. Nor is death too high a price to pay for these brief moments of ecstasy.[38]

In Strauss's account, Eve was the first lover of knowledge; the first seeker after wisdom; the first *philo-sophoi*. If man is distinguished from other animals by reason, the desire to know or the love of knowledge, then Eve was the first truly human being. In view of the close alliance between philosophy and *eros*, Eve is a particularly appropriate symbol of the love of wisdom. But Eve is also the representative of evil, of wickedness, and of the disobedience of God. However, God's prohibition was given to Adam; He had not spoken to Eve directly. She knew of it only through Adam. Strauss curiously comments that she knew of the prohibition only from 'tradition'. This is an important clue. The philosopher, the lover of knowledge must necessarily set herself against tradition, convention or the ancestral.

In the garden of Eden man is confronted with a choice between a life of submission or tutelage and a life of freedom. For love of knowledge, Eve makes the choice against God. It seems that philosophy or the love of wisdom cannot be eradicated from the human heart, and as a result evil must always find a place in her breast. For the two are coeval with one another; evil is the price we pay for philosophy. As Marx knew, there will be no need for philosophy when the evils of history are terminated. It seems that the human desire to live without evil is as intransigent and as intractable as Eve's love of knowledge. God gives man the opportunity to live without evil in the garden of Eden in order to show him that his deepest wish cannot be fulfilled. The story of the fall is 'the first part of the story of God's education of man'.[39] Man has to live with the knowledge of good and evil and suffer the consequences.

The fate of philosophy in the world is the same as the fate God inflicts on Eve. She is to be subject to the authority of Adam, the ancestral, the one who came first (at least in one out of the two accounts of man's creation provided in Genesis). If Eve is to have any freedom in the world, she must retire to the private domain and shun the glory of the public realm. Likewise, philosophy must live eternally in the shadow of the ancestral and avoid offending it for fear of its very life. If it is to enjoy a modest freedom, it must keep itself hidden and shun the glory of power and politics.[40] This is not to say (contrary to the way in which Strauss is generally understood or misunderstood) that philosophy has nothing to do with politics or nothing to offer it. On the contrary, it has a great deal to offer, so much so that any happiness man can attain depends on philosophy's success in secretly influencing the powers that be and ruling vicariously or behind the scenes, as women have always ruled over men.

After the expulsion from the garden of Eden, God gives man freedom to live in the absence of law. When Cain slays his brother Abel, God does not punish him. On the contrary, He threatens to punish severely anyone who kills him.[41] Cain was the founder of a city. Romulus, founder of Rome, also slew his brother. Like his fellow fratricide, he too gets away with it.[42] It seems that even God recognizes fratricide as necessary to the founding of a city. Strauss says implicitly and behind the veil of the commentator what Machiavelli and Hannah Arendt say openly and in their own name: 'Whatever brotherhood human beings may be capable of has grown out of fratricide, whatever political organization men have achieved has its origin in crime.'[43] Since crime is the foundation of political affairs, those who enter politics must first learn not to be good. Arendt believes that Machiavelli was the first to see the truth of this and therefore attributed to politics a domain whose laws and principles were independent of morality, and particularly of the teachings of the Church. Strauss's account of Genesis indicates that he considers these ideas to have much older origins.[44]

The race of Cain ends with the song of Lamach, who 'boasted' to his wives of the slaying of men and of being superior to God as an avenger. In contrast, the race of Seth (the replacement of Abel) cannot 'boast' a single inventor.[45] Its distinguished members are Noah and Enoch who were righteous and 'walked with God'. The contrast between the race of Cain, the founder of a city, and the race of Seth, leads Strauss to conclude that 'civilization and piety are two very different things'.[46] But he does not elaborate. It seems that those who walk with God cannot aspire to greatness. Those who aspire to greatness must renounce God. Strauss repeats Nietzsche's claim that for the Greeks the individual is marked by the pursuit of excellence, supremacy and distinction, but for the Jews the individual is marked by honoring mother and father, or living a life of obedience to the ancestral.[47] Not only are the Jews not lovers of philosophy as Spinoza observed, they have failed to found a great civilization. The latter requires not only philosophy, but craftsmanship and the arts, which are an extension of man's love of knowledge; they are part of his revolt against God and his aspiration to compete with God by remaking the world to his own liking. By their great words and great deeds (not good words and deeds), men aspire to the immortality of the gods. The Jews failed to found a great civilization because they 'walked with God'.[48]

The arts are not part of the simple life of antideluvian men. The Bible teaches that men were meant to live simply and without knowledge. Indeed knowledge succeeds only in bringing disaster upon them. Pagan religion taught the same lesson; and this shows that the similarities between religions are far greater and more significant than the differences. The Greek myth of Prometheus also tells of the disaster that befell mankind as a result of the gift of fire or knowledge offered by the philanthropist.

God, as it were, 'experimented' with the education of mankind. First, he gave them the opportunity to live as innocent children in the garden of Eden, free of evil. Then, He tried letting them live without restraint or law, but that did not work either. Rampant wickedness was the result, and God had to destroy almost every living creature with the great flood. After the flood, God made a compact with man in the form of the revelation of his Torah or law. A covenant is therefore the foundation of law. As Hobbes would say, law, which has its origin in contract, replaces the original freedom of mankind; and the exchange of law for freedom is necessary for the survival of mankind. Fallen (or 'awake' as Strauss adds, using the philosophical symbolism of Heraclitus) man needs the restraint of law. Zeus, the biblical God, and Hobbes's mortal god, all guard their law with jealousy and wrath; and in so doing, exact the required obedience.

Strauss paints Zeus and the biblical God with the same brush strokes. Both jealously demand exclusivity and forbid the worship of other gods. Both are equally willful and capricious. Just as the biblical God takes mercy and favors whom he chooses, so Zeus 'takes cognizance of men's justice and injustice only if he so wills'.[49] There is no significant difference between the two gods. Will and caprice rather than reason and wisdom are their distinguishing marks.

For Strauss, the relation of Zeus and Metis is reminiscent of 'the relation of God and wisdom in the Bible'.[50] Metis (wisdom) is Zeus's first spouse, and though not identical with him, she becomes inseparable from him. Characteristically, Strauss does not elaborate. What is implicit here, as in the Bible, is that wisdom is associated with a woman; she is erotic and desirable. Love of wisdom or philosophy is therefore not love of God. On the contrary, it is a sort of competition with Him, an attempt to possess Metis, who, being a woman, can be seduced. This deepens the opposition of Athens and Jerusalem.

Although not marked primarily by wisdom, both the pagan and the biblical gods are distinguished by justice. One wonders what Strauss could possibly mean by that. His meaning becomes transparent if we understand justice, as Hobbes did, to be a function of law, which is in turn a function of the will of the legislator. In contrast to both the pagan and the biblical gods, the god of the philosophers, does not create, give orders, or dispense justice. The god of the philosophers is 'a thinking being, pure thought that thinks itself and only itself'. As Strauss says, it is almost a 'blasphemy' to ascribe justice to the god of Aristotle.[51] The true god, the first cause, the god of the philosophers, is beyond good and evil.

Philosophy and religion confront man with two incompatible lives. A choice must be made. Strauss portrays the choice as a choice between reason and unreason, freedom and subjection, happiness and sacrifice, greatness and humility. For intelligent men it does not seem a very difficult choice to make. A life lived in blind obedience to God is inadequate not only for anyone who aspires to greatness, but for one who yearns for the fulfillment or completion of his rational or genuinely human potentialities. Strauss implies by his account of man's transgression in Genesis that man is so constituted that he cannot help but choose knowledge even though the price he must pay for his choice is high. But he does not wish to disparage or undermine the simple life of faith. On the contrary, he agrees with the Bible that it is the most appropriate life, at least for the large majority of mankind.

In 'The Mutual Influence of Theology and Philosophy', Strauss describes Western civilization as having 'two roots which are in conflict with each other, the biblical and the Greek philosophic'.[52] But Strauss has no intention of resolving or transcending this conflict. On the contrary, he regards it as 'the secret of the vitality of the West'.[53] The tone of the essay is light. It appears to describe a most amicable conflict, more akin to a friendly exchange based on a broad mutual agreement. The two conflicting parties are but parts of one Great Tradition. This is Strauss's exoteric message, and it is certainly part of his meaning, but not the whole of it.

The exoteric message is true in so far as Strauss believes that there really are two conflicting roots at the heart of Western civilization and that the conflict between them is inevitable and irresolvable. Moreover, any attempt to resolve the conflict threatens the life and vitality of the West. The disappearance of the conflict, and of the distinctive characters of the antagonists, is for Strauss symptomatic of the modern decline or 'crisis of Western civilization'.[54] It is absolutely accurate to say that the two antagonists are equally necessary for the well-being of Western civilization. However, to understand Strauss fully, we must understand what these claims *mean*.

Strauss does not wish to give the impression that the

philosophers reject revelation *tout court*. Instead, he repeats again and again that neither Greek philosophy nor the Bible can refute one another.[55] But as we shall see, his article does just that. It attempts to show that all the arguments for revelation cannot stand up before the tribunal of reason.

Strauss tries to soften this volte-face by the respectful demeanor he displays in the very act of undermining revelation. He gives the impression that revelation is too complicated for the humble abilities of the philosopher. He insists that philosophy is 'invincibly ignorant' of revelation. This is irony in the strictly Straussian sense. (For Strauss, irony is the means by which the superior hide their superiority in order not to cause offense.[56])

To concede that they are equally necessary is altogether different from considering them equals; the essay attempts to blur this distinction by the reverential tone it adopts when speaking of Jerusalem or biblical faith. A careful reading reveals that the two antagonists are not equals engaged in a friendly dispute; they have nothing in common that might serve as the grounds for such an exchange. Jerusalem represents blind obedience to the old, the traditional, the 'ancestral'. It is the prototype of the cave and of darkness. Athens is the paragon of wisdom and light. But Strauss is not suggesting that Western civilization exchange light for darkness. Enlightenment does not impress him.[57] Athens must find a way to live in the heart of darkness.

I do not wish to imply that Strauss does not genuinely believe what he says explicitly and repeats most frequently. I am merely suggesting that we understand it in the light of a careful reading of the whole. The two antagonists cannot defeat one another not because they are so equally matched, but because they are simply not playing in the same ball park. Revelation refuses to accept the authority of reason, it denounces reason as the source of wickedness. Reason refuses to accept the authority of revelation because it is unevident.

Every argument Strauss examines in favor of revelation seems to encounter a snag. An 'impressive' argument is one that relies on the intrinsic superiority of the divine law. For Jerusalem, morality or justice 'means primarily obedience to law', in the sense of divine law.[58] Strauss explains that behind this conception of justice is the 'primeval identification of the good with the ancestral'.[59] 'The ancestral' claims to have divine origin. But the contradictions between the variety of divine codes makes the 'idea of divine law' as the foundation of justice 'radically problematic'.[60] It gives rise to the 'problem of divine law'.[61] There is no way of knowing which of the competing divine codes is genuine. If we attempt to make the judgement on the basis of reason, then we have abandoned revelation altogether. If the 'revealed law agrees with the rational standard of the best law', then the revealed law is the work of Moses and not of God.[62] But Strauss tells us that everyone knows that the revealed law is 'supra-rational' which means that it is 'not itself supported by reason'.[63] In other words, 'from the point of view of reason, it is an indifferent possibility'.[64] Moreover, if law is a product of 'divine super-reason', it may as well be 'the product of human unreason'.[65]

For Strauss, 'there is no shred of evidence in favor of revelation, except the personal experience of man's encounter with God'.[66] However, he adds that such experience 'cannot be authoritative' since there are diverse interpretations – Jewish, Christian and Muslim.[67] There can be no historical proof of the 'fact of revelation', as there is proof of other historical facts such as the assassination of Caesar by Brutus and Cassius. In the latter case there is an 'impartial observer' or 'witnesses belonging to both parties'.[68] According to Strauss, this explains why there are 'pseudo-prophets' and 'pseudo-revelations' but no 'pseudo-assassinations' or 'pseudo-wars'.[69] The existence of historical proof provides us with criteria for distinguishing the genuine from the spurious. Since there are no criteria by which to distinguish between the spurious and the genuine in the case of revelation, Strauss allows us to draw the conclusion that the human experience of God does not constitute a shred of evidence for revelation.

What about the miracles? Strauss tells us that these are not a reliable source: 'no miracle was performed in the presence of first-rate physicists'.[70] Besides, miracles were meant to impress idolaters, not atheists.[71] The former are 'people who in principle admit the possibility of divine action'.[72] Idolators are men who know fear and trembling, they are not atheists 'who are beyond hope or fear like philosophers'.[73]

Philosophers refuse to exchange a life of 'free enquiry' for a life of faith, trust, 'true obedience', and 'free surrender'.[74] They cannot blindly accept what Strauss ironically refers to as the

unbroken chain of 'reliable tradition'.[75] Instead, they 'transcend
. . . the whole dimension of piety and pious obedience'.[76] They
embark on a 'free quest' for the 'beginnings, for the first things,
for the principles' in order to determine 'what is by nature good'
as opposed to what is good according to convention or ancestral
customs. They live a life devoted to understanding or *noesis*.
Strauss tells us that the latter is never 'divorced from sense
perception and reasoning based on sense perception'.[77] He gives
as evidence Plato's tendency to compare knowledge with the
crafts. He takes this to indicate that philosophical knowledge is
non-mystical, that it is a 'humble but solid kind of knowledge'
characteristic of one who feels and touches with his hands.[78]

Despite his rejection of biblical faith, Strauss shares with the
biblical authors a fundamental assumption: namely, that there is a
given whole to which man belongs, and that man's place within
the whole constitutes the permanent human situation. The latter
is the condition for all historical change, or the context in which
all historical change occurs. Furthermore, all true knowledge or
knowledge that is worth having, is of the permanent and
unchanging. The pursuit of knowledge consists of an attempt to
articulate the given whole or the given human situation. The Bible
provides but one articulation of this permanently given whole.
The philosopher knows that the biblical account is not true.

Strauss has been understood as a 'zetetic' or a skeptic 'in the
original sense of the term'.[79] A zetetic is one who regards
philosophy as quest for wisdom and not wisdom. A zetetic
recognizes that philosophy is not in possession of complete
knowledge of the whole. This is certainly true; Strauss regards
philosophy as a 'way of life' that is dedicated to the 'quest for
knowledge regarding the whole'.[80] Notice that it is quest and not
knowledge. Strauss is therefore not committed to the belief that
the whole is knowable. Nor does philosophy provide man with
solutions; it merely articulates the 'fundamental problems'.[81] All
this is true for Strauss, but it should not be exaggerated. Just
because knowledge of 'the whole' is not attainable does not mean
that philosophy can claim no certain knowledge whatsoever.[82]

On the contrary, philosophy has considerable knowledge
indeed. Philosophy may not have iron-clad solutions, but it does
have solutions. Strauss says only that the questions are more
obvious than the solutions.[83] Articulating the 'fundamental

problems' is no mean task, it points to the range of possible solutions. It determines the limits of the reasonable solutions at our disposal.

Far from being ignorant about ultimate things, philosophy knows that the God of Abraham, Isaac and Jacob is a fiction. The zetetic is not an agnostic. He is not uncertain. He knows that the consequences of his 'disobedience to revelation' will not be 'fatal'.[84] He knows that there is not a shred of evidence for revelation. The philosopher *qua* philosopher is an atheist; he is beyond fear and trembling.

For Strauss, philosophy does not suspend judgements about 'matters of utmost urgency'.[85] Strauss tells us that it is impossible to suspend judgments on such matters.[86] Philosophy knows the answer to the question of utmost urgency, namely, the question of the right way of life.[87] The philosopher knows that the philosophical way of life is the right way of life.[88] It is better or superior to the religious one.

Despite his rejection of revelation, Strauss does not wish to undermine religion. For Strauss, as for Farabi, religion is necessary to maintain order by ensuring that citizens obey the laws, not simply out of fear of being found out (it is often easy not to be found out), but out of fear or love of God. Only religious faith can ensure that men follow the rules without qualification, without ifs or buts. Only such devotion to the laws of the city can ensure the harmony and happiness of citizens. But in spite of the political usefulness of religion, Strauss is not one to go overboard in emphasizing its virtues. It is singularly lacking in the 'royal art', as Farabi would say. The latter belongs only to the philosophers.

The happiness of men in cities depends on the rule of philosophers not priests. Indeed, nothing is for Strauss less desirable than the rule of priests.[89] These godly types are likely to take advantage of God's favor, and rule over their fellow men with *His* iron fist. Priests would invariably interfere with the 'royal art' or with statesmanship by applying to politics a code not suited to the nature of public affairs. They impose on the latter absolute moral standards that are useful only in the private relations of men or among citizens.[90]

For Strauss, religion provides men with a code of the heart suitable for private intercourse, whereas philosophy provides them with a code of the mind suitable for the sorts of decisions statesmen need to make. The difference between these two codes will become more apparent below.[91] Suffice it to say here that the moral code provided by the 'royal art' is not one that involves absolute prohibitions, but one that relies heavily on ifs and buts. The two codes therefore come into conflict, a conflict that mirrors the conflict between Athens and Jerusalem. Both codes are equally necessary; Athens and Jerusalem must therefore find a way to coexist. For Strauss, the only way this can be done is for philosophy to accept 'persecution' with equanimity and keep a low profile for its own sake as well as the city's. It must find a place in the heart of Jerusalem that allows it to rule over the dark city in secret, without disturbing its pious illusions.

This means that the philosopher must appear to assent publicly to what he does not believe privately. The life of the philosopher is necessarily divided between the things of the heart and the things of the mind.[92] Doing one's duty, obeying the laws, observing the traditions of our society and its religion are things of the heart. In contrast to the things of the heart, the things of the mind are not bound to any time or place or *Weltanschauung*.[93] The mind is distinguished by free and unencumbered enquiry. The mind does not lend credence to the things of the heart. Philosophy is a way of life dedicated to the things of the mind.[94] But since philosophers are still men with a heart, they must live a dual life. Strauss does not seem perturbed by the hypocrisy this involves. Instead, he tells us that those who 'live that conflict' do not find it disconcerting, but 'reassuring and comforting'.[95]

What Strauss says of Farabi seems to be true of Strauss. As a pupil of philosophy he was attracted to ideas he abhorred as a believer. He was a man divided within himself. He was a man with a Jewish heart and a pagan mind. Frederick D. Wilhelmsen's portrait of a Straussian as a 'Hellenized Jew' is somewhat fitting:

> Given we are men of both reason and faith, we are torn to pieces by two conflicting authorities. . . . We therefore give pious obedience to the God of Moses even though we spend our lives disengaging the texts of Plato and Aristotle, knowing all the while that those texts tell us something completely contradicted by the Scriptures which are, we hold as Jews, the word of the Lord. Such men walk as did Cicero, internally denying the gods but professing them publicly. Straussians are very pious men externally and they are serious about this

external piety. An esoteric and exoteric contradiction dominates their thinking.[96]

In Wilhelmsen's view, Strauss is a Latin Averroist in the sense of one who believes that there are *two truths* that could not be reconciled or synthesized with one another. The philosopher is therefore torn apart by an inner conflict.

Wilhelmsen's view is not altogether accurate, although there is much that lends support to it. For example, Strauss was not a practicing Jew, nor was he a man particularly fond of music. But curiously, he is said to have loved Jewish synagogue music.[97] This lends credibility to the view that the conflict is a psychic condition. Strauss himself describes it as a 'drama' of the 'human soul'.[98]

There is little doubt that for Strauss, the philosopher lives a dual life. This is necessary because the philosopher is human and therefore must live in civil society and adhere to its pious illusions. However, it is only Wilhelmsen's sensibility or sensitivity that leads him to conclude that the philosopher is a man 'torn to pieces' by the conflict within. He would be torn to pieces only if he genuinely believed that there are *two truths* of equal worth. But Strauss denies that this is the case. He declares emphatically that 'there can be *only one truth*'.[99] This is why a choice must be made. Strauss insists that no one can be both philosopher and theologian at the same time. Strauss's choice is clear, he is not torn to pieces. The conclusion we must draw is *not* that there are two truths, but only one truth, which is the preserve of the philosophers, not the theologians.[100]

In Strauss's account, the philosopher does not live tragically.[101] He follows the example of Socrates not Christ. He does not weep, but laughs.[102] As we shall see in the following pages, the dual life of the philosopher is not the tragic life of one who is torn to pieces, it is the happy life, the good life, the life 'according to nature'.

We can understand the dual life of the philosopher only by careful examination of Strauss's commentaries on Socrates, Plato and Aristotle. In the next two chapters, I examine Strauss's view of the classical philosophers and particularly his conception of classic natural right. The latter sheds light on the dual life of the philosopher and the dual moral codes he must juggle.

Before turning to the classical philosophers, it is important to note why the issue of Athens and Jerusalem is at the heart of

Strauss's understanding of the debate between ancients and moderns.

For Strauss, as for the ancients, the conflict between Athens and Jerusalem cannot be reconciled. But more than that, reconciliation *must not be attempted*. A synthesis that transcends the conflict between them is deadly. It leads inevitably to the destruction of both antagonists, and hence to the destruction of civilization itself. Modernity is the attempt to affect such a synthesis, and for Strauss, this explains the present crisis of the West. Modernity therefore begins with Christian philosophers like St Thomas Aquinas, who believed that a synthesis of Jerusalem and Athens, biblical faith and Greek philosophy, is possible. For Strauss, the history of Western man is the story of the disastrous failure of this project. In the light of what I have described as the deadly conflict between Athens and Jerusalem, Strauss's conception of modernity and of the debate between ancients and moderns has to be understood anew. Suffice it to say here that the most fundamental differences between the ancients and the moderns are not what they appear to be at first blush. The single most fundamental difference between ancients and moderns is that the latter no longer believe in the need or the necessity of esoteric writing. They have parted with the wisdom of the ancients in thinking that philosophical truths are wholesome for the masses and for society as a whole. If Strauss is indignant when he speaks of the 'moderns', this is due not so much to their atheism or their moral relativism, but to the public manner in which they present it. What he objects to is the foolishness with which they dispense philosophy as if it were the gospel. This foolishness has its source primarily in Christianity and in its belief in the harmony of reason and revelation. Christianity unleashes philosophy only to be destroyed by it. In the Middle Ages, Christian philosophers labored under the illusion that philosophy can come to the aid of faith. But history has shown how blind they were. That Western man no longer believes in the existence of God is a testimony to the failure of their project. The liberation of philosophy and its emergence into the public sphere has destroyed the latter. God is dead because philosophy has killed Him.

Genuine philosophers know that what the Bible teaches is largely true: man's love of knowledge has brought him only grief. But modernity has succeeded in making things worse by bringing philosophy to the masses. Today, the secular heirs of the modern venture continue to cling to the belief that philosophical truth, regardless of its content, is salutary. They believe that philosophy can replace God and that Western civilization can withstand the death of God. They have therefore parted with the wisdom of the ancients according to which the masses need myths and illusions to cling to: they need to believe that there is an unchanging moral law sanctioned by a divine creator and backed by the powers that be. Strauss does not say any of this explicitly, because a wise man ought not to say publicly that there is no God and no unchanging moral law. He is particularly silent about the role Christianity has played in the crisis of modernity. His sense of social responsibility makes him reluctant to criticize what is still the most viable religion at the disposal of Western civilization.

In order to illustrate what is at issue between Strauss and the moderns on the question of Athens and Jerusalem, allow me to indulge in an imaginary dialogue between Strauss and Sigmund Freud. The dialogue is imaginary because Strauss is silent about Freud. I will not venture to explain the meaning of this silence. I will only note that Freud's analysis of the human condition, of politics and of religion are astoundingly close to Strauss's. More than any other modern thinker, Freud confronts the problem of Athens and Jerusalem. He differs from Strauss not so much in his analysis, but in the conclusions he draws from that analysis.[103]

In *Future of an Illusion* Freud addresses the question of Athens and Jerusalem, or what Strauss sometimes refers to as the 'theologico-political predicament'.[104] After stating his position, Freud imagines the objections of two defenders of religion, one of them he calls the 'As if' philosopher.[105] In my view, Strauss fits Freud's description of the 'As if' philosopher perfectly. In what follows I have attempted to duplicate the way Strauss would speak in an academic or quasi-public forum. His speech is neither candid nor devious, but cautious. If the effect of the dialogue is to clarify the matter (as I intend it to do), that is due to the fact that Freud is the sort of worthy opponent who would have understood Strauss. Strauss had a reputation for avoiding such opponents.[106]

Freud: There is little doubt that religion has won great conquests in taming man and making him fit for civilization. It has compensated man for the suffering and privations that a civilized life in common has imposed by instilling in men the belief that 'in the end all good is rewarded and all evil punished'.[107]

Strauss: A civilization cannot hope to sustain itself unless citizens believe that acting in the interest of their fellow men is ultimately in their own best interest or that the righteous life is the happiest, most rewarding and most profitable one. No other belief is more necessary for making man fit for civilization as you say. Indeed, I believe that was the central theme of Plato's *Laws*.

Freud: We should not forget the success of religion in exorcising the terrors of nature and particularly of death. It has entrenched the belief that death is not death or a 'return to inorganic lifelessness', but the beginning of 'a new kind of life'.[108] It has therefore provided us with psychical means by which to deal with our senseless anxiety and so has made us at home in the uncanny.[109] You yourself have noted this in your funeral speech upon the death of one of your graduate students.[110] You spoke truly and most eloquently saying, 'death is terrible, terrifying, but we cannot live as human beings if this terror grips us to the point of corroding our core'.[111]

Strauss: It is difficult for a philosopher to give a funeral speech, he can provide no comfort where it is needed.

Freud: Nor did you pretend to; you said honestly and truthfully 'it is not given to me to say words of comfort of my own'.[112] You meant to say of course that the philosopher *qua* philosopher cannot provide comfort where death is concerned. But you went on to say that the dead young man was protected against the corrosive not only by his faith, but by philosophy, which provides an alternative way of dealing with the corrosive. The philosophical way of dealing with the corrosive is to face it, understand its 'ineluctable' necessity.[113] You hoped for his sake that his soul died the death of a philosopher.[114] You meant to say a death without terror, but also without hope.

Strauss: It surprises me that despite your masterful analysis of the benefits that religion has bestowed on civilization, you venture to suggest that it should be abandoned and replaced by philosophy.

Freud: That is not surprising at all. Religion has simply outlived its usefulness and ought to be abandoned. It is no longer useful because it is no longer believed. It has been unmasked as an illusion, and it is time mankind grew up and learned to live without illusions. This in the long run is the safer course. Unless we advance fearlessly on this path, we will find ourselves in mortal danger. Once the illusions on which civilization once rested are unmasked, the enemies of civilization, thinking the latter their oppressor, will destroy it. Men must learn that civilization, far from being their oppressor, is organized to serve their interests. The death of God is bound to leave man unsettled, fearful and defenseless. It is bound to lead to the sort of period of decline that you like to refer to as the 'crisis of Western civilization'. But this crisis is a temporary ailment, inevitable in times of transition.

Strauss: Your optimism is astounding; philosophy is not pabulum for the masses, it cannot hope to replace religion.

Freud: There have in recent times been two desperate efforts to save religion, one by the fideists and one by the Averroists or the 'As if' philosophers.[115] The fideist maintains that the unreasonableness of religion is no reason to disbelieve. On the contrary, as early Fathers of the Church such as Tertullian recognized, *'credo quia absurdum'*, or 'I believe because it is absurd'. For such men the very incredulous nature of faith is precisely what makes it commendable. This surely is a 'desperate' and not particularly convincing effort to save religion. Am I to be obliged to believe *every* absurdity? And if not, why this one in particular?[116] In the second argument, civilization is grounded on a network of fictions and pious lies, but for 'practical reasons we must behave "as if" we believed these fictions'. This is particularly the case with religious doctrines because of their 'incomparable importance for the maintenance of human society'.[117] In my view, this argument is not far removed from the first, nor more convincing, but it is one that only a philosopher can put forward. Normal people would turn away from religion, they could not stand the hypocrisy of the 'as if' for it robs their lives of meaning.[118] If I understand you correctly Professor Strauss, that is precisely what you propose.

Strauss: I have in writing denounced this argument as 'either stupid or blasphemous'.[119]

Freud: You are quite right, it is utterly foolish to put forth publicly an argument of this sort as a defense of religion, for the success of religion depends on its being believed. 'As if' philosophers who are intelligent as well as merciful will naturally express their views esoterically. But this mercifulness is misplaced. Civilization runs a greater risk by clinging to religion than by replacing it with science.

Strauss: Science cannot hope to replace religion. Men have needs that cannot be satisfied by cold science. Convincing men that civilization is organized to promote their interests will fail to make them good. If the chance of being found out is small, what is to prevent people from paying lip service to justice while reaping the advantages of their injustice. Your own psychology testifies to the fact that people naturally seek pleasure; but you would have them sacrifice their pleasure for the good of the whole. Are they capable of such a sacrifice? But it is not a matter of sacrifice, you say, it is a matter of justice. They must give if they are to reap benefits. But this way of thinking far exceeds the capacities of ordinary people.

Freud: You overestimate the ability of religion to make men good. Men are not made more moral by religion. On the contrary, their weakness next to God gives them an excuse to sin, enjoy it and then do penance.[120] It is time we replaced religious motives by secular or rational ones. The time is ripe for men to be brought up strong and clear-headed, without the bitter–sweet poison of religion that leads to intellectual atrophy and makes them dead to reality. If men hope to transcend their infantilism or abandon their heavenly father as they must their earthly one, they need an 'education to reality'[121] without which they cannot face a hostile world.

Strauss: What reason is there to believe that science is not just another illusion? Does it not play the same role played by the messiah in religion and by the prince in fairy tales? Science is the new messiah, the prince of modernity!

Freud: With one difference, 'science is no illusion'.[122]

Strauss: Of course, it could not be the prince of modernity if its capacity to save us from our plight were doubted. Slowly, you modern men will become aware that science makes a bad religion. Not only does it place men at the mercy of their fellow men, it fails altogether to provide consolation for the many. Only the few can profit from the consolation of science or philosophy.

Freud: In your view, philosophy, science and reality are for the few and religion and its infantile illusions are for the many. In

that case, the philosophers must lead a dual life, they must live
as if they believed what they know to be myths and illusions.
Assuming that the secrecy of their enterprise can be maintained,
which to my mind is a very doubtful matter, how can those
who live this dual life hope to avoid neuroses and other
perversities with which their hypocrisy is likely to afflict them?

*   *   *

Strauss rejects Freud's 'modern' solution because he is not
convinced that enlightened self-interest provides man with a
sufficient motivation for virtue. One who accepts the argument
that the moral rules of civilization are beneficial can still maintain
that it would be even more beneficial to reap the benefits of
one's own injustice as well as those of living in a law-abiding
society. I am inclined to think that Strauss's objections to Freud
are quite valid. But surely one could respond that there is an
ancient solution that upholds morality even in the absence of
religion. I am referring to the rationalist arguments of Plato and
Aristotle regarding the intrinsic desirability of justice, or the view
that justice is a virtue without which the individual could not be
happy. As we shall see in the next chapter, Strauss rejects this
solution. Moreover, he denies that it was ever seriously held by
Plato, Aristotle or any of the ancients.

   In this chapter, I have tried to establish the following. First, that
in Strauss's view religion and philosophy are opposites that
cannot and should not be reconciled. The life of faith is the life of
blind unquestioning surrender, whereas the life of philosophy is
that of free enquiry. The faithful are steeped in delusions
whereas the philosophers rejoice in the truth. Religion prohibits
contemplation because it knows that as soon as one reflects, one
will recognize that religion is a fraud. However, if one reflects
further, one will realize the necessity of such swindles, and the
wisdom of the prophets who create them for love of mankind.
Recognizing this, philosophers must keep their atheistic truth
hidden; they must live a dual life endorsing publicly what they
know is but a noble fiction. As we shall see in what is to follow,
this dual life causes them no grief; on the contrary it fills their life
with laughter, inside jokes, subtle winks and pregnant pauses.[123]

4

Socrates and the Drama of Western Civilization

Reconstructing the political philosophy of Leo Strauss would be an impossible task were it not for the fact that he undoubtedly regarded classical thought as the repository of human wisdom and truth. Strauss presents himself as a classicist. He criticizes the moderns and defends the ancients; he uses 'classic natural right' as the standard by which to criticize modernity. He laments the decline of the wisdom of classical antiquity. But we cannot understand what it means to think of Strauss as a classicist unless we realize the extent to which his interpretation of the classics turns the conventional understanding of classical thought on its head.

For Strauss, the history of Western thought tells a story. Studying it will enable us to give an account of the whole, or to grasp the nature of things human, political and divine. It is the clue to the true nature of the human condition and its limitations. It reveals the causes as well as the symptoms of the decline of the West. It describes how the ascendancy of philosophy destroyed the sanctity of the ancestral. It explains why the safety, comfort and orderliness of man's pre-philosophical existence was irretrievably lost. Understanding how and why this happened is the key to understanding our own situation or the contemporary 'crisis' of Western civilization. However, understanding our predicament will not enable us to avoid the impending disaster altogether, but it might provide us with the insights necessary to prevent us from plunging full speed to our annihilation.

According to Strauss, the dangers of modernity are intimately linked to the discovery of philosophy. In the beginning, or in man's pre-philosophic understanding, the traditional, conventional, or ancestral was the ultimate standard or court of appeal. The ancestral is not just old, it is sacred, it has its origins in gods or men inspired by gods. In other words, the pre-philosophic understanding is marked by its theological character.[1] Philosophy emerges with the 'discovery' of the idea of nature (which is *not* coeval with human thought).[2] It unmasks the artificiality, fraudulence and inauthenticity of the conventional or ancestral. It sets itself apart from the comforting illusions that characterize all theological or pre-philosophical positions. It therefore threatens the security and stability of the pre-philosophical world.

There are three crucial stages in the development of Western civilization after the discovery of philosophy. In the first stage, the discovery of nature remains the privilege of rare sages, and so does not disrupt the tranquility of man's pre-philosophic existence. This stage is represented by the wise Epicurus, and to a lesser extent by his pupil Lucretius. Once philosophy is popularized, man's pre-philosophic innocence is lost. Socrates is the pivotal figure in this drama. This second stage is represented by the Aristophanean Socrates and the Sophists. In the third stage, the wisdom of the ancients reaches its zenith. This stage is represented by the mature Socrates or the Platonic–Xenophontic Socrates. The three stages describe the development of philosophy's own self-understanding; in particular, its understanding of its proper relationship to political society.

Strauss's account is meant to be logical and philosophical rather than chronological. It is an exercise in what John Gunnell has labelled 'epic political theory'.[3] This genre can best be appreciated as an imaginative story meant to shed light on the permanent features of the human predicament. It is not so much a history of ideas as a philosophy of history.

THE WALLS OF THE WORLD COLLAPSE

The story of the 'walls of the world' is an Epicurian tale describing the human predicament. It can be found in the poem *On The Nature of Things* by Lucretius, a Roman Epicurian.[4] For Strauss, the Epicurean account shares with the biblical one certain timeless and incontrovertible truths. In both accounts, loss of innocence is the result of the irresistible desire to know. Reasoning breaks through the simple happy world of man's early existence. Evil and wickedness are the result. Coercive society and divine laws backed by threat are the remedy. But unlike the biblical tale, this version is meant for the enlightened few and is told by a philosopher, or his disciple, and not by one who is lured by the charms of faith to be suspicious of reason. The Epicurian version is as follows.

In the beginning, man lived in a finite or closed universe. He experienced the world as if it had walls. The 'walls of the world' is a metaphor indicating the finiteness, stability and permanence of the world.[5] The walls afforded men protection and security; they shielded man from the inhuman universe and its infinite spaces. 'Finiteness is comforting; infinity is terrifying.'[6] In these early societies, men lived without fear and without evil. They were innocent, kind and willing to devote themselves to others in the absence of coercive social machinery or the belief in 'active gods' or gods who busy themselves with human affairs. They 'clung to the sweet light of life' not because they feared what might happen to them after death, but simply out of love of the world.[7]

Man's early innocence comes to an end when the walls of the world are torn asunder or when his salutary delusions are undermined by reasoning. Men begin to doubt whether the sun will always rise, or whether the world will come to an end. They begin to fear that the 'walls of the world will someday crumble'.[8] Their love of the world and attachment to it is the source of their distress. In Strauss's view, philosophy 'transforms the divination into a certainty' and is therefore 'productive of the deepest pain'.[9]

Once the walls of the world are broken, men become acutely aware of the fact that they live in an 'unwalled city' or an infinite universe. Naturally, these infinite spaces frighten them.[10] Fear makes them savage. Coercive society is necessary to curb their savagery, but it is not enough: 'civil government is not sufficient for orderly corporate life within society'.[11] Coercive society is a superficial solution to man's savagery because it does not penetrate to the root of the problem; it fails to address the fear that is the source of the savagery. Belief in 'active gods' alone can do this.

Religion 'originates in the actions of outstanding individuals'; it is a 'code of law prescribed for the many by higher intelligences'.[12] These are known as 'prophets'. For Strauss, prophecy is a matter of intelligence and imagination (not grace).[13] Prophets know that men are incapable of virtue, and so they appeal to their striving for material satisfaction by promising rewards for virtue and punishment for vice. Religion is necessary to assist coercive society in controlling crime. Since not all crimes can be observed and punished by law, it is necessary that potential criminals believe in the possibility that crimes undetected by law can be observed and punished by the gods.[14] But this is not all. Religion provides men with comfort. The gods are less frightening and less impersonal than blind fate. Unlike the latter, the gods can be influenced or bribed by offerings and sacrifices. Sigmund Freud expresses the same idea in *Future of an Illusion*.[15] Religion makes the world a friendlier and safer place to be: now, the continued existence of the world depends on the will of the gods. The gods invented by religion are busybodies who concern themselves with human affairs. They are easily angered and are quite capable of punishing transgressions of their will. It is in man's interest to keep them happy. The gods of political society inspire men with 'shuddering awe', but the terror they inspire is believed to be preferable to the terrors of the void. Religion counteracts the indifference of the infinite spaces to man's needs; it keeps the absurd at bay. Strauss accepts this account and regards it as the proper understanding of Epicurian philosophy. The point of Strauss's 'Notes on Lucretius' is that the latter does not fully understand his master.

In contrast to Strauss (and his Epicurus), Lucretius does not believe that the invention of the gods was such a good idea, for it made men unspeakably wicked.[16] Far from making them less savage, it fills them with fear and makes them willing to go to the most barbaric lengths to appease their gods. The story of the sacrifice of Iphigenia, Agamemnon's virgin daughter, to appease the goddess Diana is a case in point.[17] Lucretius believes that the terrors of the void are not as unbearable for ordinary humanity as people (like Strauss) are inclined to think. It is better to accept the mortality of our souls without delusion or rebellion, than to be gripped by the fear of Hades. The latter destroys our happiness and robs our pleasures of their sweetness. We are bound to be happier if we face up to the fact that the world is unsupported by wise and benevolent gods, and that there is nothing at the helm but the blind fury of the blind atoms.[18] Man will be happier living in the face of the truth than in the grip of the terrifying delusions of religion. Lucretius embarks on a campaign against fear, and the use of fear by priests and kings to augment their power.[19] His intention is to liberate the minds of men from the terror of religion, and replace it with the 'sweet solace of life' which is philosophy.[20]

Strauss's analysis of Lucretius's poem is intended to show that his attack on religion is foolish and unsound in view of his own penetrating account of the human condition. In Strauss's view, Lucretius realizes full well that the delusions of religion are sweet in comparison to the terrible truth of philosophy, and therefore, replacing one with the other does not so obviously and incontrovertibly enhance the happiness of mankind. Strauss makes much of the fact that the poem begins with the 'glad and lovely' Venus and ends with the agony of death in the plague. Strauss uncovers the significance of this beginning and ending as follows. Venus is the symbol of man's pre-philosophic or theological existence. The poem is therefore an 'ascent' from the pleasant delusions of religion to the terrible truth of philosophy.[21] The poem moves from sweet delusion to naked truth, from the gods to nature, from religion to philosophy. But this movement is intended to be a movement from the *terrors* of religion to the 'sweet solace' of philosophy, so why begin with Venus and end with plague and not the reverse?

Strauss's explanation is that the poet must have known that philosophy is more 'savage truth' than 'sweet solace'. He knew that the truth is not so sweet to those who have not been 'initiated into it', and that 'the multitude shrink from it with horror'.[22] The poet knew, as does Strauss, that philosophical truth is ugly, repulsive, terrible, frightening, depressing, dark, harsh and horrible, at least to the uninitiated.[23] He knew that the 'ascent' from pleasant delusions to truth is not an easy one: 'the movement from untruth to truth is not simply a movement from unrelieved darkness and terror to pure light and joy. On the contrary, the truth appears at first to be repulsive and depressing.'[24] Strauss means to say that it becomes sweet only to the wise. (Recall that the ascent out of the cave in Plato's *Republic* is not an easy one, and the light of the sun is at first quite blinding to one who has been dragged out of the comfort of the cave.) It seems that the love of truth is an acquired taste.

In Strauss's view, Lucretius is fully aware of the difficulty of the ascent and the repulsive nature of the truth. His intention is therefore to sweeten the 'wormwood' with 'honey', or to facilitate the difficult ascent to the truth by the beauty of his poetry.[25] His subject may be dark, but his poem is bright. The movement of the poem from Venus to the plague mirrors the emancipation of the addressee; it reflects the ascent from the charming but fallacious beliefs in the gods to the light of the truth via the art of poetry which is the honey that sweetens the wormwood.

Strauss's 'Notes on Lucretius' is a subtle but penetrating critique of the intention of the poet. However, his disagreement with Lucretius begins from a considerable base of agreement. He does not object to Lucretius's account of the origin of religion or its untruth, nor does he challenge Lucretius's account of the terrifying nature of the truth. Strauss questions the wisdom of the poet's activity. For Strauss, philosophy is the representative of the naked truth. True philosophers do not believe that the naked truth should be sweetened or made palatable. The only reason for sweetening it is to give it to children or those who are 'quite immature' and therefore unfit for it.[26] The poet's activity is therefore foolish and dangerous.

Strauss also questions the political wisdom of Lucretius's campaign against religion. In Strauss's view, the poet 'leaves us with the sting of the question as to how the unphilosophic multitude will conduct itself if it ceases to believe in gods who punish lack of patriotism and of filial piety . . .'.[27] Strauss believes that in his more lucid moments, Lucretius realized that the utility of religion is 'not altogether negligible'.[28] Nevertheless he was eager to liberate the mind from the 'terrors of religion'.[29] But surely, Strauss objects, those terrors are not so great as to make one 'swallow the naked truth'.[30] What, asks Strauss, has Lucretius accomplished by undermining the belief in Hades? He has merely succeeded in replacing the fear of Hades with the terror of the void, or of death itself. After all, only the unjust fear hell, but the fear of death grips all men, not only the unjust; it is the 'corrosive' that Strauss spoke of so eloquently in his funeral speech.[31] Lucretius has therefore succeeded only in removing a 'salutary restraint'[32] effective against criminals while making everyone else miserable, because the fear of death (understood as a return to inorganic lifelessness) is far worse than the fear of hell. Only the few or the philosophers are capable of happiness in the face of the savage truth. The happiness of the philosophers is not accessible to men who are 'dull-witted' or of 'mean capacities'.[33] Even if it were possible for every man (no matter how 'dull-witted') to live the life of the philosopher, the life 'according to nature'[34] or the life 'worthy of the gods',[35] this is not politically feasible. Philosophy, presupposes 'a high development of the arts'.[36] It requires freedom from toil or leisure that pre-political society could not afford. Philosophy is therefore parasitic on political society.

Despite his criticisms of Lucretius, Strauss regards his doctrine to be a genuinely philosophical one in the Straussian sense of the term. It does not labor under the naïve equation of the good and the ancestral.[37] It recognizes the origin of religion in the moral and political needs of man, and hence the intimate connection between religion and political society.[38] It recognizes the necessity of political society for the philosophical life. It also recognizes that the highly unnatural or unpleasant cooperation of coercive society and religion is necessary to make possible the only truly happy or pleasant life, the life of the philosopher. The Epicurian is vividly aware of the conflict between the unnatural character of political society and the natural character of the most pleasant life, the life of the philosopher, the life according to nature, the good life, or the life that affords the most solid pleasure (pleasure being the highest good by nature).[39]

In the 'unwalled city' philosophizing affords the only solace and the only real pleasure. We must therefore accept the 'disproportion' between the requirements of philosophy and those of society; one is natural and pleasant, the other unnatural and unpleasant.[40] Strauss believes that Lucretius was fully cognizant of this fact, which explains why he replaces Venus in the beginning of the poem with the 'Great Mother' at the end. Unlike Venus, the Great Mother represents political morality, the motherland and patriotism.[41] Venus does not hold sway in political society. There, Mars, the god of war, and the Great Mother hold sway. Love and family may be the foundations of civil society, but unless they are politicized into love of motherland and a desire for honor, they can threaten the survival of the city. Sigmund Freud makes the same point in *Civilization and its Discontents*. For Freud, as for Strauss, even though civil society has its origin in the family, the *eros* within the family, as well as family love in general, threaten the larger society. The latter must therefore devise means by which family love can be extended to the larger community.[42] Political society is the enemy of Venus as it is of *eros* or pleasure in general, and the highest *eros* in particular (i.e. philosophizing).

Strauss has contempt for Lucretius, but not for his doctrine. For Strauss, a genuinely philosophical doctrine is not the appropriate subject-matter for poetry. The poet Lucretius imitates the philosopher Epicurus. The imitator 'belongs as it were to a weaker and lower species than the teacher of the naked truth'.[43] By sweetening the naked truth, Lucretius's poetry introduces an element foreign to the master's doctrine. Strauss therefore suggests that Lucretius is not the 'master's pupil in every respect'.[44] He may have thought himself wiser than the master for his ability to do what the master could not, but for Strauss, Lucretius 'could as little rival Epicurus as a swallow could rival swans or kids a horse'.[45]

In spite of Lucretius's shortcomings, Strauss regards him as an ancient. He does not aspire to happiness by the 'conquest of nature'; he knows that philosophy cannot transform political society; he knows that misery is as necessary to human life as happiness.[46] I understand this to mean that the misery of the many is necessary for the happiness of the few, since only the few wise are capable of true happiness. Lucretius is a true ancient because he is not moved by charity; he has no desire to feed the hungry or clothe the naked. He aspires to live a life worthy of the gods, and he knows that 'one cannot be a god while being a benefactor of men'.[47]

Strauss makes it clear that one does not have to be an Epicurian in the sense of accepting the theories of the void and of the unholy war of the atoms to aspire to the life of the Epicurian sage, or the blessed philosopher.[48] It suffices to be willing and able to live in the face of the naked truth without fear or delusion, that is, to live as a philosopher. Strauss concurs with Lucretius's account of the nature of philosophical life: it has everything in common with the views of the Platonic–Xenophontic Socrates as Strauss understands the latter. In Strauss's view, Lucretius understood the nature of philosophical life very well. Philosophy is a way of life that enables one to transcend fear by facing the truth and accepting it without rebellion. This is possible because philosophy is a process of 'detachment' from the world and love of the world.[49] Philosophy, 'anticipating the collapse of the walls of the world, breaks through the walls of the world, abandons the attachment to the world'.[50] Only such detachment can allow the philosopher to live a life worthy of a god.

We cannot understand the philosophical way of life to which Strauss lures 'young men who love to think', unless we grasp the nature of the godlike ideal that is the standard for the philosophical life. Strauss upholds a conception of deity that he claims to share with Lucretius, the mature Socrates, Plato, Xenophon, Aristotle and Cicero, in short, the ancients. On the ancient view, real gods, if there are any, are self-sufficient. They do not suffer need. They neither love, nor need to be loved. Real gods are not benefactors of men. There is no reason to be a benefactor unless you wish to be loved. Allan Bloom put it more forcefully than his teacher when he declared that a god who loves without need (like the biblical God, I presume) is an 'imposter'![51]

The 'world' to which men find themselves attached is that of the family and the city. The philosopher must detach himself from both. He must shun love as much as politics, because the pleasures of the political life are a form of the pleasures of love.[52] In *On Tyranny*, Strauss explains that the political man must be a benefactor of his fellow citizens because he wants to be loved. The ruler is the citizen *par excellence*.[53] The life of the ruler is one of servitude, not pleasure. He must benefit his citizens if he wishes to be honored.

In Strauss's interpretation, the wise Simonides in Xenophon's *Hiero* reveals to the tyrant that his desire for honor is the political form of the common desire for love.[54] Like the desire to be loved, the desire to be honored depends on others. For Strauss, as for Lucretius and the other ancients, a life dedicated to public office is akin to the life of Sisyphus: forever trying to lay hold of something that always eludes one. Because esteem depends on others and not on oneself, the political man is not self-sufficient; it is not in his power to secure his own happiness.[55] The same reasoning leads Strauss to believe that the wise man must prefer the pleasures of eating to those of sex, since the former, unlike the latter do not depend on the cooperation of another human being.[56]

In contrast to the political man, the wise man wants neither to love nor be loved. He knows that the desire to be loved necessarily leads to servitude.[57] Instead of love, he seeks admiration, not by everyone, but by a 'competent minority'.[58] It is not necessary to be a benefactor in order to be admired. 'Admiration seems to be less mercenary than love.'[59] Besides, 'a man may be admired many generations after his death whereas he will cease to be loved once those who knew him well are dead'.[60] Love depends on proximity. To be loved is to be someone's possession, for everyone 'loves what is somehow his own'.[61] Love shackles us to space and time; it holds us captive to the Here and Now. As a result, it frustrates the philosophical process of detachment.

The same reasoning leads Lucretius to advise those who would be happy to forsake the pleasures of Venus altogether.[62] Strauss wonders if this is not too drastic a solution. He complains that the Epicurian conception of philosophy is altogether unerotic.[63] It forgets that the philosophical life, for all its detachment, consists mainly in conversations, which require the cooperation and company of others. Strauss subtly suggests that it would be possible to 'enjoy the fruit of Venus' if we 'separate sexual pleasure from love'.[64] In other words, the philosopher should seek the pleasures of sex, friendship and companionship without the shackles of love and family. This is the sort of reasoning that must lead the wise man to prefer boys to women. Strauss makes much of Socrates's charm and seductive qualities which enable him to lure beautiful and promising boys like Kleinias (not to mention Plato) away from politics and the family to a life dedicated to the philosophical *eros*.[65] There is, in all of this, more than a hint of a fashionable homosexuality.

The process of detachment is intended to make the life of the philosopher akin to that of the gods; that is, if there *are* any gods. Philosophy does not simply cast doubt on the gods of the city, it *invents new gods*! It speculates that if there *are* any gods, they are not the gods of political society, the gods of 'shuddering awe',[66] the gods who busy themselves with the affairs of men, setting down laws and threatening punishment for disobedience. The real gods must be sempiternal, blessed immortal beings who neither care about the affairs of man nor hold up the heavens nor move the stars. Their perfect bliss must be 'unmolested' by such mundane chores.[67] Such gods cannot feel love, and they do not know charity.[68] However, if there are no such gods, then 'the most divine being, the being most resplendent, most beneficent and most high in rank is the wise man with his frail happiness'.[69] Like the gods he has invented, the sage is not a benefactor except incidentally; he 'is beneficent by being what he is rather than by doing anything'.[70] This is the vision of deity that explains Strauss's claim that Socrates was guilty as charged of *inventing* new gods. It also explains why for Strauss the difference between inventing new gods and *not* believing in god or gods is not decisive.

There is a conflict between the philosopher and the city. The philosopher rejects the gods of the city and invents new gods. He renounces love of motherland, public office and love of a woman and a family. The life of the philosopher is one that is lived on the fringes of civil society, and not a life in service to it. The philosopher is in the city, but not of the city: 'he is a stranger in the most radical sense'.[71] His position in the city is not unlike that of Albert Camus's 'outsider'. The latter was condemned to death for making public his strange uncitizenly sentiments.[72] The philosopher stands in similar danger *vis-à-vis* the city. This is why so much caution and thrift in expression is absolutely necessary. Unlike Camus's absurd man, the philosopher *can* live in the face of the naked truth or the 'benign indifference'[73] of the universe without despair. Unlike the despairing antihero of Camus's novel, the philosopher is prudent enough to protect the city from his own insolence; he recognizes that the city is the prerequisite to the enjoyment of any pleasure, including the sweetest pleasures of contemplation.[74] As Pangle writes, this supremely free man who has liberated himself from the 'plastic power of custom', will 'continue to dwell among and profit from his deluded neighbors; but spiritually he will live a life apart'.[75]

THE YOUNG SOCRATES AND THE SCIENTIFIC SPIRIT

The young or early Socrates described by Aristophanes in the *Clouds* is a Sophist. The view he represents is the result of the 'publication' and the resulting vulgarization of the Epicurean view which represents the earliest appearance of philosophy, or the discovery of nature.[76]

For Strauss, Socrates is the pivotal figure, not only for understanding the classics, but for understanding ourselves. Strauss follows Nietzsche in thinking that the contemporary West is the embodiment of 'Socratic culture'. Socrates is the 'turning point' of our civilization, nay the 'vortex of world history', and therefore the 'most questionable phenomenon of antiquity'.[77] To understand ourselves, we must understand him.

Following one of the Islamic philosophers, Strauss believes that Socrates must have undergone a 'conversion'.[78] The early Socrates portrayed by Aristophanes in the *Clouds* is a Sophist. The Socrates portrayed in the dialogues of Plato and Xenophon has been converted. The Aristophanean Socrates, not the Platonic–

Xenophontic Socrates, is responsible for inaugurating what Nietzsche called 'Socratic culture' and what Strauss simply calls modernity. Therefore, in Strauss's view, Nietzsche rightly attacks the young Socrates as does Aristophanes. However, the mature Socrates, the Platonic–Xenophontic Socrates, the Socrates made 'fair', 'new' and 'noble' is a different Socrates.[79] He has learnt his lesson from Aristophanes and has seen the errors of his ways.

The young Socrates is the embodiment of the scientific spirit. He is green, foolish and degenerately modern.[80] He embodies the optimistic rationalism that characterizes modernity. In other words, he believes that the true is in perfect harmony with the good and the beautiful (i.e. there is nothing 'savage' about the truth).[81] He therefore does not consider knowledge to be dangerous for mankind. He is an optimist who believes not only that this is the best possible world, but that the best world imaginable is possible with the help of science and enlightenment.[82]

The young Socrates is a debunker of the gods. He denies that thunder, lightening and rain are caused by Zeus. He dethrones Zeus and replaces him with Vortex, Clouds and Air. He swears by the Chaos and by the Air. He compares the sounds of thunder with diarrhea and the rumblings of a human stomach. He therefore deprives the 'things aloft' of their 'awesome glamour' and 'awe-inspiring splendor'.[83] He denies that lightening bolts are Zeus's way of striking perjurers; he points to the fact that temples and oaks are more often struck by lightening than perjurers.[84] Strauss observes that Zeus has been replaced by Clouds and Air to account for rain and thunder, but 'in the case of the punishment of perjury Zeus has not been replaced by anybody or anything'.[85] Socrates's debunking of heaven has the effect of undermining justice. Piety and justice, religion and the city go together; undermining one leads to the demise of the other.[86] As we shall see, this is necessarily the case not simply because the many need fear as a motive for justice, but because Strauss believes that justice simply lacks rational support.

Aristophanes portrays the young Socrates as a teacher of rhetoric (i.e. a Sophist in the Platonic sense of the term).[87] Strepsiades, an old fool, seeks to learn from Socrates how to make the weaker argument appear the stronger, so that he can defraud his creditors in court. Socrates does not know his intention, nor does he care.[88] He quickly and imprudently reveals to Strepsiades his 'most shocking innovations'.[89] He teaches Strepsiades in a genuinely Socratic fashion: he allows him to discover the truth for himself. He stages a public debate between the 'Just Speech' and the 'Unjust Speech' (or Right and Wrong as personified by Aristophanes in the *Clouds*). As Strauss explains, 'Socrates does not teach injustice; he merely exposes his pupils to the exchange between justice and injustice'.[90] He therefore takes no responsibility for the outcome. Dialogue serves the cause of truth: whoever succeeds in the course of the dialogue must deserve to succeed.

The 'Just' and 'Unjust Speech' hurl insults at each other in a struggle to possess the mind of the listener. The 'Just Speech' is old-fashioned: he glorifies the men of old, declares that justice is with the gods, and exhorts men to obey Zeus. He champions decency, chastity, moderation and self-restraint. He recalls with nostalgia the days when boys were seen and not heard, and when deviations were severely punished. He praises training in gymnastics which is necessary to breed the sorts of warriors who fought at Marathon.[91] He objects to warm baths on the grounds that they breed effeminacy and make men cowardly.[92] He is an ascetic. Strauss observes that the 'Just Speech' spends much time telling us what we must abstain from, rather than what to do, and adds, 'not to say enjoy'.[93]

The 'Just Speech' hurls insults at the 'Unjust Speech', calling him a shameless, ribald pederast and parricide, but the 'Unjust Speech' proudly accepts these as terms of praise. The 'Unjust Speech' is modern, bold, daring, clever and debonair. He warns the listener against the 'Just Speech', saying that to choose the 'Just Speech' is to be filled with reverence and shame, to be respectful of old men, to be easily angered when mocked, and to have no relations with dancing girls.[94] He destroys the case against warm baths by pointing to the example of Herakles, the strong and courageous son of Zeus, who was known to take warm baths regularly. He declares that right does not exist; and even if it did, it is not with the gods: Zeus could not have fettered his father with impunity if right was with the gods![95] He advocates doing what the gods do and not what they say. In Strauss's words, the 'Unjust Speech' 'subverts law and justice by raising the question regarding their foundations'.[96]

Strauss knows that in any contest between the 'Just Speech' and the 'Unjust Speech', 'the Unjust Speech is doomed to win'.[97] For Strauss, Aristophanes illustrates the triumph of the 'Unjust Speech' by the result of the contest – namely, the total corruption of Strepsiades. Like John Stuart Mill, Strauss believes that the truth will triumph in the course of debate and dialogue. Unlike Mill, however, he believes this to be most unfortunate: for the triumph of the truth will consist only of the most devastating defeat of justice. Strauss considers Aristophanes to be far wiser than Mill. His play is intended to illustrate the disastrous results of unrestricted public debate, especially a debate between the 'Just' and the 'Unjust Speech'.

Socrates wreaks havoc on the city. By mocking him, Aristophanes seeks to render his 'corrupting influence' less harmful. The mature Socrates recognizes the folly of his ways. In the hands of Plato, 'Socratic discourse' becomes the highest political art. There, Socrates is portrayed using his rhetorical skills to ensure the triumph of justice. In other words, the Platonic Socrates uses his Sophistry (or his ability to make the weaker argument appear the stronger) for the sake of the city, or in the cause of justice.[98]

For Strauss, the young Socrates is the embodiment of the scientific spirit: he is 'anerotic' and 'a-music'; in other words, he is characterized by a most 'inhuman asceticism'.[99] His pupils are pale and sickly; they are not permitted to go out into the fresh air, but spend all their time in the 'think-tank' or Thinkery. His 'zeal' in the pursuit of learning leads him to lead a hard ascetic life characterized by a lack of gymnastics, sexual abstinence, frugality, endurance and continence.[100] He is concerned with truth above beauty. He fails to understand that a culture needs beauty more than it needs truth and ugliness. By the same token, he fails to recognize that the truth is ugly and destructive. His dedication to truth is altogether consuming. He is oblivious to its effects on those around him. In spite of his immoderate love of truth, Socrates is not an erotic lover of knowledge for its own sake (i.e. for the sake of the pleasures of contemplation). For the Aristophanean Socrates, knowledge is a means to the 'relief of man's estate'; it is sought for the sake of 'higher egoism', or collective selfishness.

Strauss describes the young Socrates as a Promethian benefactor of mankind (and therefore not the godlike sage that he later becomes). He offers man the light of knowledge without thinking of the unpalatable results of mass enlightenment. Socrates, like Prometheus, is a fool; only our 'modernity' leads us to labor under the illusion that a Promethian is a hero. Aristophanes knows better. The destruction of the Thinkery by fire at the end of the play is meant to teach Socrates a lesson – namely that his pious devotion to science leads inevitably to his own destruction as well as that of the city.

Strauss concludes that the young Socrates is quintessentially 'modern' in his unconcealed debunking of the gods, his suicidal dedication to truth, his rationalist optimism and his scientific asceticism. He is a pivotal figure in the drama of Western civilization. By the time he learned the errors of his ways, it was too late, he had done too much damage. Modernity is a testimony to the triumph of his scientific spirit.[101]

THE MATURE SOCRATES

The Socrates we encounter in the dialogues of Plato and Xenophon is one who has been made 'fair', 'new' and 'noble'. According to Strauss, this converted Socrates is one who has learnt his lesson from Aristophanes. He is the embodiment of ancient wisdom. To understand him, we must understand what he has learnt from Aristophanes.

It is important to establish at the outset that whatever Socrates has learnt from Aristophanes does not lead him to revoke the fruits of the discovery of nature. The 'conversion' of Socrates is a conversion to esotericism. Briefly stated, the mature Socrates realizes the damage he has caused to the city and himself by his immoderate dedication to truth. He therefore abandons his naïve optimist rationalism because he realizes that science cannot save mankind, it can only destroy it. The fair Socrates has now learnt that there is an irreconcilable conflict between the true on the one hand and the noble on the other. He knows that the truth is destructive of the noble delusions on which the city depends. He is therefore more erotic because he loves the truth for its own sake or for the pleasure of it, and not for the benefits it can bestow. The mature Socrates is more political; he realizes the extent of his dependence on the unphilosophic multitude, and hence of the need to give an account of his philosophic activity in terms that are acceptable to the city. He is a citizen, a patriot and a married man with children. In short, he has learnt a lesson in political prudence.[102] Strauss finds evidence for these claims in the Socratic dialogues of Plato and Xenophon.

The most important result of Socrates's conversion is that he is now a 'safe speaker'; in other words, he is 'radically ironic'.[103] He says different things to different people; he does not say the same things to Sophists and representatives of the political multitude that he might say to 'young men of promise' or those he might be able to lead to wisdom. He is never portrayed speaking to equals: there are no dialogues between Socrates and Plato. He therefore never reveals the truth fully.[104] Likewise, Plato and Xenophon conceal their own opinions (as well as their master's) through the dialogue. To understand the Socratic dialogues, we must pay attention not only to the speeches, but to the characters, the action and the drama.[105] Strauss approaches the dialogues as one would approach literary works. His commentaries resemble literary criticisms more than conventional textual analysis. His literary approach allows him to deal with the text much more freely and imaginatively. In the course of unpacking the literary symbols, Strauss reveals to us his own vision of what a wise man must have meant.

The most unorthodox aspect of Strauss's understanding of the Platonic–Xenophontic Socrates is his claim that he is much closer intellectually and much friendlier personally to the Sophists than the unwary reader of the dialogues might assume. Strauss's interpretation of the conversation between Socrates and Thrasymachus in the first book of Plato's *Republic* illustrates what he means.

The originality of Strauss's interpretation of Plato's *Republic* rests in his claim that Socrates does not refute Thrasymachus; on the contrary, Thrasymachus's principle 'remains victorious'.[106] Nor does Socrates deny Polymarchus's view that justice consists in benefiting friends and harming enemies. Nor does he prove that the morally just life is the happy life or that justice benefits the just man, or that justice (in the moral sense) is a good that is choiceworthy for its own sake.[107] Such orthodox views about the *Republic* are fictions inherited from Christian Neoplatonism. Nothing could be further from the truth.

Plato presents Thrasymachus as the embodiment of the 'Unjust Speech'. In contrast, Socrates is portrayed as the incarnation of the 'Just Speech', whereas Thrasymachus is depicted as a 'wild beast', Socrates is naïve and 'innocent'.[108] But this does not fool Strauss. It certainly did not fool Thrasymachus. He knew that Socrates was a 'dissembler, a man who pretends to be ignorant while in fact he knows things very well'.[109] Far from being naïve and innocent, Socrates is 'clever and tricky'.[110] Strauss suggests that this is precisely what infuriates Thrasymachus in the first book of the *Republic*. He is impatient with all that jesting. Strauss believes that Socrates might have spoken to him more openly in private, and as a result, Thrasymachus knows that Socrates agrees with him but is not telling the truth.[111]

Strauss admires the 'cleverness with which Socrates argued badly on purpose',[112] in order to show Thrasymachus that he is right, but not going about things the right way. Strauss explains that Thrasymachus's realization of this is the only thing that could have made him willing to listen silently to Socrates. Thrasymachus submits to the charm of Socrates: he 'allows' Socrates to 'tame' him into silence even though he knows the truth.[113] Strauss insists that Thrasymachus is 'tamed' by Socrates, but he is *not* 'refuted'.[114]

According to Strauss, Thrasymachus's view of justice is far from 'savage'; on the contrary, it is 'highly respectable'.[115] It is the view that is eventually enlarged and deepened in the course of the *Republic*. Thrasymachus states it as follows. Justice is a matter of obedience to law; but law is made by those in power to further their own interests. Obedience to law therefore consists in acting in accordance with the interests of those in power, or the stronger (which may be the majority). To act justly is to promote the interest of the stronger and not one's own good. However, by nature everyone seeks his own pleasure which is the only good. To act justly, or for the good of others is therefore to act contrary to nature. The city and its justice are unnatural and anti-natural; they set severe limits on man's pursuit of the natural good.[116]

Strauss contends that the *Republic* substantiates the view that justice is a fabrication, a product of art, or of human convention.[117] Contrary to popular belief, Socrates found nothing natural about justice. It is not the natural order of the human *psyche* or any such fiction. Acting justly consists in benefiting others, or acting contrary to the natural human inclination to prefer one's own good. Strauss is convinced that Socrates could not have failed to see that there is an irrevocable conflict between the good of the individual and that of the city.[118] Justice is concerned with the latter, and so inevitably conflicts with everyone's inclination to prefer their own benefit, which is 'the only natural good'.[119] Justice is an artificial device by which the city compels us to benefit our fellow citizens. And, if prudence or wisdom consists in seeking one's own good, then Thrasymachus is right in thinking that the just man is a fool, or a man duped by convention.[120] The foolishness of Thrasymachus lies in his effort to 'liberate them [mankind] from the charms which make them obtuse'.[121] This is precisely what Strauss believes to be at issue between Socrates and Thrasymachus: whereas Socrates believes justice to be a necessary evil, Thrasymachus believes it to be an unnecessary evil. Convincing Thrasymachus that it is necessary is the first step in taming him or getting him to hold his tongue.[122]

If the city is to survive, let alone flourish, it needs to cultivate the virtue of justice among its citizens. In view of this, nothing could be more salutary than the belief that the just are happy or that justice is in the interest of the one who is just. But in Strauss's view, Socrates's attempt to make this argument fails miserably; conceivably because it is an impossible argument to make. If the failure in question is missed, that is the result of the beauty and charm (if not the cleverness) of the mature Socrates who uses his Sophistic rhetoric to uphold the cause of the 'Just Speech'. At the end of the *Republic*, Plato is compelled to resort to myths about the gods and the rewards and punishments of the afterlife; Strauss understands this as a subtle acknowledgment of the failure of the argument in favor of the 'Just Speech'.

What Strauss learns from Plato is that there is nothing sacred about the rules of justice. Justice is simply a means to collective self-interest. It lacks universal validity in inter-group relations. The same rules that are useful to the preservation of the city, are necessary for the preservation of a gang of robbers, whose activities are in the service of manifest injustice. One cannot escape from this unpleasant reality by asserting that the city is just to all, while a gang of robbers is not. Everyone knows that the foundation of every city is in crime, and that foreign policy even in peace time requires espionage and other more sordid activities, because 'war casts its shadow on peace'.[123] Political societies act much like gangs of robbers:[124] they practice 'thievery' not against one another, but against the 'foreign enemy'.[125] As Strauss writes:

> Are the maxims of foreign policy essentially different from the maxims on which gangs of robbers act? Can they be different? Are cities not compelled to use force and fraud to take away from other cities what belongs to the latter, if they are to

prosper? Do they not come into being by usurping a part of the earth's surface which by nature belongs equally to all others?[126]

Strauss makes the case for Thrasymachus more eloquently than it has ever been made before.

Strauss's position is simply this. How could Socrates be said to uphold what so obviously lacks rational support? It is not plausible to believe, as Socrates is generally reputed to believe, that justice consists in harming no one. How could it be? Is it possible for justice to consist in harming no one? If that were the case, then even the best city cannot be just; for a 'city is a society which from time to time must wage war, and war is inseparable from harming innocent people'.[127] Nor did Socrates believe that enlightenment will make war obsolete. On the contrary, he understood, as did Aristophanes, that there can be no lasting peace.[128]

Far from denying Polymarchus's view of justice, as benefiting friends and harming enemies, the *Republic* confirms it. As Strauss notes, the dog-like morality of the guardians consists in being gentle to the citizens and ferocious to outsiders.[129] Justice is a matter of benefiting friends who are fellow citizens and harming enemies who are outsiders.[130] Political society is not possible without WE and THEY.[131] Mankind will always live in societies characterized by mutual hostility and antagonism. This is the logic of political societies.

According to Strauss, Aristophanes had a profound understanding of the true nature of political justice. He understood that the city must from time to time wage war. It therefore needs citizens with manliness, courage and spiritedness. He understood that most of the city's acts of justice are acts of punishment, and the latter is assisted by anger, moral indignation or spiritedness (Strauss's term is derivative from and relies on Plato's conception of spirit or the second part of the *psyche*). Aristophanes compares the sorts of qualities the city needs with those characteristic of wasps.[132] The Wasps, in Aristophanes's play of the same name, are a group of old men who are particularly patriotic and high-spirited. In their youth they distinguished themselves in war. They boast to the audience of having fearlessly crushed the Persians in battle. Now, too old for battle, they spend their time at the law courts, earning their living as jury men. By the sounds of it they are a tough bunch who have no mercy or compassion on any lawbreakers. Among them is one super-Wasp who does not need the jury-man's wage; he is independently wealthy. But for love of his city, he is more zealous than the rest. Like wasps, these men act in swarms; they are vicious, 'singularly quick to anger and ill-tempered when provoked'.[133] Waspishness is the very opposite of softness, gentleness, effeminacy and compassion. The Wasps champion the same causes as does the 'Just Speech' in the *Clouds*. Like the latter, they insist on self-discipline, self-restraint and strength. They are altogether intolerant of deviant behavior, and are quick to denounce it as subversive.[134] They are radically ascetic and will not suffer any enjoyments, pleasures or comforts.[135]

In Strauss's interpretation, Aristophanes's *Wasps* is about the disastrous consequences that result from the corruption of one super-Wasp by his *nouveau riche* son who wishes his father to cease frequenting the courts and spend his time in leisure, comfort and the pleasures of high society. The play is about the unavoidable necessity for waspishness. The latter is inseparable from the virility of the city; if it is undermined, the city is lost. The city knows this full well, and hence its understandable animosity to the pleasures of *eros*.

According to Strauss, the *Republic* contains two different concepts of justice: political justice and philosophical justice.[136] Political justice is intimately connected with waspishness. It is the virtue of citizens, and hence Strauss's reference to it as a 'citizen morality'.[137] He also refers to it as moral, political or 'vulgar' virtue.[138] The central concern of the *Republic* is not so much with justice in the vulgar or political sense, but with philosophical justice. The latter is the peculiar justice of the philosopher.

The philosopher's justice is a microcosm of the justice of the city taken as a whole. The philosopher is the most perfect reflection of the justice of the city because he is not part of the city.[139] The philosopher is not just in the same way as the citizen is just. Like the city, the philosopher gives to each his due: he does not say the same things to everyone. He does not speak to the vulgar or to the representatives of the political multitude as he speaks to 'potential philosophers'.[140] Just as the city does not benefit other cities, so the philosopher is not a benefactor – he does not benefit others except incidentally by his own beneficence. He does not by nature or without compulsion benefit the non-philosophic multitude. However, the city not only does not benefit other cities, it harms them. In this respect the philosopher is unlike the city. He neither benefits nor harms others.[141] His attitude to inferiors is not characterized by hate or the desire to harm, but simply by indifference or neglect.[142] There is no reason for the philosopher to harm others because what ordinary men 'hotly contest' is of little value to him. Human things seem 'paltry' to one who has seen the 'truly grand'.[143] The only thing he considers choiceworthy for its own sake is the philosophic *eros* or the pleasures of contemplation, friendship and conversation.[144] The mature Socrates is more erotic than the young Socrates because he has abandoned the idea of being a benefactor of mankind. Instead, he embraces knowledge for its own sake or for the pleasure of it. In doing so, he surpasses the wisdom of the Epicurean sage who loved knowledge primarily as a means to tranquility and freedom from fear.

We cannot grasp the novelty of Strauss's Socrates unless we understand that he is a thoroughgoing hedonist.[145] Only a 'comprehensive hedonistic interpretation of human life' can make sense of the life of Socrates. Only in *On Tyranny* does Strauss explicitly refer to the view of the wise as a comprehensive hedonism. There, he is commenting on a dialogue in which Simonides and not Socrates is the main speaker. Strauss suggests that we cannot be sure that the teaching in this dialogue belongs to Socrates. Anyone familiar with Strauss's other works on Xenophon is not likely to be fooled by this feeble disclaimer. Besides, Strauss tells us at the outset of the commentary that using Simonides as the main speaker was Xenophon's way of hiding his own thoughts as well as Socrates's even more scrupulously. Socratic hedonism (Strauss does not use the term) is not an ordinary garden variety type. Strauss distinguishes between the hedonism of Socrates and that of the vulgar. The latter identify the good with the greatest pleasure, and regard sex as the highest pleasure.[146] The hedonism of Strauss and his Socrates is more refined. Although not oblivious to the lower pleasures, it is cognizant of the higher pleasures: the pleasures of contemplation, friendship and conversation with equals or with young men of promise, and of course, the pleasure of being admired (not loved) by them. This highbrow hedonism continues to regard pleasure as the ultimate criterion, and identifies it with the good. It recommends virtue (in the sense of moral or political justice and nobility) only as a means to the good or pleasure (i.e. as a necessary evil). Socratic hedonism makes an important distinction between the noble and the good: whereas the latter is what all men naturally seek or long for, the former is a product of artifice; it belongs to the city and to convention, not nature.[147] This explains why Strauss regards the noble as far more 'problematic' than the good.[148]

The philosopher's conception of the good is closer to that of the vulgar than to that of the morally virtuous. According to Strauss, this is indicated by the fact that Alcibiades, who was a morally dubious character, was Socrates's lover. In other words, Socratic hedonism regards the good as something other than the morally good or noble. Because the city cannot live with this hedonistic truth, it inevitably comes to conflict with philosophy. Politics is impossible in the face of the truth. What is needed for political order is a class of men who reject hedonism altogether. These types of men Strauss calls 'citizens', and the most superior among them, 'gentlemen'. Citizens and gentlemen have no pleasures: being a citizen and especially a gentleman is a serious business. Citizenship is a 'loveless affair'.[149] The citizen must renounce the natural human dedication to pleasure. He must subordinate his own pleasures to his duties to others.

Strauss is well known for his claim that the political solution *par excellence* is the rule of gentlemen. This must be understood in the light of his conception of gentlemen as a special breed. They are people capable of harboring the noble self-deceptions without which the city cannot exist.[150] They are people who believe that the just life is the happy life, and that the life dedicated to the service of others is truly the most pleasant life. They are people who believe that the noble is choiceworthy for its own sake. The philosopher knows that these are political fictions; he knows that the good life by nature is a life dedicated to the pursuit of one's own pleasure; he knows that the life of the citizen and gentleman, the life dedicated to the service of others is indistinguishable from servitude. This is the gist of Strauss's commentaries on the writings of Xenophon.

In their Socratic dialogues, Plato and Xenophon set out to defend Socrates (as well as themselves and their activities). They therefore did their utmost to conceal his guilt. But Strauss sees through their camouflage. He embarks on his study of the Socratic dialogues armed with a motto: where there is so much smoke, there must be fire!

On careful reading, the Platonic and Xenophontic dialogues

reveal the truth of the charges against Socrates.[151] Socrates is guilty. Not only does he not believe in god or gods, he corrupts the youth with his hedonism. We learn from Xenophon that he is more seductive than the breathtakingly beautiful courtesan, Theodote.[152] Strauss refers to him as the supreme *erotikos*. Even Theodote is attracted to him. What is seductive about Socrates is not physical beauty, but the charm of his conversation and his philosophizing. He is therefore supremely capable of seducing young men away from family and politics to the slothful nobility of the philosophical life. But he does not practice his seductive art indiscriminately, he does not reveal the truth to all, but only to a few young men who have the makings of potential philosophers. He does corrupt, but only those who are wise enough to keep his secret, and noble enough to share his own elevated conception of the highest pleasure. Xenophon therefore excuses Socrates by showing that he is, despite his guilt, mindful of his social responsibilities.

The Socratic dialogues are intended to display Socrates's philosophical justice or his ability to benefit or at least not to harm those with whom he speaks. He could not do this without speaking differently to different types of people.[153] When speaking to citizens and gentlemen, Socrates does nothing to disturb their noble self-deceptions (i.e. he does not harm or corrupt them). For example, Xenophon portrays Socrates conversing with Isomachus who is reputed to be a 'perfect gentleman'. As any reader of the dialogue no doubt realizes, Isomachus is an overbearing fool. He is one of these men who knows just how everything ought to be done to the minutest detail. He instructs Socrates on the art of household management. He lectures his wife about her duties and just how to run the household, manage the servants and organize her pots and pans. But in his effort not to offend her, he tells her that she is his queen bee. He is convinced that he is a master of the art of managing a wife. He boasts to Socrates at how well he is able to manage his wife and what a perfect little wife she has become as a result of all his impeccable instruction. But Strauss speculates that he is probably the same Isomachus whose daughter married Kallias, son of Hipponikos. Within a year of the marriage, Kallias took his bride's mother for his lover and kept mother and daughter in his house. The situation was so intolerable to Isomachus's daughter that she tried to hang herself, but failed. Later she ran away or was driven out by her mother.[154] Strauss cannot assert without a doubt that this is the same Isomachus who was father-in-law to Kallias, but he is certain that Isomachus's wife was not the sweet, devoted wife her husband believed her to be, and that this fact was known to all who were listening to Socrates's report of the story of his conversation with Isomachus.[155] We are to conclude that the dialogue must have been an occasion of much hilarity for those who understood the joke.

Isomachus believes himself to be his own master as well as his wife's, and Socrates leaves his self-deception undisturbed. But Strauss tells us that the dialogue reveals the truth, though only to the few. Isomachus is his wife's slave. But that is not a fate peculiar to Isomachus, it is the *sine qua non* of being a husband. Xenophon's dialogue is not just a chuckle about the hapless Isomachus. The intent of the joke is much more far-reaching. The message is clear: to be a husband, father and citizen is to be held captive by the charms that women employ in the service of civilization. (The idea is altogether Freudian.)[156] The despotic charms of women hoodwink men into a life of never-ending servitude.[157] In this way, women assist the city in transforming natural men into citizens and gentlemen. Perfect gentlemen like Isomachus are so oblivious to their chains that they believe themselves to be masters of their households. This is a form of self-deception native to gentlemen. Strauss makes a point of telling us more than once that Socrates is *not* a gentleman.[158]

The point of all this jesting is this. By portraying Isomachus as the model of the 'perfect gentleman', Strauss casts a shadow on the noble life, the morally virtuous life, the honest life of the husband, father and citizen. He believes it to be a life of servitude, coupled with self-deception or the lie in the soul that Plato loathed so much. In other words, the sort of life that has been championed by civilization is a life fit for fools. It is the unexamined life or the life devoid of self-knowledge. There is nothing genuinely noble about it. It is a spurious nobility. Genuine nobility belongs to the philosopher who is the master not of the lie in the soul, but the noble lie. Therein lies his brand of justice.

It should be clear by now that Strauss's words have dual meanings. Just as there are higher and lower pleasures, there is genuine and spurious nobility, true virtue and vulgar virtue or citizen morality, political justice and philosophical justice, moral virtue and intellectual virtue. (Strauss certainly gives this old Aristotelian distinction a different twist.) One set of virtues refers to the city and its citizens, the other refers to the philosopher. One set of virtues is moral, conventional and artificial, whereas the other is natural and philosophical. To understand Strauss, we must determine which sense of pleasure, nobility, virtue or justice is being used, and that can be done only in the context of what is being said.

Strauss leads us to the conclusion that philosophers are 'real men' in Callicles's sense of the term.[159] They are natural men who have not been duped by the conventions of the city; they are free of the charms that hold other men captive, the charms that transform men into husbands and citizens, the charms that facilitate servitude, the charms that make men 'obtuse'!

Philosophical justice is indistinguishable from the hedonistic or erotic life of the philosopher. It transcends the city, and with it, the whole domain of morality itself. Even though it threatens the city, the philosophical life is the true or natural end for which the city exists.[160] In short, whereas political justice is a means, philosophy (or philosophical justice) is the end. It is the genuine good in relation to which all else is a means. It alone is choiceworthy for its own sake. The city and its justice, or what the city deems good (i.e. the morally good or noble), are subordinate goods: they are instrumental or ministerial to philosophy.[161] Strauss believes that the confusion of the two very different meanings of justice has led to the 'novel' belief that Plato's *Republic* is meant to show that justice in the 'vulgar' sense is choiceworthy for its own sake.[162]

Philosophy is the only good that is choiceworthy for its own sake. But philosophy is also the highest pleasure and therefore the highest manifestation of *eros*. Strauss understands *eros* as desire; more specifically, it is a longing for immortality that ranges from the desire for offspring and the desire for fame, to the desire for immortality by participation in the philosophic *eros* by which we are united with the 'unchangeable things'.[163] *Eros* threatens the city. The city cannot exist unless *eros* is repressed. As Strauss writes, 'there is a tension between *eros* and the city and hence between *eros* and justice: only through the deprecation of *eros* can the city come to its own'.[164] As the highest manifestation of *eros*, philosophy necessarily comes into conflict with the city. The conflict between philosophy and the city is therefore a species of the city's conflict with *eros* in general. Ironically, that for which the city exists poses the greatest threat to its survival.

For Strauss, a balance must be struck between the claims of the city and those of *eros*. Neither can be allowed to triumph over the other.[165] In our efforts to strike this balance, we cannot afford to make the city too soft, lest we rob her of her virility. But by the same token, life would be hell unless the claims of the city were moderated by those of *eros*.[166]

The relationship between philosophy and the city for Strauss is reminiscent of the relationship between sex and civilization for Freud. According to Freud, civilization has its origin in the family, which in turn has its source in the union of *Eros* and *Ananke*. The former refers to the masculine desire for the security of sex or sexual satisfaction, which can only be guaranteed by keeping the female readily available. *Ananke* refers to the feminine desire for offspring which by necessity forces her to seek the protection of the stronger male. Sex and necessity are therefore the parents of civilization. But civilization cannot flourish unless men expand their horizons beyond the family and towards the larger community. The task of civilization is therefore to harness man's libidinal energies for the sake of civilization. As representatives of the family and the claims of sexual love, women soon become the enemies of civilization.[167] The irony is that although *Eros* is that for which civilization was invented, it is also the greatest enemy of civilized life. For Strauss as for Freud, the city or civilization is a necessary evil. *Eros* cannot enjoy the most modest degree of satisfaction in the absence of civilization any more than philosophy can exist in the absence of the city. For both Strauss and Freud, the opposition between the two antagonists cannot be resolved, a compromise is necessary.[168] Here the resemblance between the two thinkers comes to an end. The solutions they propose are different.

Like Strauss, Freud realizes that civilization keeps natural man captive not by threats or force, but by its comforting illusions and seductive charms. For both philosophers, the success of civilization rests in its capacity to enslave men from within and not simply from without by the threat of punishment and death. Unlike Hobbes, they recognize that fear alone is not the most reliable motivation. Society must internalize its authority and rule over man from within. Both philosophers understand morality as the internalized authority of society or as something thoroughly conventional. Freud believes that civilizing man is a process of psychic oppression the violence of which causes illness and neurosis. He therefore sets out to cure the beleaguered *psyche* by a process of enlightenment. His object is not to overthrow civilization, but to make us accept it by impressing upon us its necessity.[169] In contrast, Strauss believes that the philosopher is a fool if he tampers with the civilizing process. The gentleman is not neurotic. He is so duped by civilization that he delights in his servitude. Strauss finds no reason to liberate or enlighten him. The philosopher must under no circumstances sing the praises of *eros*. On the contrary, he must come to the aid of the city; he must use his sophistic rhetoric to assist her in casting as powerful a spell as possible.

According to Strauss, Plato understood full well that the philosopher must come to the assistance of the city, not by enlightening her citizens, but by using his clever rhetoric (i.e. making the weaker argument appear the stronger) in order to vindicate the noble falsehoods that make his pleasurable life possible.[170] The philosopher must therefore be compelled to serve the city. (Remember that the philosophers in the *Republic* are compelled to leave the pleasures of the sunlight and descend into the cave.) The philosopher's service rests in his capacity to dispense the salutary myths needed for the survival of the herd. As we shall see, he is modeled after Nietzsche's superman.

The *Republic* is Plato's own attempt to serve the city. This explains the fact that it is a supremely waspish and anti-erotic dialogue. It opens with what Strauss regards as a most unconvincing 'curse on *eros*', placed in the mouth of Cephalus, the ancestral figure: old, pious, just and unerotic, the antithesis of the philosopher. Plato goes even further: he depicts the tyrant as '*Eros* incarnate'.[171] Strauss is not duped by Plato's deprecation of *eros*.

For Strauss, the *Republic* is about the proper relationship between the philosopher and the city. Thrasymachus is the symbol of the city; he is depicted as a man eager for a fight; he is angry, irascible, indignant, manly, impetuous and high-spirited. Socrates represents philosophy. The relationship between Socrates and Thrasymachus is therefore Plato's account of the ideal relationship between philosophy and the city.[172] In the *Republic* Socrates succeeds in taming Thrasymachus. But in real life, Socrates is not so successful.

The excessive wrath and indignation of the Athenians leads to the death of Socrates. However, the fault belongs not so much to

Athens as to Socrates's failure to tame her waspishness with his clever rhetoric. Instead, he taunts her with his science (he debunks her gods), threatens her with his cleverness (allows the triumph of the 'Unjust Speech'), and insults her with his neglect (he cared only for the things aloft). As a result, he fails entirely to bewitch and captivate her as the Platonic Socrates captivates Thrasymachus.

The mature Socrates tries to compensate the city for his neglect and his insolence. He is now a citizen and a married man with children. But as Strauss points out, Xenophon does not count Socrates among the married men.[173] He therefore makes it clear that Socrates is not a very assiduous husband or father.

Strauss believes that Socrates's relationship with his wife Xanthippe represents his real relationship with Athens.[174] Socrates failed to tame Xanthippe as he failed to tame Athens. Xanthippe represents the city. She is said to be ill-tempered, impossible, high-spirited, full of courage and manliness.[175] In short, she is a super-wasp. Why would the unmanly Socrates choose to marry such a woman? For Strauss, Xenophon provides the explanation. Wishing to live with human beings, Socrates chose Xanthippe because if he could succeed in taming her, he could succeed in managing everyone else.[176] Socrates was not any more successful with Xanthippe than he was with Athens. Strauss allows us to surmise that the fault is not with Xanthippe any more than it is with Athens. After all, she can only be pitied. A man like Socrates who sits around thinking and philosophizing all day could hardly be her idea of a man. A real man is supposed to act, display his strength, courage and resolve. Socrates does not even manage to support his family; he makes no effort to acquire a paying job. Instead, he uses a dubious wisdom as an excuse for sloth. Athens' opinion of Socrates must have been the same as Xanthippe's. She found his excessive wisdom insufferable. She rightly recognized the threat his philosophizing posed to her well-being.[177]

We must be careful not to go too far in identifying the views of Athens and Xanthippe with those of Strauss. For Strauss, Socrates is justly condemned, not so much for excess of wisdom, as for lack of prudence. Strauss is not surprised that Socrates was put to death. What surprises him is that he was allowed to philosophize for as long as he did!

In summary, Socrates is the pivotal figure in the drama of Western civilization. The story begins with an early state of innocence that is disrupted by the discovery of nature and the emergence of philosophy. In the beginning knowledge was the preserve of rare sages, but later, it was popularized and as a result vulgarized. Socrates was the decisive figure in this process because the scientific spirit he represented dethroned the gods and undermined the 'Just Speech'. He erroneously believed that neither the gods nor the 'Just Speech' are necessary, but that science alone is the means to salvation. Aristophanes prophesied that the outcome would be disastrous. He tried to mitigate the danger by ridiculing Socrates. But the damage was already done. Even Socrates's own conversion could not reverse it. We are the heirs of Socrates. We have deified the man that Athens so wisely condemned. The wisdom of the Platonic–Xenophontic Socrates has altogether eluded us. We are back to the Thinkery and should not be surprised if it blows up.

5

Classic Natural Right or the Teaching on Tyranny

Socrates was put to death when the amoral and apolitical nature of his philosophical life became apparent to his fellow citizens. If the philosopher is to redeem himself, he must, in justice as well as for the sake of appearances, make some contribution to the city: he must be compelled to return to the cave. But how could he possibly contribute to the well-being of the city since his truth is destructive of social life? The answer rests in the fact that philosophers, despite their shortcomings, are peculiarly fit for two tasks essential to the well-being of the city. First, their clever rhetoric (which enables them to make the weaker argument appear the stronger), can serve the city by strengthening its noble fictions. Secondly, philosophers are particularly fit to rule because they are wise. But since they are unlikely to take or be given power, they can serve the state best as advisers to those in power. What sort of political advice are they likely to give? To what standard will they appeal? For Strauss, their standard will understandably be derived from nature. They will regard political and legal justice best which comes closest to what is right by nature or to *natural right*.

Once nature is discovered, a variety of conceptions of nature emerge. Strauss identifies the following: philosophical conventionalism, vulgar conventionalism, pre-Socratic or egalitarian natural right, and Socratic, aristocratic or classic natural right. All are philosophical theories in the Straussian sense of the term. They depend on the discovery of nature. However, Strauss makes it clear that he regards classic natural right to be the pinnacle of political wisdom. Indeed, he criticizes modern relativism, nihilism and historicism in the name of classic natural right. It is therefore not in the least controversial to identify his own political philosophy with his understanding of classic natural right. We can best understand the latter by recognizing its relation to the competing conceptions of nature, and particularly its relation with conventionalism.

CONVENTIONALISM

Conventionalism has its origin in the distinction between nature and convention that is coeval with philosophy. Understandably, the discovery of nature results in the deprecation of convention. Conventionalism is the denial that what is right has any foundation in nature. It regards law and justice as purely conventional and therefore contrary to nature. Nature recognizes only the right to live a life of pleasure, which alone is supremely good by nature. The unrestrained pursuit of pleasure threatens the peace and harmony of civil society; it therefore places severe restraints on the pursuit of pleasure. But 'real men' are those who have a healthy disdain for civil society, and live a life of pleasure according to nature.[1]

Conventionalists disagree about what is most pleasant. The 'philosophical conventionalism' represented by Lucretius maintains that the philosophical life yields the greatest pleasure.[2] 'Vulgar conventionalism' emerges as a result of the 'publication' of philosophical conventionalism.[3] It replaces the higher pleasures of philosophy with the lower pleasures of wealth, power and the like; these are the sorts of pleasures that the vulgar have experienced and can appreciate. This is understandable because the many have not or cannot experience the higher pleasures; they have tasted only the lower pleasures. Vulgar conventionalism denies that the philosophical life is the most pleasant life, or the life according to nature. Instead, it maintains that the most pleasant thing is to get the better of others and rule over them. Vulgar conventionalism is embodied in the 'Unjust Speech' described in the previous chapter.[4] It is represented by men like Thrasymachus, Callicles and Hiero.

It is important to understand that the conventionalism of Thrasymachus is not Hobbesian. It refuses to accept justice in exchange for life and security. On the contrary, it is scornful of mere life; those who are 'real men' will scoff at Hobbes's solution as unworthy of themselves. Nature did not intend them to live a life of subservience, fear and misery at the hands of the many. They must therefore be clever enough to hide their injustice while practicing it on a large scale.

Conventionalism in general is hedonistic and elitist. Its hedonism consists in the claim that the pursuit of the greatest pleasure is the best and most natural end for man. Its elitism is the claim that only the natural elite or the few 'real men' can attain the pleasures of nature in the context of the unnatural conditions of civil society. For the philosophical conventionalists, only the few are wise enough for the good life; for the vulgar conventionalists, only the few are clever enough or devious enough to live the life according to nature. In either case, it is a life lived on the 'fringes of civil society', paying lip service to its unnatural ways.[5] The conventionalists were contemptuous of conventional life, the life of the many, the life lived according to ancestral custom or divine law.

Strauss makes the case for conventionalism more clearly and more compellingly than it has ever been made before. Conventionalism as presented by Strauss is far more sophisticated than is generally believed. It does not consist in an argument to the effect that there is no natural right because there is no agreement among men. Conventionalism does *not* assert that different societies have different conceptions of right and justice. (Even if this were true, the fact of diversity alone does not prove that there is no natural right, since truth is not a matter of agreement.) These arguments are simple-minded and easy to refute. The 'nerve of conventionalism' as described by Strauss is far from being so naïve.

Conventionalism makes two important claims. First, what is believed to be right is not arbitrary and does not differ dramatically from place to place. In most societies the same general sorts of rules necessarily emerge; they are required to insure peace and harmony.[6] These rough rules of social expediency men call by the name of justice. The rules of justice are 'conventional' in the sense of being unnatural; they are products of art or convention, not nature. They are contrived by the city to facilitate its survival. If they were natural they would be universal, but they are not. They are valid among members of a group, but lack universality, or validity in inter-group relations. There is nothing sacred about the rules of justice, they are simply a means to collective self-interest. The same rules that are useful to the preservation of the city, are necessary for the preservation of a gang of robbers. Justice is therefore nothing but collective self-interest.[7] As we have seen earlier, Strauss does not believe that we can escape from this unpleasant reality by saying that the city is just to all while the gang of robbers is not: the foundation of every city is in crime, and foreign policy even in peace time requires espionage, force, fraud and other sordid activities.[8]

Secondly, the rules of justice invented by the city stand in an inescapable tension with everyone's natural desire which is directed to their own good.[9] If prudence or wisdom consists in seeking one's own good, then the just man is a fool or a man duped by convention.[10] The conflict between the city and the self-interest of the individual cannot be settled. This is why religion is necessary for civil society: it reconciles the interests of individuals with those of the group by promising rewards to the just and punishment to the unjust in the life beyond.[11]

CLASSIC NATURAL RIGHT

Even though classic natural right emerges in the context of a debate with conventionalism, it shares with the latter some important characteristics. I will identify three characteristics of classic natural right. In each case I will point to its departure from conventionalism as well as its similarity to it. A careful examination of Strauss's account of natural right will make it clear that it is much closer to conventionalism than the unwary reader might assume.

First, classic natural right does not deny the conventionalist view of justice as a set of rules intended to maximize collective self-interest. Nor does it deny the conventionalist claim that there is a permanent and unavoidable conflict between the self-interest of the individual and that of the city. Nor does it deny that the city's claim to be sacred (founded by gods or men inspired by gods) is fictitious. It repudiates the vulgar conventionalists for not being wise enough to recognize how dangerous expressing these views publicly and unambiguously is to the philosopher and the city.

Secondly, classic natural right does not dissent from the conventionalist claim that the city is coercive.[12] However, it does not maintain that the coercive nature of the city necessarily leads to the conclusion that the city and its justice are unnatural. Instead, it maintains that man is so constituted that he cannot achieve the perfection of his nature without the coercion of his 'lower impulses'.[13]

Natural right rejects the vulgar conventionalist view of the good life as one dedicated to the pursuit of the pleasures of wealth, power and sex. Instead, it embraces the view of the philosophical conventionalists (like Epicurus and Lucretius), according to whom the good life or the most pleasurable life is the life of contemplation.

Strauss often repeats that the central issue in classical philosophy is that of the good life for man. This sounds so incontrovertible and so uncontentious that it is generally ignored as a platitude that only old and famous men are allowed to utter without shame. However, what Strauss means by this is by no means so banal and uncontentious. He means to say that the central issue of classical philosophy revolves around the question of who the 'real men' are. What is not contentious is that the real men are the few who can live the life according to nature or the supremely pleasant life, in spite of the city. The question that concerned the classics is who these men were. Hiero, the tyrant, believed that he was a real man, and vulgar conventionalists such as Thrasymachus were inclined to agree with him. In Strauss's interpretation, Xenophon's dialogue, *Hiero* (which presents a conversation between a tyrant and a wise man), is an argument to the effect that the wise are in truth the 'real men'. The wise Simonides shows Hiero that if the tyrant is to live a pleasant life free from fear of violent death, he must become a good tyrant, or a tyrant who is a benefactor of his city. He makes Hiero see that tyranny is a type of super-citizenship because it involves perpetual servitude to the city and its citizens; and this is certainly incompatible with the sort of pleasant life that Hiero must himself admit that 'real men' aspire to.[14]

Since the good life according to nature, or the life of the philosopher requires leisure, it is impossible in the absence of civil society.[15] Classic natural right does not therefore endorse the conventionalist denunciation of civil society as unnatural – at least not without qualification. For Strauss, the city and its justice are natural to the extent to which they are directed to the perfection of man which is according to nature. Dedication to this exalted end alone redeems the city and raises it above the association of the gang of robbers.[16]

Thirdly, classic natural right, like conventionalism, is elitist or inegalitarian.[17] It rejects pre-Socratic or egalitarian natural right. According to the latter, all men are by nature free and equal.[18] But political rule is akin to the rule of master over slave, and it is against any man's grain to be treated as a slave. Strauss maintains that egalitarian natural right is closely allied to the doctrine of a golden age or an ideal state of nature where men lived in a state of equality and freedom prior to the emergence of political rule. But for the egalitarians, innocence is not irretrievably lost, society can and must be made harmonious with nature or natural right by being based on the consent of free and equal individuals. Socratic or classical natural right considers this view of nature to be altogether fictitious. Far from being characterized by equality, nature is distinguished by hierarchy, by higher and lower, superior and inferior.

Since men are unequal from the point of view of their perfection, or in the 'decisive respect', equal rights for all are unjust and contrary to nature. Some men are naturally superior to others and according to natural right, rulers of others.[19] Subjecting what is by nature higher to what is by nature lower is acting against nature. The best regime, the one sanctioned by nature, therefore consists in the rule of the wise.

At least in theory, the doctrine of classic natural right is for Strauss identical with the absolute right of the wise to rule.[20] It finds its 'complete answer' in the rule of the wise. Wisdom, being superior not only to unwisdom but to law, it would be unnatural to limit the rule of the wise either by law or by the consent of the unwise. As Strauss writes:

It would be absurd to hamper the free flow of wisdom by any regulations; hence the rule of the wise must be *absolute rule*. It would be equally absurd to hamper the free flow of wisdom by consideration of the unwise wishes of the unwise; hence the wise rulers ought not to be responsible to their unwise subjects.[21]

The only natural right is the right of the wise to rule absolutely or in the absence of law. Strauss understands tyranny as it is commonly understood – namely, as rule in the absence of law. *Classic natural right is therefore identical with the tyranny of the wise.*

Strauss expresses the same idea about the nature of the best regime in his *On Tyranny* (a commentary on Xenophon's *Hiero*). Xenophon's dialogue portrays a wise poet, Simonides, speaking with Hiero, a tyrant. In Strauss's interpretation, the point of the dialogue is to reveal the true view of the ancients regarding tyranny.[22] By using Simonides and not Socrates as his mouthpiece, Xenophon provides himself with the opportunity to speak more candidly.

According to Strauss, Xenophon's message is this: the wise do not despise tyranny for the same reasons others find it objectionable. In other words, they do not object to the forceful or fraudulent way the tyrant came into power; nor do they object to the innumerable crimes he has committed; nor to the fact that he rules in the absence of law. What they despise about tyranny is what they despise about every form of government – namely, its failure to listen to the counsel of the wise. The wise are not so naïve as to think that political affairs can be devoid of force, fraud and injustice; nor are they naïve enough to think that a particular form of government is best. Magistrates are not made good rulers by being duly elected; nor does a king possess the art of governing simply because he has inherited his crown according to the accepted rules of succession. How one acquires power makes no difference. 'Constitutional rule', or acquiring power by constitutional means, is not essentially more legitimate than tyrannical rule.[23] Any rule is legitimate only to the extent that it 'listens to the counsel of the wise'.[24] Knowledge is alone the true title to rule.[25] Indeed,

> the rule of a tyrant who, after having come to power by means of force and fraud, or having committed any number of crimes, listens to the suggestions of reasonable men, is essentially more legitimate than the rule of elected magistrates as such.[26]

Tyranny, or rule in the absence of law, comes closest to the best regime which is absolute tyranny of the wise. In Strauss's words, 'tyrannical government can live up to the highest political standards'.[27]

Most men despise tyranny because it is rule in the absence of law. But this fact does not disturb the wise. They are painfully aware of what Strauss calls the 'problematic' character of the rule of law.[28] Strauss is not very explicit about this, but he makes it clear that absolute rule without law, if it is wise, is infinitely superior to the rule of law. Therein rests what Strauss refers to as the 'tyrannical teaching' of Plato and Xenophon.

The tyrannical teaching is a theoretical account of the best regime in accordance with natural right. Even though it is theoretical, it is not deemed to be unattainable. On the contrary, as Strauss writes,

> the best regime as the classics understand it, is not only most desirable; it is also meant to be feasible or possible, i.e. possible on earth. It is both desirable and possible because it is according to nature . . . no miraculous or non-miraculous change in human nature is required for its actualization; it does not require the abolition or extirpation of that evil or imperfection which is essential to man and to human life; it is therefore possible.[29]

For Strauss, the classic conception of the best regime has a much greater possibility of being made actual than an ideal, like that of Marx, which requires the historical transformation of human nature or the abolition of evil.

In spite of the realistic nature of the best regime, Strauss insists that it is only a theoretical ideal or a 'city in speech'. This does not mean that the best regime is unattainable. It means that the description in speech of the best regime is not meant to be a blueprint for political action. The theoretical description of the best regime is not meant to incite men to action. Philosophers need not rush out and seize power by force, fraud and crime. They must wait for favorable conditions to present themselves. The realization of the best regime depends on the 'chance' appearance of princes friendly to philosophy: 'man does not control the conditions under which it could become actual'.[30]

In practice, only an approximation of the best regime can be hoped for. The practically best regime is a compromise between wisdom and unwisdom, tyranny and consent.[31] The practically best regime is the rule under law of 'gentlemen'.[32] In this case, the law, framed by wise legislators, is freely adopted by citizens and its administration entrusted to gentlemen. The gentleman is the urban patrician who derives his income from agriculture. Like the hapless Isomachus we encountered earlier, he must be a man of moderate wealth, or wealthy enough to be free from toil to pursue noble or honorable things. He must be well-bred and public-spirited. In the practically best regime, gentlemen obey and administer the laws; they rule and are ruled in turn, to use the phrase of Aristotle. The practically best regime is a mixed regime: an aristocracy that is strengthened by the admixture of monarchical and democratic institutions.[33] This is the sort of regime described in Plato's *Laws* as well as in Aristotle's *Politics*.

The gentleman is not the same as the wise man or the philosopher. Nevertheless, Strauss describes him as a 'political reflection or imitation of the wise man'.[34] The reason is that the gentleman, like the philosopher is not among the 'vulgar', and he looks down on many things esteemed by the vulgar. However, as we have seen earlier, the gentleman and the philosopher have different conceptions of nobility. The gentleman, like Isomachus, does not understand the philosopher (the philosopher makes sure he does not), but is favorably disposed towards him and is inclined to respect him simply because he believes him to be far removed from the vulgar sort of humanity. The best regime is the tyrannical rule of the philosopher; but the practically best regime is the rule of gentlemen whose favorable disposition towards philsophers allows the latter to direct political affairs in a 'remote manner'.[35]

Whether philosophical rule is direct or indirect, it has as its foundation the doctrine of natural right. We have already established the fact that classic natural right is the absolute rule of the wise independent of the constraints of law (i.e. the tyranny of the wise). It remains to be seen what sorts of principles direct or characterize the rule of the wise. Unless we know something more concrete about the rule of the wise, we will be unable to distinguish it from any other rule. Strauss's commentary on Aristotle's account of classic natural right comes closest to providing us with the sort of concrete information that will give the classic natural right doctrine its content.

ARISTOTELIAN NATURAL RIGHT

Although Aristotle's treatment of natural right is very brief and elusive (it covers barely a page), he says two significant things about natural right on which Strauss bases his interpretation. First, natural right is part of political right and does not transcend the concrete political situation. Secondly, *all* of natural right is changeable. I will discuss Strauss's understanding of these two points in turn.

Strauss praises Aristotle for what he calls 'the spirit of his

unrivalled sobriety'.[36] Aristotle softens the socially disruptive
implications that attend the discovery of nature by making natural
right part of political right.[37] In other words, he declares the best
possible regime in the circumstances to be just by nature and
therefore 'legitimate'.[38] Strauss explains that the difference between
the best regime and the legitimate one is equivalent to the
difference between the noble and the just: 'not everything just is
noble'.[39] A certain ignobility may be just if it is deemed necessary
under the circumstances. The full import of this claim can only be
appreciated if we examine Strauss's account of Aristotle's second
claim regarding natural right.

Aristotle's second claim is that *all* of natural right is changeable.
Strauss considers two interpretations of this claim: the Thomistic
and Averroist. St Thomas Aquinas's famous interpretation of this
claim is as follows. Aristotle's statement must be understood with
a qualification. The general or first principles of natural right are
universal and immutable; only the secondary principles or more
specific rules derived from them are mutable. Strauss rejects this
interpretation as being generally 'alien' to the spirit of Aristotle as
well as contrary to Aristotle's explicit statement, which is
unqualified.[40]

Strauss regards the interpretation of Averroes and the *falasifa* or
the Islamic Aristotelians to be more plausible. (Strauss considers
Marsilius of Padua to be the only medieval representative of this
view in the Christian world.) In this interpretation, natural right
refers to the broad rules of justice that necessarily grow up in every
civil society, and without which it cannot be preserved. They are
only 'quasi-natural' because they depend on 'ubiquitious
convention'.[41] They correspond roughly to the Second Table of
the Decalogue, but include the command of divine worship.
Despite the fact that they are necessary and universally recognized,

> they are conventional for this reason: civil society is incompatible
> with any immutable rules, however basic, for in certain
> conditions the disregard of these rules may be needed for the
> preservation of society; but for pedagogic reasons, society must
> present as universally valid certain rules which are generally
> valid. Since the rules in question obtain normally, all social
> teachings proclaim these rules and not the rare exceptions. The
> effectiveness of the general rules depends on their being taught
> without qualifications, without ifs and buts. But the omission of

the qualifications which makes the rules more effective, makes them at the same time untrue. The unqualified rules are not natural right but conventional right.[42]

The view of the *falasifa* is, not untypically, esoteric. It amounts to saying that the rules that are necessary to preserve society, when regarded from a philosophical point of view, are only rules of thumb. They indicate the most successful means to achieve a given end under most circumstances. They do not obligate us absolutely. They are akin to signposts in a fog. On a clear day, when a more direct route presents itself, it is foolish to insist on following the signposts. The rules should, to use another example, be regarded by statesmen in the same manner as the almanac is regarded by a skillful navigator. Failure to calculate accurately, not to mention lack of goodwill, are bound to wreak havoc on a society that understands its moral rules as rules of thumb that do not bind unconditionally. It is therefore dangerous to make this view public. The effectiveness of the rules depends on their being regarded as absolute and unconditional. The easiest way to ensure this is to regard the rules as having intrinsic dignity and more importantly, as being backed by divine sanction.

Strauss maintains that his own interpretation of Aristotle's brief and elusive statements regarding natural right are a middle position between the Thomistic and Averroist interpretations. However, a careful examination of Strauss's view reveals that it is more accurately described as a variation or fuller account of the Averroist view.

Strauss tells us that he is 'tempted' to suggest the following. Natural right refers to just decisions in concrete situations, which are dependent on the circumstances. Such decisions do not require rules, rather, they require practical wisdom. The Averroist view is correct because it emphasizes the mutability of right and hence recognizes that civil society is incompatible with any immutable rules. However, the Averroist view is incomplete; it fails to recognize that just decisions presuppose principles of justice, and that the latter are not variable.

Strauss believes that Aristotle's discussions of slavery, of distributive and commutative justice and of the natural foundation of the city are attempts to establish such principles. Strauss suggests that these discussions can be summarized in the form of the following principles of justice or natural right. The first principle consists in the requirements of commutative and distributive justice. The second consists in the 'mere existence, the mere survival, the mere independence, of the political community'.[43] It is important to notice that these are *not* principles of conduct. According to Strauss, 'there is a universally valid hierarchy of ends, but there are no valid rules of action'.[44] *Natural right provides man not with principles of conduct, but with a hierarchy of ends.* Peace, stability and preservation of the city are lower than justice, and the latter is lower than the most noble life of the philosopher. But this hierarchy of ends does not determine which of these ends takes priority and which must be sacrificed for the sake of the other in cases of conflict. There is no principle that can tell us in advance whether the higher or the lower ends in any given situation take priority. These decisions can only be made in concrete situations, and, needless to say, require wisdom if they are to be made in accordance with natural right. Strauss indicates that the lowest, being the most urgent, frequently takes precedence over the higher:

> In extreme situations there may be conflicts between what the self-preservation of society requires and the requirements of commutative and distributive justice. In such situations, . . . the public safety is the highest law.[45]

In other words, justice may have to be sacrificed for the sake of public safety, and such sacrifices are also in accordance with the requirements of natural right. This is understandable in view of the fact that the lower is a necessary means to the highest. Without the preservation of the city, the life of the philosopher would be impossible.

By setting no limits on conduct, natural right makes it possible to consider any conduct just if it is deemed necessary under the circumstances. As Strauss writes: 'there are no limits which can be defined in advance, there are no assignable limits to what might become just reprisals'.[46] Hence, there is no way of knowing what might be needed in any given situation for the preservation of the city. Nor is Strauss referring only to extreme situations of warfare; what he says is equally true for peace, since 'war casts its shadow on peace'.[47] No society, he maintains, can survive without espionage, and similar activities that involve the suspension of the rules of justice. Strauss is uncomfortable about speaking of these 'sad exigencies', and suggests that we leave them 'covered with the veil with which they are justly covered'.[48] What is of interest is that Strauss is not willing to refer to these 'sad exigencies' as instances where men are forced to act unjustly to avoid annihilation. On the contrary, he insists that 'the exceptions are as just as the rules'.[49]

Strauss is not saying that in extreme situations the preservation of the state requires that we suspend the rules of natural justice and in so doing act unjustly. This is the view of Machiavelli.[50] For Machiavelli, the prince often has to commit injustice for the greater good of the state or its preservation. Machiavelli is sometimes commended for daring to call injustice by its name. It is interesting that the utilitarians, who made more radical suggestions, were hailed as rational liberators, whereas Machiavelli was denounced as diabolical. It seems to me that the difference is significant.

In discussing utility and justice, John Stuart Mill denies that the two are separate entities that may come into conflict with one another. He maintains that the difference between justice and utility amounts to the fact that justice arouses human sentiments that mere expediency is utterly incapable of doing.[51] The reason is that justice is the name we give to the rules without which the very being of society would be threatened. Justice is therefore the most sacred heart of utility. Like utility, justice lends itself to more and less. It is therefore right to violate an obligation of justice if that obligation has been 'overruled by a stronger obligation of justice'.[52] It seems to me that Mill's language makes it impossible to speak of a conflict between justice and utility. Greater or lesser utility is synonymous to a stronger or weaker obligation of justice. If we choose to frame an innocent man in order to appease a lynch mob and prevent riots and deaths,[53] we would describe our action not as a necessary injustice for the public safety, but as the action required by the 'stronger obligation of justice'.

Strauss's claim that 'exceptions are as just as the rules' resembles the utilitarian view more closely than the Machiavellian one. It seems to me that this way of speaking allows one to do injustice with a clear conscience.

What is significant to notice about Strauss's account of Aristotle's natural right is that the hierarchy of ends it provides does not itself determine which end takes priority in any concrete situation. It is for practical reason therefore to determine *both* the appropriate *end* as well as the *means* necessary for its attainment. So understood, *natural right places no restrictions on wisdom*. Indeed, it gives human reason much greater latitude than utilitarianism would allow.

THOMISTIC NATURAL LAW

The radically consequential nature of the classic natural right doctrine is more clearly apparent when the latter is compared to the Thomistic ideas of natural law.

Although Strauss includes St Thomas Aquinas in his Great Tradition of classic natural right, he believes that the Thomistic theory introduces 'profound changes' to classic natural right as he understands it. In a letter to Helmut Kuhn, Strauss says that he realizes that his interpretation of Aristotle on natural right goes contrary to the authority of Aquinas, but it differs 'only by a nuance'. However, he adds that 'there are sometimes subtle nuances which are of crucial importance'.[54] This is the reason, as he explains to Kuhn that he purposefully entitled his book *Natural Right*, not *Natural Law*. Elsewhere he writes that natural law is an invention of the Stoics that was later adopted by Aquinas, and that the very idea of a natural law is for him a 'contradiction in terms'.[55] This makes it clear that Strauss rejects the doctrine of natural law as having no roots in pagan wisdom. For Strauss, nature does not contain laws of conduct; unless of course, one believes that there exists a divine legislator. The pagan idea of natural right does not involve such assumptions.

Although he does not criticize Thomistic natural law openly, Strauss brings to our attention its significant departure from his own account of classic natural right. Moreover, he makes it clear that Aquinas's departure from pagan natural right is a vulgarization. An examination of what Strauss tells us are the differences between the two theories will enable us to uncover Strauss's own position on an issue that is central to current debates in moral and political philosophy.

First, whereas natural right has its source in human wisdom, natural law has its foundation in divine law or the will of God.[56] It regards individuals as proprietors of a right granted by the Creator independent of political society. Natural law is therefore not part of political right. It is a transcendent right to which political right must conform.

Elaborating on Strauss's understanding of Aquinas, Ernest Fortin explains that, for Aquinas, the individual is a member of a universal community or *cosmopolis* ruled by divine providence, the rational order of which he recognizes and to which he must give his allegiance over and above the political community to which he belongs.[57] Man is naturally part of the rational universal order, but is not *naturally* part of any particular political society. The sense of belonging to a particular political society is one that is acquired. Since the natural is higher in status than the artificial or conventional, man's allegiance to the universal community takes priority over his allegiance to the political community in cases of conflict.

Strauss believes that Aquinas's natural law refers to the rules of conduct established by God to which man is absolutely subject. In spite of Aquinas's own efforts to distinguish between natural and divine law, Strauss insists that natural law depends on divine will and not natural or unassisted human reason. Strauss enlarges on this difference in his essay 'Natural Law'.[58] He explains that natural law refers to principles of human conduct which are twofold: intrinsic and extrinsic. The intrinsic principles are habit, virtue and vice. The extrinsic principles are law (eternal, natural, human and divine) and grace. The internal principles depend on man, the external principles are the manner in which God guides man towards the good; he instructs them by law and assists them by grace.

Following Strauss, Harry Jaffa argues that natural law, unlike natural right, is a law genuinely speaking. It satisfies Aquinas's own definition of law according to which law must be rational, directed to the common good and promulgated by he who has care of the community. Since natural law is not human law, it cannot be promulgated by man; it must therefore be promulgated by God. Jaffa concludes that natural law must be God's law promulgated to man through conscience.[59]

The second difference between Strauss's classic natural right and Aquinas's natural law is that the former is known only to the few wise who have sufficiently cultivated their reason, but the latter is known to all naturally and automatically because it is promulgated by God through conscience. The idea of conscience is no part of Strauss's pagan wisdom.[60]

Thirdly, natural right and natural law have two different conceptions of the good life for man. Natural right regards the life of philosophical contemplation as the highest life for man. In contrast, Aquinas finds the natural end of man insufficient for complete happiness and fulfillment; a supernatural end is needed. Man's highest happiness rests in a life with God. In order to be fit for the life with God, man must live his earthly life in humble obedience to God's law. Strauss objects to the otherworldly character of Aquinas's natural law because it has the effect of exalting the moral life at the expense of the philosophical life or the life of 'free enquiry'.

For Strauss, moral virtue stands in relation to intellectual virtue as the city stands in relation to the philosopher, one is a means, the other the end.[61] Politics and morality are required to make the highest life possible. Moral virtue is therefore not a noble way of life desirable for its own sake. The means are choiceworthy only for the sake of the good they serve.

Strauss's view implies a radical deprecation of morality.[62] In the course of his exchange with Jacob Klein, Strauss admits that in his scheme of things morality does not enjoy a particularly high status.[63] Indeed, for Strauss, as for his Aristotle, 'intellectual perfection' is not only 'higher in dignity' than moral perfection, it 'does not require moral virtue'.[64] This means that intellectual excellence can be attained by one who does not bother with morality or the 'vulgar virtue'.[65] Strauss's contempt for the morally virtuous man takes on extreme proportions when he describes the just or moral man who is not also a philosopher as a 'mutilated human being'![66]

The fourth and most important difference between natural law and natural right follows from the others. If morality is instrumental, then its goodness depends on its success in securing the end it serves. It is therefore unlikely to have a fixed character, but must vary with the circumstances. Accordingly, natural right contains no principles of human conduct; *all* of it is changeable: what is right depends on the results of actions in concrete situations. Even though natural right contains a fixed hierarchy of ends, it does not insist on giving priority to the highest end. It leaves human reason free to choose both the end and the means appropriate in the circumstances. In contrast, the principles of natural law are principles of human conduct.[67] They refer to the Second Table of the Decalogue. They are immutable and unchanging – they 'suffer no exceptions'.[68] They specify certain types of actions as forbidden without qualification: law is not encumbered with ifs and buts. According to Strauss, Aquinas considers moral principles to have a compulsory character that they did not have for Aristotle: they do not just encourage and discourage, they command and forbid.[69]

Ernest Fortin explains the Straussian understanding of what is at issue between Aristotle and Aquinas as follows:

> The decisive question, then, and the real issue between Aquinas and Aristotle, is not whether moral principles are subject to change but whether there are *any* moral principles from which one is never allowed to deviate and which retain their obligatory character even in the most extreme situations. . . .[70]

And later he writes that for Aquinas,

> the very possibility that the common good or the preservation of society should at times compel one to act in a manner contrary to these principles is eliminated once and for all. Between the requirements of justice and those of civil society there is a fundamental and necessary harmony.[71]

As we have seen, such a harmony is denied by the Straussian teaching.

It is my contention that Strauss's classic natural right is a thoroughly consequential theory. Like every consequential theory, it maintains the primacy or priority of the *good* over the *right* or just.[72] The *good* is understood as the end to which all action is a means; it is a state of affairs deemed desirable, excellent, noble, or worthy of pursuit for its own sake. The *right* on the other hand, refers to action meant to bring about the good or end in question. Right is therefore subordinate to good.[73] The relation of the right to the good is that of means to end. The rightness of any action depends not on the nature of the action, but on its consequences or results, and these depend on the circumstances. Moral reasoning is therefore instrumental, it is a means–end type of rationality.

Strauss's whole understanding of morality is instrumental in the extreme. Morality, along with politics, is good only in so far as it makes the philosophical life, the good *par excellence*, possible.

Consequential theories differ from one another only in what they regard as the good or end of action. In Strauss's view, the utilitarian conception of the good or the 'greatest happiness of the greatest number', is simply too vulgar.

The problem with which classic natural right must deal is the same problem with which utilitarianism is confronted. A consequential morality is likely to wreak havoc on society if widely known and practiced. Even a society of good-willed citizens is unlikely to achieve felicific results if each individual were to determine the rightness of each action depending on his calculation of its results or consequences, not only for himself, but for everyone in the society that may be affected by it. This understanding of utilitarianism, generally known as 'act utilitarianism', has fallen into disrepute on purely consequential grounds. It fails to achieve the ends, which on its own assumption are worthy of pursuit for their own sake.[74] Indeed, it threatens the very order of society on which depends the possibility of achieving any kind of good for man whatsoever. If act utilitarianism were meant only as a morality for those in power, the difficulty is not likely to be alleviated especially if this were publicly known. Citizens are not likely to take kindly to a dual standard. If those in power were to act on consequential grounds, they would invariably act contrary to the laws whenever doing so were felicific. Citizens in such a society would live in a state of constant anxiety, not knowing how they are likely to be treated by the authorities.

Following Austin, some contemporary utilitarians have responded to this criticism by saying that utility (or whatever is deemed as the ultimate good or highest end) is the measure of the rules in force within a given society, and not the measure of individual actions. The latter are to be judged by their conformity or nonconformity to the rules. The rules must be strictly adhered to by most citizens if they are to produce the most optimific results (i.e. results that maximize utility). This so-called 'rule utilitarian' solution has its shortcomings. If utility is the end of action, it would be foolish to adhere strictly to rules in cases where much more optimific results can be achieved by departing from them. In response to this, the rule utilitarian generally replies that the damage done to the rules by even a single breach undermines the respect for the rules on which the very existence of the political order depends. No amount of good that can be achieved by a single breach can outweigh the damage done to the social practices and institutions without which a society would plunge into Hobbes's wretched state of nature. In objection to this claim it may be argued that not every breach of the rules need necessarily threaten political order. This is particularly true if the breaches are kept secret.[75] *This* is the solution that Strauss adopts and it explains why he insists on esotericism.

Strauss's classic natural right doctrine finds itself in the same predicament as utilitarianism – it is convinced that consequentialism is the most rational approach to politics and morality, but at the same time, it is painfully aware of the fact that this truth threatens the well-being and stability of civil society. It is the sort of doctrine that can easily be abused if publicly known and widely practiced. One way of avoiding the difficulty is to follow Aquinas in substituting for natural right a non-consequential doctrine that insists on the strict adherence to rules. But Strauss rejects this solution, not just because he considers it false or unphilosophical, but because he is convinced that it is not optimific.

Strauss's criticisms of Aquinas's natural law are subtle, but not undetectable. In Strauss's view, Aquinas has failed to recognize the radical, threatening and destructive nature of a transcendent natural law independent of political right. It has the tendency to demote political society, undermine its dignity, status and authority, and as a result, threatens its very survival. If there is a moral order higher than that of the state that is more worthy of their allegiance, men are likely to disregard the conventional rules whenever they come into conflict with the higher law. Indeed, natural law goes so far as to declare that positive laws that are contrary to natural law are so unjust as not to be binding laws at all.

Strauss praises Marsilius of Padua in rejecting the natural law view, according to which unjust laws are not, properly speaking, laws and so do not place us under obligation.[76] Strauss endorses the complaints of Marsilius against the politically radical nature of natural law. He criticizes it, just as Hobbes did, for dividing sovereignty between the secular and sacred domains, or between kings and priests. He argues that this does not advance the cause of peace, and so undermines the essential purpose of the state. In short, natural law encourages anarchy and chaos because it forgets that 'any regime is better than anarchy'.[77]

Strauss endorses Marsilius's view, saying that it is not without respectability. He believes that it gets support from the New Testament. The latter recognizes 'in the strongest terms' the duty of obedience to human government 'which beareth not the sword in vain'. God has placed it on earth to execute his wrath on the evildoers. Even Christian slaves dare not demand to be set free.[78]

Strauss objects to natural law not just for being too radical, but for being too timid. It excessively restricts the 'latitude' of prudent statesmen in forbidding certain types of actions that may be necessary for the protection of the state. Its otherworldly nature puts a great strain upon the political order because it makes absolute demands on it that are oblivious to its limitations. Strauss praises Marsilius who, unlike Aquinas, recognized, as did Machiavelli (although Strauss does not make the comparison), that Christian virtue is incompatible with political power. As Strauss puts it, 'the demands of the Sermon on the mount cannot be reconciled with the status and the duties of governors. . . .'[79] Deferring to Aristotle in a rather scholastic manner, Strauss remarks, in the same context, that a natural law that would suffer deformed children to live is certainly not natural, being contrary to Aristotle's judgement on the matter.[80] It seems that Strauss cannot help agreeing with Machiavelli and Nietzsche that Christianity is inferior to pagan religion because it has the effect of rendering the world weak.[81]

Strauss does not criticize natural law openly. On the contrary, he tries to blur the distinction between it and natural right. Since the public dissemination of natural law is beneficial, it should not be openly undermined. As the *falasifa* were well aware, the efficacy of the conventional rules of conduct depends on their being regarded as binding without qualifications, without ifs and buts. But there is no reason for philosophers to mistake a salutary delusion for the truth. Aquinas dispenses with esotericism because he has mistaken a noble lie for the truth. Granted that philosophical truth is dangerous when made public, it is most useful when it is the preserve of philosophers who have the ear of the powerful. What is needed is natural law for the masses and classic natural right for philosophers and those in power. Religion for the many and philosophy for the few. Natural law is therefore objectionable not just because it is too radical, but because it is too timid. It banishes philosophy because it does not have the fortitude to withstand its hard truths.

Aquinas is usually credited with having reconciled Aristotle with the Bible. But for Strauss, such a reconciliation is impossible. Far from making Aristotle compatible with the Bible, Aquinas has succeeded only in baptizing Aristotle.[82] He banished philosophy altogether and replaced it with theology. Fortin points out that Aquinas was repudiated by the Latin Averroists who 'objected to the enslavement of the very philosophy that they could credit with having made them free'.[83] This is reminiscent of Strauss's remark, noted earlier, that Christianity (unlike Islam and Judaism), did a disservice to philosophy: by bringing it close to its bosom, it subjected it to ecclesiastical supervision, and as a result, deprived it of the freedom that is its very essence.[84]

John Roos and E. A. Goerner have challenged the Straussian interpretation of Aquinas.[85] They have argued what would seem curious to anyone unfamiliar with the Straussian literature, that Aquinas shares more in common with Aristotle than is generally believed. What is remarkable about their account is the extent to which they defer to the Straussian assumptions regarding the unquestionable superiority of Strauss's pagan ideas. They re-interpret Aquinas's natural law as an Aristotelian (i.e. Straussian) natural right theory in disguise. Contrary to Strauss and Fortin, they argue that Christianity may not have been quite as friendly to philosophy as was surmised and that Aquinas may have been forced to write esoterically. Indeed, they maintain that Aquinas's natural law is but an exoteric doctrine meant to camouflage a fully-fledged Aristotelian philosophy.

Both Roos and Goerner attempt to show that there is an incongruity between Aquinas's account of natural law and his account of justice and the virtues. Whereas the former is rigid and legalistic, the latter manifests all the radically metamorphic qualities of Aristotle's natural right. Roos holds that Aquinas separates justice and the common good, and regards the latter to consist in peace and preservation. Roos argues that this is the clue to understanding what Aquinas means when he tells us that in administering the law, a judge must have the intention of the lawgiver in mind – and *that* is *always* directed to the common good in contradistinction to justice.[86] It is therefore admissible for a judge to act contrary to the letter of the law as well as to justice in order to uphold and defend the common good. *It is even right for a judge to find a man guilty whom he knows to be innocent* if 'respect' for positive law is at stake! Roos provides other examples intended to show that Aquinas did not consider the natural law to be absolutely binding in all circumstances, especially when the preservation or even the dignity of the state is at stake. Curiously, all this is meant to *vindicate* Aquinas by showing that he all but matches the unrivaled wisdom of Aristotle.

Goerner's arguments follow along the same lines as Roos's, but illustrate more vividly the lavish extravagance of the Straussian faith in the radical superiority of the wise. Goerner refers to Aquinas's account of the nature of justice as a quiet 'revolution' in the midst of a long discourse full of the most excruciatingly fine distinctions and balanced discriminations that would put all but the most 'alert and cautious' reader to sleep. Central to this quiet revolution are the concepts of *gnome* and *epiekeia*. These two concepts refer to the virtues of the wise who are able to judge according to *gnome* or natural reason itself and not according to common law. *Epiekeia* or equity is not subordinate to legal justice, unless the latter is understood broadly as obedience to the intention of a just legislator, which cannot be formulated in any set of rules. Moses's dispensing of the natural law prohibition against divorce because it was unsuitable to the hardheartedness of the people is used as an illustration of *gnome*. In Goerner's account, the judgement of one who possesses *gnome* is likened by Thomas to divine providence itself. On the conventional Straussian account of natural law, God alone can suspend its absolutely binding obligation, as when he orders Abraham to kill Isaac. Goerner's argument has the effect of saying that Aquinas believes there are men whose judgements are equal to God's. Indeed, Goerner suggests that the relation between the eugonomic man and God, is not a filial relation but a 'friendly communion'.[87] Within the Aristotelian context implied, friendship indicates equality. Natural law is but a pale reflection of natural right that remains necessary not only for 'the bad man', but because the wise cannot always be found and in 'dark times' are not listened to.

In conclusion, classic natural right is theoretically identical with the absolute right of the wise to rule in the absence of law – that is, it is identical with the tyrannical teaching. In practice, the best regime strictly speaking is unattainable, but a close approximation of its exists in the rule of gentlemen, or any other regime (even a tyranny), where those in power listen to the advice of the wise. This 'diluted' or practical natural right is the standard of judgement. Following the sobriety of Aristotle, Strauss deems just or right by nature whatever is the best possible under the circumstances. Since not everything just is noble, a wise man should be ready to endorse many a regime that falls short of nobility, or, if the circumstances warrant, one that is ignoble.

According to Strauss, this diluted version of classic natural right is the origin of the later distinction between primary and secondary natural right.[88] In this view, the primary natural right is applicable to man's state of innocence in the garden of Eden prior to the fall. It prohibits tyranny, patriarchalism, private property, and on some accounts, even government.[89] In contrast, the secondary natural right appropriate to man's fallen condition permits government, private property, patriarchalism and even tyranny. The secondary natural right has been in force since man was banished from the garden of Eden. It is both a remedy and a punishment for wickedness. Strauss points to a close resemblance between his diluted natural right and secondary natural right. However, there is one important difference between the two which he brings to our attention:

> If the principles valid in civil society are diluted natural right, they are much less venerable than if they are regarded as secondary natural right, i.e. as divinely established and involving an absolute duty for fallen man. Only in the latter case is justice, as it is commonly understood, unquestionably good. Only in the latter case does natural right in the strict sense or the primary natural right cease to be dynamite for civil society.[90]

Strauss is brief but not altogether cryptic. It seems that the difference between Strauss's natural right and the secondary natural right can best be understood by their attitude towards the *status quo*, and by deduction, to revolution. Although Strauss's classic natural right very often upholds the *status quo*, it is not *in principle* anti-revolutionary. It must necessarily look favorably on a revolution that would bring a city closer to the rule of the philosophers (in its practicable or diluted form). *In practice*, however, it will lend support to *any* regime, no matter how ignoble, if it is deemed necessary in the circumstances, and the means required to overthrow it are likely to result in even greater turmoil and disorder. However, if conditions permit the transformation of a bad regime into a good one (i.e. the rule of gentlemen guided by philosophers), then there would be no reason for the advocate of natural right to cling to the *status quo*. For being wise means recognizing that the old or ancestral is not venerable simply for being old.

It is a well-known fact that Strauss is a conservative. But the nature of his conservatism is ill-appreciated. Strauss is not a Burkean conservative. He does not regard the old as venerable because it is old. His conservatism is radical, and even revolutionary. It consists of a vision of a good society: orderly, law-abiding, patriotic, heroic, proud and strong – a society lead by gentlemen under the guidance of the wise. But he does not believe that such a society can be brought about by human will alone, i.e. by revolution. The wise cannot be the vanguard of a revolution because a revolution cannot be successful unless it has the support of the multitude, and the latter are invariably suspicious of the wise. Nor are the wise in the business of revolution; what they value above all is the peace and tranquility necessary for their contemplative lives. They must therefore wait until an opportunity presents itself for those friendly to philosophers to seize power, or for those in power to listen to the advice of the wise: theirs is a quiet revolution.

Understanding the character of natural right is indispensable for appreciating Strauss's critique of modernity. Strauss's classic natural right shares with modernity more than he would care to admit. In practice, it follows Machiavelli and Hobbes in making peace, stability and preservation the supreme ends of politics, and sanctioning whatever means are necessary to attain them.

6

Machiavelli's Subversion of Esotericism

Strauss considers our present political predicament to be one of 'crisis'; in particular, it is a crisis occasioned by what he calls 'modernity'. Simply stated, 'modernity' is the revolution against the wisdom of antiquity; a revolution that Strauss undoubtedly believes to be not only ill-conceived and foolish, but ultimately disastrous for the continued survival of Western civilization. We cannot understand what Strauss means by modernity without first grasping the central role he attributes to Machiavelli in this revolution.

Those who consider Strauss's exposition of the esoteric style of writing to be a hermeneutic for the study of ancient texts, not surprisingly, complain about the arbitrariness of this hermeneutic. Strauss's penchant for arriving at conclusions based on Machiavelli's silences lead his critics to maintain that Strauss asserts whatever he pleases.[1] His apparent precision and meticulousness seems to be but a cover for his resolve to fit Machiavelli into his preconceived view of the tradition of political philosophy.[2] That Strauss completely ignores not only recent scholarship on Machiavelli but the whole intellectual life of Italy at the time is yet another source of criticism of Strauss's methods.[3]

If we take Strauss too seriously as an historian of ideas, we will find ourselves embroiled in endless disputes with his students about what Machiavelli may or may not have thought. Although not unimportant or unpleasant, such disputes cannot shed light on Strauss's own political ideas, or his own unique vision of the drama of Western civilization. Here, as throughout this book, I will continue to ignore any serious contribution Strauss might have made to the history of political thought. I will not take issue with Strauss's interpretation of Machiavelli. Nor will I dispute the method by which he reaches his conclusions. Instead, I will consider his unconventional scholarly style as a necessary component of his own esoteric philosophy.

114

Commentators on Strauss's Machiavelli believe that Strauss's thesis in *Thoughts on Machiavelli* is remarkably simple, though puzzling. It amounts to the following. First, Machiavelli writes boldly and without any technical language, his writing appears transparent and easy to read, yet, in reality, his true meaning is hidden; he writes esoterically. Secondly, what Machiavelli aims to hide is the extent to which he is violently anti-Christian, morally unscrupulous and diabolical. The upshot of it all is that he is knowingly and intentionally a teacher of evil; he is a conscious, deliberate and subversive atheist bent on destroying Christianity. He is the first 'modern' political philosopher; he leads the revolution against the Western tradition of political thought, and so initiates the decline of Western civilization. He is far more Machiavellian than anyone ever dreamed possible.[4] But all this entirely misses the point.

There are two serious difficulties with the accepted view of Strauss's Machiavelli that leave commentators genuinely perplexed. First, as a writer, Machiavelli is, not surprisingly, regarded as one of the boldest and 'one of the most honest of all time'.[5] Commentators wonder if Strauss's ingenuity is not wasted in the lengths to which he goes to uncover in the strangest places what Machiavelli says so boldly elsewhere. How much more boldly could Machiavelli have expressed himself? What more could he have said? And has he not said enough to have himself vilified for all time? Has not Machiavellism come to be synonymous with diabolical cleverness? It is surely daring for a scholar to suggest that Machiavelli, of all men, is a secretive writer who had much to hide and who succeeded in his intention to conceal his thoughts with great skill, and that only the most meticulous scholarship and the most laborious attention to detail can begin to uncover the arcane thoughts of Machiavelli. But paradoxically, when Strauss's unconventional methods are brought to bear on Machiavelli's text, the results are commonplace: there is nothing new about the specter of the diabolical Machiavelli. What then is the meaning of Strauss's work?

The second puzzling thing about the received interpretation of Strauss's Machiavelli is the deep and apparently genuine admiration that Strauss seems to have for the man he has so unconditionally castigated. Strauss seems to couple his condemnation of Machiavelli with a deep admiration of his genius; he considers Machiavelli to have a spirit so 'intrepid' and a mind so 'noble' that they could not possibly be fathomed by the modern scientists of society who would claim him as their own.[6] What is the meaning of such superlative praise?

If we are to penetrate the real meaning of Strauss's thoughts on Machiavelli, we must heed the warnings that Strauss's students have directed at their master's critics. It seems that the contents of Strauss's book on Machiavelli do not make themselves readily available to the unsuspecting reader.[7] One particularly enthusiastic reviewer remarks that it is necessary to kiss goodbye to six months of one's life if one hopes to come to terms with this book.[8] Allan Bloom portrays the book as 'unprepossessing', 'suffused with a tension', and so complex as to be 'mind-boggling'.[9] Harvey Mansfield describes it as an 'achievement' for even the most adept readers; but more to the point is Mansfield's remark that Strauss's book is an *exoteric* book in contrast to Machiavelli's book which, following Strauss, he regards as esoteric. He explains this as follows:

> *Thoughts on Machiavelli* is an exoteric book, that is, a book containing much that is appreciably esoteric to any ordinary reader stated in a manner either so elusive or so challenging as to cause him to give up trying to understand it. In this it is to be distinguished from the books with which it is concerned, Machiavelli's *Prince* and *Discourses on Livy*. These are esoteric books because almost all readers, and especially scholarly readers, believe they understand them, and only Strauss has shown they do not.[10]

Mansfield seems to be contradicting my view that Strauss is an esoteric writer. However, attending to the meaning of his words reveals that he endorses it. As Strauss has told us, Machiavelli's books are esoteric in a way that is particularly ingenious and difficult to detect because Machiavelli *appears* to write so simply, clearly and openly, that everyone believes they understand them; but in reality, his real intention is so well hidden that it has eluded even the best scholars. Machiavelli's work is also esoteric in another sense. It contains no exoteric philosophy, no salutary teaching, no noble lies, no pious frauds. In contrast, Strauss's book can be regarded as exoteric, *not because it contains no hidden meaning, but because it also contains a salutary exoteric teaching.*

Strauss's book can only be understood if the exoteric teaching is distinguished from the esoteric one. Even though some of Strauss's students are aware of the esoteric nature of Strauss's book, none have been either willing or daring enough to reveal the exact nature or content of the esoteric philosophy it entails. This can be done only by paying careful attention to what Strauss says, and placing it in the context of his whole intellectual enterprise.

We need not become distracted by the abundance of particulars or confused by the rhetoric or perplexed by the way he seems to 'forget the holy war of mankind in the petty squabbles of pedants'.[11] Nor should we dismiss Strauss as a scholar who is afflicted with a bizarre passion for details. Instead, we should recognize these idiosyncrasies as necessary components of his esoteric philosophy. In so doing, we would begin to penetrate beyond the surface to the deeper truth that he means to communicate only to the few. Surely he does not go to all these great lengths in order to arrive at the unoriginal conclusion that Machiavelli is really Machiavellian, and that the 'old fashioned view' of Machiavelli as a teacher of evil is even truer than was previously imagined. Strauss himself alerts us to the fact that the old fashioned view is 'not exhaustive', and that it is only a convenient starting place that will enable us to penetrate the 'deeper truth' about Machiavelli.[12] A more careful examination of what Strauss has to say reveals the deeper truth in question.

My thesis regarding Strauss's Machiavelli is as follows. First, following the wise men of antiquity, Strauss used Machiavelli as his mouthpiece in order to avoid pronouncing unpleasant, unsalutary and dangerous truths in his own name. Instead, Strauss avails himself of the 'immunity of the commentator' which allows him to express truths that he believes a wise man dare not speak openly. He refers to Machiavelli's conception of the relationship between politics and morality as shocking, repugnant, evil, irreligious, diabolical and dangerous, but never as *false*. On the contrary, he thinks it a true account of the real nature of politics, but one that a wise man dare not express openly, except through the mouth of a madman, a slave, a sophist or a devil, like Machiavelli.

Secondly, contrary to what Strauss's commentators believe, Strauss does not criticize Machiavelli so much for being anti-Christian, as for having been ultimately seduced by Christianity.

So much so that he uses a secular model of Christianity for his own political philosophy.

Thirdly, what Machiavelli hides is not so much the extent to which he is anti-Christian, but the extent to which he is opposed to the pagan tradition of Greek philosophy. Machiavelli is not the admirer of the ancients that he pretends to be. The truly anti-pagan nature of Machiavelli's work is more cleverly concealed than its anti-Christian implications. Contrary to his declared love of pagan antiquity, Machiavelli accelerates the Christian revolt against the aristocratic tradition of Greek philosophy, a tradition that Strauss identifies with Western civility itself. I will discuss each of these three claims in turn.

POLITICS AND MORALITY

According to Strauss, Machiavelli is a man who doubts the 'common view' according to which 'morality can and ought to control political life'.[13] Instead, he regards the political domain as free from the restraints of morality. Whatever accomplishes the ends of politics is right and ought to be done regardless of its moral nature. In politics, the end justifies the means. Every civilization has its foundation in crime.

Strauss tells us that we cannot appreciate the novelty of Machiavelli's doctrine unless we approach it from a pre-modern perspective. From the point of view of classical and biblical heritage, Machiavelli is 'surprising', 'new', 'unexpected' and 'strange'; but from our own perspective he looks 'old', 'our own', and therefore 'good'. Interpreters of Strauss have drastically misunderstood what Strauss means by saying that the novelty of Machiavelli is one that can only be appreciated from a pre-modern perspective. They believe him to mean that we have been so corrupted by Machiavelli that we no longer find his terrible counsels shocking. In contrast, the ancients are bound to be alarmed by a doctrine so new, so unfamiliar and hitherto unknown. Strauss certainly says as much, but his meaning is not as transparent as his moral indignation and his generally animated rhetoric would lead us to believe.

Strauss does not believe that Machiavelli's political doctrine was unknown to the ancients. On the contrary, Machiavelli's conception of the relationship of politics and morality is 'as old as political society itself'.[14] Strauss means that only in the light of the verbal reserve of the ancients does Machiavelli really appear 'new', 'surprising', 'unexpected' and 'strange'.[15] What is novel and unprecedented is not the content of Machiavelli's teaching, but 'the shocking frankness of speech which he sometimes employs or affects'.[16] Looked at from the perspective of Strauss's ancients, Machiavelli is shocking, not because of what he has to say, but because of the manner in which he says it, openly and in his own name:

> Machiavelli proclaims openly and triumphantly a corrupting doctrine which ancient writers had taught covertly, or with all signs of repugnance. He says in his own name shocking things which ancient writers had said though the mouths of their characters. Machiavelli alone has dared to utter the evil doctrine in a book and in his own name.[17]

Strauss makes the same point in *On Tyranny*. He declares that Xenophon's *Hiero* was the model Machiavelli deliberately set out to imitate.[18] He learns from Xenophon that a man who would advise tyrants must be or appear to be utterly unscrupulous. Machiavelli learnt his lesson from Xenophon, but he 'certainly did not apply it in the spirit of its originator'.[19] Xenophon does not separate moderation or prudence from wisdom or insight.[20] He makes his Simonides reveal his freedom from morality, and so shows himself to be a man who understands 'political things', not by speech, but by his silence regarding Hiero's innumerable crimes. Xenophon conceals his own thoughts even further in the form of the dialogue; he does not even use Socrates as his main spokesman – the latter is too easily identified with Xenophon himself. All this reveals that what he has to say is 'a philosophic teaching of the sort that a truly wise man would not care to present in his own name'.[21] It can only be elicited by a careful examination of the setting, the action, the context of the conversation and the characters employed (as Strauss attempts to do). He is moderate or prudent about dispensing his wisdom because he knows that not all truths are harmless. In contrast, Machiavelli proclaims his tyrannical teaching from the rooftops. He is less 'politic'. He has insight or wisdom, but no moderation or thrift in expression.[22] He 'dares to utter the evil doctrine in his own name'. He therefore subverts the very *genre* he pretends to imitate. Strauss regards the difference in form to be 'decisive'.

Machiavelli does not dissent from the ancients in the content of his thought on the issue of politics and morality. Ancient philosophers taught the same doctrine, only covertly.[23] Even the divine Plato seems to have taught a doctrine of political conspiracy and tyrannicide.[24] Machiavelli's conception of the relation between politics and morality may well go against the 'common view' but it is by no means a novel doctrine.[25]

It is clear that philosophers have always known that crime is indispensable to the founding of a civilization. For Strauss, every society needs an 'ideology' precisely to hide its foundation in crime, because 'a self-respecting society cannot become reconciled to the notion that its foundation was laid in crime'.[26] Strauss would have us believe that the truth of Machiavelli's view is authenticated by the Bible. The Biblical God punishes Cain only mildly for slaying his brother Abel, but threatens to punish severely anyone who would kill Cain. Cain was the founder of a civilization. We must therefore conclude that the 'common view' which upholds the contrary, belongs only to common, ordinary or vulgar men, and is not shared by philosophers.

In *Thoughts on Machiavelli* Strauss follows the wise ancients in teaching covertly Machiavelli's true doctrine about politics and morality. Strauss would have us believe that there are exceptions to Machiavelli's claim that all political societies have their foundation in crime. He declares that the United States of America is an exception that might refute the truth of Machiavelli's doctrine. He asserts that it is 'the only country in the world which was founded explicitly in opposition to Machiavellian principles'.[27] He quotes Thomas Paine according to whom the foundation of the United States is in freedom and justice rather than in the sword; unlike the governments of the old world, it is a government founded on a moral theory, on universal peace and indefeasible rights. In quoting Paine against Machiavelli, Strauss appears to be contrasting the good and the evil, the exalted and the vulgar. However, the contrast does not belong to Strauss, but to Paine, the patriot, and those of us who have more reverence for truth than for patriotism will disregard it. Indeed, Strauss gives us every reason to do so; no sooner does he point to an exception to Machiavelli's claim, he subverts it by reminding us of the Louisiana Purchase and the fate of the Red Indians. Strauss makes the case for Machiavelli subtly, but more eloquently than he does for Paine. Without telling us, he leads us to discover yet another proof for the 'contention that there cannot be a great and glorious nation without the equivalent of the murder of Remus by Romulus'.[28] The only exception turns out *not* to be an exception after all. We must therefore conclude that the foundation of *every* political society is in crime. Strauss teaches us in the very same manner that he contends that Machiavelli teaches or, more accurately, corrupts. When the truth is kept hidden, it can only be discovered by effort. But once discovered, it is believed to be one's own. Strauss gives the following example: Machiavelli tells us of the crimes of Moses who was forced to 'massacre innumerable human beings' if they opposed his law.[29] Strauss wonders if Moses's law was not God's; he thinks that Machiavelli implies the crimes must belong to God! Strauss brings this to our attention as one example among many where Machiavelli conceals his blasphemy and so 'compels the reader to think the blasphemy by himself and thus to become Machiavelli's accomplice'.[30] For Strauss, 'concealment as practiced by Machiavelli is an instrument of corruption or seduction'.[31] However, we must notice that Strauss reports Machiavelli's words but makes no effort to come to Moses's defense; he provides no reason to dispel the blasphemy. His 'obtrusive silence', here as elsewhere, is disturbing. It makes the wary reader wonder whether the deviousness in question really belongs to Machiavelli. I am inclined to think that Strauss's own seductive method of teaching is modeled after the method he attributes to Machiavelli.[32] This might explain why Strauss's avid followers typically report an experience of sudden catharsis, transformation, awakening, or revelation upon their first encounter with Strauss. At the same time, they deny that Strauss has taught them anything; they insist that he has merely inspired them to attain the most profound insights independently.

MACHIAVELLI AND CHRISTIANITY

Strauss accuses Machiavelli of being an enemy of the Bible who sets out intentionally to destroy Christianity. Strauss brings to our attention that Machiavelli's praise of religion is only the reverse side of his 'indifference to the truth of religion'.[33] In other words,

Machiavelli praises religion only because he believes it to be indispensable to political order; he praises it only for its usefulness.

Unless men are appeased by religious hopes and frightened by religious fears, they would be less likely to defer to the ruling class, and society would be in a state of constant turmoil. Machiavelli believes with Marx that religion is the opium of the people. But unlike Marx, Machiavelli believes that the opium will always be necessary because of the unchanging nature of both men and the world. The world is characterized by scarcity, whereas human desires are limitless; as a result, they crave a satisfaction that is impossible.[34] Religion is useful for curbing man's unlimited cravings, hence making them moderate enough to be satisfied with the little that politics can realistically offer.

Machiavelli's animosity to Christianity is due to the fact that he considers it politically less useful than pagan religion, and maybe even the most useless of all religions. Far from having a salutary effect on political order, it tends to be divisive; it sets men against one another and against the state. The jealous God of the Bible demands 'zealous love' and insists on adherence to His commands regardless of their effects. In contrast, pagan religion leaves human prudence free to choose the wisest course of action.[35] But worst of all, Christianity contributes to sloth. Its otherworldly nature promotes general indifference to worldly glory and civic virtue. It tends to make men trust in God's providence and not in their own skills. The Romans tried Fortuna whereas the Christians trust in her because they have replaced her by a good and just God.[36] Whereas paganism is conducive to the strength of the world, Christianity renders it weak.[37]

Strauss shows how Machiavelli openly sheds doubt on the truth of Biblical religion. He argues that his intention is to consciously undermine it. He says that the Christian religion is of human origin, and consists only of poetic fables.[38] He denies the existence of God by denying that the argument that the universe had a beginning has any force.[39] Furthermore, he takes the 'side of Aristotle as over against the Bible' on the question of the eternity of the universe.[40] Strauss therefore declares Machiavelli an enemy of the Bible.[41]

Commentators understand Strauss to be accusing Machiavelli of being a zealous and committed atheist, an enemy of religion in general and of Christianity in particular. It cannot be denied that Strauss so considers Machiavelli, but it is not clear that this is the source of his condemnation. Strauss is hardly a champion of Biblical religion himself. Strauss's vociferous condemnation of Machiavelli hides the true nature of Strauss's own teaching.

It is not entirely false to think that Strauss laments the decay of Christian morality. He does genuinely lament its decay among the many. Christianity may not be as useful as other religions, nevertheless it is the dominant religion of the West, and as such it is both foolish and cruel to undermine it publicly as Machiavelli does.

The real reason Strauss rails against Machiavelli is that he makes his disapproval of Christianity much too easy to detect. He does not follow the ancient wisdom of writing esoterically on these matters. Machiavelli is being very devious when he pretends to be following the authority of Livy in belittling religion. Livy does not mock religion although he puts words mocking religion 'into the mouths of plebeians who mock religion'.[42] But Machiavelli says these words in his own name and pretends to be following Livy in doing so. Strauss shows numerous instances where Machiavelli quotes words of Livy which the historian put into the mouthes of his characters.

Machiavelli constantly pretends to 'defer' to Livy's authority, 'cherish' it, 'harken' to it in filial affection', in 'patient docility', in 'pious reverence', when all the while he is subverting it.[43] He only appeals to the 'prejudice in favour of antiquity'; he knows that he must make the new seem old if it is to be palatable.[44] This reveals to Strauss the extent to which Machiavelli is a master of the esoteric art he sets out to subvert:

> Time and again we have become bewildered by the fact that the man who is more responsible than any other man for the break with the Great Tradition should in the very act of breaking prove to be the heir, the by no means unworthy heir, to that supreme art of writing which that tradition manifested at its peak.[45]

Machiavelli is esoteric because he pretends to follow Livy in the very act of subverting him. Conversely, he pretends to denounce Christianity while mimicking it.

Strauss's real criticism of Machiavelli has little to do with the anti-Christian nature of his central doctrine. Far from criticizing Machiavelli for being anti-Christian, Strauss believes Machiavelli is very much under the spell of Christianity. The latter is the model both for his own philosophizing as well as for his politics. Strauss does not make this explicit, and it is likely to be missed in the midst of his rhetoric against Machiavelli's conscious intention to destroy Christianity.

Strauss believes that Machiavelli's political model is Christian, not pagan. What Machiavelli subverts is not so much Christianity as pagan philosophy. According to Strauss, Machiavelli appears to deny one of the central assumptions of the Bible, according to which there was in the beginning a Golden Age where men were good and from which they have fallen. Machiavelli pretends to follow the traditional view that progress is a return to the foundations, but in reality he introduces an entirely new doctrine. Machiavelli's new doctrine consists in the following. There never was a golden age in which men were good. Men have always been corrupt from the very beginning. If they seemed good, that is only due to terror. Princes must therefore instill fear and terror into the hearts of men if they hope to make them good. In doing so, they not only return to the terror accompanying the foundation, but to the 'terror inherent in man's situation'.[46]

Strauss explains that

> Machiavelli's return to the beginning means a return to the primeval or original terror which precedes every man-made terror, which explains why the founder must use terror. . . . In the beginning there was terror. In the beginning men were good, i.e., they were willing to obey because they were afraid and easily frightened. The primacy of Love must be replaced by the primacy of Terror if Republics are to be established in accordance with nature and on the basis of knowledge of nature.[47]

In the light of Strauss's own interpretation of the biblical beginning, we know that Strauss does not think the biblical account regarding man's goodness to be reasonable. On the contrary, he considers the first transgression to be shockingly unfounded.[48] It is founded neither in the evil nature of man nor in the malevolent nature of God. The Bible provides us with no answer. Reason would have us side with Machiavelli in thinking that men were not good in the beginning; if they appeared good, that is probably because they feared God, because they experienced the terror that 'precedes every man-made terror'. We must therefore conclude that Strauss does not believe that the Bible really begins with the idea of man's perfection, but the reverse. Machiavelli's politics therefore follows what Strauss regards as a reasonable interpretation of the biblical account of man's situation. He uses the biblical account of man as the model for his politics.[49]

Strauss casts doubt on Machiavelli's claim that unarmed prophets cannot succeed. He maintains that Machiavelli could not possibly believe this since he is himself an unarmed prophet. Strauss suggests that Machiavelli models himself after Christ: an unarmed prophet whose success must have inspired Machiavelli with awe and admiration.[50] The triumph of Christianity over paganism must have encouraged a man, who, like Machiavelli, wanted to introduce 'new modes and orders', or to change the way men thought about good and evil, honor and dishonor. Machiavelli portrayed the change he wished to make in terms of a return to the virtues of antiquity, but Strauss uncovers this claim as a fraud.

Strauss repeats again and again that Machiavelli is the enemy of the Great Tradition; that he leads a conscious revolt against it with the aim of undermining it. Commentators err in thinking that Strauss's conception of the Great Tradition embraces both the Bible and classical philosophy.[51] Strauss's account of Machiavelli's politics reveals otherwise. In the very act of asserting that Machiavelli subverts the Bible, Strauss shows the extent to which he mimics it. Machiavelli's politics has as its foundation the biblical conception of man according to which he can be kept from depravity only by the terror that God's power and wrath can instill in his heart. Machiavelli's prince must therefore mimic the biblical God and inspire his subjects with the same primeval terror. Machiavelli rejects good beginnings, but Strauss 'silently denies' that the biblical beginning was good by the powerful manner in which he portrays the similarity between Machiavelli's politics and biblical beginnings.[52] The perfection of man is therefore not envisaged by Christianity, it is envisaged only by classical philosophy. It comes at the *end* and not at the beginning.[53] It is the result of the full cultivation of man's highest potentialities – namely, intellectual virtue as understood by Aristotle. Machiavelli's revolt against the Great Tradition is not so much a revolt against Christianity as a revolt against the tradition of classical Greek philosophy which alone constitutes the Great Tradition.

MACHIAVELLI'S REVOLT AGAINST THE CLASSICAL TRADITION OF GREEK PHILOSOPHY

The real source of Strauss's critique of Machiavelli rests in the anti-classical rather than in the anti-Christian nature of his thought. Machiavelli is the leader of the modern revolution against ancient wisdom. He is eminently qualified to play this leading role because he is a true student of the ancients. One cannot successfully revolt against that which one does not understand. This explains why Strauss makes Machiavelli the subject of his severest condemnation as well as his most exalted praise.

According to Strauss, Machiavelli's esotericism rests on the fact that he hides his conscious intention to subvert the wisdom of antiquity and to introduce 'new modes and orders'. Being well versed in the tradition he sets out to undermine, Machiavelli knows that men are generally suspicious of anything new; the latter must therefore be painted with the colors of the old if it is to be received without hostility. To use the authority of the ancients in the very act of subverting it, requires not only a thoroughgoing acquaintance with the content of ancient wisdom, but also a mastery of the ancient art of writing. Machiavelli testifies to the fact that he was a devoted student of antiquity in a famous letter: in the evening, upon entering his study, he put on regal and courtly clothes and thus properly dressed, he 'fed himself on that nourishment which alone was his and for which he was born; there he united himself wholly with the ancients, and thus did not fear poverty, forgot every anguish, and was not frightened by death'.[54] In Strauss's view, the overwhelming success of his revolution against antiquity is due precisely to the fact that it was an inside job!

Strauss identifies Machiavelli's revolt against antiquity with modernity itself. For Strauss, Machiavelli's revolution opens the way to the Enlightenment and the whole 'modern project'. If we are to grasp what Strauss means by modernity, we must first understand what aspects of antiquity Machiavelli succeeded in subverting. It seems to me that the most important are as follows. First, by making politics autonomous, he rejects contemplation as the end beyond politics for which the latter exists. He therefore undermines the life of reason in favor of the life of action and politics. Characteristically, his ideals tend to be Roman rather than Greek. Secondly, he breaks with the aristocratic tradition and exalts the multitude. Thirdly, while being a master of the esoteric art of writing, he overthrows the ancient understanding of philosophy as esoteric. Instead, he makes philosophy a public instrument of propaganda for the service of the state. I will discuss each of these points in turn.

Strauss laments the fact that Machiavelli makes politics an autonomous realm sufficient unto itself and independent of other domains of human life, especially morality. This is generally misunderstood to be a celebration of the view that politics should be subordinated to the demands of morality. But this for Strauss is not possible. What Strauss laments is not the expulsion of morality from politics, but the banishment of contemplation as the end which hallows and sanctifies that necessary but repugnant domain of human life, namely politics. What contemporary scholars educated by Machiavelli have forgotten is that the state in and of itself is unworthy, partial and abominable. They have forgotten that there are ends far more worthy than the state, ends for which the state alone exists and which alone make the abomination, the partiality, the waspishness and the injustice of the state tolerable, and even honorable and according to nature. Modern scholars corrupted by Machiavelli believe that his patriotism justifies his terrible counsels. As Strauss writes,

> the indifference to the distinction between right and wrong which springs from devotion to one's country is less repulsive than the indifference to that distinction which springs from exclusive preoccupation with one's own ease or glory. But precisely for this reason it is more seductive and therefore more dangerous.[55]

What Strauss says here of patriotism he says elsewhere of political justice in general. Both amount to nothing more than collective self-interest.[56] Strauss remarks that we cannot justify Machiavelli's 'terrible counsels' by referring to his patriotism. To do this is to see the virtue of patriotism while being 'blind to that which is higher than patriotism, or to that which both hallows and limits patriotism'.[57] Strauss does not in this context tell us what the good that hallows patriotism is, but we know from what he says elsewhere that the highest end is the philosophical life or the perfection of man's rational capacities. Strauss identifies this with the common good, although there is little that is 'common' about it. For Strauss, the inevitable nastiness of politics cannot be transcended, but it can be excused or made respectable if politics is made a means to a higher end. The higher end not only limits patriotism but 'hallows' it, and by implication, its 'terrible counsels'. What for Strauss is abominable about Machiavelli is not that he is willing to counsel princes to commit atrocities but to commit them *only* in the name of patriotism and not something higher.[58]

Strauss makes the same point in his debate with Carl Schmitt in Germany in 1932.[59] Schmitt takes a position not unlike Machiavelli's regarding the autonomy of politics from morality. In his reply to Schmitt, Strauss does not argue that politics must be subordinated to the demands of morality, but only that politics cannot be a supreme or self-sufficient end; and that it exists only to make higher ends possible.[60]

What is at issue between Strauss and Machiavelli is that Machiavelli couples his rejection of contemplation as the end of politics with a rejection of the whole aristocratic Greek tradition. Strauss seems positively offended by the fact that Machiavelli prefers the 'more democratic and less stable Roman polity' to the 'less democratic and more stable Spartan polity'.[61] This for Strauss is decisive in the understanding of Machiavelli as the first modern. Strauss links Machiavelli's preference of Rome over Sparta to the anti-aristocratic sentiment, that more than anything else, characterizes modernity. He writes:

> It may easily appear that Machiavelli was the first philosopher who questioned in the name of the multitude or of democracy the aristocratic prejudice or the aristocratic premise which informed classical philosophy. He preferred the more democratic Roman polity to the less democratic Spartan polity. He expresses the opinion that the purpose of the people is more honest, or more just, than the purpose of the great. It is true that he did not favour the rule of the multitude: all simple regimes are bad; . . .[62]

Strauss is a man who chooses his words carefully. He does not say that Machiavelli is definitely the first modern or the first to undermine the 'aristocratic or oligarchic republicanism of the classical tradition'. He says only that he *appears* to be the first. It does not take much ingenuity to surmise that Christianity and not Machiavelli was the first to do this. We must conclude that Machiavelli's bias in favor of the multitude is Christian and that Machiavelli completes rather than begins the revolt against classical antiquity.[63] Modernity therefore begins with Christianity and not with Machiavelli. Strauss is unwilling to say this openly not only because it might be distasteful for a Jew to criticize Christianity as the source of all the ills of modernity, but because Strauss is reluctant to criticize the dominant religion of the West. Despite all its shortcomings, Christianity is still better than no religion at all. Strauss does *genuinely* lament its decline among the many.

There is a further significance to Machiavelli's preference of Rome. It points to his celebration of the active life in contradistinction to the contemplative or philosophical life. What is at issue between Strauss and Machiavelli can be described as follows. Strauss adheres to a tripartite sort of Platonic anthropology of human types, each with a morality appropriate to it. First, there are the most noble philosophers who seek wisdom for its own sake.[64] Then there are citizens, gentlemen and lovers of honor. Among these are a few who are not ordinary citizens, gentlemen or lovers of honor, but super-citizens: they are men who aspire not only to honor, but to greatness and worldly immortality. These are the men that Machiavelli aims to teach by what Strauss calls a process of brutalization. To be great they must learn not to be good. They must shed the effeminacy of their Christian inhibitions and soar to the manly realm of politics where excellence is measured not by good intentions or purity of heart, but by one's success and concrete achievements. Finally, there are the ordinary men whose concern is security, self-preservation and ultimately, pleasure. A religion full-blown with a belief in an afterlife is needed for them, if they are to be prevented from tearing the state apart in their never-ending quest to satisfy their insatiable desires.

Strauss's disagreement with Machiavelli has to do with the group of men he most admires. For Strauss, the philosopher is the highest and most noble type, since he is dedicated to the highest activity of which man is capable, namely, contemplation. What is at issue has been well captured by Hannah Arendt's distinction between the *vita activa* and the *vita contemplativa*.[65] Plato and Aristotle gave priority to the life of contemplation. In contrast, Machiavelli gives priority to the life of action. Strauss understands this as a decline.

Strauss regards Machiavelli as one who has lowered the standard of politics. Strauss recognizes two natural ends of politics. The first or lower end is that of the survival of the group in a condition of health, security and modest wealth. The second or higher end is to make possible the life of the philosopher, or what Strauss simply calls the good life for man. The first end of the political order is a necessary means to the second. Having banished the second, or higher end, Machiavelli has lowered the standard of politics by confining it to the less exalted ends of security, peace and preservation. Thus, it is not surprising that Machiavelli advises those who would be great to attend to the needs and desires of the multitude; the latter make and unmake princes and greatness rests largely on one's ability to appease them or to appear to appease them. This is what Strauss means by saying that Machiavelli shows an unforgivable preference for the multitude as against the few or most noble philosophers.

At the bottom of Machiavelli's celebration of politics and patriotism as ends in themselves, is his disregard for the contemplative life. For all his praise of the ancients and his insistence on the need to imitate them, Machiavelli is silent about ancient philosophy.[66] Strauss is struck by this blatant omission. He understands the reason for it to be Machiavelli's intention to break with the esoteric and prudent forms of expression that distinguish the ancient philosophers. Nor is this departure simply a stylistic matter. Strauss insists that 'one cannot radically change the mode of a teaching without radically changing its substance'.[67] By abandoning the esoteric nature of philosophy, Machiavelli undermines philosophy itself. He turns it into an object of mass consumption or an instrument of public propaganda in the service of the state. Instead of being the exalted end for which the political is tolerated, philosophy becomes the handmaid of the powers that be. Philosophy cannot be considered fit for mass consumption without a significant change in the conception of philosophy as well as that of society. The public dissemination of philosophy is therefore concomitant with the democratization of society. As society becomes democratic, philosophy becomes propaganda.

Machiavelli himself says that he is only making public what the ancients had taught covertly. Strauss does not disagree that this is precisely what Machiavelli is doing. What he takes issue with is Machiavelli's claim that his teaching is not novel. It is not possible to write openly what ancient writers taught covertly without introducing 'new modes and orders'. Machiavelli's dissemination of philosophy to the masses opens the way to the Enlightenment, nay, it is identical with Enlightenment. Enlightenment is 'the project' of modernity *par excellence*: its goal is to fight against the Kingdom of Darkness. It believes falsely, that mass enlightenment is the solution to man's political dilemmas. Moreover, this modern project is conceived as a conscious and heroic effort on man's part to take control of his destiny and to master Fortuna. According to Strauss, Machiavelli replaces the biblical God with Fortuna, and the Christian idea of providence with the modern idea of not trusting to chance, and taking one's fate in one's own hands. Having deposed both God and chance, man becomes the sole master over nature; his destiny depends only on himself. The result is the technological society where man's inventions have become his masters and his destroyers.

Commentators have objected that Strauss's identification of Machiavelli with modernity and Enlightenment is 'overdone'.[68] Dante Germino provides a nearly exhaustive list of all the traditional assumptions that make up part of Machiavelli's intellectual baggage: the consistency of human nature, the cyclical view of history, the preference for a mixed regime, and the need for a civil religion are examples. Germino's concrete and well-documented argument must, however, remain irrelevant to Strauss. Machiavelli initiates the Enlightenment because he abandons esoteric writing and makes philosophy public; and so, contrary to the ancients, believes that philosophical truth is salutary or that no one will be harmed by hearing the truth. For Strauss, this is the key ingredient that characterizes the Enlightenment.

Strauss does not deny Machiavelli's affinity to the ancients. In the final analysis, Strauss does not regard Machiavelli as the true champion of modernity. That role he reserves for Hobbes. Machiavelli is only the first of the moderns, the leader of the revolution against antiquity. What is so devilish about Machiavelli, what is for Strauss so inexcusable, is that he once lived among the great men of antiquity. He is a devil precisely because he was once an angel. This is the meaning of Strauss's praise of Machiavelli as a fallen angel, and it explains why Strauss makes

Machiavelli the subject of the most severe condemnation as well as the most exalted praise.[69]

In conclusion, Strauss's view of Machiavelli is more interesting than the orthodox account of it allows. I have made three claims which uncover the hidden meaning of Strauss's *Thoughts on Machiavelli*. First, far from condemning Machiavelli's understanding of the relation between politics and morality, Strauss takes its truth for granted. What he finds shocking is the open and public manner in which Machiavelli expresses himself. Following the wise men of antiquity to whom Machiavelli pretends to defer, Strauss is resolved to keep this dangerous truth hidden. It may not be altogether a coincidence that the first words of the first chapter of Strauss's book are: 'we shall not shock anyone'. Secondly, the same holds true for Strauss's castigation of Machiavelli's anti-Christian sentiments. Machiavelli is a teacher of evil, not because he doubts the truth of Christianity, but because he expresses this doubt publicly. It is both wicked and foolish to undermine religion publicly, since, by Machiavelli's own admission, religion is necessary for political stability. Thirdly, Strauss's substantive criticism of Machiavelli lies in the fact that he launches a revolt against the tradition of Greek philosophy. The autonomy of politics frees it not only from the rigid standards of morality, but makes it a supreme end in itself and not a means to a higher end, namely, the cultivation of intellectual excellence or contemplation for the few. This raises important questions. Why is contemplation the highest end which politics must serve? Is it not conceivable that there is a plurality of equal and incommensurable goods that politics must serve? And why is it unreasonable to demand that politics be subordinated to the ends of morality? Is not morality a good end rather than just a means to peace, survival and preservation? Strauss provides few, if any, answers to these questions in his writings. One must suppose that ideas that are covertly held and transmitted need no argument.

7

Hobbes and the Character of Modernity

One of the central themes of Strauss's work is to analyze the character of 'modernity' and explain how it ultimately led to the 'crisis' of our time. If we are to understand Strauss, we must examine what he means by 'modernity' and by 'crisis'. Although he does not express it this way, his view can be described as follows. A civilization is not made of oak and rock but of individuals. Its foundation is in the hearts and minds of men. Its health depends on the psychic health or depravity of its constituents. A civilization is healthy when it is inspired by an idea, a purpose and a project that animates all those within its compass. A civilization begins to decline and decay and ultimately vanishes when the individuals within it no longer believe in the idea or ideas that are its guiding light. For Strauss, 'modernity' is not essentially an historical or chronological category.[1] It refers primarily to the set of ideas that in the last two hundred years have gained ascendancy and become the guiding light and inspiration directing Western civilization. The crisis of modern Western civilization consists in the fact that these ideas have now lost their power; we no longer believe in them. This is not altogether surprising, for the ideas that have been our guiding lights were ill-conceived from the start. Disillusioned, we are beginning to wander aimlessly; and this aimlessness is symptomatic of an impending catastrophe.

Strauss is a modern prophet, warning of impending doom and bringing ancient wisdom. From the perspective of old wisdom, the ideas that have been the guiding lights of our civilization are tragically flawed. They must now be supplemented or moderated by the sobriety of the ancients. The quarrel between 'ancients' and 'moderns' has led to the triumph of the moderns; but their ascendancy may well prove our undoing. What then is modernity and what is at issue between the ancients and the moderns?

Modernity is fundamentally the subversion of ancient wisdom;

more particularly, the subversion of the esoteric philosophy. Although Machiavelli leads this revolt, he is not the quintessential modern. He is the great 'Columbus' who discovers the continent on which 'Hobbes could erect his structure'.[2] The quintessentially modern philosopher is Hobbes. He is the key to understanding the real character of modernity.

Hobbes was well aware that he was a rebel against the tradition of Western political thought. He associated that tradition with Socrates, Plato, Aristotle, Cicero, Seneca, Tacitus and Plutarch. But in spite of his open revolt, he shared with the tradition the concern for the good political order; however, he departed from the tradition in significant ways. He was the founder of the novel doctrines of 'political hedonism' and 'political atheism', which together completely overthrew ancient wisdom and gave modernity its distinctive character.[3]

Hobbes denied the 'idealism' of the tradition or the view that the noble and the just are independent of the pleasant and preferable to it. Instead, he embraced the Epicurian view that the pleasant is the highest good by nature and that the noble and just are desirable only in so far as they are conducive to pleasure. Hedonism is an ancient doctrine, but Hobbes gives it an entirely new twist. He maintains that it can be made the foundation of a good political order. What is absolutely novel about Hobbes's doctrine is that it transforms the previously apolitical character of ancient hedonism. Hedonists such as Epicurus were not political; they lived on the fringes of society. They were aware that the life according to nature, the life dedicated to the pursuit of pleasure, whether high- or low-brow, is incompatible with civil society. In the ancient view, 'political hedonism' is highly paradoxical if not altogether contradictory.

Hobbes's originality rests on the fact that he accepted the premises of the hedonists, but rejected their conclusions. He accepted their conception of the good as pleasure, but denied that such a conception of good poses any threat to the state. On the contrary, he maintained that the hedonist conception of the good is the most solid and the most natural foundation for politics. For Hobbes, there is no political good that transcends the multiplicity of human desires and appetites. He declared that the state was but the sum total of individuals, and that the collective good is therefore none other than the maximum satisfaction of individual appetites. Nor did he think that the sheer diversity or multiplicity of these appetites will necessarily come into conflict. He believed that they could be made fully compatible with one another. According to Strauss, this explains why Hobbes tries 'to instill the spirit of political idealism into the hedonistic tradition'.[4] To do this, he had to deny what both the hedonists and idealists of antiquity regarded as an incontrovertible fact – namely, the inevitable conflict between the interests of individuals and those of the whole. The ancients regarded the community as more than the sum of individuals, and the good of the whole as distinct from the maximum satisfaction of individual desires and interests. They believed that the good of the whole requires the sacrifice of individual interests, if not their lives. The hedonist conception of the good therefore cannot be the foundation of politics; it poses a threat to collective life. This was recognized both by the hedonists and by their opponents. It explains why they led a retiring and quiet life, keeping largely to themselves. Only the most uncouth ventured to sully the public realm with their hedonism. In Strauss's view, Hobbes's unrivaled novelty rests on having liberated hedonism form its previously hidden, private or apolitical character, and transformed it into a political doctrine.

Even though Hobbes begins with a conception of man as a thoroughly depraved, antisocial, self-centered egoist with limitless desires for power and pleasure, he does not despair of politics. Moral depravity is for him no obstacle to political excellence. As Strauss writes, 'It is hard for us to understand how Hobbes could be so hopeful where there was so much cause for despair.'[5] Far from despairing, Hobbes's expectations of politics are extravagant. In Strauss's view, such expectations are unprecedented in the history of political thought. The explanation is that Hobbes believed that the good political order can be constructed with flawed human material. As Kant put it, it is possible to establish a good political order 'even for a nation of devils, provided they have sense'.[6] This means that moral virtue is not necessary for a good and just society. Devils will suffice provided that they are guided by enlightened selfishness.

If Hobbes's state of nature can be said to replace the biblical condition of man after the fall, then civil society can be said to replace the state of grace.[7] Civil society is man's only salvation from the solitary, poor, nasty, brutish and short life in the state of nature. Nor is it a compromise between the best and the worst of all possible worlds as hedonists of old were inclined to believe.

On the contrary, it alone ensures the maximum satisfaction of insatiable human appetites. Indeed, the fundamental purpose or end of the state is 'commodious living'; it sets out to 'furnish the citizens abundantly with all good things . . . which are conducive to delectation'.[8] Strauss explains that this is possible only because Hobbes believed in the limitless conquest of nature.[9] The latter is, in Strauss's view, one of the great hallmarks of modernity. Modernity is animated by man's determination to conquer chance and become the complete master of his destiny. Machiavelli's desire to subdue Fortuna is the same idea in its embryonic form. It takes a more radical form in Hobbes's faith in the scientific revolution's ability to force nature to yield to human desire. The idea is central to what Strauss calls the 'modern project'. The latter is the full-blown version of the determination to triumph over nature and conquer chance.

The 'modern project' that has animated Western civilization for the last 200 years aims to establish an affluent universal society that subsumes a multiplicity of cultures. It is a vision of a world in which both scarcity and the ravages of war are absent.[10] In Strauss's view, Hobbes is the true father of this ill-conceived dream. It is true that Hobbes did not envisage either a universal community or the abolition of either war or capital punishment; nevertheless, Strauss argues that these are logically required by his conception of politics. Men enter into society in order to safeguard their lives, and particularly to avoid violent death. The continued existence of both capital punishment and war are therefore incompatible with the ends of society. War can only be abolished if men cease to live in distinct groups characterized by mutual hatred and hostility. It is the failure of this modern project and of the belief in the viability of this project that is the source of the 'crisis' of modernity. Hobbes's philosophy is only the first stage or 'wave' of modernity.[11] He represents modernity in its youthful exuberance – confident, bold, full of expectation and undaunted by self-doubt. As Strauss puts it, there is in Hobbes's work a conspicuous absence of the 'Scipionic dream' that reminds men of the ultimate futility of all that men do.[12]

In Strauss's view, Hobbes's political hedonism is a doctrine that 'has revolutionized human life everywhere on a scale never yet approached by any other teaching'.[13] Indeed, political hedonism gives the whole of modernity its character. For Strauss, what is characteristic of modernity is the belief that mastery over nature can replace mastery over oneself. In other words, a society that overcomes scarcity through the technological mastery over nature does not require the virtue of moderation and self-restraint. On the contrary, perpetual consumption, greed and love of luxury are not only harmless, they are beneficial. They may be private vices, but they are also public benefits. Although Strauss does not refer to him, Bernard de Mandeville expresses most colorfully Strauss's sentiments regarding this quintessentially modern phenomenon. In *Fable of the Bees*, or 'private vices, public benefits' as the poem is sub-titled, Mandeville writes:

> Thus every Part was full of vice,
> Yet the whole Mass a Paradise;
> Such were the Blessings of the State;
> Their Crimes conspir'd to make them great:
> And Virtue, who from Politicks
> Had learn'd a Thousand Cunning Tricks
> Was, by their happy influence,
> Made Friends with Vice: And ever since,
> The worst of all the Multitude
> Did something for the Common Good.[14]

In Strauss's view, the idea that man's most hateful qualities fit him for the happiest and most flourishing society is the brainchild of Hobbes. And no one can fail to see that the idea of a happy and harmonious society held together by greed, self-indulgence and the basest instinct of mankind is irresistible. Men have never failed to be lured by easy solutions and magical cures, or by the belief that it is possible to achieve excellence without effort.

Strauss is not alone in finding modernity obsessed with easy solutions. Sheldon Wolin and Jürgen Habermas have pointed to this phenomenon as a hallmark of modernity. Wolin has noted the ascendancy of methodological and organizational ideas. Politics has become a matter of organization, and political science a matter of method. Wolin surmises that: 'method, like organization, is the salvation of puny men, the compensatory device for individual foibles, the gadget which allows mediocrity to transcend its limitations'.[15]

Similarly, Habermas has observed that the trend in political science is to assume that individual morality plays no significant role in politics. The individual or the individual *psyche* is no longer the unit of analysis in politics. Habermas points out that the whole conception of order changes as the domain being ordered shifts from the individual *psyche* to the external conditions. The result is that 'the order of virtuous conduct is changed into the regulation of social intercourse':

> The engineers of the correct order can disregard the categories of ethical social intercourse and confine themselves to the construction of conditions under which human beings, just like objects within nature, will necessarily behave in a calculable manner.[16]

It seems to be taken for granted today that the political problem *par excellence* is organizational not moral. As critics of Karl Popper have observed, Popper's 'social engineer' is charged with the improvement of society, but he has none of the characteristics of the great legislators, who are said to have the ability of writing their laws on people's hearts.[17] Plato had taught that even the best legal organization and the best set of laws will fail to provide even a modestly just society unless these laws are inscribed in the hearts of citizens. Citizens inclined to take advantage of loopholes in the laws will spend their days making more laws to remedy the loopholes of old laws and then newer laws to remedy the new laws *ad infinitum*. The process would be as hopeless as cutting off a hydra's head – twelve more will grow in its place![18]

In the ancient view, the most ingenious social organization and the best set of laws will not allow the state to transcend the limitations of its human material. But in Hobbes's view, as Strauss understands him, the state can be constructed like a machine that flourishes, not despite its morally flawed human material, but because of it. This is the essence of Hobbes's political hedonism. The idea is as seductive as the advertisements that promise a healthy and trim figure without diet or exercise.

Hobbes's political hedonism bequeathed to modernity two connected but equally misguided ideas that in Strauss's view will prove to be the undoing of Western civilization. First, there is no conflict between the interests of individuals and those of the whole. Individuals need not be prepared to sacrifice their interests for the community. On the contrary, they can expect to further their private interests by being a part of civil society. Furthermore, concern with their private interests, pleasure and the pursuit of wealth, is not a threat to the well-being of the commonwealth. The second idea is closely connected to the first. It is the idea that a technological society would provide a successful means to the realization of the modern end of politics, namely, the maximum satisfaction of desires. Indeed, the first idea is parasitic on the second. For Strauss, it is plausible to argue that the function of civil society is to maximize the satisfaction of our desires and appetites *only* if the technological mastery over nature is believed to be possible.

Strauss believes that the ancients knew that the mastery over nature cannot replace the mastery over oneself. The ancients were wise enough to foresee the pitfalls of modern Western civilization. Strauss is convinced that the ancients knew the truth of which we have now become so painfully aware, but of which Hobbes was totally oblivious – namely, that a civilization that is committed to the unlimited technological mastery over nature threatens the survival of man. Strauss's claim may seem extravagant, but an examination of the myth of Prometheus as told by Plato in the *Protagoras* may give some plausibility to his thesis. Strauss often points to this myth, and it may well be useful to examine Plato's account of it.

According to Protagoras, there was once a time when no mortal creatures existed. Then the gods formed the mortal creatures. When they were ready to bring them into the light, they charged Prometheus and Epimetheus with the task of allotting to them powers and equipping them with the means of survival. Epimetheus begged Prometheus to allow him to make the distribution. It was then agreed that Epimetheus would complete the task and Prometheus would inspect it. Epimetheus ensured the survival of each species by giving it either strength or speed or fertility. He also provided each species with furs, feathers or thick skin to protect it from the elements. Epimetheus, however, made a grave error. He distributed all the available powers to the brutes and forgot the needs of man.

When Prometheus came to inspect the work, he found man 'naked, unshod, unbedded and unarmed'.[19] To save him from complete annihilation, Prometheus stole fire and with it the gift of skill in the arts from the dwelling of Athena and Hephaestus. Consequently, man was able to develop a sufficient amount of 'technical skill' to provide himself with nurture. However, lacking strength, men continued to be devoured, and so their continued survival was endangered. Realizing that they could not be self-sufficient, men attempted to come together in cities. This attempt, however, proved unsuccessful.

Protagoras explains than men injured one another and so were unable to live in society 'for want of political skill'.[20] As it became evident that technical skill alone was not sufficient to prevent the total destruction of the race, Zeus resolved to give man the highest gift he could offer – namely, the art of politics.

Fearing the total destruction of the race, Zeus sent Hermes to impart to men the qualities of respect for others and a sense of justice, so as to bring order to our cities and create a bond of friendship and union.[21]

The myth teaches the hard truth that our society is only as good as ourselves, and that there are no easy solutions or magical cures to political problems. Technical skill or the mastery over nature cannot replace the mastery over oneself. No society can exist in conditions of peace, order and harmony without just individuals, or individuals willing to sacrifice their own interests for the sake of the collective good. No amount of technical skill in the arts and crafts that are conducive to 'commodious living' can possibly save us from annihilation if we are unjust. Strauss is not alone in thinking that the ancients understood something of our present predicament. Interpreting the myth, Werner Jaeger explains that

> the civilization which could be produced by Promethean man by subduing the elementary forces of nature was a mere technical civilization. It resulted in violence and destruction and humanity seemed about to perish miserably through its own invention.[22]

In other words, unless technical ability is governed and hence restrained by knowledge of right, it threatens to devour its own creators. This is one of the central themes of Strauss's work and the reason for his critique of modernity. The latter frees technology from all moral and political restraint.[23] Modern man seems to have an undaunted faith in technology or the use of science to master nature. This unrestrained passion for the mastery of nature has brought us to the brink of annihilation. Modernity follows Hobbes in thinking of technology as a means to the satisfaction of human desires and appetites. But this is a never-ending project, because desires and appetites are by their very nature insatiable.

It is therefore not surprising that modernity is committed to the endless mastery over the infinite spaces for its own sake: for the sake of mastery. Since man is a part of nature, the mastery over nature leads to the mastery of man over man, and hence to tyranny and the dehumanization of man. Strauss maintains that the ancients knew this. They knew that man's inventions inevitably 'become his masters and destroyers'.[24] That is one of the reasons they rejected the 'modern project' of a universal affluent society. The latter presupposes the publicization of science and hence its vulgarization into technology. Scientists cannot make their science public without expecting it to be used by the herd for its own purposes. The publicization of science therefore threatens the tranquility of society and debases the quest for knowledge into a quest for mastery.

The modern liberation of the passions is premised on technology's capacity to minister to human desires. Modernity begins with the liberation of the 'useful' passions, but ends by refusing to put any restraint over any passions unless they are conclusively and indubitably proven to be harmful to the interests of others. It therefore develops an aversion to restraint *qua* restraint, and embraces a conception of liberty that is almost indistinguishable from license. It fails to see that the liberation of the passions is destructive of the well-being and preservation of society. Society cannot hope to preserve itself without the virtue of self-restraint, or the capacity of just men to subordinate their own interests to those of the whole. This is why Sophists like Protagoras and Thrasymachus agree with Socrates that just individuals are necessary for the survival of the collectivity. It is precisely this agreement between Socrates and Thrasymachus that, in Strauss's view, enables Socrates to shame Thrasymachus into silence in the first book of Plato's *Republic*.[25]

Hobbes is not a new Thrasymachus; he cannot be shamed into silence. He is convinced that the publication of his doctrine will not threaten the peace, order and preservation of the political community. In Strauss's view, Hobbes believed he had discovered a liberating truth; one that need not be kept hidden.

Hobbes's political hedonism is not unconnected to his other outrageously novel doctrine, that of 'political atheism'. Like hedonism, atheism is not a novel doctrine, but according to Strauss, *'political* atheism', like *political* hedonism, has no equivalent in the ancient world. Strauss admires Edmund Burke for recognizing the nature of this 'epoch-making change', regarding which Burke wrote:

> Boldness formerly was not the character of atheists as such. They were even of a character nearly the reverse; they were formerly like the old Epicureans, rather an unenterprising race. But of late they have grown active, designing, turbulent, and seditious.[26]

What is 'political' about modern atheism is that it is public, overt and unconcealed; as such, it is a 'distinctly modern phenomenon'. Strauss explains that the reason for this change in the character of atheism is due to the fact that the moderns, following Hobbes, no longer believe that religion is necessary to the peace, order and stability of political society. As Strauss writes: 'No pre-modern atheist doubted that social life required belief in, and worship of, God or gods.'[27] Political hedonism coupled with political atheism makes the esotericism of antiquity entirely superfluous. It is, therefore, no exaggeration to say that modernity is characterized above all else by its openness.

Hobbes is quintessentially modern precisely because he drops all decorum, all appearances and all esotericism. Strauss describes him as 'that impudent, impish, and iconoclastic extremist, that first plebeian philosopher, who is so enjoyable a writer because of his almost boyish straightforwardness, his never failing humanity, and his marvelous clarity and force'.[28]

For Hobbes, the esoteric writing of antiquity was dispensable because moral virtue and fear of the Lord are unnecessary for the construction of a good political order. There is no need to restrain selfishness and egoism or to promote moral goodness and the readiness for self-sacrifice. Myths about the afterlife are unnecessary to restrain self-interest; the latter, far from being a menace to political order, is most advantageous to it as long as it is informed. Enlightened self-interest is the true foundation of political society. Enlightenment is, therefore, the true handmaid of political well-being. Myths and pious lies can in these modern times be dispensed with. Philosophy poses no threat to the city; on the contrary, it is its best ally.

Hobbes's novel doctrines succeeded in changing altogether the ancient conceptions of man, society, politics, virtue and even philosophy itself. But Hobbes could not have exerted this monumental influence without the mediation of the 'judicious Locke' who refrained from mentioning Hobbes's 'justly decried name'.[29] Hobbes was much too outrageous a writer to have exerted his influence single-handedly; men are generally suspicious of novelty, as Machiavelli knew so well.

In Strauss's view, Locke's political teaching is the same as Hobbes's in decisive respects. Locke shares Hobbes's view of man and of the state of nature. Man is not a creature who is endowed by his creator with a moral law inscribed in his heart or conscience.[30] For Strauss, man's conscience was traditionally regarded as the voice of God within and the sanction for the moral law. Like Hobbes, Locke regards conscience as nothing more than private opinion. The only sanction for the law of nature is the right to the executive power of the law of nature. Without the latter, the law of nature would be but empty words. Locke's state of nature, like Hobbes's is characterized by 'want of society'. It is a condition of war, full of fear and danger.[31] Contrary to the traditional Christian belief, God has not given us all things richly. On the contrary, the state of nature is not a state of plenty but of penury, where men are 'needy and wretched'. The gifts of nature are worthless; everything of value is the result of human labour or toil. Civil society is the salvation from this miserable condition of life. It liberates labor from the confines of nature by the invention of money which secures comfortable self-preservation. The latter is the end of the state; but it requires not so much knives and guns as victuals.[32] Civil society makes possible the quest for unlimited appropriation.[33] Strauss writes:

> the burden of his chapter on property is that covetousness and concupiscence, far from being essentially evil or foolish, are, if properly channeled, eminently beneficial and reasonable. . . . By building civil society on 'the low but solid ground' of selfishness, or of certain 'private vices', one will achieve much greater 'public benefits' than by futilely appealing to virtue which is by nature 'unendowed'.[34]

Locke had complained that the ancient philosophers had left virtue 'unendowed' because they could not establish the connection between personal happiness and the moral law. Christianity alone ensures that the scales are weighted heavily on the side of virtue. Strauss suggests that this is the reason that the 'judicious Locke' did not write as openly and as candidly as that impish schoolboy whose philosophy he followed so diligently.

Unlike Hobbes, Locke was cautious in the manner in which he expressed himself. Even though he regarded the law of nature, as did Hobbes, to be no more than instrumental rules conducive to public happiness, he adhered outwardly to natural law in the traditional Christian sense as a moral law backed by Divine sanction.

Strauss genuinely admires Locke's caution and indicates that he had learnt it from the ancients. In his *Reasonableness of Christianity*, Locke observes that Socrates opposed and laughed at Greek polytheism, and we see how they rewarded him for it. In contrast, Plato, and other sober philosophers, were 'fain' in 'their outward professions and worship' to 'go with the herd'.[35] Locke seems to endorse Strauss's own view of the differences between Socrates and Plato, and to follow Strauss in admiring the caution of the latter. Strauss points out that Locke did not regard 'the conduct of the ancient philosophers as reprehensible'.[36] On the contrary, he believed that

cautious speech is legitimate if unqualified frankness would hinder a noble work one is trying to achieve or expose one to persecution or endanger the public peace; and legitimate caution is perfectly compatible with going with the herd in one's outward professions or with using ambiguous language or with so involving one's sense that one cannot easily be understood.[37]

Strauss appears to castigate Locke for following Hobbes and not the Bible, but all the while he is paying him a compliment; for he (Locke) combines boldness of thought with the moderation of speech characteristic of the ancient philosophers. Like the latter, he thought it legitimate to use noble prejudices for a good cause. He knew that the well-being of society depends on the belief in the existence of a natural law promulgated by an Almighty God with sufficient power to enforce it with rewards and punishments in the afterlife. He knew that unassisted reason could not show a connection between virtue and personal prosperity in this life because such a connection does not exist.[38] Like Strauss, he knew that there is a clear connection between 'public happiness' or 'the prosperity and temporal happiness of a people' and the general compliance with 'several moral rules'. He also knew that these rules cannot be considered instrumental or hypothetical, since their effectiveness depends on their being regarded as absolute and applicable at all times without qualification.

Despite a significant residue of ancient wisdom, Locke's philosophy is, in Strauss's view, thoroughly modern. For Locke, the end of civil society is not excellence, but 'commodious living'.[39] Selfishness and the basest instincts of mankind are the low but solid foundations of the state.[40] Locke's philosophy involves a 'negation of nature'; movement towards happiness is still movement away from the state of nature.[41] Locke's judicious caution therefore serves only to entrench modernity by making Hobbes's ideas respectable.

Strauss's interpretation of Hobbes and Locke is not what is at issue here. They are simply characters in a drama that explains how we have come to live in a world so different from that of the ancients. The ideas he attributes to them are at the heart of modernity as Strauss understands it. They help to explain what is at issue between ancients and moderns, which is the central theme of Strauss's work.

The fundamental differences between ancients and moderns follow from the assumptions implied by the doctrines of political hedonism and political atheism; doctrines that overturn ancient wisdom. First, for the moderns, the function of society is the maximum satisfaction of desires. Secondly, the conquest of nature is a viable means to this end. Thirdly, the assumption is that the liberation of the passions is not harmful to society, because there is no conflict between the interests of the individual and those of the whole. Fourthly, religion is not necessary to ensure the required self-restraint beneficial for society; enlightened self-interest is sufficient for accomplishing this end. From these fundamental assumptions several other elements emerge that define the character of modernity. These can be summarized as follows: (i) the inviolability of the individual, (ii) the disappearance of the public realm, (iii) the transformation of the idea of virtue, (iv) the rejection of nature, (v) value relativism, and (vi) openness or the rejection of esotericism. I shall discuss each of these in turn.

(i) In opposition to the ancients, the moderns reject the idea that there is an inevitable conflict between the interests of the individual and that of the whole. They affirm the inviolability of the individual: an idea that is at the heart of the modern conception of natural rights. Society exists in order to safeguard the rights of individuals. The rights of the individual are inalienable and cannot be sacrificed for the sake of the whole. The whole exists for the sake of the individual and not the reverse. The asocial nature of man and the foundation of civil society in consent serves to reaffirm the priority of the individual.

For the ancients, man is a political animal; he is endowed by nature with potentialities for excellence that can be brought to fruition only in the context of political community. Reared in the proper setting, he is the most excellent of creatures; but left uncultivated, he is capable of depravity that far surpasses anything ever encountered in the animal kingdom. Political community is therefore necessary for man to be fully human. Its purpose is to make possible the highest life for man, which is that of intellectual excellence. Its existence and preservation must be given priority over that of the individual. The community is prior to the individual because the fully human individual cannot exist outside the context of civil society. Political society has an exalted end, though one that can only be realized by the few.

The political problem *par excellence* is to make man morally virtuous. For the ancients, moral virtue consists fundamentally in self-restraint or the subordination of what Plato describes as the 'multiform beast within' to the rule of reason. The health of both individuals and collectivities depends on the subordination of the 'lower' to the 'higher'. The morally virtuous man is one who is ready and willing to sacrifice his interests and perhaps even his life to the whole. This understanding of moral virtue is logically necessary in view of the impossibility of reconciling the interests of the individual with that of the whole.

(ii)   The ancient secret to the socialization of the individual was well understood by Machiavelli. He explained that selfish ambition is the key to social success. The pursuit of honor and glory was the ancient way of mobilizing selfishness for the sake of the common good. Machiavelli railed against Christianity because its private or feminine conception of virtue deprived the state of the salutary effects of the heroic or manly virtues and so rendered the state weak.

Modernity follows Machiavelli in expelling contemplation or the 'highest end' of politics altogether. But it goes even further than

Machiavelli; it eliminates glory from the public realm and makes the base desires of the multitude the end of the state. In the modern view, the purpose of the state is to provide its citizens with all the good things conducive to delectation. It regards private life and not public life as the means to satisfaction. In *The Political Philosophy of Hobbes*, Strauss explains that Hobbes looked at the desire for honor and glory with suspicion. Far from thinking them a solid foundation of the state, he thought of them as the cause of war. Men are by these passions (Hobbes did not consider them virtues) dazzled and made blind.[42] They are inseparable from vanity, which he regarded as the root of all evil. Instead of vanity, Hobbes trusted fear, and particularly the fear of violent death. Unlike vanity, fear made men wise. He therefore considered fear the sufficient motive for all right behavior. Strauss concludes that in doing so Hobbes discredits the aristocratic or heroic virtues, because fear and honor are irreconcilable.[43]

Hobbes replaces the pursuit of honor with the pursuit of wealth. The modern state must therefore free its citizens from public life so that they can pursue a private life of consumption and wealth. In other words, the function of the state is to maximize freedom, understood as absence of external restraint, to pursue private interests. Locke is credited with making the pursuit of wealth beyond what is necessary for a good life, respectable.

The ancients could not have dreamed of a political order founded in greed, consumption and the unrestrained pursuit of wealth. Two ideas at the heart of political hedonism make this new world conceivable; first, the belief that the basest instinct of mankind are a sufficiently solid foundation of civil society; secondly, the view that man's insatiable appetites can indeed be satisfied through the technical mastery over nature. In Strauss's view, the modern project is doomed to fail: selfishness cannot be mobilized for social purposes because it cannot transcend the inevitable conflict between the interests of individuals and those of the community. The selfish pursuit of honor and glory is a more viable and more prudent means to social success because it does not attempt to fly in the face of the truth about political things.

It is important not to misconstrue Strauss's regret at the disappearance of the public realm. Hannah Arendt too laments its disappearance in modern times; indeed, it is the central theme of her work. But her reasons for doing so are different from Strauss's.

She laments it because she values the manly virtues of display and virtuosity for their own sake. She thinks that the state's most exalted function is that of creating a public space in which citizens can pursue a modest immortality through great words and great deeds.[44] In contrast, Strauss laments the disappearance of the public realm primarily for the sake of the end it serves – namely, the preservation of the state without which the highest end of contemplation is unattainable.

(iii)   The modern conception of human virtue in general and justice in particular differs dramatically from that of the ancients. In Aristotle's view, virtue consists in magnanimity (or the virtues that contribute to individual excellence, albeit of the few) and justice (or the other-regarding virtues). The moderns reduce all virtues to justice, and leave magnanimity altogether out of account.[45] Self-regarding vices are of no concern to the state; not only can their presence not harm it, they are believed to be beneficial to the commonweal.

Not only do the moderns leave out of account what Aristotle regarded as the higher or superior part of virtue, they alter the complexion of justice itself. The moderns make justice identical with the social virtue of peaceableness, humanity and benevolence. In turn, vice becomes identical with offending others, vanity, pride and *amour propre*.[46]

(iv)   In the ancient view, nature is the standard and measure that is higher in dignity than civil society. A radically hierarchical nature indicates that the wise or superior should rule over the unwise or inferior. Wisdom is the title to sovereignty and must take precedence over consent.[47] Society must be organized with a view to the best, who are necessarily the few. In contrast, the moderns are characterized by animosity to nature and determination to thwart her, master her and make her yield to human will. They reject the natural hierarchy in favor of egalitarianism. They make consent the title to sovereignty and give it precedence over wisdom. The modern state therefore takes its bearings from the lowest common denominator, or the base life of the many.

(v)   Classical political philosophy is the quest for the good life according to nature. It presupposes that there is a good life for man dictated by nature, the superiority of which is immediately recognized by reason, at least that of the wise. Modernity follows Hobbes in denying that there is a good knowable by reason that is distinct from appetite or desire. It is not so much the hedonism of this position to which Strauss objects, but the publication of that hedonism in the form of Hobbes's political hedonism. The hedonism of the ancient Epicurians is necessarily vulgarized when published. Among the ancients it was moderated by the highest pleasure, that of contemplation. But for the vulgar hedonist, all pleasures are of equal worth. The belief that all pleasures are equal easily leads to the belief that all 'values' are of equal worth. As we shall see, this value relativism leads to the sort of 'nihilism' that Strauss associates with the more advanced stages of modernity.

In the final analysis, political hedonism makes the base life of the many the highest end of the political community. In so far as modernity exorcises from its political horizon the excellence of which only the few are capable, it can be made public without risk to the philosopher.

(vi) Despite the differences between modern and ancient political philosophy, the former nevertheless retains many of the unsettling truths of the latter, but it denies that these pose any danger to society.

For the ancients, philosophy harbors a profound indifference to the 'philosophies' of civil society because it doubts that there can be a rational justification of morality. In so doing, it threatens the well-being of the state because it undermines patriotism. For the moderns, the terrible truths of philosophy pose no threat to the peace, order and preservation of the city. That God is dead, and that there is no universal moral law backed by divine sanctions, can in these bold modern times be expressed publicly. The noble myths of old are no longer necessary in this brave new world. Enlightened self-interest and not myth are now of the essence. Philosophy can now become the city's best ally. This is precisely why modernity can dispense with esotericism, which for Strauss is identical to classical philosophy or ancient wisdom. This is the meaning of Strauss's often repeated claim that modernity consists above all else in the eclipse of classical political philosophy. But from Strauss's ancient perspective, modernity deludes itself into thinking that philosophical skepticism can be unleashed on a society without causing it any harm.

Although modern philosophy is public, it cannot be described as exoteric because it abolishes the distinction between esoteric and exoteric. Exoteric philosophy is the public form that ancient philosophy assumed when it ventured out into the public realm: it is 'political' philosophy. As Strauss never tires of repeating, modernity is the eclipse of political philosophy. Modern philosophy is not exoteric or political, because the latter presupposes the distinction between esoteric and exoteric that is a necessary part of ancient wisdom, whereas modernity is predicated on the abolition of the distinction itself. In Strauss's view, modernity replaces philosophy with propaganda, which is the public dissemination of doctrines (such as political hedonism and the mastery of nature) that are neither salutary nor possible.[48]

8

The Crisis of Modernity

Modernity is not identical to the crisis of Western civilization. It is a set of ill-conceived ideas that ultimately lead to that crisis. In its heyday or golden age, modernity is bold and self-confident. The first crisis of modernity erupts when confident exuberance gives way to self-doubt. Jean-Jacques Rousseau articulates this doubt, and Strauss therefore regards him as the representative of the first crisis of modernity.

Rousseau's denunciation of the character of modernity does not bring an end to modernity and a return to ancient sobriety. Despite his criticism of modernity, Rousseau does not abandon its fundamental premises, but forces it into a more radical direction. In so doing, he advances modernity, giving it new life, new confidence and a new vitality. This advanced modernity is manifest in the works of Hegel and Marx. It consists of a far more radical revolt against nature than was dreamt of by Hobbes. The project of advanced modernity is the complete triumph over nature, the transformation of human nature, and the creation of a universal and homogeneous state.

As long as the project of modernity is believed to be possible and good, it animates and inspires Western civilization. The second crisis of modernity, or the crisis of our time is the result of our loss of faith in the modern project. Western civilization is in crisis because it is unsure of itself. It no longer believes in the nobility of its own project. It has sunk into despair and nihilism. Value-free social science is a manifestation of that nihilism, but modern social science is oblivious to the trauma that it embodies. In this chapter I will describe Strauss's conception of the first crisis of modernity, the subsequent radicalization of the modern project, and the second crisis of modernity or the crisis of our time. Whether Strauss's interpretation of historical figures such as Rousseau, Hegel and Marx is accurate is not at issue. I will regard them simply as vehicles which enable Strauss to express his own conception of the modern world and what he believes to be the source of its malaise. Here as elsewhere, I will not pass judgement on Strauss's ideas. My intention is to express his views in a clear and systematic fashion that will do justice to the originality of his position.

ROUSSEAU AND THE FIRST CRISIS OF MODERNITY

Rousseau was not the first to feel that 'the modern venture was a radical error and to seek the remedy in a return to classical thought'.[1] Strauss mentions Jonathan Swift, but does not elaborate except to say that, unlike Swift, Rousseau was not a 'reactionary', which means that he was not entirely true to the ancients. Rousseau shares the ancient understanding of the political problem, but he rejects the solution. In the final analysis, Rousseau 'abandoned himself to modernity'.[2] Understanding the ancient content of Rousseau's thought on the one hand, and its modern content on the other, illustrates what Strauss believes is at issue between ancients and moderns.

Strauss's account of the ancient content of Rousseau's thought is one of the clearest and most concise accounts of Strauss's view of the ancient understanding of the nature of politics and its relation to philosophy.

Rousseau rejects Hobbes's political hedonism. He denies that enlightened self-interest can be the foundation of civil society. He is therefore critical of the modern liberation of acquisitiveness and greed. Society cannot be erected on self-interest, no matter how enlightened. The city needs virtue in the old sense of self-restraint, courage, steadfastness and loyalty. Societies must defend themselves against external enemies. They must therefore have citizens with courage, conviction, loyalty and devotion to the common good. Self-interested calculators are incapable of glorious or extraordinary acts of self-sacrifice.

To survive at all, let alone thrive, societies must cultivate citizens who are devoted to the common good and willing to place it ahead of their own interests. If they hope to inspire such love and devotion, societies must have a way of life that is unique and distinctive. What is required are national and exclusive institutions animated by a national 'philosophy'.[3] The latter is 'a way of thinking that is not transferable to other societies'.[4] In short, society must be animated by 'a spirit of patriotism' which is quite compatible with 'national hatreds', a 'warlike spirit', or what Strauss likes to refer to as 'waspishness'.[5]

Rousseau shares the ancient conception of the city, of philosophy, and of the conflict between them.[6] Like the ancients, he understands the conflict as a necessary consequence of the nature of the antagonists. Whereas society is 'closed', exclusive and particular, philosophy or science is 'cosmopolitan' or universalistic. Philosophy is therefore indifferent to the petty differences between nationalities: 'Science or philosophy necessarily weakens the power of the national "philosophies" and therewith the attachment of the citizens to the particular way of life, or the manners of their community.'[7]

The plight of Gulliver among the Lilliputians is particularly illustrative of the danger that philosophy presents to the city. Gulliver's physical superiority to the Lilliputians represents the superiority of the philosopher.[8] A man of Gulliver's intelligence could not help but be indifferent to the trivial matters to which the Lilliputians attached unspeakable importance. A man who is indifferent to the very things that the Lilliputians are ready to die for, cannot be trusted. When the Emperor's grandson cut his finger in the course of breaking his breakfast egg on the big end, the Emperor passed a law forbidding the breaking of eggs at the big end. However, there were among his subjects some very committed Big-Endians who would rather die than obey such a law! Luckily, the neighbouring Belfuscu was sympathetic to their cause and gave them refuge, and this was the cause of many wars between the two cities.[9] The national 'philosophies' are to the philosophers what the dispute between the Lilliputians and the Big-Endians is to Gulliver. The Lilliputians can hardly be blamed for considering Gulliver dangerous. The cold and dispassionate rationalism of philosophy is destructive of the national 'philosophies'.

Society requires entrenched opinions, certainty and unquestioning loyalty. Only in this manner can it hope to elicit conformity, obedience and voluntary compliance to the laws of the community. In contrast, the philosopher must 'follow his own genius with sincerity'.[10]

Perhaps most importantly, Rousseau followed the ancients in thinking that political virtue requires the support of religion: 'Virtue apparently requires support by faith or theism, although not necessarily by monotheism.'[11] And, 'society requires that its members adhere without question to certain religious beliefs'.[12] It seems that 'these salutary certainties' or 'sacred dogmas' are threatened by philosophy or science. The latter fosters a dangerous skepticism. Moreover, philosophy or science is dedicated to the pursuit of truth as such, 'regardless of its utility', and so may well lead to dangerous and harmful truths.[13]

Philosophy is dangerous to the city for other reasons. Science and philosophy require leisure, 'which is falsely distinguished from idleness'. The city requires that its citizens be productive, active and busy contributing to the common good. As Rousseau put it, 'every idle citizen is a scoundrel'. The good citizen is devoted to his fellow citizens and to his duties to them; in contrast, the scientist or philosopher, 'selfishly pursues his pleasure'.[14]

Despite Rousseau's apparently passionate attack on science and philosophy in the *First Discourse*, Strauss argues that he should not be understood to have unconditionally castigated science and philosophy as enemies of virtue and the city. He explains that what is under attack is not science as such,

> but popularized science or the diffusion of scientific knowledge. . . . Science must remain the preserve of a small minority; it must be kept secret from the common man. Since every book is accessible not only to the small minority but to all who can read, Rousseau was forced by his principle to present his philosophic or scientific teaching with a great deal of reserve.[15]

Strauss maintains that the intent of the *First Discourse* is 'to warn away from science, not all men, but only the common men'.[16] He suggests that when Rousseau rejects science as simply bad, he speaks as a common man addressing common men – not philosophers or 'those who are not subjugated by the opinions of their century, of their country, or of their society'.[17] Rousseau looks down on society because he recognizes that its foundations are in 'the needs of the body' whereas he finds in the 'joys and raptures' of 'pure and disinterested contemplation' a 'perfect happiness and a godlike self-sufficiency'.[18] Rousseau follows the ancients in regarding philosophy as the supreme pleasure for which only the few are fit; it is therefore not something he is willing to renounce.

Despite the danger that philosophy poses to the city, Rousseau believes, with the ancients, that it could be made to serve the city in a useful and even necessary capacity. For example, philosophy can be useful to a corrupt society: it can discover 'palliatives' for the 'prevailing abuses', it can undermine the sacred dogmas and ultimately lead to the collapse of a bad city. In other words, philosophy is good for a bad society, but bad for a good one. After the revolution, it must retreat, it must remain the hidden preserve of the few 'great geniuses', 'privileged souls' or 'true philosophers'. It is good for the latter, but bad for 'the peoples' or 'the public' or 'the common men' or '*les hommes vulgaires*'.[19] But all this is true only of popularized philosophy or the diffusion of the scientific or theoretical aspect of philosophy. There is another aspect of philosophy that can be useful even to a good society. If we distinguish between two parts or aspects of philosophy, we can see how philosophy can be made useful to the city, not just in times of corruption, but at all times.

Strauss suggests that Rousseau recognizes what the ancients have always known, namely that there are two parts to philosophy: a purely theoretical science or wisdom which Strauss thinks we can call 'metaphysics', and a political or practical science which Strauss calls 'Socratic wisdom'.[20] (Strauss has the Platonic Socrates in mind.) Socratic wisdom is 'ancillary' or subordinate to pure or theoretical science. It consists in placing theoretical science in the service of the city and of virtue. Virtue is the 'sublime science of the simple souls'.[21] The function of Socratic wisdom is to use the intelligence and cleverness acquired from theoretical science in order to defend the 'science of the simple souls' against sophistry.[22] This is a necessary task even in a good society, because virtue, like innocence, is easily lost, and requires constant vigilance if it is to be sustained. Socratic wisdom is not for the sake of Socrates, who is not a simple soul; it is for the sake of the simple souls or the people. The true philosopher is therefore the 'guardian' of virtue, and hence of the city itself.[23]

In contrast to 'Socratic wisdom', the theoretical part of science does not serve society. It is dedicated to the pursuit of truth for its own sake regardless of its utility. It invariably leads to harmful truths and to even more harmful skepticism. This part of science must remain the preserve of 'the few who are by nature destined to guide the peoples',[24] it must remain 'esoteric'.[25]

For Strauss, Rousseau shares the ancient understanding of the 'fundamental problem of civil society'.[26] His doctrine of the legislator is quintessentially classical and serves to clarify what the ancients regarded as the fundamental political problem. The legislator plays an important role in civil society that is not unlike that of the philosopher. The legislator is the father of a nation; he is a man of superior intelligence who ascribes 'divine origin to a code which he has devised' and convinces the people of its goodness.[27] Strauss comments that: 'It goes without saying that the arguments by which the legislator convinces the citizens of his divine mission or of the divine sanction of his code are necessarily of doubtful solidity.'[28] Supposedly, the 'simple souls' will be unable to detect the 'doubtful solidity' of these arguments.

We are led to conclude that the well-being of society depends on 'a specific obfuscation against which philosophy necessarily revolts'.[29] Nor does this obfuscation ever become unnecessary. One might think that the legislator is needed only in the infancy of society; once its legal code is established, the wise legislation will be accepted on account of its proved wisdom and the belief in the superhuman origin of the code will be unnecessary. But Strauss denies that this is possible:

> this suggestion overlooks the fact that the living respect for old laws, 'the prejudice of antiquity' which is indispensable for the health of society, can only with difficulty survive the public questioning of the accounts regarding their origin. . . . Society has a continuous need for at least an equivalent to the mysterious and awe-inspiring action of the legislator.[30]

The problem of political society is that man does not by nature submit to the collectivity or give up his interests for the sake of the whole. He must therefore be 'collectivized', made virtuous, or fit for society. But the process by which he is so transformed involves continuous obfuscation. However, the success of the process depends on forgetting that the transformation is possible only through myth and obfuscation. As Nietzsche maintained, forgetfulness is necessary for life.[31] Philosophy recommends the substitution of its own sober wakefulness for a forgetful stupor. And this, to say the least, is highly paradoxical.

Strauss's admiration for Rousseau has its source in the fact that he shares the ancient account of the 'fundamental problem of civil society' and understands the solution offered by the ancients. But alas, the spell of modernity makes him unwilling to accept that solution. He therefore renounces the doctrine of the legislator in the name of the quintessentially modern doctrine of individual freedom and democratic sovereignty. In so doing, Rousseau forces modernity to become far more radical than ever before.

Rousseau departs from the ancients and radicalizes modernity in the following way. First, he regards nature in general, and the nature of man in particular, as 'subhuman' and sets out to transform it. Secondly, he insists on the radical independence of the individual, and therefore, believes that a free and virtuous society requires democracy or equality.[32]

Unlike the ancients, Rousseau does not find in nature the roots of civil society. He turns to nature only to reject it. Man in the state of nature has no given or fixed nature as such, he is infinitely malleable. His humanity or rationality is acquired, not natural. Reason emerges in the process of satisfying bodily wants. In the early stages of human history, these wants are easy to satisfy. With the increase in population, this is no longer the case, and man is forced to think in order to survive. Man is therefore shaped by the circumstances of his existence. He is the product of blind fate. Rousseau, however, wishes man to become master of his fate by mastering the blind forces that have shaped him.[33] In this way, man shapes himself in the process of overcoming nature in his quest for self-preservation.[34] Nature is something to be overcome. Rousseau therefore radicalizes the modern revolt against nature. The first signs of that revolt are to be found in Hobbes's denial of the hierarchical character of nature and his insistence on the radical equality of all men. But Hobbes recognized that nature and human nature still set limits to what man could achieve by means of political artifice. For Rousseau, nature is putty. It sets no limits on what people may do or achieve. This explains the radical nature of modern politics. Modernity abandons every shred of caution and moderation in political affairs because of the grandiose nature of its expectations. Rousseau's desire to transform or master nature advances modernity or inaugurates what Strauss calls the second 'wave' of modernity.[35] (Strauss's three 'waves' of modernity are reminiscent of the three 'waves' of Book v of Plato's *Republic*. They are waves of laughter as well as obstacles to the realization of the best regime or of the only human happiness that is available to man *qua* man.)

The second way in which Rousseau advances modernity is by

rejecting the ancient solution to the political problem. The problem is how to reconcile duty and inclination or civil society and selfishness. The solution is to introduce or pray for a legislator with Socratic wisdom capable of convincing the people by obfuscation and clever rhetoric to adopt his code. Rousseau rejects the classical solution because it threatens the freedom and sovereignty of the people. In his novel view, politics becomes a matter of submitting to laws one has made for oneself. Individual consent is not only the root of legal obligation, as it was for Hobbes and Locke, it is the source of law and legislation itself. Rousseau clings to the 'primacy of the individual' far more tenaciously than either Hobbes or Locke.[36] He believes in the possibility of a much more perfect reconciliation between individual inclinations and the necessities of social life.

ADVANCED MODERNITY

I will use the term 'advanced modernity' to refer to a more radical phase of modernity which Strauss believes Rousseau's philosophy made possible. In its advanced stage, modernity is bolder and more self-confident than it was in its early incarnation. Its project is more grandiose than anything that the fathers of modernity could have imagined. Advanced modernity is characterized by an unrivaled optimism that is reflected in the belief in progress. According to Strauss, the idea of progress consisted in the following elements. First, the development of human thought as a whole was to progress to a level that would surpass all previous thought. This new-found enlightenment was not to be limited to the few, but was to be widely diffused throughout the population. Secondly, there was to be a 'necessary parallelism between intellectual and social progress': social and political institutions would reflect the newly acquired enlightenment of the population.[37] Thirdly, progress involved the perfection of the understanding in relation to the arts and crafts.[38] This means that 'philosophy or science was no longer to be understood as essentially contemplative and proud, but as active and charitable'.[39] It was to be cultivated for 'the relief of man's estate'.[40] The mastery over nature was believed to contribute not only to universal prosperity, but also to universal freedom and justice. This ideal was articulated by Hegel and Marx.

The project of advanced modernity is most succinctly summed up in the establishment of a universal, affluent and homogeneous state, characterized by freedom, justice and equality. For such a state, evil and war are distant memories of a barbaric past to which it is impossible to return. There will be no 'telluric catastrophes', but only a 'solid floor below which man can no longer sink'.[41]

The *same* modern project animates modernity, East and West. His preference for the United States over the Soviet Union notwithstanding, Strauss believes that the two superpowers are animated by the same ill-conceived and ultimately deadly dream. Both the United States and the Soviet Union aspire to world dominion: they want to subdue the world and make it prosperous.[42] According to Strauss, this goal is expressed in the term 'underdeveloped nations': 'the expression implies the resolve to develop them fully, i.e. to make them either Communist or Western, and this despite the fact that the West claims to stand for cultural pluralism'.[43] The Americans believe that the whole globe has to be democratic if it is to be safe for Western democracy.[44] It seems that the pluralistic ideology of the West is a fraud, though not a particularly pious one.

Since the leading ideologies of East and West have the same roots, Strauss remarks that the possible victory of communism does not mean the 'triumph of Eastern despotism over Western culture'.[45] On the contrary, he thinks it would be the victory of the West, for the communist manifesto is a synthesis of British industry, French Revolution and German philosophy.[46]

All this is not to say that there is no difference between the United States and the Soviet Union. It is only to say that the difference is not in the nature of their dream. The difference lies in how much of freedom and morality they are willing to sacrifice in order to attain their end.[47]

THE CRISIS OF OUR TIME

A civilization must be animated by a set of ideas that is believed to be noble or superior to those of any other society. A civilization is lost when its founding ideas, ideals and beliefs begin to lose their grip in the hearts and minds of its citizens. As long as the project of modernity was believed to be possible, it provided Western civilization with its life and vitality.

The second crisis of modernity, the crisis of our time, seems to Strauss to be far more serious and deadly than the first. As with the first crisis, the second crisis is the result of the doubt of the project of modernity. This time, however, doubt has not been replaced by new faith, but has entrenched itself and turned into nihilism.

The crisis of the West 'consists in the West's having become uncertain of its purpose'.[48] The purpose of the West as Strauss understands it is the creation of a prosperous society embracing equally all human beings, a universal league of free and equal nations each consisting of free and equal men and women. Western Civilization no longer believes in either the nobility or the viability of its own project.[49] For Strauss, this is not surprising in view of the untenability of the modern project. It is inevitable that a civilization motivated by such an ill-conceived ideal will in time discover this fact. The discovery is bound to be accompanied by despair, nihilism, hopelessness and decline. This is the phenomenon that Strauss understands as the 'crisis' of the West. The crisis is not the same as defeat or destruction: the West could very well go down in honor, 'certain of its purpose'. Crisis is atrophy from within. In what follows, I hope to explain Strauss's understanding of how and why this crisis has come about, and what, if anything, we can do to save our civilization from annihilation.

First, the West has lost its optimistic belief in progress which is at the heart of its project. Modern natural science predicts a possible end to the existence of the earth and a certain end to its inhabitability.[50] (Strauss seems to believe in the plausibility of this view, since he doubts the Aristotelian belief in the eternity of the world.)

Secondly, as the United Nations has illustrated, a league of nations cannot succeed in abolishing wars, in particular wars of aggression. To do this, it must assume that the present boundaries are just. But as Strauss remarks, this is a 'pious fraud whose fraudulence is more evident than its piety'.[51] The whole idea flies in the face of historical experience. Men have lived, and always will live, in societies characterized by mutual antagonisms and hostilities. There are limits to human gregariousness: the capacity to identify with fellow citizens is impossible in the absence of a closed community with shared values and a common enemy. Citizens of a universal state are rootless and lack identity, having no fellow citizens to identify with. For Strauss there can only be closed societies.[52] Strauss implies that citizenship, like friendship, requires a certain exclusivity. In the final analysis, citizens of a universal society are Hobbesian men in the state of nature. The modern ideal of a universal society flies in the face of what Strauss calls 'rootedness in the soil' or *Bodenstandigkeit*. According to Strauss, modern man is suffering from an acutely painful homelessness. Modern philosophers such as Heidegger wish to introduce 'an entirely novel kind of *Bodenstandigkeit*: a *Bodenstandigkeit* beyond the most extreme *Bodenlosigkeit*, a being at home beyond the most extreme homelessness'.[53] Strauss has forebodings about this novel conception of rootedness. Rootedness in a universal state is for him indistinguishable from homelessness. But worse than that, Strauss realizes, as Heidegger seems also to have realized, that universalism and internationalism cannot succeed in destroying the parochial nature of man and of his nationalism. Internationalism is therefore nationalism on a large scale.[54] For Strauss, the dream of the universal and prosperous society is dangerously close to the horror of modern tyranny. The universalism of modernity and the 'unlimited or uncontrolled progress of technology has made universal and perpetual tyranny a serious possibility'.[55] The Nazis are a case in point: their brand of universality was a peculiarly rooted one – it was a universality that failed altogether to reach any level of pluralism, it failed to transcend its rootedness in German soil. Strauss does not think this is an isolated phenomenon, as is evidenced by his criticism of American pluralism, or its lack thereof. The American desire to make the world safe for democracy is potentially as oppressive as the German desire to make the world ready for the master race. For Strauss, planetary rule, no matter what form it takes is oppressively tyrannical. Universalism and pluralism do not so much succeed in transcending natural human rootedness, they only pervert it.[56]

The third factor in the crisis is the loss of faith in the miraculous effects of prosperity. The West seems to have slowly discovered or rediscovered the fact that prosperity does not have the effect of making man good. The enormous success of modern science and its conquest over nature has succeeded in providing man with a power over nature that is hitherto unsurpassed. But his newly acquired power has not been accompanied by a 'corresponding increase in wisdom and goodness'.[57] The 'barbarization' that we have witnessed in our own century is a case in point.[58] Modern man has no idea what to do with all his power. The liberation of science in the form of technology can only spell disaster. We have failed to learn the lesson of Socrates and his Thinkery. Modern man is destined to be victimized by his own inventions.

Fourthly, the West has lost its purpose because the modern project is without direction. In the beginning, the modern project was directed to the relief of man's estate. It therefore pre-supposed that man has a nature with given needs, the satisfaction of which gives the modern project its rationale. However, the conquest of nature led to the conquest of human nature, and this undermined the assumption which gave the conquest its goal, and which also set limits to the modern project. Once human nature is regarded as part of the nature to be conquered, 'the natural needs of men could no longer direct the conquest'.[59] Recent debates on genetic engineering are an excellent example of the aimlessness to which Strauss points.[60]

The fifth component of the crisis is the most comprehensive of all, so much so that Strauss regards it as identical with the crisis itself. The West is in decline because it has fallen prey to nihilism. Nihilism is simply the belief that all values or ends are of equal worth, or that there is nothing intrinsically more noble or good than any other. The values of our own civilization are not superior to those of any other, because all values are equally groundless and hence equally worthless. All values are conventions, ideologies, interpretations, fictions or products of will to power. Nihilism is a profound indifference to the distinctions between good and evil, noble and base.

Strauss is not suggesting that to be healthy a society must believe in the viability of a universal and prosperous society. But it must believe that its own ideals and principles, *whatever they are*, are superior to any others and therefore worthy of the ultimate sacrifice. Men cannot be expected to fight and die for an ideal that they believe to be arbitrary, unfounded and not intrinsically superior to that of any other society or group. Human beings seem to have what Nietzsche called a 'god-forming instinct', or a tendency to objectify their values or attribute to them transcendent sources independent of human volition. Nihilism is the erosion of this god-forming instinct: it reveals what the philosopher or truth lover has always known – namely that the values of our society are groundless. What is the source of this nihilism? And how has it come to have such a hold on Western civilization?

Strauss sometimes uses the terms nihilism, historicism and relativism as if they describe one and the same phenomenon. But a careful reading of his work reveals important distinctions between these three concepts. In what is to follow, I will show that for Strauss, historicism, relativism and nihilism are three distinct, though not unrelated stages in the demise of Western civilization.

For Strauss, historicism is strictly speaking not identical to nihilism, although it plays a central role in the march towards nihilism. Historicism is the claim that all values, ideologies and regimes are historically relative to time and place. They are all fraudulent attempts to justify injustice and inequality. However, there is an absolutely just order of things that awaits man at the end of the historical process.

Even though historicism is largely responsible for modern nihilism, and hence the modern crisis, it is not itself nihilistic, but quite the contrary. Strauss points out that historicism does not 'belong to a skeptical tradition'.[61] Skepticism is the denial of the possibility of genuine knowledge that transcends time or history; but historicism regards history as the custodian of an absolute and enduring truth. Far from denying the possibility of genuine knowledge about the right and the good, historicism maintains that such knowledge is imbedded in history. In Strauss's view, historicism does not deny the universal or absolute, it merely places it at the end of the historical process.[62] In so doing, it preserves the transcendence of the truth, but in a radically altered form. It is not satisfied with the belief that has characterized all human societies throughout history, namely, that their own beliefs, values and principles are a reflection of a transcendent reality. It believes that the ideal, universal and absolute can be made actual. Historicism is therefore born out of the most extravagant optimism.

Strauss understands historicism not as a form of relativism, but as a particularly insidious and dangerous form of absolutism: it aims at the global project of replacing the plurality of truths with its own single truth. Therein lie the seeds of a peculiarly modern tyranny (i.e. a global one). The absolutism of History is far more radical than that of God. History is more jealous and more tyrannical than the God of the Old Testament: being incarnate in political leaders and regimes, it can take its revenge much more effectively than any god.[63]

Men such as Hegel believed themselves to be the confidants of History, but History has proved to be colossally disappointing. It has refused to reveal its secret, perhaps because it does not have one. If the historical dialectic has no end or goal, then all that is left is the 'depressing spectacle of a disgraceful variety of thoughts and beliefs'.[64] History can tell us only that thought is linked to the historical situation and changes with that situation. It cannot tell us whether the change or choice is a good or a bad one, because history is a 'meaningless web', a 'tale told by an idiot'.[65]

When history proves to be disappointing, historicism gives way to relativism and nihilism.[66] Strauss describes Max Weber as a man who experienced this disappointment, and therefore turned away from the historical school.[67] Weber was the founder of social science or the study of the multiplicity of historical 'caves'. Social science inherits from historicism a 'cave' that has been thoroughly debased, because it has been robbed of that alone which gives it life – namely, the belief that it is not a mere fiction, a manifestation of the will to power, without foundation or reality, suspended by nothing, unrooted in the eternal. In other words, historicism destroys the 'protecting atmosphere within which life or culture or action is alone possible'.[68] Nor can the cave be exalted as a necessary stage in the actualization of the universal: for the atrophy of historicism left behind it social scientists who no longer believe in the end of history, the possibility of the universal state, or the modern project.

Social science begins with relativism or the acceptance of a permanent, irresolvable and deadly conflict between the plurality of 'values' that sustain different societies. 'Values' refer roughly to the goods or ends that are to guide human life; they also refer to what is morally good, right and just. Social science cannot provide us with any knowledge of values because such knowledge is not available to man. There is no rational foundation for choosing between diverse values. From a rational point of view, all values are of equal worth. Nevertheless, we must choose. Of course, there are goals that we cannot legitimately choose because they are fantastic, unattainable and impossible. Peace and universal happiness are an example – they are unattainable because they fly in the face of the irresolvable conflict of the plurality of values that inspire the lives of different people in different societies. Weber wanted men to be committed, not because what they are committed to is worth commitment, but merely for the sake of the commitment itself.

The relativism of social science differs from nihilism only by being inauthentic. For Strauss, the most objectionable aspect of value-free social science is that it is oblivious to the nihilism at its heart. The relativist turns a blind eye to the human implications of his relativism.

Existentialism is an authentic or self-conscious relativism: it is sensitive to the seriousness of nihilism. The existentialist is a relativist with *angst*.[69] Strauss describes Heidegger as the most outstanding philosopher of our time who gives expression to the *angst* that is a natural result of nihilism.[70] But *angst* is not an invention of existentialism: it is not just a 'modern' experience. In an unpublished, but widely circulated lecture, Strauss wonders why it is that a human experience that is totally understandable, and certainly not new, has become for us *the* fundamental human experience. Strauss's work as a whole suggests the following answer. The human *angst* is the natural result of the collapse of the 'walls of the world'. It has its source in our awareness of our mortality, our finitude or our 'throwness' as Heidegger would say. That this is the consuming human experience of our time is the natural consequence of the fact that the traditional remedies for this *angst* no longer exist. There are two traditional remedies for this human experience: religion and philosophy. In the days of old, religion consoled the many, philosophy the few. But modernity is characterized by the undoing of religion by philosophy. The modern project of enlightenment or the publication of philosophy is ill-conceived because philosophy is ill-equipped to provide consolation for the many.

Strauss has often repeated that the crisis of Western civilization is identical with the decline of political philosophy.[71] Indeed, he goes so far as to say that the eclipse of political philosophy and its transformation into 'ideology' is the 'core of that crisis'.[72] At first, this seems preposterous, but not untypical: men of ideas generally overestimate the importance of ideas in shaping history. But Strauss does not mean to say that the well-being of Western civilization is inseparably linked to the well-being of a particular academic discipline. Political philosophy is not an academic discipline or a purely theoretical pursuit. Strauss is often seriously misunderstood on this point.[73]

Contrary to Kojève's belief, Strauss does not depart from him on the matter of the relation between political philosophy and politics (or the political philosopher and the tyrant).[74] For Strauss as for Kojève, political philosophy does not belong in a secluded tower removed from political practice. Its role is to influence and direct that practice. What must remain hidden is *philosophy*, not *political philosophy*. As we have seen, the latter is the political or exoteric garb in which philosophy appears in the world. Its object is to dispense the salutary myths necessary for the survival and well-being of the city.

The crisis of the West is the direct consequence of the fact that there are no salutary lies. Modernity dispenses with noble illusions. It believes that a civilization can be built on the basis of mass enlightenment. Political philosophy gives way to social science. Noble illusion gives way to naked truth.

What Strauss said in a lecture to a group of young Jewish students about Judaism, he could equally well have said about Western civilization as a whole. Strauss defined Jewishness in terms of faith in Judaism. When asked about Jews who do not believe in the truth of Judaism, he resorted to a Jewish prayer about redemption and the Kingdom of God. He treated Judaism with reverence and piety, yet the gist of what he said was that the history of the Jewish people is a testimony to the fact that there is no redemption. But it is better to live by a 'noble delusion' than 'wallow in the sordid truth'.[75]

Western civilization has two roots: the Bible and Greek philosophy.[76] Biblical faith provides Western civilization with its noble delusions. Political philosophy uses its clever rhetoric to sustain these delusions in the very act of introducing contrary principles that cater to the sordid business of political survival. The West has declined because there is no longer anything to sustain it. The clever obfuscations of political philosophy are deemed unnecessary. Machiavelli subverted the esoteric philosophy of the ancients: he shouted the truth about political things from the rooftops. He liberated philosophy, and in so doing allowed it to wreak havoc on the noble delusions of faith. But Machiavelli did not liberate philosophy single-handedly; he was assisted by the Christian philosophers who were foolish enough to believe that philosophy will come to the aid of faith. The atrophy of Christian faith is a historical testimony to the unreality of their hopes. The two roots of Western civilization are at odds. In its effort to dissolve the tension between them, modernity allows them to destroy one another, and this will prove to be the undoing of Western civilization.

I am not suggesting that Strauss is either a historicist or a nihilist in his sense of the terms. First, Strauss is not a historicist because he does not believe that truth or reality is historical. For Strauss, there is a permanent truth behind the variety of historical interpretations, ideologies, *Weltanschauung*, or 'caves'. Philosophy is the attempt to grasp the truth behind the multiplicity of 'caves', or the attempt to elicit the 'universal or essential structure' common to all historical worlds.[77] Strauss objects to historicism because it succumbs to the fictions of the cave and wallows in its darkness. It attempts to exalt the cave and undermine philosophy by declaring that all philosophies are but fictions, ideologies interpretations, or will to power. But the attempt to exalt the cave necessarily fails, for the cave cannot be exalted without simultaneously being debased. Historicism undermines the cave because it robs it of that alone which gives it life – namely, the belief that its truth is not a mere fiction or a manifestation of the will to power, without foundation in the eternal or absolute. Nor does historicism succeed in demonstrating the impossibility of philosophy: for the claim that all values are historical is a philosophical claim. It is a claim that cannot be made by one who is in the grip of the illusions of the cave.

Although Strauss does not express it this way, he certainly believes that historicism is right in thinking that politics is ideology, interpretation and will to power. However, historicism is mistaken in believing that there is no 'text' behind the multiplicity of interpretations, or that there is no 'nature' behind all historical 'caves'.[78] For Strauss, as we have seen, the 'nature' behind all caves is not the sort of nature that lends support to any of their idiosyncrasies but one that makes the creation of these idiosyncrasies as necessary as the belief that the universe lends them support.

Secondly, Strauss is not a relativist or nihilist in the sense described above. He is not indifferent to all ends. As we have seen, he regards a certain end or a certain way of life as by nature superior to all others. This is not a moral superiority, it is a superiority of pleasure, and in his view, of excellence. Strauss is genuine in railing against nihilism and relativism, but not because he is himself a champion of inviolable moral principles. We have seen previously that he is not. He rails against relativism because it is dangerous to the well-being of any society. He champions natural rights, as he does natural law, because they are useful. But as he himself writes, 'utility and truth are two entirely different things'.[79]

I am not suggesting that the only ground on which Strauss objects to relativism and nihilism is social utility. Strauss *does* believe that nature provides man with standards. But as we have seen, these *are not moral standards*. The distinction between good and evil is a matter of convention and citizen morality, not nature.

In summary, Strauss finds Rousseau keenly aware of the flaw at the heart of the modern project launched by Hobbes. Rousseau doubts that enlightened self-interest can be made the foundation of political society. But in spite of all his ancient wisdom, Rousseau advances modernity by rejecting the ancient solution to *the* political problem – namely, the conflict between individual and collective interests. Rousseau opts for a reconciliation of the individual and the community that is far more optimistic and complete than Hobbes would have dreamed possible. Rousseau therefore radicalizes the modern project by extending the conquest over nature to a conquest over human nature. Rousseau returns to nature only to reject her: nature sets no limits on what is humanly possible, for man's nature is infinitely malleable. The political problem will henceforth be solved by the transformation of human nature. Rousseau therefore represents not only the first crisis of modernity, but the solution to that crisis. From Rousseau, the modern project acquires new life and a new vitality. In its advanced stage, represented by Marx and Hegel, the modern project consists of the creation of a prosperous universal society of equal men and women. But the loss of faith in this project soon leads to the crisis of our time. According to Strauss, the modern crisis was inevitable because the modern project was ill-conceived from the beginning. Strauss's sobering insights into the human predicament are as follows. Prosperity does not make man good. Technology will only succeed in making us victims of our own inventions. All attempts to establish a free and prosperous universal society will inevitably lead to global tyranny and to the sort of 'barbarization' we have already witnessed in our century. There are no final solutions to political problems. Men will always live in separate societies characterized by mutual hatred, antagonism and animosity, fueled by an irrational attachment to their own culture, customs and ways. War will always be with us. We must be satisfied with the little consolation of ancient wisdom according to which politics is the art of transforming natural man into citizen, and this requires constant vigilance and reinforcement, not to mention noble lies and obfuscations. The state must appear to be supremely honorable, nay, sacred. This 'protecting atmosphere' (Strauss borrows the phrase from Nietzsche) is necessary for political life; it is necessary if some men are to sacrifice their lives for the safety and security of others. By exploding the 'protecting atmosphere', nihilism has threatened the political life of Western civilization.

9

Post-Modernity: Plato or Nietzsche?

Strauss does not explicitly propose a 'solution' to the crisis of modernity. Nevertheless, his diagnosis of the ills of modernity in terms of the revolt against nature points to how the effects of the crisis can be undermined. Whatever 'solution' is implicit in Strauss's writings, it must be construed in terms of the reinstatement of nature as a standard. Only the latter can begin to reverse the modern subversion of nature.

One question remains: in his effort to transcend modernity, does Strauss look to Plato or to Nietzsche? Does he look back to the restoration of ancient wisdom or does he look forward to a new era? In what follows I will show that how we answer this question is immaterial, because the ancients to whom Strauss appeals have been transfigured by Nietzsche.

If we are fully to understand Strauss, we must recognize that his greatest intellectual debt is to Nietzsche. Although Strauss has linked Nietzsche with modernity, Nietzsche is not strictly speaking a modern philosopher in the Straussian sense. Strauss regards Nietzsche as the modern philosopher of *nature*.[1] At first blush, this sounds like a contradiction in terms, because Strauss has described modernity as a revolt against nature. However, according to Strauss, the revolt against nature ultimately leads to a deeply felt alienation that forces those who experience it, like Nietzsche, to return to the desecrated skeletal remains of nature.[2] Nietzsche replaces the modern revolt against nature with an affirmation of a nature that is beautiful and strong. He transcends relativism by replacing the modern supremacy of history with the supremacy of nature.[3] He therefore holds out the hope of transcending modernity altogether. Since he is not, strictly speaking, a modern, I suggest that Nietzsche is best understood as the philosopher of post-modernity.

I will use the term post-modernity to refer to a new era in the making. This is the era represented by Nietzsche and Strauss.

Implicit in Strauss's work is a 'project' for post-modernity. The post-modern project must temper the effects of modernity and mitigate some of the damage modernity has inflicted on Western civilization. If it is to transcend modernity, post-modernity must reinstate nature; it must restore a world of strength, beauty and nobility that has been dealt a deathly blow in the course of Western civilization. In launching his post-modern project, Strauss looks primarily to Nietzsche.

Nothing reveals the extent of Strauss's intellectual debt to Nietzsche more than the fact that he subtly identifies Nietzsche as the modern champion of ancient wisdom. Strauss's writings on Nietzsche are very condensed, if not cryptic. Nevertheless, Strauss's essay 'A Note on the Plan of Nietzsche's *Beyond Good and Evil*' is not only one of the most penetrating and most consistent accounts of Nietzsche's philosophy, it reveals the extent to which Strauss's own ideas have their foundation in Nietzsche's thought. I will summarize Strauss's interpretation of Nietzsche as clearly as I can.

In Strauss's view, Nietzsche is a genuine philosopher because he *discovers* a truth that transcends all historical truths. Nietzsche's view of truth is often regarded as contradictory. On the one hand, Nietzsche rejects the correspondence theory of truth according to which the truth refers to a reality independent of human making. In opposition to the correspondence theory, Nietzsche declares all truth to be a product of human creativity. But in spite of this, Nietzsche proceeds to reveal to us all sorts of things about nature, man and history that he obviously does not regard simply as inventions of his own. By the same token, Nietzsche rejects all notions of objective good, yet he insists on distinguishing between master and slave, noble and base. Nietzsche appears to be trapped in a self-defeating contradiction. His conception of truth appears to leave his own message without foundation or support; there is no reason to regard it as being truer than any other philosophical position. Although he does not say so in so many words, Strauss finds this contradiction so blatant, so ordinary, and so obvious, that it could not have been missed by a mind as great as Nietzsche's. Nietzsche must have meant something different. Strauss suggests an interpretation that resolves the contradiction. He understands Nietzsche's view of truth as follows. 'Truth', especially where morality is concerned, is a human creation. From the moral point of view, nature is chaotic and meaningless. Every morality is based on 'some tyranny against nature', it is a fiction, an ideology, an expression of the will to power that imposes order on chaos.[4] In short, order and truth originate in man's creative acts or will to power.[5] However, there is a truth that transcends all man-made truths. The latter is the truth about all 'truths'; and *that* is not a human creation. This is the truth which philosophy seeks to grasp: it seeks to get a hold of the 'text' as opposed to the interpretations.[6] According to Strauss, Nietzsche's *Beyond Good and Evil* is a genuinely philosophical work that ascends to a truth beyond all man-made truths, or a truth beyond all human creativity and will to power. Strauss describes it as 'transmoral'.[7] As we shall see, Strauss means that the truth in question transcends morality, it is beyond good and evil, which are components of man-made truth.

Nietzsche makes three philosophical discoveries about all truths. First, he discovers that the 'text' is inaccessible; everything is interpretation. Secondly, he discovers that the truth (i.e. the human creation) is 'life-giving'.[8] Man cannot live in the face of chaos any more than he can live with perfect self-knowledge.[9] Life needs a protective atmosphere of illusion in order to thrive. Thirdly, he discovers that no truth is everlasting, all truths eventually perish when they are no longer 'life-giving'. For example, God is dead because the 'God truth' (if I can call it that) is no longer life-giving. This is the import of saying that God is dead: Nietzsche does not say that God does not exist. The idea that God is dead implies that God (or the God truth) once lived. It means that there was a point in time when the 'God truth' was life-giving.

Armed with this conception of truth, Strauss believes that Nietzsche provides us with a profound understanding of the crisis of the West. In Strauss's interpretation, Nietzsche's diagnosis can be described as follows. Western civilization is in decline because the morality on which it has relied is in a state of atrophy. That morality is the 'rationalist morality', the 'plebeian morality', the 'morality of timidity', or the 'morality of the herd'. (It is most commonly translated as the 'slave morality'.) The atrophy of the plebeian morality, like the atrophy of any other morality, is due to the fact that it is no longer life-giving. It was once vital and life-giving, it served to protect the 'human-herd' or the 'large majority of men'. Its standard of goodness was utility for the herd. The 'common good' refers to the good of the herd or majority, and nothing else. The plebeian morality did not esteem independence, superiority and inequality, except to the extent to which they were believed to serve the herd. The morality of the herd was timid, weak and Christian. It was primarily a morality of compassion for those who have been neglected by nature.[10] The downfall of the timid morality is the result of its own compassion becoming too indiscriminate. The timid morality is bent on the abolition of all suffering, and this is impossible without undermining the safety and well-being of the herd. The timid morality therefore contains the seeds of its own destruction: its own timidity is the reason for its demise. As Strauss explains, the morality of the herd upholds the 'common good' which, he explains, is 'the good of a particular society or tribe; it demanded therefore hostility to the tribe's external and internal enemies and in particular to the criminals'.[11] The herd morality loses its grip when it fails to defend the herd, and sides instead with the criminal. It does this as soon as it 'becomes afraid of inflicting punishment' and is 'satisfied with making the criminals harmless'.[12] Once it abolishes fear, the morality of timidity becomes 'superfluous'. What is needed is a new morality that does not shrink from cruelty because it is aware of the great things man owes to suffering.[13]

In Strauss's interpretation of Nietzsche, the plebeian morality is in decay not only because of its own timidity, but also because God is dead, or because the 'God truth' on which it relies is no longer life-giving. The plebeian morality is characterized by 'the god-forming instinct', or the tendency to project its values beyond itself, to a higher or transcendent realm like God or the Platonic Forms.[14] It is oblivious to the will to power, to human creativity and to what Strauss calls 'the problematic character of morality'.[15] Not being well traveled, the plebeian morality is not aware of the endless variety of moralities.

Unlike the plebeian morality, historicism is well traveled or fully cognizant of the variety of moralities, and hence of the problematic nature of morality. No less than Strauss, Nietzsche recognizes the bankruptcy of historicism.[16] However, Nietzsche credits historicism with one virtue: that of having made intellectual probity possible. It has made possible Nietzsche's discovery of the truth about all truths. Historicism is therefore a necessary prerequisite to the defeat of the plebeian morality and the emergence of a superior morality. The 'historical sense' mediates between the two moralities: it shatters the illusions of one in order to make the 'intellectual probity' of the other possible.[17]

Strauss does not regard Nietzsche as an existentialist. Having arrived at nihilism, Nietzsche does not despair: he refuses to divinize the Nothing.[18] Nor does Nietzsche make a virtue of probity, or what existentialists call authenticity.[19] On the contrary, Nietzsche launches the most radical attack on the love of truth. Strauss draws attention to the fact that *Beyond Good and Evil* begins with questioning the love of truth.[20] Nietzsche understands that the truth (i.e. the truth about all truths) is not 'attractive', 'lovable', or 'life-giving', but 'deadly'. According to Strauss, Nietzsche does his best to 'break the power of the deadly truth': he discovers something life-giving at the heart of the deadly truth – the will to power, which is made possible only by the Nothing or the deadly truth itself.[21]

In *Natural Right and History*, Strauss reflects on Nietzsche's dilemma:

> According to Nietzsche, the theoretical analysis of human life that realizes the relativity of all comprehensive views and thus depreciates them would make human life impossible, for it would destroy the protecting atmosphere within which life or culture or action is alone possible. . . . To avert the danger to life, Nietzsche could choose one of two ways: he could insist on the strictly esoteric character of the theoretical analysis of life – that is, restore the Platonic notion of the noble delusion – or else he could deny the possibility of theory proper and so conceive of thought as essentially subservient to, or dependent on, life or fate. If not Nietzsche himself, at any rate his successors adopted the second alternative.[22]

Those who conceive of thought as subservient or dependent on life are the 'radical historicists' who deny the very possibility of genuine philosophy – that is, they deny the possibility of a theoretical analysis that transcends all historically bound horizons. Radical historicism abandons the idea that history has a goal or end. It recognizes no Archimedean points, either outside of history or at the end of history. Radical historicists believe that all philosophizing takes place within the cave. Strauss's 'Note on the Plan of Nietzsche's *Beyond Good and Evil*', denies that radical historicism is the heir of Nietzsche. The point of the essay is to tell us that far from radicalizing historicism, Nietzsche 'restores the Platonic notion of the noble delusion'.

Nietzsche's thought is often believed to be contradictory in its insistence on myth and illusion on the one hand, and its celebration of truth on the other. Strauss resolves the difficulty by attributing to Nietzsche the esoteric thesis. In other words, he attributes to Nietzsche the belief that only the few can withstand the deadly truth, the rest need myths and illusions.[23] The esoteric thesis succeeds in resolving the contradictory things Nietzsche says about the truth – namely, that it is good and that it is terrible.

In Strauss's interpretation, Nietzsche expects the philosophers of the future to 'create' a new morality (commonly known as the Master Morality) built on the Will to Power. The new morality will be fully conscious of itself as a celebration of human creativity and will require no other foundation. The new values will be products of a free creative act. They will be complete and self-sufficient. They will not be images of some other transcendent reality that robs them of *their* reality by turning them into mere appearances. The new philosophers will not allow the knowledge of the groundlessness of their morality to debase it, for they will not be enslaved by the love of truth. They will regard their creation as the only reality. They will abolish the whole distinction between appearance and reality. The new breed of philosophers will be the *Führers* of the future who will subjugate nature and establish a new order, for every morality is based on some tyranny over nature. The new philosophers will possess a superabundance of will to power, and will be characterized by an 'atheistic religiosity'.[24] This is what Strauss means when he says that *Beyond Good and Evil* is a 'vindication of God'.[25] The new philosophers will be creators of a new 'God truth' which needs to be preceded by an interregnum of atheism.

According to Strauss, even though the new values that the philosophers of the future will create will be products of a free creative act, Nietzsche nevertheless demands that the new order be in accordance with nature.[26] Nature recognizes a higher and lower, superior and inferior: 'there is an order of rank of the natures, at the summit of the hierarchy is the "complementary man"'.[27] The complementary man (more commonly known as the superman) is the philosopher, who possesses a superabundance of Will to Power, and who is the highest and most spiritual manifestation of the Will to Power. Strauss remarks that he is the 'peak' in whom 'the rest of existence is justified'.[28] The project of the 'highest natures' is to 'maintain in the world the order of rank'.[29]

This may sound puzzling: how can nature which is chaos and meaninglessness contain an order of rank? Has Nietzsche not declared all values to be human creations? Strauss's interpretation resolves the difficulty as follows. Nature *is* chaos, and all values *are* human creations, including the superior morality of nature. However, there is one natural end for man – that of being a creator of order, of values and of moralities. The natural man *par excellence* is the philosopher, the interpreter of the nonexistent 'text'. The philosopher is the maker of the myths necessary for the life of man. Only in the light of Strauss's understanding of Plato can we appreciate why Strauss regards Nietzsche's anti-Platonism as a grave exaggeration.[30] In spite of Nietzsche's polemics against Socrates and Plato, Strauss maintains that Nietzsche's *Beyond Good and Evil* is a very Platonic work.[31] In Strauss's view, Nietzsche returns to the classics. That is to say, the classics as transfigured by the Straussian interpretation.

Strauss concludes that in the final analysis, Nietzsche could not do without nature. But he realized that nature was a 'problem' because of the limitless character of the modern conquest of nature. Strauss explains that because of that conquest, 'people have come to think of abolishing suffering and inequality. Yet suffering and inequality are the prerequisites of human greatness'; they must therefore be brought back: 'Hitherto suffering and inequality have been taken for granted, as "given," as imposed on man. Henceforth, they must be willed'.[32] Nature would then owe its being to an act of human will. Everything is will to power. There is no 'text' because there would be no 'nature' were it not for an act of will by 'the highest natures'.[33] Nietzsche is a modern philosopher of nature because in the context of modernity, *nature must be willed*.

What becomes clear is that Strauss owes more to Nietzsche than to any other philosopher.[34] All the major themes of Strauss's work echo Nietzsche, or a Nietzsche that has been made ruthlessly clear and consistent. Consider the following. First, Strauss's critique of historicism relies heavily on Nietzsche's criticism of historicism and Hegelianism in *Use and Abuse of History*. Secondly, Strauss follows Nietzsche in tracing the ills of modernity to its suicidal devotion to truth. Like Nietzsche, he exalts illusion as necessary for life. Thirdly, Strauss shares Nietzsche's view of (the early) Socrates. Fourthly, Strauss's conception of the philosopher is modeled after Nietzsche's superman.

First, Nietzsche lamented that the great individuals of the past are now replaced by the 'historical process'.[35] He deplored the fact that the effect of historicism was to replace the great individuals by the masses. The masses, he complains, are poor copies of the great individuals painted on bad paper from worn out plates! Their only usefulness is to serve as a contrast to the great men and as tools for their existence.[36] Strauss shares Nietzsche's contempt for the masses; he too believes that they are but the tools for the existence of the few. Like Nietzsche, Strauss rails against historicism for depriving the great individuals of their rightful place. In particular, he abhors the historicist approach to the history of ideas because it reverses the natural order of things: it regards the great men as reflections of their times. Strauss attempts to put an end to this unfortunate predicament by understanding the great thinkers of the past 'as they understood themselves', which is to say, as great men, as men *against* their time, and not men *of* their time.[37] Understanding the great thinkers 'as they understood themselves' means understanding their work as they intended it to be understood, as timeless and not as reflecting any particular *Weltanschauung*.

Nietzsche preceded Strauss in denouncing historicism for being self-contradictory. Nietzsche argued that historicism exempts itself from the verdict it imposes on all other ages and systems of thought: it believes all life and thought to be historical except its own. It is Nietzsche who first complained of the self-righteousness of historicism: it understands itself as the pinnacle of evolution, of history, or the world process. It is Nietzsche who argued that historicism ends with the idolatry of success, which in turn leads to a most uncritical attitude: how can one criticize what is necessary, or what could not have been otherwise?[38] Historicism ends by approving everything, or regarding all things as being of equal worth. It therefore launches us on the road to nihilism in the Straussian sense.

Secondly, Strauss's fundamental insight into the 'crisis' of modernity is Nietzschean. Like Nietzsche, Strauss traces the ills of modernity to its unquenchable quest for truth – its immoderate, excessive and suicidal devotion to knowledge. Scientific knowledge, for example, threatens us with extinction; yet we are convinced that only more knowledge can save us. For Strauss, as for Nietzsche, what is true of scientific knowledge is equally true of philosophical knowledge. Like Nietzsche, Strauss forces us to think the unthinkable. He forces us to question the goodness of truth and knowledge for mankind. Nihilism, understood not as the indifference to all values, but as the insight into the groundlessness of law, justice and morality, is a 'deadly truth'. We are therefore confronted with a choice between this deadly truth and a life-giving myth. Unless we are bent on self-annihilation, we must choose the life-giving myth. Truth is not good for man; in Strauss's view, even the Bible taught us that!

Nietzsche is not a relativist or a nihilist in the Straussian sense because he does not believe that all values are of equal worth, and so is not indifferent to all values. But he is fully aware of the *angst* of the self-conscious nihilist. (This is the same *angst* that ensues upon the collapse of the walls of the world.) Modernity lacks the means by which to deal with the human *angst*, instead, it surrenders to nihilism. Nietzsche is not a modern precisely because he does not despair – he refuses to surrender to nihilism. On the contrary, he does his best to 'break the power of the deadly truth'.[39] He affirms life in spite of the truth of nihilism. But he is not an existentialist who makes a virtue out of intellectual probity.[40] On the contrary, he is the greatest critic of the modern devotion to truth regardless of the cost. It is Nietzsche who wrote that 'the search for truth is often thoughtlessly praised'.[41] Like Strauss's ancients, Nietzsche celebrates myth, art and illusion. Nietzsche denounces the 'historical sense' because 'it destroys illusions and robs existing things of the only atmosphere in which they can live'.[42] According to Nietzsche, life needs forgetfulness: 'a thing can live only through a pious illusion'.[43] For Strauss as for Nietzsche, the danger in which we find ourselves is a result of the fact that science now rules life, and science is the enemy of illusion, religion and art. Science strips man of the protecting veil of illusions. For Nietzsche, the modern 'savant' is a plebeian who does not understand this; if he did, he would have more compassion and spare the people his science.[44] This is reminiscent of Strauss's 'considerate few' who write esoterically in order not to bring destruction upon the multitude.

Thirdly, Strauss borrows Nietzsche's view of Socrates. Nietzsche believes that Socrates is the originator of Western man's deadly quest for truth. He wonders if Socrates was not an ordinary criminal, for he was inclined to believe criminologists according to whom the typical criminal is ugly. Socrates was known to be ugly. Nietzsche speculates that Socrates was an envious plebeian who purposely set out to destroy a beautiful world of nobility, beauty, art and instinct.[45] He used rationality as his weapon: by means of dialectic, the 'rabble comes to the top'. Dialectics is chosen where there are no other means: 'where authority is still part of a good tradition, one does not "reason" but commands'.[46] Reasoning destroys authority and demystifies life. Socrates wanted to make 'existence appear intelligible'. He was a 'mystagogue of science' who introduced mankind to a 'never-suspected universal craving for knowledge'.[47] He was the 'Pied Piper of Athens', a 'crank' who invented the 'theoretical man', a 'form of existence without precedent'. He attributed to knowledge 'the power of a panacea' and conceived of error as 'absolute evil'.[48] He believed in reason whatever the cost: he made reason a tyrant.[49] He was 'the distinctive nonmystic' who never experienced the 'sweet madness of artistic enthusiasm', for his 'eye was forbidden to look with approval into the Dionysian abysses'.[50] Modernity is the heir of Socrates and must pay the price.

As we have seen, Strauss echoes Nietzsche's sentiments when he describes the young Socrates as 'anerotic' and 'a-music', 'the first theoretical man', and 'the incarnation of the spirit of science', founder of the belief in progress and the salutary effects of enlightenment.[51] Strauss does not believe that Plato (or the mature Socrates) fell prey to the aspirations of the rabble. Unlike Socrates, Plato was not a plebeian. The whole point of Strauss's essay on Nietzsche is to show that, Nietzsche's anti-Socratism notwithstanding, *Beyond Good and Evil* is a 'very Platonic work'.[52] As we have seen, Strauss regards Plato (or his 'converted' Socrates) as '*erotikos*', a man intoxicated by the supreme *eros*. One would surmise that such a man was not forbidden to look with approval into the Dionysian abyss.

For Strauss as for Nietzsche, morality is a function of necessity coupled with art and illusion. No civilization can withstand the radical questioning of its morality. By making reason a tyrant, Socrates destroyed the morality of the ancient Greeks. He laughed at their inability to give an account of their instinctive sense of nobility. Nietzsche suspects that the 'mysterious ironist' could not provide a rational account of morality himself. Even with the greatest philosophical might of all time at his disposal, Plato could not prove the identity of reason, virtue and happiness. Nietzsche regards the identity as 'bizarre' and contrary to the instincts of the more ancient Greeks.[53] Strauss denies that Plato *really* tried to provide proof for such a bizarre identity. He believes that Plato could not have failed to see what he and Nietzsche saw so clearly – namely, that morality cannot give an account of itself. This is the dark truth at the heart of all moralities: the 'Just Speech' cannot be required to give a rational account of itself without being destroyed by the 'Unjust Speech'.[54]

Fourthly, Strauss's philosopher is modeled after Nietzsche's superman. Like the latter, the philosopher is the creator of the needed or necessary truths that ensure the survival of the herd. For morality is a matter of collective self-interest.[55] The philosopher, like the superman, fashions the opinions, attitude and sensibilities of the vulgar; he determines their art, their feelings and their very horizon of possibility. But neither the philosopher nor the superman partake of the illusions they create for the consumption of the herd. They alone have the intestinal fortitude to withstand the deadly truth that transcends all man-made truths.

For Strauss as for Nietzsche, the philosopher–superman will not create just any illusion: his fiction will have its roots firmly planted in nature. The modern conquest of nature coupled with the timid morality threatens the superior type. From this point of view, Darwin's claim that nature exalts the higher type by ensuring the survival of the fittest seems implausible: this may well be the intention of nature, but human activity interferes with the process. The weak and inferior, by sheer numbers, have managed to thrive. Christianity has also come to the assistance of the lower type by suffering the deformed to live. The philosophers of the future must will back nature at a time when nature has become a 'problem', or when it has come very close to being annihilated by human conquest. The new morality created by the philosophers of the future will be a superior morality. It will reintroduce nature as a standard of appeal. The nature in question will not be one that has been humbled by Christianity. It will be strong, heartless and even terrible. The project of post-modernity is to reintroduce rank and hierarchy in place of the modern egalitarianism which serves only to perpetuate and exalt mediocrity.[56] Strauss believes that Nietzsche failed to give effect to his ideas because of the distortion his philosophy suffered at the hands of the Nazis.[57] (And, unlike Strauss, he had no disciples to carry out the work.)

We are led to conclude that Strauss's greatest intellectual debt is to Nietzsche. It is no use protesting that Strauss's real intellectual debt is to Plato and the ancients. For as we have seen, the ancients to whom Strauss appeals have been transfigured by Nietzsche. That Strauss insists on appealing to Plato rather than Nietzsche should not surprise us. He has learnt a lesson in political prudence from Machiavelli. He has learnt to use the 'prejudice in favor of antiquity' to establish 'new modes and orders'.

10

Esotericism Betrayed

Throughout this study, I have attempted to elicit and unravel the political ideas of Leo Strauss from the midst of his many detailed commentaries on the history of Western political thought. In this chapter, I should like to make a few comments about the status of my interpretation of Strauss, in the light of recent controversies among his own followers.

The recent debate between Harry Jaffa and Thomas Pangle in the pages of the *Claremont Review* illustrates the radical disagreement among Straussians regarding the true nature of Strauss's legacy.[1] It has been observed that my interpretation of Leo Strauss sides with Pangle against Jaffa. But this is not the case. The interpretation of Strauss that I am proposing transcends the conflict between his students. Indeed, it explains why this conflict is inevitable and perfectly understandable. Before explaining why this is so, let me first describe what I believe to be at issue between Jaffa and Pangle.

In his Introduction to *Studies in Platonic Political Philosophy*, Pangle provides a picture of Strauss's Socrates that comes close to suggesting some of the things which I have expressed explicitly in this work. In reviewing Pangle's Introduction, Jaffa expresses shock and alarm. He finds Pangle's interpretation completely foreign to his own understanding of his teacher and friend of 30 years. Jaffa observes that such a vision of Strauss is Nietzschean,[2] and he denounces Pangle for having perverted the legacy of Leo Strauss.

Pangle maintains that Jaffa has distorted his interpretation of Strauss 'beyond recognition'.[3] But in the course of his response to Jaffa, Pangle makes the same claims that Jaffa had attributed to him in the first place. I am therefore not convinced by Pangle's disclaimer. As I see it, the only distortion Jaffa is guilty of is that of coming to the heart of the matter. Indeed, Jaffa's approach to Pangle's text closely resembles my own approach to Strauss's text. As Jaffa writes, 'I thought it best to expound his [Pangle's] true argument, without going through the wearisome process of disentangling it from its sophistical cocoon.'[4] (It should be added that Pangle's cocoon is not as intricate or as tightly woven as Strauss's.) If I hope to explain what is at issue between Jaffa and Pangle, I must also ignore Pangle's cocoon and come to the heart of the matter.

The controversy between Jaffa and Pangle revolves around three aspects of Strauss's thought. First, Pangle believes that Strauss (or his Socrates) distinguishes between virtue, nobility and justice (in their moral sense) and the good, understood as the pleasant, the useful and the healthful.[5] According to Pangle (and his Strauss), the noble and the just necessarily come into conflict with the good or the pleasant. The noble is good only to the extent that it is useful or instrumental to the non-moral good. The relationship between the noble and the good is therefore 'problematic'. Although Pangle does not say so, he implies that pleasure is the natural and superior good, whereas virtue is an artificial or conventional good that is subordinate, derivative and instrumental to the good by nature. What he actually says is that over a long period of time, and due to the 'plastic power of custom', the concern with being noble or being thought noble has

> gained such strength that it now competes with man's natural, spontaneous, and uninvented desires, and obfuscates the calculation which naturally serves and guides the latter. Yet through piercing, uncompromising thought and iron self-discipline some men can liberate themselves from the sway of opinion and learn to content themselves with the pursuit of the pleasures that are truly or intrinsically sweet. Since man does, by nature, need the assistance of society, the truly free man will continue to dwell among and profit from his deluded neighbors; but spiritually, he will live a life apart.[6]

It is therefore hardly a distortion to follow Jaffa in maintaining that Pangle regards the noble and the just as artificial goods necessitated by civil society, which require some men to sacrifice themselves in order that others may enjoy personal pleasure, security and comfort, or what is really good by nature.[7] In contrast to Pangle, Jaffa believes that nobility, virtue and justice in the moral sense are real or natural goods and that Strauss has always upheld this to be the case.

Secondly, according to Pangle, the 'Socratic turn' (following

Strauss, I have referred to this 'turn' in Chapter 4 as 'the conversion of Socrates') does not involve a fundamental change in the core of the Aristophanean Socrates. The 'Socratic turn' refers to Socrates's shift of emphasis from the things aloft to the moral and political realm. Pangle explains that Socrates turns his attention away from the attempt to unravel the mysteries of the universe to the question of justice because he has learned an important lesson in political prudence from Aristophanes. His attention to political matters is a result of his awareness of his own dependence on the political community. Socrates does not turn to the moral and political realm because he came to believe that the latter 'can be made philosophic'.[8] In other words, his turn to political matters was not the result of his believing that there can exist a moral and political order that is rationally and philosophically justifiable. As Pangle writes, 'not for one moment does Socrates suppose that moral and political virtue can be made philosophic, or that a healthy society can be come rational, and thus cease to be a "closed" society'.[9]

For Pangle, all political societies are by definition 'closed' societies. Politics is characterized by what Strauss refers to as a love of 'one's own': political societies love their traditions and beliefs because they are their own, and not because they are good or noble from an objective point of view. Philosophy threatens political society because it loves the good that transcends 'one's own'. Politics is by its nature parochial, whereas philosophy is cosmopolitan. Although Pangle is not explicit, he implies that philosophy cannot lend support to any political regime or its 'citizen morality' because it cannot give a rational account of morality, no matter what its nature.

In contrast to Pangle, Jaffa believes that the Platonic Socrates differs from the Aristophanean Socrates not only in his rhetoric, but in the substance of his thought. His attention to moral and political matters is not simply a display of skill in concocting myths to hide the true nature of philosophy. The difference is substantial. The Platonic Socrates has discovered 'the ground in nature for human excellence', understood in a moral and not only in a philosophical sense.[10] According to Jaffa, Strauss taught that we must not simply love 'our own' because it is our own, but must make the good our own.

The same issue is at the heart of the recent exchange between Jaffa and Pangle on the American founders, in the pages of the

National Review.[11] In Jaffa's view, the foundations of the American nation are not Lockian or 'modern' in the Straussian sense, but Aristotelian and classical. The founders believed that the health of the nation rests on virtue and self-restraint; they denounced the abandonment to the pursuit of pleasure and wealth; they upheld natural law and classic natural right. (Jaffa understands natural law and classic natural right to be harmonious, in contrast to my interpretation of Strauss on this matter in Chapter 5.)[12]

On the other hand, Pangle believes that the American nation has its roots in a specifically 'modern', egalitarian and individualistic conception of the Rights of Man.[13] The American Nation is characterized most of all by a passion for political liberty. Only on the grounds of the latter can philosophy thrive. Pangle defends the claims of philosophy against what he understands to be the 'closed' nature of the political. He believes that political values must be tempered by the spirit of philosophical doubt. He fears that the belief that the principles of our society coincide with the true and rational principles will lead to an 'obscurantist fever', from which will emerge the 'germ of nihilism'.[14] Pangle explains that nihilism is a

> process by which high principles self-destruct or devaluate themselves. In one of its principle manifestations, it is the process by which the supposedly rational principles, which however are suspected by their adherents of lacking rational validity, come to be trumpeted ever more hysterically even as the voice of reason in the soul steadily eats away those principles' hold on the heart.[15]

Pangle seems to think that the heart must learn to withstand the skepticism of the mind if the 'obscurantist fever' and the 'germ of nihilism' are to be avoided. It seems as though he is advocating that every American citizen must learn to live with the tension between the 'things of the heart' and the 'things of the mind'. But as we have seen, Strauss believes that only the few can learn to live with this inner conflict.

I am inclined to think that Pangle is far more 'liberal' than Strauss. However, his liberalism does not appear to be grounded in John Stuart Mill's belief that no one is privy to the whole truth, but only to parts of the truth, especially in moral and political affairs. Instead, Pangle's liberalism seems to have its source in the skeptical philosophy of Leo Strauss which doubts that there are any moral truths. In Straussian terms, Pangle's public defense of the claims of philosophy against those of politics may be said to follow more closely the impolitic example of Socrates rather than that of the more judicious Plato.

The third matter that is at issue between Jaffa and Pangle is the relationship between reason and revelation, Athens and Jerusalem, or Greek philosophy and the Bible. According to Pangle, Jerusalem claims to have final and satisfactory answers on ultimate questions. However, it appeals not to reason, but to the realm of the miraculous or supernatural.[16] In contrast, Athens denies that it has any satisfactory answers on the most important questions: it pleads Socratic ignorance. However, it questions Jerusalem's claim to knowledge. In the course of its rational questioning, it reveals the 'thin ice' on which faith skates. But this does not, according to Pangle, amount to the refutation of faith: the pious still cling to their faith. Pangle attempts to soften the opposition between faith and reason by saying that philosophy cannot refute revelation because philosophy itself rests on faith in reason,[17] and as a result must show respect for faith and accord it a status equal to that of reason and philosophy.

Strauss's argument is more radical and more complex than Pangle's version allows. The fact that the pious cling to their piety despite the philosopher's effort to show them that it lacks rational ground, need not lead one to conclude that philosophy cannot refute faith and so must defer to it in submissive humility. The real reason that the philosopher treats piety with reverence is not that he cannot refute it, or that he regards it as a mystery that transcends the competence of reason, or that he is painfully aware of his own ignorance about the whole. When all is said and done about the philosopher's ignorance, it still remains the case that he knows a fundamental and irrevocable truth about political society – namely, that it needs religion to maintain a measure of inner peace and tranquility. And *that* is the reason that the philosopher must accord to faith its due.

Jaffa sees through the veneer of Pangle's not so esoteric writing. He understands Pangle to be admitting the superiority of philosophy to faith, whereas Jaffa believes that

Strauss denied that the answer of Plato and Aristotle (or either of them) was evidently superior to the answer of the Bible.

Indeed, no classical philosopher ever attempted the kind of argument that might have proved the superiority of reason to revelation.[18]

According to Jaffa, Strauss accorded to faith and reason an equal dignity, and denied that either was superior to the other. Besides, Strauss realized that if revelation is refuted by reason, then the philosopher would have attained wisdom and this would mean the triumph of 'the unqualified claim of wisdom to rule'.[19] Jaffa understands this as the claim of the 'universal tyrant' or the tyranny of the universal and homogeneous state that Strauss has so unequivocally opposed. But there is no reason to think that absolute rule need necessarily be global. It is only the *global* nature of absolute philosophical rule, and not the absolute nature of the rule in question, to which Strauss objects. (Kojève does not fully understand the nature of his own debate with Strauss. Like Jaffa, he believes that Strauss rejects tyranny altogether.) In Jaffa's view, revelation is necessary to keep philosophy humble and to ensure that it is not disfigured by the lust for power. Despite the wisdom of Jaffa's position, there is little evidence for it in the writings of Leo Strauss. As we have seen, Strauss believes that philosophy *has* refuted faith and *has* an absolute right to rule unhampered by law, even if these are 'truths' that must be kept hidden.

It might seem that the evidence I have brought forth from Strauss's writings more effectively supports an interpretation of Strauss that is closer to Pangle's than to Jaffa's. But a plausible interpretation of Strauss cannot simply ignore Jaffa's view. An adequate interpretation must explain how such disparate views regarding the legacy of Strauss could have emerged among his followers.

In reflecting on the meaning of the controversy between Jaffa and Pangle, it is necessary to recall Strauss's conception of a 'teaching'. As I have explained earlier, a 'teaching' consists of a teacher and one who is being taught. The content of the 'teaching' depends on *who* is being taught. According to Strauss, the Socratic dialogues of Plato and Xenophon portray not so much the philosophy of Socrates, as the various 'teachings' of Socrates. Socrates is depicted speaking to different people differently. Strauss believes that if we are to understand the Platonic and Xenophontic dialogues, or if we hope to grasp the significance of what Socrates is saying, we must note carefully to *whom* Socrates is speaking. Strauss also reminds us that there are no dialogues between Socrates and Plato: in other words, there are no dialogues depicting wise men speaking to one another. The task of the scholar is to recreate the unwritten dialogue of the wise over the ages, and this is no mean task.[20]

Strauss's students testify to the fact that Strauss followed the example of his Socrates by speaking differently to different students. In his memorial to Leo Strauss, Ted A. Blanton said that Strauss spoke to different people differently, telling each what he believed they needed to hear.[21] It is important to understand that speaking differently to different people does not mean expressing the same truths to all in different ways or using different language or metaphors depending on the ability and inclination of the one being taught. It means *literally* teaching different people different things.

It is my contention that Strauss taught students such as Jaffa and Pangle different things. He taught students like Jaffa to take morality and religion, honor and nobility, gentlemanship and statesmanship seriously, and to regard them as necessary components of genuine human excellence that are good by nature. On the other hand, he taught students like Pangle that the sorts of things that the gentleman and statesman take seriously are little more than artificial goods to which the philosopher must nevertheless pay lip service, nay, show great reverence, for they are necessary to the well-being of the city on which he himself must rely. In short, Strauss taught some of his students to be statesmen and gentlemen while teaching others to be philosophers.

In maintaining that Strauss taught his students different things, I do not rely simply on the testimony of his students, or on the observable differences between them. I believe that teaching different students different things is an integral part of Strauss's political thought. Strauss believed that the city needs at least two kinds of men: the philosopher and the gentleman or statesman. (I will use the terms citizen, gentleman and statesman interchangeably, since Strauss regards them as instances of the same type in varying intensity.) In teaching, Strauss therefore sought to cultivate two different types of men. I am inclined to think that the two types of men correspond to Strauss's two roots of Western civilization: the Bible and Greek philosophy. Indeed, Strauss's version regarding the proper relation between these two types of men mirrors his understanding of the relation between the two roots of Western civilization.

As I have argued above,[22] Strauss was absolutely earnest in maintaining that Western civilization had two equally vital though conflicting roots – the Bible and Greek philosophy, or Jerusalem and Athens. He believed that the vitality of the West depends on the coexistence of these two visions of what alone 'is needful' for the good life. Yet these two conceptions of the good life were not only diverse but antagonistic: one insisted on blind obedience, the other on free enquiry. Strauss was opposed to any effort to harmonize, reconcile or synthesize them. He thought that harmony cannot be achieved without radically altering the distinctive character of the antagonists. Their distinctive characters are necessary in performing their different, but equally vital roles, in the life of our civilization. The Bible provides the West with moral standards to govern the relations between citizens. Biblical religion, like most religions, secures obedience to law even in situations where there is a good chance of not being found out. The gentleman is the incarnation of the overwhelming success of traditional religion in shaping natural man into a being fit for civilized life. The gentleman is pious, honorable and upright. He is a good father, an assiduous husband and a patriotic citizen. Moreover, he is not virtuous simply out of fear of punishment (here or in the hereafter), but out of love of his family, his city, his ancestral heritage and, not least, his own honor and reputation. Such a man can be trusted with political power. This is why Strauss believed that *the* solution to the political problem is the rule of gentlemen. However, Strauss also believed that the rule of gentlemen is not sufficient to the happiness of men in cities. Only the rule of the philosopher can ensure the latter. Philosophy provides the city with that which the honorable and pious alone cannot provide. Philosophy supplements the city's religious or conventional right with a standard that it derives from nature. Philosophy is necessary because the ancestral laws of justice that are useful in governing the relations between citizens are not applicable in inter-group relations. Philosophy understands the nastiness of politics and the requirements of political survival. The city therefore needs philosophy, but the latter threatens the ancestral or religious element on which the city's internal order and stability depends. This is why Athens and Jerusalem must find a way to coexist. Despite the danger that the 'publication' of philosophy might inflict on the city, philosophy cannot be banished; for there can be no happiness for men in cities without the rule of philosophers. Athens must therefore find a way to live and rule in the heart of Jerusalem without disturbing the latter's pious illusions.

The difference between Athens and Jerusalem corresponds to the difference between the code of the heart and the code of the mind; the latter belongs to the philosopher, whereas the former belongs to the gentleman. As I have argued, Strauss believes that a viable political order requires religion as well as philosophy, a code of the heart and a code of the mind. But because these two foundations are not in harmony with one another, what are needed are two different types of men: the gentleman and the philosopher. For Strauss, the good regime consists of the rule of gentlemen who are friendly to philosophers and who are therefore willing to listen to their advice. Strauss's vision of the relationship between these two types of men is embodied in his understanding of the relationship between Socrates, the philosopher, and Isomachus, the perfect gentleman.[23] As we have seen, the friendship of the gentleman and the philosopher is predicated on the fact that the gentleman ill-understands the philosopher. The gentleman is naïve and innocent: he believes that life must be governed by the right and the honorable under all circumstances. The philosopher, on the other hand, knows that the right is only good when it is useful. The gentleman is given to self-deception or a total lack of self-knowledge: he is oblivious to the beast that dwells within him, the multiform beast that is kept at bay only by the civilizing process and its elaborate art of obfuscation. In contrast, the philosopher knows the truth: he knows that civilization is only a thin veneer that masks the bestial nature of man. In short, the philosopher is privy to the terrible truth about things human and divine. It is absolutely mandatory for the philosopher to keep his philosophy hidden; for, were it to become known to the gentleman he would naturally feel betrayed. The result would be the dissolution of their friendship, and this would certainly undermine the happiness of men in cities, and maybe even the 'vitality' of the West.

The success of the friendship between the gentleman and the philosopher therefore rest on the esotericism of philosophy, or on the philosopher's ability to exercise a great deal of thrift and moderation in his speech. But failing to exercise the necessary caution, and daring to follow the poor example of Socrates by openly defending the claims of philosophy against the city, he is sure to relive anew the conflict between philosophy and the city. Once betrayed, esotericism harms the city as much as the philosopher. For it is the case, according to Strauss, that the city needs the philosopher as much as the philosopher needs the city.

The debate between Jaffa and Pangle is just one instance of the deepening division among Strauss's followers, but more examples of similar debates can readily be found.[24] The division is between what I shall call the 'philosophical' Straussians and the 'political' Straussians. The former are philosophers, the latter are gentlemen. The philosophers understand Strauss's esoteric philosophy, the gentlemen mistake the exoteric philosophy for the whole of Strauss's philosophy. The philosophers are Nietzscheans, even if they refuse to admit it, the gentlemen are advocates of natural law, and other ancestral myths. Jaffa accuses Pangle of being 'intoxicated' with a little philosophy.[25] In Jaffa's view, Pangle has had too much wine. But for Strauss, there is nothing wrong with having too much wine – philosophizing is hardly possible without it; as he tells us (in *What Is Political Philosophy?*), political philosophy is moderate speech about immoderate, not to say 'shameless' and 'intoxicated' thoughts. Unless the 'charms' with which civilized life holds us captive are loosened, we cannot philosophize. Strauss hoped that the philosopher would be able to combine intoxication in thought with moderation in speech: in other words, he hoped that philosophy can remain esoteric.

The rift within the ranks of Straussians is indicative of the dissolution of the friendship between the philosophers and the gentlemen, and hence the failure of Strauss's political programme. What has gone wrong? Are the philosophers betraying their trust? Is Pangle guilty of the 'publication' of philosophy, which is one step away from its vulgarization? I do not believe that Pangle is purposely betraying the trust. From what he writes, it is clear that he believes himself to be serving the city as the Straussian philosopher should – namely by taming its 'waspishness' with a little philosophical *eros*. But how much is too much? Perhaps Strauss has given his philosophers too fine a line on which to tread. Perhaps he overestimated the philosopher's capacity for thrift and caution in expression. Besides, esotericism is not impenetrable, not even for the gentleman. Strauss underestimated the gentleman if he thought that he would defer to the authority of the philosopher but never realize that the principles that guide the philosopher's wisdom are not always honorable. In any case, the schism between the political and the philosophical Straussians is a testimony to the failure of esotericism. But how could Strauss not have suspected that it would come to this?

11

The Wise and the Vulgar: A Criticism of Leo Strauss

Strauss's ideas may be perverse, but they are not frivolous. They deserve serious attention for several reasons, not least among them is the fact that they have proved to be overwhelmingly popular. The converts are attracted to Strauss because he offers them ready-made answers to all the difficult questions; and if they travel in the right circles, they need not fear ridicule, for their 'philosophy kit' will always save the day. But it is also possible to appreciate Strauss without being or becoming one of his converts. No matter how bizarre his commentaries on the Great Books might be, they are nevertheless full of valuable insights. They challenge those who are not in search of a philosophy kit to see for themselves. Besides, the commentaries are not so much interpretations, as dialogues with the text: dialogues that force the text and the reader to surrender to the Straussian logic. For those who refuse to surrender their critical intellect and submit to his seductive charms, Strauss is a challenge that is as intriguing as Nietzsche, Freud or Machiavelli. Like Nietzsche, he forces us to question the goodness of knowledge, he makes us wonder how or if we could give an account of our moral beliefs. Like Freud, he forces us to look into the dark depths of our *psyches*. And, like Machiavelli, he forces us to come to terms with the nastiness of politics.

What is unfortunate is that Strauss corrupts; and that, more than the power of his intellect, is the source of his attraction. Strauss seduces young men into thinking that they belong to a special and privileged class of individuals that transcend ordinary humanity and the rules applicable to other people. In criticizing Strauss, I focus primarily on the vulgar nature of his vision of the philosopher–superman.

Strauss is often criticized for being both elitist and anti-democratic. Unlike others, I do not object to Strauss for being either elitist or anti-democratic. Nor do I believe that elitism is necessarily incompatible with democracy. On the contrary, the existence of an elite that exercises sound leadership may well enhance, rather than undermine the democratic process. John Plamenatz provides a vivid example:[1] imagine a society of 100 men and women who govern themselves by assembling periodically and making all decisions and laws as one body politic: theirs is a direct rather than a representative democracy. Imagine also that 10 of these men and women habitually do most of the talking in the assembly: they identify the issues and debate the pros and cons of the various policies or courses of action. One cannot deny that such informed and intelligent debate can only have the effect of bringing the issues to light and allowing the rest of the community to make more informed decisions or to vote more intelligently than might otherwise have been the case. It would seem from this example that there is nothing in the nature of an elite that is inherently incompatible with democratic government. Strauss's elitism is not necessarily anti-democratic. Besides, Strauss makes it clear that he is not an enemy of democracy. He also believes that (despite all evidence to the contrary) Plato's anti-democratic posture has been highly exaggerated.[2] For Strauss, democratic society provides the sort of freedom that is necessary to the unhampered pursuit of the philosophical life, and he is sure that Plato must have recognized this.

Strauss is elitist, but he is not anti-democratic. His political programme consists in cultivating an elite that would exercise leadership as politicians, statesmen and judges, *as well as* a philosophical elite that would exert influence on them. The political elite is composed of gentlemen, the philosophical elite only plays the part; but, armed with the prestige of the university professorship and the respectability of the social scientist, the 'philosophers' of our time are in a position to exert far more influence than someone like Socrates, who was despised and ridiculed. My objections to Strauss are not directed at his elitism, but at the *nature* of the philosophical elite he envisions, and on the influence they are likely to exert on their friends in power.

Strauss's elitism is among the most radical that has ever been encountered in the history of Western thought. Woven throughout Strauss's philosophy is the theme of the dramatic gap between the wise and the vulgar. The wise are those who are capable of experiencing the truth in peace, whereas the vulgar are destroyed by it. The wise are capable of living happily in the face of the naked truth, whereas the vulgar need noble delusions. The wise are those who fabricate the noble lies, the vulgar are those who consume them. The differences between the vulgar and the wise (I will for the moment leave the gentlemen and statesmen out of account) are for Strauss quite fantastic. The vulgar are self-seeking lovers of pleasure and wealth. They are Hobbesian men seeking power after power ending only in death. They can only be motivated to moral virtue by laws that threaten severe punishments and by the terrors of Hades. In contrast, the philosophers are almost godlike in comparison to ordinary men. They know that there is no God and no support in the universe for the laws that men make. They know that Hades is a necessary but noble fiction meant for the vulgar. Yet in spite of this they have no desire to harm others or get the better of them, even when they can do so with impunity. They are possessed of what might seem to be an incomprehensible nobility. Their justice is not a result of philanthropy or love of mankind. Nor is it motivated by fear of the earthly or heavenly powers. Strauss explains their nobility by saying that they place little stock in the things that ordinary men 'hotly contest'. It is not that they do not love pleasure; on the contrary, they wish to lead the most pleasant life (for they believe that pleasure is the only truly natural good). However, unlike the vulgar, they have experienced not only the lower pleasures of eating, drinking, sex, wealth and power, but the *eros* of philosophy. According to Strauss, in relation to the pleasures of the philosophical life, all the other pleasures pale into insignificance. What other men so 'hotly contest' appear 'paltry' to those who have seen the 'truly grand'. This is meant to explain their unusual nobility.

Strauss considered the gap between the vulgar and the wise to be so great, that one of his students, Allan Bloom, likened it to the difference between Gulliver and the Lilliputians. Although neither Strauss nor Bloom brings this example to our attention, reflections on some aspects of Swift's tale reveals a hidden message that has already been confirmed by the study of Strauss's classic natural right above. When Gulliver urinates all over the palace, the Lilliputians are shocked and horrified. But they soon realize that Gulliver's scandalous conduct was the salvation of the city, for it saves not only the palace from being engulfed in flames, but all of Lilliput! The moral of the story is that the rules that apply to the Lilliputians do not apply to Gulliver. Strauss seduces us into thinking that morality is akin to taboo: there is nothing intrinsically despicable about it when viewed from the point of view of nature and reason. What makes Gulliver's conduct shocking is that it flies in the face of the ancestral, but one who has been immersed in Straussian wisdom is too sophisticated to identify the ancestral with the good! Strauss castigates Machiavelli for corrupting his readers by allowing them to discover his truths for themselves. But Strauss seduces his readers to his way of thinking, in the same manner. He allows them to 'discover' the very things he wishes to teach. By reflection on the plight of Gulliver we are led to surmise that acting immorally for the sake of the public good is necessary, reasonable and even merciful. So if we are in a position to condemn an innocent man to appease a lynch mob threatening to destroy our society, we can congratulate ourselves on our mercifulness. But this savage truth ought not be too widely published, for it will shock and scandalize (not to mention corrupt) those who are 'duped' by 'citizen morality'. But those who are not so 'dull-witted' will recognize that if kept secret, immoral conduct often serves the public good, and in such cases is of no greater gravity than Gulliver's urinating over the palace. There is one rule for citizens and another for the wise and the powerful.

Strauss believed that the two different sets of standards correspond not only to two different types of people, but also to two different sets of situations: domestic and foreign. The rules that are useful in domestic affairs are not effective in foreign policy and international affairs. Religion and morality are good for the relations among citizens, but they are a hindrance to the city's quest for greatness. Like Machiavelli, Strauss believed that political greatness is a function of power. Moral ideals have no place in politics. As we have seen, the 'justice' of the city consists in doing good to friends and evil to enemies. Strauss seems to think that the logic of international affairs requires and even justifies the existence of two sets of standards and two types of men. According to Strauss, not only Machiavelli, but Thucydides recognized the conflict between the 'private' and the 'public', that is, domestic and international affairs.[3] But unlike Machiavelli, he was a cautious writer who disclosed these dangerous truths with articulate silences and pregnant indications. For example, he silently conveyed to us that the Greeks encountered disaster in

Sicily, not because the gods looked unkindly on their injustice, but only because they *believed* that the gods would be displeased at their injustice; and this *belief* prevented them from performing as well as they might have done. Religion and morality are useful in ensuring amicable relations between citizens, but they are stumbling blocks for those who would aspire to true greatness. This is why Strauss and Machiavelli must educate those who would be great by a process of 'brutalization'.

But of course, all this is very questionable. It is not reasonable to think that a city can become truly great by preying on its neighbors and treating other cities with savage brutality. Even in international affairs, greatness is not simply a matter of power, but of power properly and rightly used. Greatness in the international arena is the macrocosmic version of honor and reputation in domestic life. The man of honor is not identical with the perfectly just man or the perfectly unjust man. But on the whole, one who would be honored must bear greater resemblance to the perfectly just man than to the perfectly unjust man. It may be objected that to be honored one need only *appear* to be just. In Plato's *Republic* Glaucon paints a picture of a perfectly unjust man with a reputation for justice. But Glaucon's picture is a gross exaggeration that is impossible in real life. Keeping one's injustice secret is not an easy matter. No one can get the better of others time and again and still expect to have an untarnished reputation. It is impossible to deceive people indefinitely. In time one's character will be found out.

The greatness of cities, like the honor and reputation of individuals, depends on the regard and admiration of others. And it is highly unlikely for even the mightiest of cities to be admired for being truly great if it displays a callous indifference to justice. The most powerful nations in the world know that they will not be admired or counted as truly great unless they are perceived to use their power in ways that do not simply serve their own ends. This is why they go to such lengths to justify their injustices by appealing to standards that are universally recognized. They will describe an invasion of a small and relatively helpless nation as the liberation of a people from the rule of an oppressive tyrant. They will attempt to justify a war of aggression by accusing the other party of striking the first blow. They will try to justify the usurpation of land from its rightful owners by arguing that they were there first. I am not saying that morality holds sway in international affairs. What I am saying is that it is never ignored, and that even the mightiest nations go to great lengths to justify the use of their power by appealing to moral standards that others are likely to recognize. If greatness could be secured by power alone, all this talk would be unnecessary. The manner in which international disputes are carried out testifies to the fact that there is a universal moral law that is recognized, even if it is perpetually abused. And the mightiest nations cannot continually disregard it and still expect to be great. For greatness, like honor and reputation, depends on the perceptions of others, who will no doubt see through the lame excuses of those who are bent only on augmenting their own power at all cost. Even if the Nazis had been more successful than they were, they could never have been great.

Strauss's radical deprecation of morality in international affairs corresponds to his deprecation of morality in his account of human excellence in general. As we have seen, Strauss regards the highest human type, the philosopher, as one whose excellence 'does not require moral virtue'. Indeed, the justice of the philosopher is said to mirror that of the city, for the philosopher is not a citizen, but a stranger. He is quick to add that the philosopher, unlike the city, has no reason for harming anyone, for he has little regard for the things that other men hotly contest. But as Alexandre Kojève has shown, in Strauss's own account the philosopher seeks not simply the pleasure of contemplation, but immortality. He wishes to be admired by a 'competent minority', which means that in spite of what Strauss says, the philosopher too seeks honor and glory.[4] Since this is the case, he will be motivated to harm those who would stand in his way, and his 'wisdom' is ill-equipped to provide him with reasons for self-restraint.

Strauss does not take Plato's conception of the tripartite *psyche* very seriously. He believes that Plato was not describing the nature of the human *psyche*, but the different kinds of men in the world: the lovers of knowledge (the philosophers), the lovers of honor and reputation (the gentlemen and statesmen), and the lovers of pleasure (the vulgar). This is the foundation of Strauss's belief that there is an unbridgeable gap that separates the vulgar from the wise. The standards that apply to the philosophers do not apply to the vulgar, just as what is fitting for people is not appropriate for dogs. For surely, people are allowed to do things that are forbidden to dogs. This explains why Strauss can attribute to words such as nobility, justice and gentlemanliness more than one sense. The meaning depends on *whose* nobility, justice or gentlemanliness is at issue. Strauss notwithstanding, this may well be *the biggest lie of all*, what Plato called the 'lie in the soul' or self-deception. Are Strauss's philosophers not deceiving themselves in thinking that they are far removed from ordinary humanity? Is this not the most self-congratulatory and self-serving lie? Is it not closer to the truth to think that the theory of the tripartite *psyche* describes a continuum *within* the *psyche* itself?

Experience does not suggest that there exist men who are pure embodiments of rationality, devoid of appetites. Nor is the world populated by men who are simply bundles of appetites, devoid of reason. If there were men of pure reason, they would be anomalies. Strauss would not be impressed with this objection, for he regards the philosopher as a truly rare phenomenon. But what is not so rare is the specter of Strauss's ever increasing followers believing themselves to be the rare exceptions.

Plato was not an egalitarian. He believed that there were decisive differences among human beings that made some more fit to rule, or more fit for political power than others. But contrary to Strauss's claims, what makes some people more fit to rule is not the fact that they are able to live in the face of the benign indifference of the universe, or the fact that they are not likely to allow the moral rules of conduct to restrict the 'latitude' of their 'prudent' statesmanship. What makes some more fit to rule is a moral superiority, or a superiority in justice. Their moral superiority is due to the fact that their justice is not simply a result of habit, or fear of Hades. (Nor are they just because they have fallen prey to the charms that transform men into citizens.) Their justice is a product of wisdom or the knowledge that the just life is the truly happy life and that justice is its own reward. Far from thinking that vice is the true liberator of the mind, they identify wisdom with justice. Their wisdom consists in *knowing* that one who is free of vice, one who is not malicious, envious, hateful or vindictive, is, simply speaking, better off.[5] This profound insight into the nature of human happiness is a special asset to those who would hold political power because the latter provides so many opportunities of doing injustice with impunity. Therefore, only those possessed of such knowledge could withstand the temptations of power. Strauss's philosophers are not possessed of such knowledge; on the contrary, they believe that the equation of the true, the good, the beautiful and the useful is highly 'problematic'. They believe that Plato never intended to show that the just man, in the moral or 'vulgar' sense is the happy man; the only 'justice' that is choiceworthy for its own sake is 'philosophical justice' which is identical with the pursuit of the pleasures of the contemplative life coupled with the 'justice' of giving to each his due by saying different things to different people.

Strauss may have paid lip-service to the rule of law, but in reality his esoteric philosophy subverts it. He believes himself to be following Plato in pointing esoterically to the 'problematic' nature of law. It is true that Plato believed that even the best set of laws cannot guarantee a just political order. Good laws need good judges to administer them. Because injustice so often manifests itself in the abuse of the procedural justice, the moral rectitude of the administrators of the law is as important as the goodness of the laws themselves. Law therefore needs to be supplemented by wisdom and virtue. But Strauss adds a highly original, if not perverse, twist to the Platonic sobriety about the shortcomings of law. As I have shown in Chapter 5, Strauss supplements law with the sort of wisdom that 'does not require moral virtue'. The wisdom with which Strauss supplements law is consequential not moral. It is the kind of 'wisdom' that subverts the principles on which law is founded. Of course, it may be objected that consequentialism in politics is nothing new. And I am certainly willing to concede that no self-respecting moral and political philosophy can disregard the consequences of action, or can give an account of right independent of consequences. But there is an important difference (that is more than a 'nuance') between according consequences a rightful place in one's moral and political philosophy, and making them the sole determinants of the rightness of actions. The idea that evil should not be done in the hope that good will come of it is at the heart of the moral traditions of the West.[6] If modernity is understood in terms of the erosion of the moral foundations of Western civilization, then Strauss is the quintessential 'modern'. His radical deprecation of morality embodies the very 'crisis' of the West that he describes.

Strauss follows Nietzsche in thinking that modernity consists fundamentally in the triumph over nature. The conquest of nature has become so successful in our time that nature has almost been completely eclipsed. I have argued that Strauss joins Nietzsche in launching the project of post-modernity. The latter consists in the reinstatement of nature. But if nature is to be reinstated, it must be *willed*. It is the task of the philosophers or supermen of the future to *will* back nature by the superabundance of their will to power. The nature that they will reinstate is cruel, harsh and merciless. It consists of different standards for different people. It mirrors their profoundly hierarchical conception of nature. But contrary to Strauss's convictions, the philosopher–superman does not revive a banished reality, he creates a world of his own making. Far from being a yea-sayer, the philosopher–superman wishes to overthrow reality. For in reality the differences between men do not resemble the differences between Gulliver and the Lilliputians.

It is ironic that the 'young men who love to think' and who are destined to become the heirs of Strauss are characterized by their willingness to accept Strauss's authority without question. Strauss has subtly taught them that the wise recognize these truths instantly, to question them is by definition to remove oneself from the elect. This seems particularly comical in view of Strauss's definition of philosophy as that which rises up against authority.

The corruptive nature of Strauss's doctrine is the real reason that so many succumb without question to his charm. The idea that there is no higher excellence than that of the philosopher seduces those who embrace it into thinking of themselves as gods among men, exempt from the restraints to which the rest of humanity is subject. They come to believe that philosophical excellence is the supreme end in relation to which all else is a means. Moreover, Strauss assures them that the excellence of the philosopher is one that 'does not require moral virtue'.[7] Moral virtue is not constitutive of the end, it is only the instrument for its attainment. Everything is therefore permitted to the philosopher in his efforts to seek his own good. Strauss teaches his philosophers that the political community exists only to make their life possible. They repeat after their master that the end of the city is the good life for man, confident that no one understands the true meaning of this commonplace tenet of political thought. They are under the impression that they have discovered for themselves a dark and delicious, but very dangerous truth. In the final analysis, Strauss's philosophers are but 'heroic Epicurians', to use the phrase of Harry Jaffa, living on the fringe of civil society and paying lip-service to its ways while pursuing their own pleasure and glory. But anyone whose critical intellect is left intact will find it difficult to see how the company of men who are 'unduped' by 'citizen morality' can be pleasurable, let alone noble.

The nobility of Strauss's philosopher can only be spurious. The lavish extravagance of Strauss's faith in the nobility of the wise is quite unwarranted in view of his own understanding of the hedonistic nature of his philosophers, supermen or great 'immoralists' as Nietzsche would say. The Straussian philosophers are thoroughgoing hedonists, and even if their hedonism is of the highbrow variety, it is hedonism nevertheless, and so is committed to the doctrine that pleasure is the highest good. The transition from the higher to the lower pleasures is an easy one to make. Besides, Strauss gives no reason why his noble philosophers need not pursue the lower pleasures with as much tenacity and dedication as they pursue the philosophical *eros*. His idea of philosophy as *eros* is a splendid excuse for being one of the Hugh Hefners of the philosophical set.[8] The transition from 'shameless' or 'intoxicated' thoughts to shameless deeds is almost natural. It is an understatement to say that Strauss's conception of nobility lends itself to vulgarization. It is impossible for men who harbor Strauss's contempt for morality not to fall into the most fearful depths of depravity. This is most unfortunate, for it serves to undermine Strauss's contribution to political philosophy.

Notes

The following abbreviations of books by Strauss are used in the Notes:

AAPL   *The Argument and the Action of Plato's Laws* (Chicago, Ill.: University of Chicago Press, 1975).

CM   *City and Man* (Chicago, Ill.: University of Chicago Press, 1964).

HPP   *History of Political Philosophy*, ed. Leo Strauss and Joseph Cropsey, 1st edn (Chicago, Ill.: Rand McNally, 1963); 2nd edn (Chicago, Ill.: University of Chicago Press, 1973).

LAM   *Liberalism Ancient and Modern* (New York: Basic Books, 1968).

NRH   *Natural Right and History* (Chicago, Ill.: University of Chicago Press, 1953).

OT   *On Tyranny*, first published 1963, later revised and enlarged (Ithaca, N.Y.: Cornell University Press, 1968).

PAW   *Persecution and the Art of Writing* (Westport, Conn.: Greenwood Press, 1952).

PPH   *The Political Philosophy of Hobbes* (Chicago, Ill.: University of Chicago Press, 1952; first published by The Clarendon Press, Oxford, 1936).

SA   *Socrates and Aristophanes* (Chicago, Ill.: University of Chicago Press, 1966).

SCR   *Spinoza's Critique of Religion*, trans. from the German by E. M. Sinclair (New York: Schocken, 1965; first published by Akademie-Verlag, Berlin, 1930).

SPPP   *Studies in Platonic Political Philosophy*, ed. with an Introduction by T. L. Pangle (Chicago, Ill.: University of Chicago Press, 1983).

TM   *Thoughts on Machiavelli* (Chicago: University of Chicago Press, 1958).

WIPP   *What is Political Philosophy?* (New York: Free Press, 1959; repr. Westport, Conn.: Greenwood Press, 1973).

XS   *Xenophon's Socrates* (London: Cornell University Press, 1972).

XSD   *Xenophon's Socratic Discourse* (London: Cornell University Press, 1970).

Notes to Chapter 1: Leo Strauss: Teacher and Philosopher

1. Lewis A. Coser, *Refugee Scholars in America: Their Impact and Their Experiences* (New Haven, Conn.: Yale University Press, 1984). Coser refers to Strauss as the only refugee scholar who managed to attract a 'brilliant galaxy of disciples who created an academic cult around his teaching' (p. 4).
2. The most recent and most complete bibliography of Strauss's work can be found in *SPPP*. Other compilations of Strauss's work can be found in Joseph Cropsey, 'Leo Strauss: A Bibliography and Memorial,

1899–1973', *Interpretation*, vol. 5, no. 2 (1975) pp. 133–47; Joseph Cropsey (ed.), *Ancients and Moderns: Essays on the Tradition of Political Philosophy in Honor of Leo Strauss* (New York: Basic Books, 1964); David L. Schaefer, Jr, 'The Legacy of Leo Strauss: A Bibliographic Introduction', *Intercollegiate Review*, vol. 9, no. 3 (Summer 1974) pp. 139–48. The latter is an excellent and informative introduction to Strauss's work.

3. For some devastating reviews of Strauss's books see Terence Irwin's review of *XS* in *Philosophical Review*, vol. 83 (1974) pp. 409–13. One of Strauss's claims to fame is having resurrected Xenophon by emphasizing his importance for understanding Socrates. Irwin comments that Strauss succeeds only in reminding us of 'how unexciting Xenophon can be'. Worse than that, Strauss's interpretation is a 'tedious paraphrase' that 'reduces the amusing episodes to a uniform level of dullness' (p. 409). See also Trevor J. Saunders's review of Strauss's *AAPL*, in *Political Theory*, vol. 4 (1976) pp. 239–42. Strauss is described as sailing 'serenely across the surface of the text, skirting obvious rocks and crashing on submerged ones without knowing he is doing so' (p. 242); see also J. W. Yolton, 'Locke on the Law of Nature', *Philosophical Review*, vol. 67 (1958) pp. 477–98. Yolton points to innumerable examples of careless scholarship and a tendency to quote out of context; see also Victor Gourevitch, 'Philosophy and Politics II', *Review of Metaphysics*, vol. 22, no. 2 (December 1968) pp. 281–328, which is the second part of a two-part study of Strauss's work: the list of errors occurs on pp. 326–8; see also the criticisms of M. F. Burnyeat, 'Sphinx Without a Secret', a recent review of Strauss's *SPPP*, in *New York Review of Books*, vol. 32, no. 9 (30 May 1985) pp. 30–6, a penetrating and comprehensive critique of Straussian scholarship *and* philosophy.

4. Upon his death the *National Review* reported in its editorial comment that Leo Strauss had deeply impressed several generations of political philosophers, many of whom 'occupy high posts in major universities all across the nation' (vol. 25, (9 November 1973) p. 1226). Since his death in 1973, Strauss's popularity has been gaining momentum, and is now as visible in Canada as in the United States.

5. Werner J. Dannhauser, 'Leo Strauss: Becoming Naïve Again', *American Scholar*, vol. 44 (1974–5) pp. 636–42, esp. p. 637.

6. Jacob Klein and Leo Strauss, 'A Giving of Accounts', in *The College*, vol. 22 (April 1970) pp. 1–5. *The College* is a publication of St John's College, Annapolis, Maryland, where Strauss was the Scott Buchanan Distinguished Scholar-in-Residence at the time of his death. In this autobiographical piece, Strauss describes Marburg as a neo-Kantian center founded by Herman Cohen. He tells us that the school was 'in a state of disintegration' due to the increasing power of Husserl's phenomenological approach.

7. Strauss was raised as an Orthodox Jew and had a gymnasium education. He says that he was converted to Zionism ('simple, straightforward political Zionism') at the age of 17. From his studies at the Academy of Jewish Research came his first book, translated

from the German edition of 1930 into English as *Spinoza's Critique of Religion*.

8. There he wrote *On Tyranny* (1948), enlarged and revised with an essay by Alexandre Kojève in 1963, one of three books Strauss was to write on Xenophon. The others were *Xenophon's Socrates* (1972), an interpretation of Xenophon's *Memorabilia*, and *Xenophon's Socratic Discourse* (1970), an interpretation of Xenophon's *Oeconomicus*.

9. When he arrived from California to Annapolis in 1969 a 'spontaneous champagne party greeted him, his wife and adopted daughter and son-in-law at the railroad station between trains'. This is reported by George Anastaplo, 'On Leo Strauss: A Yahrzeit Remembrance', *University of Chicago Magazine*, vol. 67 (Winter 1974) p. 35.

10. See, for example, 'The Achievement of Leo Strauss,' *National Review*, vol. 25 (7 December 1973) pp. 1347–57, contributions by Walter Berns, Herbert J. Storing, Harry V. Jaffa and Werner J. Dannhauser; Allan Bloom, 'Leo Strauss: September 20, 1899–October 18, 1973', *Political Theory*, vol. 2, no. 4 (November 1974) pp. 372–92, is an excellent intellectual biography; Schaefer, 'The Legacy of Leo Strauss', is a concise introduction to his most famous works and their themes; Cropsey, 'Leo Strauss: A Bibliography and Memorial', is still among the most complete bibliographies available: Cropsey was a colleague of Strauss, and is his literary executor; Anastaplo, 'A Yahrzeit Remembrance', pp. 31–8, provides interesting descriptions of Strauss as a man; Dannhauser, 'Becoming Naïve Again', provides a detailed description of what it was like to be a graduate student at Chicago and to attend Leo Strauss's seminar in political philosophy; see also Jacob Klein, J. Winfree Smith, Ted A. Blanton and Laurence Berns in 'Memorials to Leo Strauss', *St. John's Review* (formerly *The College*), vol. 25, no. 4 (January 1974) pp. 1–5: Blanton tells us that he was 'charmed' by Strauss, and that in time he hoped to train his eyes to see in the texts what Strauss saw; Laurence Berns, 'Leo Strauss 1899–1973', *Independent Journal of Philosophy*, vol. 2 (1978) pp. 1–3; a very interesting and more detached article is Milton Himmelfarb's 'On Leo Strauss', *Commentary*, vol. 58, no. 2 (May 1974) pp. 60–6.

11. Jaffa, 'The Achievement of Leo Strauss', p. 1353. See also André Liebich, 'Straussianism and Ideology', in Anthony Parel (ed.), *Ideology, Philosophy and Politics* (Waterloo, Ontario: Wilfrid Laurier University Press, 1983), an outstanding work that attempts to come to grips with Strauss's conservatism. Liebich is puzzled by the comparison of Strauss with Machiavelli. For reasons that will become apparent below, this comparison is by no means unwarranted; on the contrary, it is quite appropriate (see Chapter 6).

12. Jaffa, 'The Achievement of Leo Strauss', p. 1355.

13. Anastaplo, 'A Yahrzeit Remembrance', p. 30.

14. Berns, 'The Achievement of Leo Strauss', p. 1347.

15. Storing, 'The Achievement of Leo Strauss', p. 1348.

16. Anastaplo, 'A Yahrzeit Remembrance, p. 36.

17. Ibid., p. 33.

18. Dannhauser, 'Becoming Naïve Again', p. 637.

19. Ibid.
20. Ibid., p. 639.
21. Ibid., p. 638. The Straussians are characterized by an overwhelming self-confidence that often bespeaks an embarrassing lack of modesty. In 'The Achievement of Leo Strauss' p. 1348, Storing explains this phenomenon as follows: 'If Strauss's students have sometimes displayed an unseemly self-assurance, the source is not so much pride of truth as relief that they have not allowed political science to make them more stupid than they need to be.'
22. Dannhauser, 'Becoming Naïve Again' p. 641. Dannhauser contrasts Strauss's formality and aloofness with his own style and that of many other Straussian teachers who believe in 'entering the life' of their students. However, Anastaplo reports that Strauss was not always so aloof. He established 'intimate ties' with his students earlier in his career but confessed to Anastaplo that a man of 50 could establish relations with 25-year-old graduate students that a man of 65 simply could not. See Anastaplo, 'A Yahrzeit Remembrance', p. 33.
23. Dannhauser, 'Becoming Naïve Again', p. 639, certainly felt a great deal of satisfaction from belonging to a group and went so far as to say that Strauss was responsible for much of the happiness in his life (p. 640).
24. Leo Strauss, 'An Unspoken Prologue to a Public Lecture at St. John's [In Honor of Jacob Klein, 1899–1978]', *Interpretation*, vol. 7, no. 3 (September 1978) pp. 1–3. This tribute was unspoken by Strauss since his death preceded that of Klein's. It was, however, prepared for the occasion of Klein's 60th birthday, and the editors of the journal above saw fit to publish it as a tribute to Klein upon his death. Strauss points to an interesting difference between himself and Klein. He says that Klein had an 'idiosyncratic abhorrence of publicity'. When they were in their twenties, they worked together with a group of other young men in the Prussian State Library in Berlin and relaxed together in a coffe-house close by the library. Klein was eager not to appear as part of a group of intellectuals; 'idle and inefficient young men of business or of the lucrative professions or any other kind of drones' were, however, acceptable. In contrast, Strauss did not mind the publicity; he reports that on such occasions he used to derive enjoyment from exclaiming as loud as he could 'Nietzsche!'
25. Dannhauser, 'Becoming Naïve Again', p. 640.
26. Strauss frequently uses this expression particularly in connection with the work of Maimonides. See his 'How to Begin to Study *The Guide of the Perplexed*', an introduction to Shlomo Pines's translation of Maimonides, *Guide of the Perplexed* (Chicago, Ill.: University of Chicago Press, 1963) pp. xi–lvi.
27. Dannhauser, 'Becoming Naïve Again', p. 640.
28. Eugene F. Miller, 'Leo Strauss: The Recovery of Political Philosophy', in Anthony de Crespigny and Kenneth Minogue (eds), *Contemporary Political Philosophers* (New York and London: Dodd-Mead and Methuen, 1975) p. 68.

29. Yolton, 'Locke on the Law of Nature'; Dante Germino, 'Second Thoughts on Leo Strauss's Machiavelli', *Journal of Politics*, vol. 28 (1966) pp. 794–817; Harvey C. Mansfield, Jr, 'Strauss's Machiavelli', *Political Theory*, vol. 3, no. 4 (November 1975) pp. 372–83; J. G. A. Pocock, 'Prophet and Inquisitor', *Political Theory*, vol. 3, no. 4 (November 1975) pp. 385–401; Edward Andrew, 'Descent to the Cave', *Review of Politics*, vol. 45, no. 4 (October 1983) pp. 510–35; Burnyeat, 'Sphinx Without a Secret', takes Strauss's interpretation of Plato and Aristotle to task; George H. Sabine, review of Strauss's *PAW* in *Ethics*, vol. 63 (1952–3) pp. 220–2.

30. *PAW*, pp. 30, 16; see also *WIPP*, pp. 231ff.; *OT*, pp. 28–66; *CM*, pp. 50–62; Alexandre Kojève, 'L'Action Politique des Philosophes', *Critiques*, VI, p. 46.

31. *OT*, p. 26: Strauss is said to have taught his students 'truths' that it is 'dangerous or unfitting to leave in the open'. See 'The Achievement of Leo Strauss', p. 1352.

32. It is not difficult to see why such a claim has aroused a furor among historians of ideas. It implies that only those who can decode the hidden message are privy to the true understanding of the history of political thought.

33. Americans are prone to overestimate the extent of the freedom they enjoy. Outsiders are often able to see more clearly that freedom in America is not as great as it is reputed to be. Writing to Löwith, Strauss remarks, 'life here in this country is terribly hard for people like me. One must struggle for the most modest working conditions, and one is defeated in every battle. I would like to print my study of Socratic politics, which you mention. But it is impossible to print it here. . . . Here, what does not fit the pattern is lost' ('Correspondence Concerning Modernity: Karl Löwith and Leo Strauss', *Independent Journal of Philosophy*, vol. 4 (1983) p. 105).

34. *WIPP*, p. 222.

35. Commenting on my paper, 'The Esoteric Philosophy of Leo Strauss', in *Political Theory*, vol. 13, no. 3 (August 1985) pp. 315–37, which was originally presented at the Canadian Political Science Association, Guelph, Ontario, 1984, Ernest L. Fortin argued that Strauss is not an esoteric writer on the grounds that Strauss does not tell us that he writes esoterically. Even if it were the case that Strauss does not say that his own commentaries are esoteric, that would not be sufficient reason to conclude that he does not write esoterically. However, Strauss *does say explicitly* that his own commentaries mirror the esotericism of the works they discuss (see *OT*, p. 27).

36. *OT*, p. 27.

37. Ibid.

38. Cropsey (ed.), *Ancients and Moderns*, Preface, p. viii.

39. Bloom, 'Leo Strauss'.

40. For the 'Platonic' critique of religion, see Chapter 3.

41. Bloom, 'Leo Strauss', p. 383.

42. Ibid.

43. Ibid., p. 385.

44. Ibid., p. 390.

45. Miller, 'The Recovery of Political Philosophy', p. 69.
46. Schaefer, 'The Legacy of Leo Strauss', p. 140.
47. James Steintrager, 'Political Philosophy, Political Theology, and Morality', *Thomist*, vol. 32 (July 1968) p. 309.
48. Ibid., p. 311.
49. Dannhauser, 'Becoming Naïve Again', p. 641.
50. Nathan Tarcov, 'Philosophy & History: Tradition and Interpretation in the Work of Leo Strauss', *Polity*, vol. 16, no. 1 (1983) p. 10; see also Warren Harbison, 'Irony and Deception', *Independent Journal of Philosophy*, vol. 2 (1978) pp. 89–94; and Willmoore Kendall, review of Cropsey (ed.), *Ancients and Moderns*, in *American Political Science Review*, vol. 61, no. 3 (September 1967) pp. 783–84. Both Harbison and Kendall deny that Strauss has any teaching or political philosophy as such. Harbison pleads Socratic ignorance for Strauss and his followers; a similar view is expressed by von Hiram Caton, 'Der Hermeneutische Weg von Leo Strauss', *Philosophisches Jahrbuch*, vol. 80 (1973) pp. 171–82. I follow Strauss in regarding Socratic ignorance with a great deal of irony.
51. Harry Jaffa, 'The Legacy of Leo Strauss', a review of Thomas L. Pangle's 'Introduction' to Leo Strauss, *SPPP*, in the *Claremont Review*, vol. 3, no. 3 (Fall 1984) pp. 14–21. Pangle's response appears in the same review (Spring 1985). A reply to Pangle by a defender of Jaffa, John A. Wettergreen, appears in vol. 4, no. 2 (Summer 1985). For a discussion of this debate, see Chapter 10.
52. John G. Gunnell, 'The Myth of the Tradition', *American Political Science Review*, vol. 72 (1978) pp. 122–34; see also his 'Political Theory and Politics: The case of Leo Strauss', in *Political Theory*, vol. 13, no. 3 (August 1985) pp. 339–61. Gunnell regards Strauss as one of several contemporary political thinkers who use the history of political thought as a vehicle for understanding our modern political predicament and diagnosing its ills. Hannah Arendt and Eric Voegelin are among the most renowned. Gunnell has aptly named this genre 'the myth of the tradition' or 'epic political theory', and maintains that writers in this genre assume that Western political thought can be viewed as a continuous historical narrative that begins with the ancient Greeks and evolves in a discernible pattern that explains where our political ideas came from and how we have come to think as we do. There are as many versions of the narrative as there are writers within this genre. In Strauss's version of the narrative, political philosophy was born with Socrates, developed by Plato and Aristotle and continued until the seventeenth century where it met a deathly blow. There is much truth in what Gunnell has to say, but we must be careful not to cast the debate between the ancients and the moderns in too historical a light, even though Strauss gives us ample reason for doing so. In principle the debate between ancients and moderns can take place in any historical period, and Strauss points to earlier versions of the debate. Gunnell has no doubt that Strauss sides with the ancients. He compares Strauss's work with Aristophanes's *Frogs*, an epic drama where Aeschylus is brought

forth from the underworld to do battle with Euripides. In the dramatic confrontation, the old teaching is vindicated. Strauss himself invites a comparison with Swift's *Battle of the Books*: see 'The Crisis of Our Time', and 'The Crisis of Political Philosophy', in Howard J. Spaeth (ed.), *The Predicament of Modern Politics* (Detroit, Mich.: University of Detroit Press, 1964) pp. 41–54, 91–103. Swift, with his characteristic wit and satire heaps praises upon the great ancients, whose very eloquence makes their modern opponents seem like a travesty of real humanity. Like Strauss, Swift heaps unspeakable insults on the moderns while showering the ancients with exorbitant praise. This is not to say that what is at issue between ancients and moderns is simple or obvious. Gunnell notes Strauss's elusiveness (p. 122).

53. See, for example, Tarcov, 'Tradition and Interpretation in the Work of Leo Strauss'. This is a response to Gunnell. Although this is an excellent article in many ways, it is unconvincing. Tarcov argues that Strauss does not wish to return to the ancients, which is true in the sense that Strauss does not think that such a return is possible. But Strauss surely thinks there is much that we can learn from the ancients; they can not only enable us to understand the source of our modern malaise, but also show us how we might postpone, if not avoid, the inevitable decline of our civilization. Tarcov goes too far in saying that Strauss does not necessarily prefer the ancients, that his wish is merely to 'reopen the quarrel' (p. 7); James F. Ward, 'Experience and Political Philosophy: Notes on Reading Leo Strauss', *Polity*, vol. 13, no. 4 (Summer 1981) p. 679: Ward argues that Strauss does not wish to replace modern with ancient science. This is certainly not true for political science, which for Strauss is always an integral part of any adequate understanding of science. See also Victor Gourevitch, 'Philosophy and Politics: I', and 'Philosophy and Politics: II', in *Review of Metaphysics*, vol. 22, no. 1 (September 1968) pp. 58–84, and vol. 22, no. 2 (December 1968) pp. 281–325, respectively. This is one of the best and by far the most comprehensive study of Strauss's work as a whole. Gourevitch erroneously believes that Strauss departs from the ancients by taking a much more skeptical position than is characteristic of the latter. He fails to note, however, the extent to which Strauss's understanding of the ancients is far more skeptical than they are generally believed to be (p. 325). See also Richard Kennington, 'Strauss's *Natural Right and History*', *Review of Metaphysics*, vol. 35 (September 1981) pp. 57–86. Kennington believes that Strauss's *Natural Right and History* is not a vindication of the ancients against the moderns, but merely a 'disclosure of fundamental alternatives' (p. 60). These authors are right in thinking that Strauss does not believe classical political philosophy will provide us with 'solutions' to our contemporary problems. But it must be added that Strauss does not think solutions are always necessarily available. Political philosophy enables us always to *understand*, but not always to *solve* problems. Chance and good fortune must coincide with understanding to make the latter possible. And in Strauss's

view, it is the classical understanding of the problems that alone can enable us to recognize the *opportunities* in which fortune might permit a partial 'solution'; for human problems there are no *final* solutions.

54. Kennington, 'Strauss's *Natural Right and History*' follows a complicated trail of misdirection and manages to write a commentary on Strauss that is more elusive than the original; Robert J. McShea, 'Leo Strauss on Machiavelli', *Western Political Quarterly*, vol. 16 (1963) pp. 782–97: McShea's article is interesting but when it hits the mark it seems quite by accident; cf. Laurence Lampert, 'The Argument of Leo Strauss in *What is Political Philosophy?*', *Modern Age*, vol. 22, no. 1 (Winter 1978) pp. 38–46: this work does not use Strauss's method to study his work, it simply takes into account that Strauss writes esoterically and therefore must be read with great care.

55. *WIPP*, p. 223.

56. *OT*, p. 27.

57. *WIPP*, p. 222.

58. Ibid., p. 225.

59. Sabine, review of Strauss's *PAW*, p. 220.

60. John H. Schaar and Sheldon S. Wolin, 'Essays on the Scientific Study of Politics: A Critique', a review essay of Herbert Storing (ed.), *Essays on the Scientific Study of Politics* (New York: Holt, Rinehart & Winston, 1962), in *American Political Science Review*, vol. 57 (1963) pp. 125–60; the book under review includes Strauss's famous 'Epilogue'. Schaar and Wolin note that the 'volume is of such uniform texture that it might have been written by one hand. In assumptions, method, style of argument, and even vocabulary, syntax and metaphor, the five essays are as one' (p. 126). All the contributors except Leo Strauss received their doctorates at the University of Chicago where Strauss was teaching. The review is followed by responses from Strauss and his students.

In recent years there have been cases where Straussians have dissented from the interpretations of Strauss. But where this is the case, they nevertheless maintain intact the Straussian assumptions and ideas to the very last detail. Their disagreement with Strauss is confined to whether a thinker in question was wise enough to think the things that Strauss taught them wise men ought to think. See for example Nathan Tarcov, *Locke's Education for Liberty* (Chicago, Ill.: University of Chicago Press, 1984). Tarcov's esoteric thesis consists in the claim that Locke's wisdom ought not be underestimated since his liberal education is intended to create a sort of aristocracy in disguise. Following Strauss, Tarcov expresses himself with utmost caution and reserve. See my review of Tarcov's book in *Interchange*, the Journal of the Ontario Institute for Studies in Education, vol. 17, no. 3 (1986). Another example is E. A. Goerner's interpretation of Aquinas. See his 'On Thomistic Natural Law: The Bad Man's View of Thomistic Natural Right', and 'Thomistic Natural Right: The Good Man's View of Thomistic Natural Law', both in *Political Theory*, vol. 7, no. 1 (February 1975) pp. 101–22, and vol. 11, no. 3 (August 1983) pp. 393–418 respectively, and also discussed in Chapter 5 below, pp. 110–11.

61. I will not be concerned with the debates regarding the adequacy of Strauss's method as a vehicle for understanding the history of thought. See J. G. A. Pocock, *The Machiavellian Moment: Florentine Political Thought and the Atlantic Republican Tradition* (Princeton, N.J.: Princeton University Press, 1975); Quentin Skinner, 'The Ideological Context of Hobbes's Political Thought', *Historical Journal*, vol. 9 (1966) pp. 286–317; Nathan Tarcov has replied to Pocock and Skinner in a review of Pocock's *Machiavellian Moment*, in *Political Science Quarterly*, vol. 91 (Summer 1976) pp. 380–2; and Nathan Tarcov, 'Political Thought in Early Modern Europe, II: The Age of Reformation', *Journal of Modern History*, vol. 54 (March 1982) pp. 56–65; see also Nathan Tarcov, 'Quentin Skinner's Method and Machiavelli's Prince', *Ethics*, vol. 92 (July 1982) pp. 692–709.
62. Klein and Strauss, 'Giving of Accounts', p. 4.
63. Strauss believed that knowledge of the whole is what philosophy is fundamentally concerned with.
64. *WIPP*, p. 231.
65. *CM*, p. 115: on the dual meaning of justice; *OT*, p. 105: on the two meanings of virtue; *XSD*, p. 161: on the two meanings of gentlemanliness; 'Farabi's Plato', in *Louis Ginsberg: Jubilee Volume* (New York: American Academy of Jewish Research, 1954) pp. 385–8: on the dual meanings of nobility and virtue.
66. *OT*, p. 26.
67. Burnyeat, 'Sphinx Without a Secret', p. 30.
68. Stephen Toulmin is reported to have been worried that the state department's policy planning staff know more about Leo Strauss than about the realities of the day; see Burnyeat, 'Sphinx Without a Secret', p. 30.
69. See the *Claremont Review of Books*, a quarterly publication of the Claremont Institute for the Study of Statesmanship and Political Philosophy.
70. I have this from a reliable source.
71. Stanley Rothman, 'The Revival of Classical Political Philosophy: A Critique', *American Political Science Review*, vol. 56, no. 2 (June 1962) pp. 341–59, with a reply by Joseph Cropsey.
72. Ibid., p. 358.
73. 'What is Liberal Education?' in *LAM*, p. 5.
74. Jaffa, 'The Achievement of Leo Strauss', p. 1355.

Notes to Chapter 2: Esoteric Philosophy and Ancient Wisdom

1. *PAW*, pp. 7, 8. It is important to note that for Strauss the terms philosophy and science are synonymous, as are the terms city, *polis*, society and the world. I will follow Strauss in using these terms interchangeably.
2. Nietzsche, *Uses and Abuses of Hitory*, trans. Adrian Collins (New York: Library of Liberal Arts, Bobbs-Merrill, 1957), sec. vi, p. 41; cf. *OT*, p. 24; *PAW*, p. 159; *NRH*, p. 33; *WIPP*, pp. 66, 101. In spite of

the extent to which I am inclined to sympathize with this sentiment, admitting that no man can altogether transcend his time is a matter of honesty not historicism. Even Strauss was to some extent a man of his time. Many of his central ideas reflect his German intellectual milieu. For example, he was, like Heidegger, concerned with the idea of *Bodenstandigkeit*, or rootedness in the soil (see Chapter 8). Like his contemporaries Hannah Arendt and Eric Voegelin, he was enchanted by antiquity and disenchanted by 'modernity'. Like Arendt he was concerned with immortality rather than eternity; he also shared with her views about politics that they both held in common with Machiavelli (with one difference: Strauss was reluctant to make these views public). The view that Western civilization is in 'crisis' is common to many writers after the Second World War. The similarities between Strauss's ideas and those of Nietzsche and Freud are also striking (see Chapters 3, 4 and 9).

3. *WIPP*, p. 221–2, my italics.
4. Ibid., p. 221; 'Farabi's Plato', in *Louis Ginsberg: Jubilee Volume* (New York: American Academy of Jewish Research, 1954) p. 393; 'Political Philosophy and the Crisis of Our Time', in George J. Graham, Jr, and George W. Carey (eds), *The Post-Behavioral Era* (New York: David McKay, 1972) p. 242. The latter is based on two lectures, 'The Crisis of Our Time', and 'The Crisis of Political Philosophy', published in Howard J. Spaeth (ed.), *The Predicament of Modern Politics* (Detroit, Mich.: University of Detroit Press, 1964).
5. *WIPP*, p. 10.
6. Ibid., p. 221, my italics.
7. Ibid., p. 222.
8. J. S. Mill, *On Liberty* (New York: Library of Liberal Arts, Bobbs-Merrill, 1956: first published 1859) p. 21.
9. Ibid., p. 43.
10. *WIPP*, p. 222.
11. Strauss, 'Farabi's Plato', p. 362; a shorter and less explicit version of this piece appears as the Introduction to *PAW*. It is understandable that the former is more explicit on the question of morality than the latter in view of the fact that it is less accessible and directed to a more limited audience.
12. *PAW*, p. 18. Strauss's interpretation of Socrates relies heavily on Al Farabi and other Islamic philosophers. For example, he follows Al Farabi in maintaining that Plato was an esoteric writer, in denying any relevance to the differences between Plato and Aristotle, and in believing that Plato did not believe in an afterlife, except as a useful myth. He follows Al Razi in maintaining that Socrates underwent an important change or conversion in the course of his life. See *SA*; cf. Muhammad b. Zakariyya al-Razi, 'The Philosophic Way of Life', in Paul Kraus, 'Raziana I', *Orientalia*, vol. 4 (1935) pp. 300–34.
13. *Paw*, p. 17.
14. *WIPP*, p. 29.
15. Ibid., p. 32.

16. I am borrowing the expression from *SCR*, p. 48.
17. *WIPP*, p. 33.
18. Leo Strauss, 'Marsilius of Padua', in *HPP*, 1st edn, p. 229.
19. *PAW*, p. 14.
20. Strauss tells us that the same is true for Farabi. Anything he might say about immortality must be regarded as 'prudential accommodations to the accepted dogma' (Strauss, 'Farabi's Plato', p. 375).
21. *PAW*, p. 18.
22. *WIPP*, p. 10.
23. Ibid., p. 221; Strauss, 'Farabi's Plato', p. 393; Strauss 'Political Philosophy and the Crisis of Our Time', p. 242.
24. *WIPP*, p. 93.
25. Ibid.
26. *CM*, p. 53,
27. Ibid.
28. *WIPP*, pp. 93–4.
29. Leo Strauss, 'Philosophy as Rigorous Science and Political Philosophy', in *SPPP*, p. 37; *OT*, p. 26.
30. *OT*, p. 26.
31. Ibid.
32. Ibid.
33. *WIPP*, pp. 31–2.
34. Ibid., p. 31.
35. Ibid.
36. Ibid.
37. Ibid., p. 32.
38. Ibid.
39. Ibid.
40. Ibid., p. 40.
41. *PAW*, p. 30; Strauss, 'Farabi's Plato', p. 382. When Strauss says that what a writer says most frequently or in the largest number of passages is not an indication of what he really believes, we must not take this to mean that what a writer says most frequently is the reverse of what he really thinks. He simply means to say that what esoteric writers say most frequently or in the largest number of passages must be interpreted in light of how they qualify it in the course of repeating it. Repetitions frequently include additions and qualifications which are very important for any interpreter, not just a Straussian one. In interpreting Strauss, I will certainly take into account not only what he says most frequently, but how he qualifies it and what he says in the course of repeating it throughout the corpus of his work. I will under no circumstances reverse what he says clearly and explicitly. I regard this as an abuse of what Strauss says about interpretation, although it is the sort of abuse to which his method readily lends itself.
42. *PAW*, p. 30, my italics.
43. Strauss, 'Plato', in *CM*.

44. In Chapter 6 I show how Strauss uses Machiavelli to utter 'truths' that he is reluctant to utter in his own name.
45. *PAW*, p. 24.
46. See discussion of the 'crisis' in Chapter 8.
47. *PAW*, p. 24.
48. Ibid., p. 14.
49. *WIPP*, p. 154.
50. *PAW*, p. 17.
51. *WIPP*, p. 34.
52. *AAPL*.
53. Harry Jaffa, 'The Achievement of Leo Strauss', *National Review*, vol. 25 (7 December 1973) p. 1355.
54. *LAM*, p. 24.
55. M. F. Burnyeat is the only critic of Strauss who seems to have recognized this fully. See his 'Sphinx Without a Secret', *New York Review of Books*, vol. 32, no. 9 (30 May 1985) pp. 30–6.
56. *PAW*, p. 13.
57. Ibid., p. 15.
58. Strauss, 'Farabi's Plato', p. 388.
59. Ibid., pp. 385–9; for other references to the dual meanings of justice, virtue and gentlemanliness, see *CM*, p. 115; *OT*, p. 105; *XSD*, p. 161.
60. Ibid., p. 385.
61. Ibid., pp. 385, 386, 387.
62. Ibid., p. 365.
63. Ibid., p. 374.
64. Ibid.
65. Ibid.
66. Frederick D. Wilhelmsen, *Christianity and Political Philosophy* (Athens: University of Georgia Press, 1978) p. 211.
67. The metaphor is from Plato's allegory of the ship, *Republic*, 488ff.
68. *OT*, p. 26.
69. Leo Strauss, 'How to Begin to Study *The Guide of the Perplexed*', an introduction to Maimonides, *The Guide of the Perplexed*, trans. Shlomo Pines (Chicago, Ill.: University of Chicago Press, 1963) pp. xi–lvi, reprinted in *LAM*.
70. *PAW*, p. 21.
71. Joseph J. Carpino, review of Frederick D. Wilhelmsen, *Christianity and Political Philosophy*, in *Interpretation*, vol. 8, nos 2 & 3 (May 1980) p. 217.
72. *PAW*, p. 20.
73. See, for example, Edward Andrew, 'Descent to the Cave', *Review of Politics*, vol. 45, no. 4 (October 1983) pp. 510–35.
74. For example, see my discussions above of 'What is Political Philosophy?' and 'On a Forgotten Kind of Writing', both in *WIPP*, and the Introduction to *OT*.
75. See Chapters 6 and 5 respectively.
76. Walter Berns, 'The Achievement of Leo Strauss', p. 1347.

Notes to Chapter 3: Philosophy's Hidden Revolt against God

1. Leo Strauss, 'Jerusalem and Athens', *Commentary*, June 1967, pp. 45–57, esp. p. 46; reprinted with minor additions in *SPPP*. All references are to the latter.
2. *NRH*, p. 81.
3. *CM*, p. 65; Plato's *Laws*, bk 10; see also my 'Idea of Nature', in S. B. Drury and R. Knopff (eds), *Law and Politics: Readings in Legal and Political Thought* (Calgary: Detselig Enterprises, 1980).
4. *NRH*, p. 85.
5. Ibid., pp. 85, 93; see also 'On Plato's *Apology of Socrates* and *Crito'*, in *SPPP*, pp. 38–66, and *SA*. See also Harry Neumann, 'Civic Piety and Socratic Atheism: An interpretation of Strauss's *Socrates and Aristophanes'*, *Independent Journal of Philosophy*, vol. 2 (1978) pp. 33–7; for Strauss's view of Socrates see Chapter 4 below.
6. *NRH*, p. 93.
7. Ibid., p. 84.
8. Ibid., p. 85.
9. Interestingly, these are the hallmarks of modernity; as we shall see below, Strauss believes that the ills of modernity stem primarily from the 'publication' of philosophy.
10. *NRH*, p. 74.
11. Ibid., p. 75.
12. Ibid.
13. Ibid., p. 76.
14. Leo Strauss, 'The Mutual Influence of Theology and Philosophy', part of a series of lectures given at the University of Chicago in the early 1950s, published posthumously in *Independent Journal of Philosophy*, vol. 3 (1979) pp. 111–18, esp. p. 113.
15. Ibid., p. 113.
16. Frederick D. Wilhelmsen, *Christianity and Political Philosophy* (Athens: University of Georgia Press, 1978) p. 218; see also R. Sokolowski, *The God of Faith and Reason: Foundations of Christian Theology* (Notre Dame, Ill.: Notre Dame Press, 1982) pp. 157–64. For Straussian responses to these criticisms see Joseph J. Carpino's review of Wilhelmsen's book in *Interpretation*, vol. 8, nos 2 & 3 (May 1980) pp. 204–22; and Walter Nicgorski's review of Sokolowski's book in *Claremont Review*, vol. 4, no. 2 (Summer 1985) pp. 18–21; see also 'Memorials to Leo Strauss', *St. John's Review*, vol. 25, no. 4 (January 1974): Jacob Klein tells us that Strauss was once an Orthodox Jew, but he 'later changed his religious orientation *radically*, tying the question of god or of gods to his political reasoning, without letting his own life be dependent on any divinity or on any religious rites' (p. 2, my italics). Laurence Berns points to the fact that even though Strauss was a Jew, he insisted that 'there is no such thing as a Jewish philosophy' (p. 5).
17. Strauss has been described as one who replaces argument by exegesis; and while this is quite true, I believe that it is not an ineffective way to argue; see M. F. Burnyeat, 'Sphinx Without a Secret', *New York Review of Books*, vol. 32, no. 9 (30 May 1985) pp. 30–6.

18. Strauss, 'Jerusalem and Athens', and 'On the Interpretation of Genesis', a lecture given by Strauss in the 'Works of the Mind' series at University College, University of Chicago, 25 January 1957, posthumously published in *L'Homme: Revue Française d'Anthropologie*, vol. xxi, no. 1 (Janvier–Mars 1981) pp. 5–20.
19. Strauss, 'Genesis', p. 7.
20. Ibid., pp. 7, 9, 10; Strauss's description of the biblical account as an 'unlikely tale' mirrors Plato's description of his own account of creation in the *Timaeus* as a 'probable or likely tale'. Compare *Timaeus*, 29D, and 'Jerusalem and Athens', p. 166. In the Platonic account, the world consisted in the beginning of a pre-existing or primal chaos (*Timaeus*, 30A–B), but the world as we know it is the work of an intelligent Demiurge or master-craftsman. The Platonic Demiurge is a rational principle that imposed order on pre-existing matter according to the ideas or forms accessible to intelligence. The Demiurge makes the best of a bad situation, as it were, but he does not create the world out of nothing. In this way, evil can easily be explained as the result of the shortcomings of matter or the pre-existing material with which he had to work. In Strauss's interpretation, the biblical account is more intelligible if it is understood as formation rather than as creation out of nothing.
21. For Strauss, the biblical God is mysterious and inscrutable; see his 'Mutual Influence', p. 112; 'Genesis', pp. 7, 20; 'Jerusalem and Athens', pp. 157, 162.
22. Strauss, 'Genesis', p. 20.
23. Ibid., p. 7.
24. Strauss, 'Mutual Influence', p. 112.
25. Strauss, 'Genesis', p. 15, also pp. 16, 18.
26. Deuteronomy 4: 15–19.
27. Strauss, 'Genesis', p. 15, also pp. 16, 18.
28. Ibid., p. 15.
29. Ibid., p. 19.
30. Ibid., p. 7.
31. Strauss, 'Jerusalem and Athens', p. 157.
32. Strauss, 'Genesis', p. 18.
33. Ibid.
34. Ibid.
35. Strauss, 'Jerusalem and Athens', p. 157.
36. *PAW*, p. 24.
37. Hegel, *Lectures on the Philosophy of Religion*, trans. E. B. Speirs and J. Burdon Sanderson, 3 vols (London: Routledge & Kegan Paul, 1895, 1962) vol. iii, p. 54; see also discussion of this in Emil L. Fackenheim, *The Religious Dimension in Hegel's Thought* (Boston, Mass.: Beacon Press, 1970) p. 133. Compare Hegel's view with Jacob Boehme, *Six Theosophic Points*, trans. J. R. Earle (Michigan: Ann Arbor Press, 1958).
38. *WIPP*, p. 11; Strauss, 'Mutual Influence', pp. 112, 113; *NRH*, p. 75.
39. Strauss, 'Jerusalem and Athens', p. 157.
40. See Arlene W. Saxonhouse, 'The Philosopher and the Female in the

Political Thought of Plato', *Political Theory*, vol. 4, no. 2 (1976) pp. 195–213; see also her 'Eros and the Female in Greek Political Thought: An Interpretation of Plato's Symposium', *Political Theory*, vol. 12, no. 1 (1984) pp. 5–27.

41. Strauss, 'Jerusalem and Athens', p. 157, also pp. 158–9.
42. Ibid., pp. 157–8.
43. Hannah Arendt, *On Revolution* (New York: Viking Press, 1965, 1963) p. 10.
44. For a more detailed discussion, see Chapter 6.
45. 'Jerusalem and Athens', p. 158.
46. Ibid., p. 158.
47. Ibid., p. 148.
48. Ibid., p. 158; Strauss, 'Zionism in Max Nordau', *The Jew: Essays from Martin Buber's Journal, Der Jude 1916–1928*, selected, edited and introduced by Arthur A. Cohen (Alabama: Alabama University Press, 1980) pp. 120–6; Strauss, 'Introductory Essay for Hermann Cohen, *Religion of Reason out of the Sources of Judaism*', in *SPPP*, pp. 233–47; Strauss, 'Why We Remain Jews: Can Jewish Faith and History Still Speak to Us?' a lecture given on 4 February 1962 at the Hillel Foundation, and widely circulated in spite of the fact that the covering note on the transcription emphasizes its private character, and states that 'recipients are emphatically requested not to seek to increase the circulation of the transcription'.
49. Strauss, 'Jerusalem and Athens', p. 164.
50. Ibid., p. 164; *NRH*, pp. 93–4.
51. Strauss, 'Jerusalem and Athens', p. 165.
52. Strauss, 'Mutual Influence', p. 113.
53. Ibid.
54. See Chapter 8.
55. Strauss, 'Mutual Influence', pp. 117, 114: this need not be regarded as an instance where Strauss says the opposite of what he thinks; it can be understood to mean that neither philosophy nor the Bible can show that 'it is the one thing needful', and for Strauss, this is as it should be, since both are necessary.
56. *CM*, p. 51: 'Irony is then the noble dissimulation of one's worth, of one's superiority. We may say, it is the humanity peculiar to the superior man: he spares the feelings of his inferiors by not displaying his superiority.'
57. *TM*, p. 173.
58. Strauss, 'Mutual Influence', p. 111.
59. Ibid.
60. Ibid.
61. Ibid.
62. Ibid., pp. 115, 116.
63. Ibid., p. 115.
64. Ibid.
65. Ibid., p. 116; for Strauss, the divine law is irrational: the reason for this is not made clear here, but it will become evident in Chapter 5 when we examine Strauss's conception of a truly rational or

philosophical ethics. Suffice it to say here that the divine law demands certain conduct from man regardless of the circumstances or the consequences. In a divine law conception of ethics there are certain things that man is not permitted to do, come what may. In contrast, Strauss believes that a philosophical (i.e. secular) ethic cannot admit such absolute prohibitions.

66. Strauss, 'Mutual Influence', p. 114.
67. Ibid.
68. Ibid., p. 115.
69. Ibid.
70. Ibid.
71. Ibid., p. 116.
72. Ibid., p. 117.
73. Ibid.
74. Ibid., p. 116.
75. Ibid., p. 115.
76. Ibid., p. 111.
77. Ibid., p. 112.
78. Ibid.
79. *OT*, pp. 210–18; Victor Gourevitch, 'Philosophy and Politics: II', the second part of a two-part study of Strauss's thought, *Review of Metaphysics*, vol. 22, no. 2 (December 1968) p. 325; James F. Ward, 'Experience and Political Philosophy: Notes on Reading Leo Strauss', *Polity*, vol. 13, no. 4 (Summer 1981) p. 681.
80. Strauss, 'Mutual Influence', p. 113.
81. Ibid., p. 116.
82. *WIPP*, p. 23.
83. Strauss, 'Mutual Influence', p. 113.
84. Ibid.
85. Ibid.
86. Ibid.
87. Ibid.
88. Ibid., pp. 113, 114.
89. Strauss, 'Marsilius of Padua', *HPP*; see also Walter Berns, *The First Amendment and the Future of American Democracy* (New York: Basic Books, 1976) p. 22, on the rule of priests. Strauss shares the sentiment of Marsilius of Padua in abhorring the rule of priests; he adds that Marsilius follows the tradition of Machiavelli. In Chapter 6, I argue that Strauss shares the sentiments of Machiavelli on religion and the rule of priests.
90. The grounds on which Strauss rejects Thomistic ethics in favor of Aristotelian ethics are discussed in Chapter 5.
91. See G. E. M. Anscombe, 'Modern Moral Philosophy', in W. D. Hudson (ed,), *The Is/Ought Problem* (London: Macmillan, 1973) pp. 175–95. This excellent essay is more articulate than anything Strauss has written on the issue. John Finnis disagrees with this position, see his *Natural Law and Natural Rights* (Oxford: Clarendon Press, 1980), and his *The Fundamentals of Ethics* (Oxford: Clarendon

Press, 1983), and my review of it in *Review of Politics*, vol. 47, no. 3 (July 1985) pp. 432–6.

92. Leo Strauss, 'An Unspoken Prologue to a Public Lecture at St. John's [In Honor of Jacob Klein, 1899–1978]', *Interpretation*, vol. 7, no. 3 (September 1978) pp. 1–3; see esp. p. 1. Strauss wrote the piece on the occasion of Klein's 60th birthday. On the death of Klein, the editors of *Interpretation* saw fit to publish this piece in Klein's honor. The same theme of 'heart and mind' can be found in Strauss's funeral speech, delivered upon the death of one of his graduate students, 6 December 1961, quoted in George Anastaplo, 'On Leo Strauss: A Yahrzeit Remembrance', *University of Chicago Magazine*, vol. 67 (Winter 1974) p. 38.

93. *OT*, p. 92: the wise man is not interested in the things that are bound by space and time, he wishes to 'liberate himself from the shackles of the Here and Now'; see also *LAM*, p. 85.

94. Strauss, 'Mutual Influence', p. 113.

95. Ibid., p. 111.

96. Wilhelmsen, *Christianity and Political Philosophy*, pp. 211. Wilhelmsen argues against Strauss in a Thomistic fashion, saying that reason would be unreasonable were it not to admit elements that it could not fully account for.

97. Anastaplo, 'A Yahrzeit Remembrance', p. 34.

98. Strauss, 'Mutual Influence', p. 114.

99. Ibid., my italics.

100. Strauss, 'Jerusalem and Athens', p. 172.

101. Strauss, 'Mutual Influence', p. 117.

102. *CM*, p. 61.

103. Strauss testifies to the central importance of this issue in his autobiographical Preface to the English translation of *SCR*, p. 1: he describes himself as being 'in the grip of the theologico-political predicament'. Joseph Cropsey testifies to the importance of this issue for Strauss in his comments following Strauss's lecture 'Why We Remain Jews'. The gist of Cropsey's remarks is that Strauss speaks about Jerusalem and Athens even when we least expect it.

104. Preface to *SCR*, p. 1.

105. Sigmund Freud, *Future of an Illusion* (New York: Doubleday, 1957) pp. 43, 56–7.

106. Ernest L. Fortin, 'Gadamer on Strauss: An Interview', *Interpretation*, vol. 12, no. 1 (January 1984) pp. 1–13. Gadamer comments that, in real life, Strauss avoided confrontations with worthy opponents. He reports that he tried on many occasions to engage Strauss in a debate on matters of importance to both of them, without success (p. 13). The noteworthy exception to this is Strauss's exchange with Alexandre Kojève, published in *OT*.

107. Freud, *Future of an Illusion*, p. 26.

108. Ibid.

109. Ibid., p. 22.

110. Anastaplo, 'A Yahrzeit Remembrance', p. 38.

111. Ibid.
112. Ibid.
113. Ibid.
114. Ibid.; see also *SCR*, pp. 38ff; *NRH*, pp. 112–13; see also Chapter 4 on Strauss's Epicurian view of death, pp. 62ff.
115. Freud, *Future of an Illusion*, p. 43. Freud does not use the terms fideist and Averroist; these are terms commonly used today to refer to these positions.
116. Ibid., p. 42.
117. Ibid., pp. 43–4.
118. Ibid., pp. 56–7.
119. Strauss, 'Mutual Influence', p. 114.
120. Freud, *Future of an Illusion*, pp. 61–2; for a contemporary exposition of this view see Kai Nielsen, *Ethics Without God* (London: Pemberton Books, 1973).
121. Ibid., p. 81.
122. Ibid., p. 92.
123. *CM*, p. 61: Strauss regards Socrates as a 'comic' rather than a tragic figure because he laughs, unlike Christ who weeps.

Notes to Chapter 4: Socrates and the Drama of Western Civilization

1. By way of example, Strauss declares that the idea of nature is absent from the Old Testament: *NRH*, p. 81; Strauss, 'Natural Law', *Encyclopedia of the Social Sciences*, vol. 12, p. 80; Strauss echoes the theme of his lecture 'On the Interpretation of Genesis' ('Works of the Mind' series, University College University of Chicago, 25 January 1957, posthumously published in *L'Homme: Revue Française d'Anthropologie*, vol. xxi, no. 1 (Janvier–Mars 1981) pp. 5–20) discussed above – namely, that the Bible is anti-nature and anti-philosophy.
2. Ibid., pp. 81–97.
3. John Gunnell, 'Political Theory and Politics: The Case of Leo Strauss', *Political Theory*, vol. 13, no. 3 (August 1985) pp. 339–61.
4. Strauss discusses the poem briefly in *NRH*, pp. 112–13, and in greater detail in 'Notes on Lucretius', which appears in *LAM*, pp. 76–139.
5. *NRH*, p. 112.
6. *LAM*, p. 92.
7. Ibid., p. 84.
8. Ibid., p. 85.
9. Ibid.
10. This is Blaise Pascal's expression.
11. *SCR*, p. 47.
12. Ibid.
13. Ibid.
14. *LAM*, p. 127.
15. Ibid., pp. 96, 100; Sigmund Freud, *Future of an Illusion*, trans. W. D. Robson Scott and revised by James Strachey (New York: Doubleday, 1964) p. 23.

16. *NRH*, p. 113.
17. *LAM*, p. 79.
18. Ibid., pp. 96, 122.
19. Ibid., pp. 79, 82, 91, 106; *SCR*, p. 49.
20. *LAM*, p. 79.
21. Ibid., p. 83.
22. Ibid.
23. Ibid., pp. 83, 84, 92, 122, 130–1, 135.
24. Ibid., p. 83.
25. Ibid., pp. 83–4.
26. Ibid., p. 84.
27. Ibid., p. 100.
28. Ibid., p. 127.
29. Ibid., pp. 79, 82, 84, 91, 106.
30. Ibid., p. 84.
31. Ibid., p. 111, and funeral speech from George Anastaplo, 'On Leo Strauss: A Yahrzeit Remembrance', *University of Chicago Magazine*, vol. 67 (Winter 1974) p. 38.
32. *LAM*, p. 105.
33. Ibid., p. 107.
34. Ibid., p. 131.
35. Ibid., p. 107.
36. Ibid., p. 131.
37. Ibid., p. 85: Strauss comments that the equation is doubtful to any well-traveled man who has observed the diversity of laws and religions from place to place.
38. Ibid., p. 131: Strauss writes that 'fear of punishment and fear of the gods belong together'.
39. *NRH*, p. 112.
40. Ibid., pp. 112–13.
41. *LAM*, p. 100; see also Harry Neumann, 'The Unpopularity of Epicurean Materialism: An Interpretation of Lucretius', *The Modern Schoolman*, vol. 45 (May 1968) pp. 299–311; Neumann regards Venus as the foundation of the city.
42. *LAM*, p. 131; cf. Sigmund Freud, *Civilization and its Discontents*, trans. James Strachey (New York: W. W. Norton, 1961) pp. 50ff.
43. *LAM*, p. 83.
44. Ibid., p. 92.
45. Ibid., p. 104; compare with what Strauss says on pp. 83, 92.
46. Ibid., p. 131.
47. Ibid., pp. 133, 131; also *OT*, p. 93.
48. *LAM*, p. 91.
49. Ibid., p. 85.
50. Ibid.
51. Allan Bloom with Harry V. Jaffa, *Shakespeare's Politics* (Chicago, Ill.: University of Chicago Press, 1964) p. 51.
52. *OT*, pp. 91, 92.
53. Ibid., p. 101.
54. Ibid., p. 91.

55. *LAM*, p. 112.
56. *OT*, p. 93.
57. Ibid., p. 91.
58. Ibid.
59. Ibid., p. 92.
60. Ibid.
61. Ibid.
62. *LAM*, pp. 118, 119; cf. Lucretius, *On the Nature of the Universe*, trans. R. E. Latham (Harmondsworth: Penguin Books, 1951) bk IV.
63. *LAM*, p. 119.
64. Ibid.
65. Thomas L. Pangle, 'Introduction' to Leo Strauss, *SPPP*, p. 16; see esp. *XS*, pp. 85–9, where Strauss makes much of Socrates's seductive powers and irresistible charm; see also *SPPP*, p. 47: Strauss refers to Socrates as *'erotikos'*.
66. *LAM*, p. 128.
67. Ibid., p. 130.
68. Ibid., pp. 119, 131; see also *CM*, p. 73: a wise man is not a benefactor.
69. *LAM*, p. 131.
70. Ibid.
71. *OT*, p. 81.
72. Albert Camus, *The Outsider*, trans. Stuart Gilbert (Harmondsworth: Penguin Books, 1942); see also Walter Berns's discussion of Camus's novel in his *For Capital Punishment* (New York: Basic Books, 1979) pp. 156ff.; Berns finds Camus's anti-hero despicable because he is 'self-sufficient', or unmoved by love or hate, 'like an animal or a god', notice the Straussian conception of deity. Gods and animals have in common the fact that they are beyond good and evil, they are not subject to moral laws. Berns's argument is developed purely from the point of view of social utility: his point is that Mersault is despicable because society cannot survive without men who cry at their mother's funeral.
73. This is Camus's phrase.
74. *OT*, p. 100.
75. Pangle, 'Introduction' to *SPPP*, p. 12.
76. *NRH*, p. 112.
77. *SA*, pp. 6–7; reviewers of this book who are not familiar with Strauss's other work are baffled by it; see, for example, Douglas J. Stewart's review in *The Classical World*, vol. 60 (November 1966–7) pp. 119–20. Stewart is perplexed by Strauss's fascination with what happens off stage. See also Michael J. O'Brien's review in *Phoenix*, vol. 21 (1967) pp. 231–2.
78. Muhammad b. Zakariyya al-Razi, 'The Philosophic Way of Life', printed in Arabic in Paul Kraus, 'Raziana I', *Orientalia*, vol. 4, pp. 300–34. Al-Razi describes Socrates as an ascetic who used to spend his time in the wilderness, did not eat meat, and did not consort with either kings or dancing girls. However, Socrates underwent a 'conversion' that led him to abandon his asceticism, emerge from the wilderness, eat meat, and consort with kings and dancing girls. But Razi defends

Socrates and himself (known to be an admirer and follower of Socrates) against the charges of corruption and irreligion. Razi also says that the meaning of his essay on Socrates cannot be fully understood unless it is read in the context of all his other writings. I am indebted to Yusuf Umar for assistance with medieval Arabic.

79. *SA*, p. 3.
80. Ibid., pp. 7, 8, 314.
81. Ibid.
82. Ibid., p. 7.
83. Ibid., p. 19.
84. Ibid.
85. Ibid.
86. Ibid.
87. Ibid., p. 15.
88. Ibid., p. 26.
89. Ibid., p. 22.
90. Ibid., p. 29.
91. Ibid., pp. 8, 30.
92. Ibid., p. 31.
93. Ibid., p. 30.
94. Ibid.
95. Ibid.
96. Ibid., p. 31.
97. Ibid., p. 29.
98. *CM*, p. 84.
99. *SA*, p. 15.
100. Ibid., p. 20.
101. For an original interpretation of *SA*, see Harry Neumann, 'Civic Piety and Socratic Atheism: An Interpretation of Strauss's *Socrates and Aristophanes*', *Independent Journal of Philosophy*, vol. 2 (1978) pp. 33–7. Neumann suggests a further link between the early Socrates and contemporary 'Socratic culture'. He asserts that Socrates was not simply an atheist, but an inventor of new gods inspired by 'atheist imaginations' (p. 37). Socrates destroys the gods of the city and replaces them with new 'global deities'. The old gods were attached to the city. They were 'martial' gods, strong, courageous and patriotic (p. 34). They preferred manliness to effeminacy, anger to compassion, Ares (god of war) to Aphrodite (goddess of love). The old gods were meant to be obeyed not imitated; and they were to be obeyed simply because they were the gods of Athens. In contrast, the Clouds with which Socrates consorts are universal or global goddesses, free from allegiance to any city. They are represented by Aristophanes as women to indicate their effeminacy. This sets them apart from the gods of the city and their 'martial horizon' (p. 34). On the new cosmopolitan perspective our city is worthy of love and allegiance only to the extent to which it partakes or participates in the 'cosmopolitan moralities'. The new deities are therefore to be imitated, not obeyed. Socrates is the inventor of these new global goddesses, and thus,

does not believe them to be really divine; he knows they are products of his own mind. The new goddesses invented by Socrates have the effect of transporting into the religious domain the universalism characteristic of science. Socrates therefore sets the stage on which reason and revelation contend, and on which their reconciliation can be conceived. In ancient times, philosophy or science and religion were perceived as opposites, much like *nomos* and *physis*. They were not contenders in the same arena. To speak of a contest between them, let alone a reconciliation of opposites, is to introduce a dialectic that presupposes the transformation of the antagonists. We fail to recognize Socrates as an atheist because we are his heirs; our conception of religion has been contaminated by his cosmopolitanism. Neumann goes further. He maintains that universalistic or cosmopolitan religions are impious. They lead to the destruction of all religions, and with them, all moral restraint! In another article, Neumann interprets Joseph Conrad's *Heart of Darkness* as a display of the savagery in which the 'pious atheism' of the universalistic or cosmopolitan religions inevitably ends. See 'Atheistic Freedom and the International Society for the Suppression of Savage Customs: An Interpretation of Conrad's *Heart of Darkness*', *Interpretation*, vol. 4, no. 2 (Winter 1974) pp. 107–14. The implication is that Christian universalism, or what Nietzsche believed to be Platonism for the masses, is responsible for the barbarism of modern times. Although not substantiated by the text in question, Neumann's message is consistent with what Strauss says about modernity. The difference is that Neumann, unlike Strauss, attributes these cosmopolitan ideas not to Christianity, but to classical antiquity itself. He is therefore truer to the Nietzschian claim that Christianity is but Platonism for the masses.

102. *SA*, pp. 7, 313, 314.
103. *CM*, p. 53.
104. Ibid., p. 54; see also *LAM*, p. 7. The same seems to be true of Strauss. He is well known for seeking out young men of promise who absorb his teaching without the 'midwifery of critical analysis', to use a phrase from Edward Andrew's 'Descent to the Cave', *Review of Politics*, vol. 45, no. 4 (October 1983) pp. 510–35.
105. *CM*, p. 59. Strauss compares Plato's dialogues to Shakespeare's plays. Macbeth for example appears to teach that the violation of the sacred law of life is self-destructive. But Strauss does not think that the play really aims to teach that this is true for all men. He remarks that Macbeth is only a certain kind of man! We are to surmise that the lesson does not apply equally to all men, and that the powerful and the wise are beyond good and evil. *This* doctrine will be corroborated by what he says about natural right (see Chapter 5).
106. *CM*, p. 84.
107. Ibid., p. 83.
108. Ibid., p. 75.
109. Ibid.
110. Ibid.

111. Ibid., p. 77.
112. Ibid., p. 84.
113. Ibid., p. 85.
114. Ibid., pp. 74, 75, 80, 83, 84.
115. Ibid., p. 75.
116. Ibid., pp. 83, 87.
117. Ibid., pp. 87, 102; *NRH*, p. 106.
118. *CM*, p. 88.
119. Ibid.
120. Ibid., p. 88; *NRH*, p. 107.
121. *CM*, pp. 59–60; these are the same 'charms' that are said to 'obstruct the philosophic effort' in *OT*, p. 26.
122. *CM*, p. 83, see also, pp. 85, 107.
123. *NRH*, p. 106.
124. *CM*, p. 100.
125. Ibid., p. 97.
126. *NRH*, p. 106.
127. *CM*, p. 75; *WIPP*, p. 34; Arlene W. Saxonhouse enlarges on this theme in 'The Unspoken Theme in Plato's *Gorgias*: War', *Interpretation*, vol. 11, no. 2 (May 1983) pp. 139–69.
128. Aristophanes, *Lysistrata*, trans. Alan H. Sommerstein (Harmondsworth: Penguin Books, 1973); see also Strauss's commentary on the play in *SA*, esp. pp. 210–13. In the *Lysistrata*, the women represent peace and the men represent war. Strauss believes that the triumph of peace over war as a result of the women's sexual strike is modest. Aristophanes realizes that there can be no lasting peace. Every peace is not only preceded by war, but followed by war. Strauss bases his interpretation on the fact that the play ends with a tribute to the 'utterly warlike Athena', who neither gives birth nor was herself born in the normal fashion. (She emerged from Zeus's skull after he had swallowed her mother, Metis, fearing that she would bear a son that would overthrow him, as the oracle had indicated.)
129. *CM*, p. 97; *NRH*, p. 150, note.
130. *CM*, pp. 87, 97; *OT*, p. 94; *XS*, p. 50; *XSD*, p. 85; *NRH*, p. 150, note; Allan Bloom enlarges on this point in the 'Interpretive Essay', of his translation of *The Republic of Plato* (New York: Basic Books, 1968) pp. 317–18.
131. *CM*, p. 111.
132. Aristophanes, *Wasps*, trans. David Barret (Harmondsworth: Penguin Books, 1964); *SA*, pp. 112–35.
133. Ibid., p. 127.
134. Ibid., p. 118.
135. Ibid., p. 122.
136. *CM*, pp. 115, 116, 127, 137: the two concepts of justice correspond to two concepts of virtue, nobility and gentlemanliness.
137. Ibid., pp. 87, 97; *XSD*, p. 85; *OT*, p. 94; *NRH*, p. 150, note.
138. 'On Plato's *Apology of Socrates* and *Crito*', in *SPPP*, p. 54; *XSD*, p. 161; *CM*, p. 27.
139. *CM*, p. 125; Strauss tells us that philosophers are not part of the

city, but are already firmly settled in the Islands of the Blessed while they are still alive. The Islands of the Blessed was a place where the gods lived a happy and carefree life and where the earth was said to bear honey-sweet fruit three times a year.

140. Ibid., p. 128.
141. An exception is Socrates's revenge on Anytos, his accuser: *XS*, p. 140: 'Availing himself of a privilege which according to Homer some men who are about to die enjoy, he prophesied that . . . Anytos' son, . . . would fall victim to some disgraceful desire. Xenophon adds that this prophesy came true.'
142. *CM*, p. 125.
143. Ibid.
144. Ibid., pp. 111–12.
145. *OT*, p. 97.
146. Ibid.
147. Ibid., p. 96; *XS*, p. 76.
148. *XS*, p. 76; see also Thomas L. Pangle's 'Interpretive Essay', in his translation of *The Laws of Plato* (New York: Basic Books, 1980); for Pangle as for Strauss, the Athenian stranger subtly reveals the 'problematic' nature of law.
149. *OT*, pp. 97, 100.
150. See Harry Neumann's review of *XSD*, in *Journal of the History of Philosophy*, vol. 9 (1971) pp. 239–43; see also his review of *XS*, in *Journal of the History of Philosophy*, vol. 12 (1974) pp. 252–6; and Stanley Rosen's review of *XS*, in *The Classical World*, vol. 66 (May 1973) pp. 470–1; and Christopher Bruell, 'Strauss on Xenophon's Socrates', *Political Science Reviewer*, vol. 14 (Fall 1984) pp. 263–318; Bruell is so deeply struck by the complexity and subtlety of Strauss's style of writing that his commentary follows the text chapter by chapter.
151. Bloom enlarges on this idea in his 'Interpretive Essay', p. 309.
152. *XS*, pp. 85–7.
153. Ibid., pp. 103, 122, 123.
154. *XSD*, pp. 157–8.
155. Ibid., p. 158.
156. Freud, *Civilization and Its Discontents*, p. 50.
157. *XSD*, p. 177; although Neumann does not make the comparison with Freud, he is aware of Strauss's meaning in his review of *XSD*, in *Journal of the History of Philosophy* (1971) p. 242.
158. *XS*, pp. 158, 143; *XSD*, pp. 132, 159; *OT*, p. 43: Strauss explains that 'the wise man' is not necessarily a gentleman in the ordinary sense. Strauss uses the term 'gentleman' in two senses, just as he uses terms such as justice, virtue and nobility. Recognizing this is the key to understanding Strauss.
159. Saxonhouse's commentary on the *Gorgias* follows Strauss's example in regarding Socrates as a very clever Sophist; so much so, that she believes Callicles to be afraid of him ('The Unspoken Theme in Plato's *Gorgias*' (May 1983) p. 161).
160. *OT*, p. 88; *CM*, pp. 83, 88, 91; as with other words there are two

meanings to the term 'common good': in its political sense it refers to collective interest; in its philosophical sense it refers to a good that is not in the least 'common' but is nevertheless the end to which the state is a means – namely, philosophy; see Seth Bernardete, 'Leo Strauss's *The City and Man*', *Political Science Reviewer*, vol. 8 (Fall 1978) pp. 1–20; Bernardete's article is less explicit than the original, but he does make the astute observation that it makes sense to talk of the common good as knowledge because it is the only good that is not by nature private (p. 7).

161. *CM*, pp. 89, 111, 112, 107, 83; *OT*, pp. 88, 96; *AAPL*, p. 160.
162. *CM*, p. 89; remember that 'novel' is not a term of praise in Strauss's vocabulary.
163. Ibid., pp. 110, 112.
164. Ibid., p. 111.
165. *SA*, p. 212.
166. Ibid., pp. 254–5.
167. Freud, *Civilization and Its Discontents*, pp. 48ff.
168. *SA*, p. 212.
169. Freud, *Civilization and Its Discontents*, p. 90; Freud points to the error of assuming that limitless repression of the psyche is possible; besides, it is irrational to opt for more repression than is necessary to achieve the benefits of civilized life.
170. *XSD*, p. 166.
171. *CM*, pp. 111, 116, 117, 118.
172. Ibid., p. 78.
173. *OT*, p. 210; *XS*, p. 178.
174. *OT*, p. 221; *XS*, p. 89.
175. *XS*, pp. 41–2, 146.
176. Ibid., p. 147.
177. Thomas G. West, *Plato's Apology of Socrates* (Ithaca, N.Y., and London: Cornell University Press, 1979), follows Strauss's interpretation: West notes that the image of Socrates as a gadfly is particularly appropriate in view of the parasitic nature of the philosopher *vis-à-vis* the city (p. 177); see also Stewart Umphrey's discussion of West in '*Eros* and *Thumos*', *Interpretation*, vol. 10 (May and September 1982) pp. 353–422, and West's reply to Umphrey in 'Defending Socrates and Defending Politics', in Thomas B. Silver and Peter W. Schramm (eds), *Natural Right and Political Right: Essays in Honor of Harry V. Jaffa* (Durham, N.C.: Carolina Academic Press, 1984) pp. 235–49; see also West's 'Introduction' to *Plato and Aristophanes: Four Texts On Socrates*, Plato's *Euthyphro, Apology* and *Crito* and Aristophanes's *Clouds* translated with notes by T. G. West and Grace Starry West (Ithaca, N.Y., and London: Cornell University Press, 1984); George Anastaplo, 'Human Being and Citizen: A Beginning to the Study of Plato's *Apology of Socrates*', in Joseph Cropsey (ed.), *Ancients and Moderns: Essays on the Tradition of Political Philosophy in Honor of Leo Strauss* (New York: Basic Books, 1964) pp. 16–49, relies heavily on Strauss; Eva Brann, 'The Offense of Socrates: A Re-Reading of Plato's *Apology*', *Interpretation*, vol. 7,

no. 2 (May 1978) pp. 1–32, also relies heavily on Strauss although he is not mentioned; Harry Neumann, 'Plato's Defense of Socrates: An Interpretation of Ancient and Modern Sophistry', *Liberal Education*, vol. 56 (1970) pp. 458–75.

Notes to Chapter 5: Classic Natural Right or the Teaching on Tyranny

1. *NRH*, pp. 93–117.
2. Ibid., pp. 112–13.
3. Ibid., p. 115.
4. Ibid., p. 114; *SA*, pp. 29–31.
5. *NRH*, p. 113.
6. Ibid., p. 158.
7. Ibid., pp. 105–6.
8. Ibid.
9. Ibid., p. 107.
10. Ibid., pp. 113, 107; Harry Jaffa has recently cast doubt on this in the context of his commentary on Thomas L. Pangle's 'Introduction' to *SPPP* ('The Legacy of Leo Strauss', in *Claremont Review*, vol. 3, no. 3 (Fall 1984) pp. 14–21). Jaffa argues that the position of Straussians like Pangle is indistinguishable from 'heroic Epicurianism'. Jaffa believes that these ideas are not Strauss's, but have been attributed to him by unworthy spokesmen.
11. *NRH*, p. 107.
12. Ibid., p. 132.
13. Ibid., pp. 132–3.
14. *OT*, pp. 52, 53, 55, 61, 91, 97, 98, 99.
15. *NRH*, p. 97.
16. Ibid., p. 134.
17. Ibid., p. 135.
18. Ibid., p. 118.
19. Ibid., pp. 134–5.
20. Ibid., p. 144. In *NRH* Strauss draws distinctions between Plato and Aristotle that he abandons in his later work.
21. Ibid., p. 140, my italics.
22. *OT*, p. 69.
23. Ibid., p. 76.
24. Ibid., p. 77.
25. Ibid., p. 76.
26. Ibid., pp. 76–7.
27. Ibid., p. 70.
28. Ibid., p. 79; Strauss believes this to be the central theme of Plato's *Laws*: see *WIPP*, pp. 31–2; *AAPL*; see also Pangle's 'Interpretive Essay', in his translation of *The Laws of Plato* (New York: Basic Books, 1980).
29. *NRH*, p. 139.
30. Ibid.
31. Ibid., p. 141.

32. Ibid., p. 142; *XS*, p. 51.
33. *NRH*, p. 142.
34. Ibid.
35. Ibid., p. 152.
36. Ibid., p. 156.
37. Ibid., p. 157.
38. Ibid., p. 139.
39. Ibid., p. 140; for an elaboration of this point, see Harry V. Jaffa, *Thomism and Aristotelianism* (Westport, Conn.: Greenwood Press, 1952, 1979) pp. 182ff.
40. *NRH*, p. 157.
41. Ibid., p. 158; see also Strauss's essay 'Marsilius of Padua' in *HPP*.
42. *NRH*, p. 158.
43. Ibid., p. 160.
44. Ibid., p. 162.
45. Ibid., p. 160.
46. Ibid.
47. Ibid.
48. Ibid.
49. Ibid.
50. See, for example, Dante Germino, 'Second Thoughts on Leo Strauss's Machiavelli', *Journal of Politics*, vol. 28 (1966) pp. 794–817.
51. J. S. Mill, in S. Gorovitz (ed.), *Utilitarianism* (New York: Bobbs-Merrill, 1971) ch. 5, p. 49.
52. Ibid., p. 44.
53. The example is from H. J. McCloskey, 'A Note on Utilitarian Punishment', *Mind*, vol. 72 (1963) p. 599; see also his 'An Examination of Restricted Utilitarianism', *Philosophical Review*, vol. 66 (1957) pp. 465–85.
54. Leo Strauss, 'Letter to Helmut Kuhn', *Independent Journal of Philosophy*, vol. 2 (1978) pp. 23–6, esp. p. 24.
55. Leo Strauss, 'Natural Law', in the *Encyclopedia of the Social Sciences*, vol. 12, p. 80, also reprinted in *SPPP*.
56. Ibid., pp. 82ff.; Ernest Fortin elaborates the same themes in his article 'St. Thomas Aquinas', *HPP*, 2nd edn; Jaffa also follows Strauss's interpretation in his *Thomism and Aristotelianism*; the Straussian interpretation has recently been undermined by the work of John Finnis, *Natural Law and Natural Rights* (Oxford: Clarendon Press, 1980); see also Ernest Fortin, 'The New Rights Theory and the Natural Law', *Review of Politics*, vol. 44 (1982) pp. 590–612, and the 'Communications' between Fortin and E. A. Goerner in the same journal, vol. 45 (1983) pp. 443–4. What is at issue between Finnis and Fortin is not just the correct interpretation of Aquinas, but whether it is right to live according to the principles of natural law or those of Strauss's classic natural right.
57. Fortin, 'St. Thomas Aquinas', *HPP*, 2nd edn.
58. Strauss, 'Natural Law', p. 83.
59. See Jaffa, *Thomism and Aristotelianism*.
60. Ibid., pp. 172–3.

61. *NRH*, p. 151; *OT*, p. 96: Simonides is said to recommend moral virtue only as a means; *CM*, pp. 83, 107: justice is described as a necessary evil; *AAPL*, p. 160: politics is described as not noble, but necessary.
62. Jaffa recognizes this but makes little of it; see *Thomism and Aristotelianism*, p. 31.
63. 'A Giving of Accounts: Jacob Klein and Leo Strauss', this exchange between Strauss and Klein took place at St John's College, Annapolis, 30 Janaury 1970, and was printed in *The College*, vol. 22 (April 1970) pp. 1–5, esp. p. 4.
64. *NRH*, pp. 163–4.
65. Ibid., p. 151; *CM*, p. 27; *XSD*, p. 161; *SPPP*, p. 54; cf. Aristotle's *Politics*, 1323 B 11.
66. *NRH*, p. 151.
67. Strauss, 'Natural Law', p. 83.
68. *NRH*, p. 163.
69. For a more eloquent version of this argument see G. E. M. Anscombe, 'Modern Moral Philosophy', in W. D. Hudson (ed.), *The Is/Ought Problem* (London: Macmillan Press, 1973).
70. Fortin, 'St. Thomas Aquinas', *HPP*, 2nd edn, p. 241.
71. Ibid., p. 242.
72. *NRH*, p. 95.
73. See Bernard Williams for a penetrating critique of consequential ethics, in J. J. C. Smart and Bernard Williams, *Utilitarianism For & Against* (Cambridge: Cambridge University Press, 1973).
74. See Bernard Williams, *Morality: An Introduction to Ethics* (New York: Harper & Row, 1972); G. J. Warnock, *The Object of Morality* (London: Methuen, 1971); D. H. Hodgson, *Consequences of Utilitarianism* (Oxford: Clarendon Press, 1967).
75. J. J. C. Smart, 'Extreme and Restricted Utilitarianism', in Philippa Foot (ed.), *Theories of Ethics* (Oxford: Oxford University Press, 1967) pp. 171–83.
76. Strauss, 'Marsilius of Padua', *HPP*, 1st edn, pp. 230–1.
77. Ibid., p. 230.
78. Ibid., p. 239.
79. Ibid.
80. Ibid., p. 243.
81. *TM*, p. 206; see also Chapters 6 and 9 below.
82. Jaffa, for example, complains that Aquinas attributes to Aristotle ideas he does not hold, in *Thomism and Aristotelianism*; Fortin makes the same claim in 'St. Thomas Aquinas', *HPP*, 2nd edn, p. 228.
83. Fortin, 'St. Thomas Aquinas', *HPP*, 2nd edn, p. 247.
84. This is discussed in greater detail in Chapter 3.
85. E. A. Goerner, 'On Thomistic Natural Law: The Bad Man's View of Thomistic Natural Right', *Political Theory*, vol. 7, no. 1 (February 1979) pp. 101–22, and by the same author, 'Thomistic Natural Right: The Good Man's View of Thomistic Natural Law', *Political Theory*, vol. 11, no. 3 (August 1983) pp. 393–418. Goerner follows John Roos, 'Natural Right and Natural Law', delivered at the Annual Meeting of the Political Science Association (1975), in maintaining that Aquinas's

natural law doctrine is only exoteric, and that, in reality, he holds a classic natural right doctrine indistinguishable from that of (Strauss's) Aristotle.

86. Roos, 'Natural Right and Natural Law', p. 12.
87. Goerner, 'Thomistic Natural Right: The Good Man's View of Thomistic Natural Law', p. 416.
88. *NRH*, p. 153.
89. See Ernst Troeltsch, *The Social Teaching of the Christian Churches*, trans. Olive Wyon (London: Allen & Unwin, 1956); Hooker, *Laws of Ecclesiastical Polity*, bk I, chap. x, sec. 13; see also my 'Transcendence of Natural Law', in S. B. Drury and R. Knopff (eds), *Law and Politics: Readings in Legal and Political Thought* (Calgary: Detselig Enterprises, 1980).
90. *NRH*, p. 153.

Notes to Chapter 6: Machiavelli's Subversion of Esotericism

1. See J. G. A. Pocock, 'Prophet and Inquisitor', *Political Theory*, vol. 3, no. 4 (November 1975) pp. 385–401; see also Felix Gilbert's review of Leo Strauss's *Thoughts on Machiavelli*, in *Yale Review*, vol. 48 (1959) pp. 466–9.
2. John Gunnell, 'The Myth of the Tradition', *American Political Science Review*, vol. 72 (1978) pp. 122–34, esp. p. 133.
3. Herbert Butterfield's review of Strauss's *Thoughts on Machiavelli*, in *Journal of Politics*, vol. 22 (November 1960) pp. 728–30; Carl J. Friedrich, 'Teacher of Evil', *New Leader*, vol. 42 (12 October 1959) pp. 27–8; see also G. L. Mosse's review in *American Historical Review*, vol. 64, no. 4 (July 1959) pp. 954–5.
4. See Pocock, Gilbert, Gunnell, Butterfield, Friedrich and Mosse, notes 1–3 above; see also J. Hallowell's review of Strauss's *Thoughts on Machiavelli*, in *Midwest Journal of Political Science*, vol. 3 (1959) pp. 300–3; Willmoore Kendall's review of the same work in *Philosophical Review*, vol. 75, no. 2 (1966) pp. 247–54; Robert J. McShea, 'Leo Strauss on Machiavelli', *Western Political Quarterly*, vol. 16 (1963) pp. 782–97; Dante Germino, 'Second Thoughts on Leo Strauss's Machiavelli', *Journal of Politics*, vol. 28 (1966) pp. 794–817.
5. Dante Germino quotes Gaetano Mosca and concurs with his judgement (p. 816); Pocock, Gilbert and Butterfield express similar sentiments.
6. *TM*, pp. 121, 201.
7. See Harvey C. Mansfield, Jr, 'Strauss' Machiavelli', *Political Theory*, vol. 3, no. 4 (November 1975) pp. 372–84, a reply to Pocock; see also Allan Bloom, 'Leo Strauss: September 20, 1899–October 18, 1973', *Political Theory*, vol. 2, no. 4 (November 1974) pp. 372–92.
8. See Kendall's review.
9. Bloom, 'Leo Strauss', p. 391.
10. Mansfield, 'Strauss' Machiavelli', p. 372.
11. *PAW*, p. 24.

12. *TM*, p. 10.
13. Ibid., p. 43.
14. Ibid.
15. Ibid., p. 12.
16. Ibid., p. 69.
17. Ibid., p. 10, see also p. 59, note 12.
18. *OT*, pp. 23, 57.
19. Ibid., p. 57.
20. Ibid.
21. Ibid., p. 34; *TM*, p. 139.
22. *OT*, p. 57: Strauss says that Xenophon refuses to separate 'moderation' (prudence) from 'wisdom' (insight).
23. *TM*, pp. 10, 78, 88, 139.
24. Ibid., p. 27.
25. Ibid., p. 42.
26. *NRH*, p. 130.
27. *TM*, p. 47.
28. Ibid., p. 14.
29. Ibid., p. 114.
30. Ibid., p. 50.
31. Ibid.
32. Ibid.
33. Ibid., p. 12.
34. Ibid., p. 230.
35. Ibid., p. 157.
36. Ibid., p. 152.
37. Ibid., p. 206.
38. Ibid., p. 51.
39. **Ibid.**, p. 31; cf. Machiavelli, *Discourses* ii, 5.
40. *TM*, p. 32.
41. Ibid., p. 42.
42. Ibid., p. 151.
43. Ibid., p. 93, see also pp. 139, 141, 151. Compare Strauss's claim that Machiavelli subverts not only the authority of Livy, but authority in general, with his discussion of the emergence of philosophy in opposition to authority, convention and the ancestral (*NHR*, p. 85).
44. *TM*, p. 136, see also pp. 124, 158.
45. Ibid., p. 120.
46. Ibid., p. 167.
47. Ibid.
48. See the discussion of Strauss's 'On the Interpretation of Genesis', in Chapter 3.
49. *TM*, pp. 167, 173, 206.
50. Ibid., p. 173.
51. Strauss himself tries to blur the distinction; see, for example, his *PPH*, pp. vii–viii.
52. *TM*, p. 167; see Strauss's 'Machiavelli and Classical Literature', *Review of National Literatures*, vol. 1, no. 1 (Spring 1970) pp. 7–25, esp. p. 10: Strauss says that the Great Tradition is founded by Socrates and culminates in the work of Aristotle.

53. *NRH*, p. 97: strictly speaking philosophy assumes that man's beginnings are imperfect: man's perfection comes at the end, in the form of the excellence of the contemplative life. Strauss is offended by Machiavelli's refusal to give this pagan sort of perfection a place in the political scheme of things.
54. *TM*, p. 121, also p. 120.
55. Ibid., p. 11.
56. *NRH*, p. 105.
57. *TM*, p. 11.
58. Willmoore Kendall, 'Who Killed Political Philosophy?' *National Review*, vol. 8, no. 11 (March 1960) pp. 174–5: Kendall compares Strauss's approach to political philosophy to that of a detective with a dead body trying to uncover the author of the crime. But what he uncovers is not a single criminal, but a syndicate, led and masterminded by Machiavelli. The detective realizes that the crime does not consist in the murder, but in the creation of a world in which the murder is not a crime. Machiavelli is the man responsible for a world in which killing is not a crime. Kendall's account is accurate only to the extent that it sees Machiavelli as the enemy of political philosophy, as Strauss understands it. However, his account is misleading in so far as it sets up too great an opposition between Strauss and Machiavelli.
59. Carl Schmitt, *The Concept of the Political*, trans. George Schwab, with comments by Leo Strauss (New Brunswick, N.J.: Rutgers University Press, 1976).
60. Ibid., p. 91.
61. *TM*, p. 95, see also pp. 88, 107, 137, 152.
62. Ibid., p. 127.
63. Ibid., p. 206.
64. See Strauss's debate with Alexandre Kojève in Strauss's *OT*.
65. Hannah Arendt, *The Human Condition* (Chicago, Ill.: University of Chicago Press, 1958).
66. *TM*, p. 88.
67. Ibid., p. 59.
68. Germino, 'Second Thoughts on Leo Strauss's Machiavelli', p. 809, note 34.
69. *TM*, p. 13.

Notes to Chapter 7: Hobbes and the Character of Modernity

1. Leo Strauss, 'Progress or Return? The Contemporary Crisis in Western Civilization', *Modern Judaism*, vol. 1 (1981) pp. 17–45, based on two of three public lectures delivered at the B'nai B'rith Hillel Foundation, University of Chicago, 5 November 1952.
2. *NRH*, p. 177.
3. Quentin Skinner denies the claim that Hobbes is radically novel: see his 'The Ideological Context of Hobbes's Political Thought', *Historical Journal*, vol. 9, no. 3 (1966) pp. 286–317.
4. *NRH*, p. 169.
5. Ibid., p. 175.

6. Ibid., p. 193.
7. Ibid., p. 184.
8. Ibid., p. 189; Hobbes, *De Cive*, i, 2, 5, 7.
9. *NRH*, p. 175.
10. Leo Strauss, 'The Crisis of Our Time', and 'The Crisis of Political Philosophy', in Harold J. Spaeth (ed.), *The Predicament of Modern Politics* (Detroit, Mich.: University of Detroit Press, 1964).
11. Leo Strauss, 'The Three Waves of Modernity', in Hilail Gildin (ed.), *Political Philosophy: Six Essays by Leo Strauss* (Indianapolis, Ind., and New York: Bobbs-Merrill/Pegasus, 1975).
12. *NRH*, p. 177.
13. Ibid., p. 169.
14. Bernard de Mandeville, *Fable of the Bees*, ed. F. B. Kaye (London: Oxford University Press, 1924), vol. i, p. 4; see also discussion of Mandeville in Arthur Lovejoy, *Reflections on Human Nature* (Baltimore, Md.: The Johns Hopkins University Press, 1961) p. 41.
15. Sheldon Wolin, *Politics and Vision* (Boston, Mass.: Little, Brown, 1960) p. 383.
16. Jürgen Habermas, *Theory and Practice*, trans. John Viertel (Boston, Mass.: Beacon Press, 1973) p. 43.
17. R. Jordan, 'The Revolt against Philosophy: The Spell of Popper', in John Wild (ed.), *Return to Reason* (Chicago, Ill.: Henry Regnery, 1953).
18. Plato, *Republic*, bk. ix, 426e–427a.
19. Plato, *Protagoras*, 321, trans. W. K. C. Guthrie.
20. Ibid., 322b.
21. Ibid., 322c.
22. Werner Jaeger, 'Praise of Law: The Origins of Philosophy and the Greeks', in Paul Sayre (ed.), *Interpretations of Modern Legal Philosophies* (New York: Oxford University Press, 1947) p. 362.
23. *WIPP*, p. 37.
24. *TM*, p. 299; see also discussion of this in George Grant, 'Tyranny and Wisdom', in his *Technology and Empire* (Toronto: House of Anansi, 1969).
25. *CN*, pp. 75, 77.
26. *NRH*, p. 169; Edmund Burke, *Works*, vol. iii, p. 377.
27. *NRH*, p. 169.
28. Ibid., p. 160.
29. Ibid., p. 166.
30. For a contrary view, see my 'John Locke: Natural Law and Innate Ideas', *Dialogue*, vol. 19, no. 4 (December 1980) pp. 531–45.
31. For an alternate view, see J. W. Yolton, 'Locke on the Law of Nature', *Philosophical Review*, vol. 67 (1958) pp. 477–98.
32. *NRH*, p. 235.
33. Strauss's view is developed at much greater length by one of his former students – see Richard H. Cox, *Locke on War and Peace* (Oxford: Clarendon Press, 1960); for a discussion and criticism of Cox, see John Dunn, *The Political Thought of John Locke* (Cambridge: Cambridge University Press, 1969) esp. ch. 12; my own understanding

of Locke on the matter of appropriation differs considerably from Strauss's; see my 'Locke and Nozick on Property', *Political Studies*, vol. 30, no. 1 (March 1982) pp. 28–41.

34. *NRH*, p. 247.
35. Ibid., pp. 207–8; Locke, *Reasonableness of Christianity* (1695), pp. 35, 42, 54, 58, 59, 64, 135–6.
36. *NRH*, p. 208.
37. Ibid., pp. 208–9.
38. Ibid., p. 213.
39. Ibid., pp. 234ff.
40. Ibid., p. 251.
41. Ibid., p. 250.
42. *PPH*, p. 111.
43. Ibid., p. 113.
44. Hannah Arendt, *The Human Condition* (Chicago, Ill.: University of Chicago Press, 1958).
45. *NRH*, p. 187.
46. Ibid., p. 186.
47. Ibid.
48. Some of the aspects of modernity to which Strauss points have been noted by other contemporary political analysts. That technology or the mastery over nature is one of the prime hallmarks of modernity is the theme of the work of writers such as George Grant, *Technology and Empire*, Jean Jacques Ellul, *The Technological Society*, trans. John Wilkinson (New York: Vintage Books, 1964), and Michael Oakeshott, *Rationalism and Politics* (London: Methuen, 1962). Eric Voegelin also understands modernity in terms of the 'gnostic' project of self-salvation through technology; see *The New Science of Politics* (Chicago, Ill.: University of Chicago Press, 1952). That one of the distinctive features of modernity is the shrinking of the public realm, and hence the decline of the pursuit of honor and glory in favor of the pursuit of wealth and private interests, is the central theme of the political thought of Hannah Arendt. The Mandevillian character of modernity has been recognized by writers such as Arthur Lovejoy, *Reflections on Human Nature*, (Baltimore, Md.: Johns Hopkins Press, 1961) and condemned as the height of foolishness by writers like Patrick Devlin, in *The Enforcement of Morals* (Oxford: Oxford University Press, 1965), and other critics of modern liberalism. The increasing democratization of society and the increasing proliferation of private rights and privileges is an aspect of modernity that is widely recognized. It is greeted by many with open arms, but treated with dismay, if not trepidation, by writers such as Ortega Y. Gasset in *The Revolt of the Masses* (New York: W. W. Norton, 1932). But only Strauss links these changes to the eclipse of the esoteric philosophy of the ancients.

Notes to Chapter 8: The Crisis of Modernity

1. *NRH*, p. 252.

2. Ibid.; Strauss also refers to Swift's *Battle of the Books*.
3. Ibid., p. 257.
4. Ibid.
5. Ibid.
6. Ibid., pp. 256–7.
7. Ibid., p. 257.
8. Allan Bloom, 'An Outline of Gulliver's Travels', in Joseph Cropsey (ed.), *Ancients and Moderns: Essays on the Tradition of Political Philosophy in Honor of Leo Strauss* (New York: Basic Books, 1964).
9. Jonathan Swift, *Gulliver's Travels and Other Writings* (New York: The Modern Library, 1958).
10. *NRH*, p. 258.
11. Ibid., p. 255.
12. Ibid., p. 258.
13. Ibid.
14. Ibid., p. 257.
15. Ibid., p. 260.
16. Ibid.
17. Ibid., p. 261.
18. Ibid.
19. Ibid., pp. 259–60.
20. Ibid., p. 262.
21. Ibid., p. 256.
22. Ibid., p. 262.
23. Ibid., p. 263.
24. Ibid.
25. Ibid.
26. Ibid., p. 288.
27. Ibid., p. 287.
28. Ibid.
29. Ibid.
30. Ibid.
31. Nietzsche, *Use and Abuse of History*, trans. Adrian Collins (New York: Bobbs-Merrill, Library of Liberal Arts, 1949, 1957) pp. 6, 7.
32. *NRH*, pp. 254, 256.
33. Ibid., p. 273.
34. Ibid., p. 274.
35. Leo Strauss, 'The Three Waves of Modernity', in Hilail Gilden (ed.), *Political Philosophy: Six Essays by Leo Strauss* (New York: Bobbs-Merrill, 1975).
36. *NRH*, pp. 277, 282.
37. Leo Strauss, 'Progress or Return? The Contemporary Crisis in Western Civilization', *Modern Judaism*, vol. 1 (1981) p. 27.
38. Ibid., p. 24.
39. *CM*, pp. 3–4.
40. Leo Strauss, 'Political Philosophy and the Crisis of Our Time', in George J. Graham, Jr, and George W. Carey (eds), *The Post-Behavioral Era* (New York: David McKay, 1972) p. 219; Strauss, 'Progress', p. 27; *NRH*, p. 23. The phrase is Bacon's.
41. Strauss, 'Progress', pp. 26–7.

42. *CM*, p. 6.
43. Ibid.
44. Ibid., p. 4.
45. *CM*, p. 3.
46. Ibid.
47. Ibid., p. 5.
48. Ibid., p. 3; 'Crisis', p. 218.
49. Strauss, 'Crisis', p. 223.
50. Strauss, 'Progress', p. 26.
51. *CM*, p. 6; Strauss, 'Crisis', p. 220.
52. See Leo Strauss, 'Correspondence Concerning Modernity: Karl Löwith and Leo Strauss', *Independent Journal of Philosophy*, vol. 4 (1983) p. 107.
53. *SPPP*, pp. 33–4.
54. Heidegger, 'Letter on Humanism', trans. Edgar Lohner, in William Barrett and Henry D. Aiken (eds), *Philosophy in the Twentieth Century* (New York: Random House, 1962) p. 288.
55. *NRH*, p. 23; for an original development of this theme, see Harry Neumann, 'Atheistic Freedom and the International Society for the Suppression of Savage Customs: An Interpretation of Conrad's *Heart Of Darkness*', *Interpretation*, vol. 4, no. 2 (Winter 1974) pp. 107–14. Neumann argues that universalism in ethics and religion leads to the worst attrocities, and that Conrad's novel illustrates the truth of this.
56. Heidegger believes that Greek philosophy laid the foundations for modern rootlessness, and hence for the modern crisis (*SPPP*, p. 33). It is true that for Strauss, philosophy transcends the roots of political society; it is an attempt to reach the universal truth about the human condition that transcends all ideologies and nationalities. This is one reason that Strauss describes the philosopher as a stranger. However, for Strauss, the danger rests not so much in philosophy itself as in the 'publication' of philosophy. Christianity is particularly instrumental in the 'publication' and hence the vulgarization of philosophy. Christianity is for Strauss, as it was for Nietzsche, Platonism for the masses because it introduces into religion, and eventually into politics, the universalistic element of philosophy – i.e. an element that transcends all particularity. But political society is particular and parochial by nature. Universalism succeeds only in perverting it, as the modern project illustrates. Strauss is at his most cautious when he speaks of Christianity; it is no wonder that his conception of its role in the decline of Western civilization has been missed. See, for example, George Grant, 'Tyranny and Wisdom: A Comment on the Controversy Between Leo Strauss and Alexandre Kojève', *Social Research*, vol. 31 (1964) pp. 45–72, reprinted in his *Technology and Empire* (Toronto: House of Anansi, 1969).
57. Strauss, 'Progress', p. 27.
58. Ibid., p. 29.
59. *CM*, p. 7.
60. See Jonathan Glover, *What Sort of People Should There Be?* (New York: Penguin Books, 1984); see also my review of Glover's book in *Review of Politics*, vol. 47, no. 2 (April 1985) pp. 285–8.
61. *NRH*, p. 20.

62. Ibid., p. 15.
63. Nicola Chiaromonte emphasizes this point, see 'On Modern Tyranny: A Critique of Western Intellectuals', *Dissent*, vol. 16 (March–April 1969) p. 148.
64. *NRH*, p. 18.
65. Ibid.
66. Ibid., p. 17.
67. Ibid.; see also Chapter 2.
68. *WIPP*, p. 221.
69. Unpublished lecture on Heidegger and existentalism, widely circulated.
70. Ibid.; see also *WIPP*, pp. 241, 246; *SCR*, p. 10; Jacob Klein and Leo Strauss, 'A Giving of Accounts', *The College*, vol. 22 (April 1970) p. 3.
71. Strauss, 'Crisis', p. 217.
72. Ibid., p. 218.
73. Alexandre Kojève is an example.
74. See Strauss's exchange with Kojève in *OT*.
75. Strauss, 'Why We Remain Jews: Can Jewish Faith and History Still Speak to Us?', unpublished lecture delivered on 4 February 1962 at the B'Nai B'Rith Hillel Foundation, University of Chicago.
76. Strauss, 'Progress', p. 28; 'The Mutual Influence of Theology and Philosophy', *Independent Journal of Philosophy*, vol. 3 (1979) pp. 111–18.
77. *SPPP*, p. 31.
78. Ibid., p. 178.
79. *NRH*, p. 6.

Notes to Chapter 9: Post-Modernity: Plato or Nietzsche?

1. *SPPP*, p. 189; Strauss, 'Relativism', in Helmut Schoeck and J. W. Wiggins (eds), *Relativism and the Study of Man* (Princeton, N.J.: Van Nostrand, 1961) pp. 153ff.; Leo Strauss, 'The Three Waves of Modernity', in Hilail Gildin (ed.), *Political Philosophy: Six Essays by Leo Strauss* (New York: Bobbs-Merrill, 1975) p. 97.
2. Strauss, 'Relativism', p. 153.
3. Ibid.
4. Ibid., p. 182.
5. Ibid., p. 177.
6. Ibid.
7. Ibid.
8. Ibid.
9. Ibid., p. 188.
10. Ibid., p. 188; see also Nietzsche, *Beyond Good and Evil*, aphorism no. 219.
11. *SPPP*, p. 184.
12. Ibid.; this is the thesis of Walter Berns's book *For Capital Punishment* (New York: Basic Books, 1979). Berns laments the fact that Western civilization has become soft, timid and irresolute. It is

reluctant to inflict punishment or to act on its convictions. Berns warns that a society that fails to uphold its principles, whatever they are, and severely punish those who deviate from them, is doomed. Berns says nothing about the goodness of the principles on which the strong and resolute are supposed to act.

13. *SPPP*, p. 188.
14. Ibid., p. 183; cf. Nietzsche, *Will to Power*, no. 1038.
15. *SPPP*, p. 188.
16. Nietzsche, *Use and Abuse of History*, trans. Adrian Collins (New York: Bobbs-Merrill, Library of the Liberal Arts, 1949).
17. *SPPP*, p. 188.
18. Ibid., p. 181.
19. Ibid., p. 188.
20. Ibid., p. 176.
21. Ibid., p. 177.
22. *NRH*, p. 26.
23. Strauss is not alone in attributing this thesis to Nietzsche. See, for example, John T. Wilcox, *Truth and Value in Nietzsche: A Study of His Metaethics and Epistemology* (Ann Arbor: The University of Michigan Press, 1974).
24. Ibid., p. 179.
25. *SPPP*, p. 178.
26. Ibid., p. 189.
27. Ibid., p. 190.
28. Ibid., p. 189.
29. Ibid., p. 187.
30. Ibid., p. 185.
31. *SPPP*, p. 175.
32. Ibid., p. 190.
33. Ibid.
34. Timothy Fuller describes this as a preposterous claim in 'The Achievement of Leo Strauss: A Response to Burnyeat, Drury and Gunnell', a paper presented at the Western Political Science Association Meetings, Eugene, Oregon, 20 March 1986.
35. Nietzsche, *Use and Abuse of History*, pp. 30, 41, 55.
36. Ibid., p. 61.
37. Nietzsche expresses the same idea; ibid., p. 41.
38. Ibid., pp. 62, 52.
39. *SPPP*, p. 177; *SCR*, p. 12; see also Strauss, 'Relativism', p. 153.
40. *SPPP*, p. 188.
41. Nietzsche, *Use and Abuse of History*, p. 35.
42. Ibid., p. 42; cf. *NRH*, p. 26; see also Strauss's essay 'The Three Waves of Modernity', pp. 95ff.
43. Ibid., p. 42.
44. Ibid., p. 47.
45. Herber Spiegelberg (ed.), *The Socratic Enigma* (New York: Bobbs-Merrill, 1964). Some of Nietzsche's writings on Socrates are collected in this volume (see p. 251).
46. Ibid., p. 261.

47. Ibid., p. 255; Nietzsche, *The Birth of Tragedy*, trans. Francis Golffing (New York: Doubleday Anchor Books, 1956) p. 93.
48. Spiegelberg, *Socratic Enigma*, p. 255.
49. Ibid., p. 261.
50. Ibid., pp. 252–3.
51. *SA*, p. 7.
52. *SPPP*, p. 175; see also Werner J. Dannhauser, *Nietzsche's View of Socrates* (London: Cornell University Press, 1974), which follows Strauss's view of the relationship of Nietzsche to Socrates and Plato.
53. Spiegelberg, *Socratic Enigma*, pp. 259–60.
54. See Chapter 4 above.
55. Nietzsche, *Beyond Good and Evil*, nos 113, 201; as we have seen, this is also Strauss's view (see Chapter 5 above).
56. Nietzsche, *Beyond Good and Evil*, no. 221. Nietzsche writes: 'Moralities must be forced to bow first of all before the *order of rank*; . . . it is immoral to say: "what is right for one is fair for the other".' And in aphorism 228: 'the demand of one morality for all is detrimental for higher men; in short, that there is an order of rank between man and man, hence also between morality and morality'. As we have seen, Strauss echoes Nietzsche when he distinguishes between the justice, virtue and nobility of the citizen and gentleman on the one hand, and that of the philosopher on the other.
57. Leo Strauss, 'Progress or Return? The Contemporary Crisis in Western Civilization', *Modern Judaism*, vol. 1 (1981) p. 28.

Notes to Chapter 10: Esotericism Betrayed

1. Harry V. Jaffa, 'The Legacy of Leo Strauss', *Claremont Review*, vol. 3, no. 3 (Fall 1984) pp. 14–21; see also Pangle's response in the same review, vol. 4, no. 1 (Spring 1985) pp. 18–20, followed by a response from Jaffa, '"The Legacy of Leo Strauss" Defended', pp. 20–4.
2. Although Pangle does not refer to Strauss as a Nietzschian in his written work, Jaffa refers to a public lecture by Pangle delivered at Claremont in which Pangle declares that Nietzsche was *the* philosopher according to Strauss, and that it is in Nietzschian or historicist terms that we must look for a solution to the dilemmas of modern man (*Claremont Review*, vol. 4, no. 1 (Spring 1985) p. 20.
3. Pangle, *Claremont Review*, vol. 4, no. 1 (Spring 1985) p. 18.
4. Ibid., p. 20.
5. *SPPP*, p. 10.
6. Ibid., p. 12.
7. Jaffa, *Claremont Review*, vol. 4, no. 1 (Spring 1985) p. 21.
8. *SPPP*, p. 15.
9. Ibid., pp. 14–15.
10. Jaffa, *Claremont Review*, vol. 4, no. 1 (Spring 1985) p. 22; see Pangle's 'Patriotism American Style', and Jaffa's reply, 'Our Ancient Faith' *National Review*, 29 November 1985, pp. 30–6.
11. *National Review*, 20 November 1985.

12. Jaffa is a very prolific author; his books include *The Crisis of the House Divided: An Interpretation of the Issues in the Lincoln–Douglas Debates* (Chicago, Ill.: University of Chicago Press, 1959); *Equality and Liberty: Theory and Practice in American Politics* (Oxford: Oxford University Press, 1965); *The Conditions of Freedom: Essays in Political Philosophy* (Baltimore, Md., and London: The Johns Hopkins University Press, 1975); *How To Think About the American Revolution: A Bicentenial Celebration* (Durham, N.C.: Carolina Academic Press, 1978); *American Conservatism and the American Founding* (Durham, N.C.: Carolina Academic Press, 1984).
13. *National Review*, 20 November 1985, p. 32.
14. Ibid.
15. Ibid.
16. *SPPP*, p. 20.
17. Ibid., p. 22.
18. Jaffa, *Claremont Review*, vol. 4, no. 1 (Spring, 1985) p. 23.
19. Ibid., p. 24.
20. *LAM*, p. 7.
21. 'Memorials to Leo Strauss', *St. John's Review*, vol. 25, no. 4 (January 1974) p. 3.
22. See Chapter 3 above.
23. See Chapter 4 above.
24. For instance, see the exchange between Thomas G. West and Gregory B. Smith, 'Natural Right and America's Future', *Claremont Review*, vol. 4, no. 3 (Fall 1985) pp. 28–31; see also the exchange between Harry Jaffa and Walter Berns, 'A Reply to Harry Jaffa', *National Review*, 22 January 1982, and Jaffa's *American Conservatism*, pp. 148–56; see also Charles R. Kesler, 'Is Conservatism Un-American?' *National Review*, vol. 38, no. 5 (22 March 1985) pp. 28–37.
25. Jaffa, *Claremont Review*, vol. 4, no. 1 (Spring 1985) p. 20.

Notes to Chapter 11: The Wise and the Vulgar

1. John Plamenatz, *Democracy and Illusion* (London: Longman, 1973).
2. *CM*, p. 131.
3. *CM*, pp. 153, 192, 193, 195, 197.
4. *OT*, pp. 143–88.
5. Philippa Foot is the most eloquent contemporary exponent of this view; see her 'Moral Beliefs', in Philippa Foot (ed.), *Theories of Ethics* (Oxford: Oxford University Press, 1967).
6. John Finnis, *Natural Law and Natural Rights* (Oxford: Clarendon Press, 1980), and Finnis, *The Fundamentals of Ethics* (Oxford: Clarendon Press, 1983).
7. Contrary to what Strauss thinks, Aristotle does not attest to this; see, for example, *Politics*, 1323 B 11: 'what is true of the felicity of individuals is also true of that of communities, and that therefore the state which is morally best is the state which is happy and "does

well". To "do well" is impossible unless you also "do right" ' (Ernest Barker's translation).

8. See, for example, Werner J. Danhauser, 'On Teaching Politics Today', *Commentary*, March 1975, p. 74, where he writes: 'I lecture to hundreds, and my practiced eye roams freely and fiercely over bosom after bosom.'

Select Bibliography

WORKS ON STRAUSS

Anastaplo, George, 'On Leo Strauss: A Yahrzeit Remembrance', *University of Chicago Magazine*, vol. 67 (Winter 1974) pp. 30–8. Very interesting and very chatty. A good reflection of the spirit and excitement Strauss was able to generate.

Andrew, Edward, 'Descent to the Cave', *Review of Politics*, vol. 45, no. 4 (October 1983) pp. 510–35. Begins with the assumption that the Straussian interpretation of Plato considers political philosophy to belong to a transcendent realm beyond politics. Shows evidence in Plato's work to the contrary.

Beleval, M. Yvon, 'Pour une Sociologie de la Philosophie', in *Critique*, vol. 68–9 (October 1953) pp. 853–66. A review of Strauss's *Persecution and the Art of Writing*.

Benardete, Seth, 'Leo Strauss's *The City and Man*', *Political Science Reviewer*, vol. 8 (Fall 1978) pp. 1–20. Suggests that 'the city' is Athens and 'the man' is Socrates, and that the book is about the conflict between philosophy and the city, nature and convention or law. Benardete writes in a Straussian style that does not readily disclose itself.

Berns, Laurence, 'Leo Strauss 1899–1973', *Independent Journal of Philosophy*, vol. 2 (1978) pp. 1–3 (originally in *The College*, January 1974). The same issue of the *Journal* includes Strauss's correspondence with Hans-Georg Gadamer and Helmut Kuhn. The former correspondence sheds light on Strauss's method and his anti-relativism, while the latter comes to the heart of Strauss's conception of classic natural right and its distance from the natural law and natural rights tradition.

Berns, Walter, 'The Achievement of Leo Strauss', *National Review*, vol. 25 (7 December 1973). Includes contributions by Herbert J. Storing, Harry V. Jaffa and Werner J. Dannhauser.

Bloom, Allan, 'Leo Strauss: September 20, 1899–October 18, 1973', *Political Theory*, vol. 2, no. 4 (November 1974) pp. 372–92. An important article. Reveals the deepening esotericism of the books of his 'ripeness'.

Bruell, Christopher, 'Strauss on Xenophon's Socrates', *Political Science Reviewer*, vol. 14 (Fall 1984) pp. 263–318. A detailed, chapter-by-chapter commentary on Strauss's *Xenophon's Socratic Discourse*.

Burnyeat, M. F., 'Sphinx Without a Secret', *New York Review*, vol. 32, no. 9 (30 May 1985) pp. 30–6. Followed by 'The Studies of Leo Strauss: An Exchange', vol. 32, no. 15 (10 October 1985). Includes replies to Burnyeat by Joseph Cropsey, Harry V. Jaffa, Allan Bloom, Thomas L. Pangle, and a rejoinder by Burnyeat. The latter's article is not just a review of *Studies in Platonic Political Philosophy*, but a comprehensive critique of Strauss's philosophy as a whole, and of his interpretation of Plato in particular. Argues against Strauss's understanding of the

244 *Select Bibliography*

Platonic conception of justice as doing good to friends and evil to
enemies.

Butterfield, Herbert, review of *Thoughts on Machiavelli*, in *Journal of
Politics*, vol. 22 (November 1960) pp. 728–30.

Caton, Hiram, 'Der Hermeneutische Weg von Leo Strauss', *Philosophisches
Jahrbuch*, vol. 80 (1973) pp. 171–82. A favorable treatment. Recognizes
that the aim of political philosophy for Strauss is *action*. Regards
Strauss as a 'zetetic' or skeptic.

Chiaromonte, Nicola, 'On Modern Tyranny: A Critique of Western
Intellectuals', *Dissent*, vol. 16 (March–April 1969) pp. 137–50. Defines
modern tyranny as the 'irresistible tendency of contemporary society
toward autocratic yet impersonal forms of organization'. Develops
Strauss's ideas regarding the global and universalistic character of
modern tyranny.

Cropsey, Joseph, 'Leo Strauss: A Bibliography and Memorial, 1899–1973',
Interpretation, vol. 5, no. 2 (1975) pp. 133–47. Believes that Strauss
taught modesty.

Dannhauser, Werner J., 'Leo Strauss: Becoming Naïve Again', *American
Scholar*, vol. 44 (1974–5) pp. 636–42. A classic account of the spell that
Strauss cast on his students.

Deane, Herbert A., review of Strauss's *What is Political Philosophy?* in
American Political Science Review, vol. 55 (1961) pp. 149–51. See also
Harry V. Jaffa's response in the next issue, vol. 55 (1961) p. 599. Deane
raises an interesting point: is it not the case that much of what Strauss
attributes to the 'moderns' belongs equally to the Church Fathers who
made the decisive break with classical philosophy?

Drury, S. B., a review of Nathan Tarcov's *Locke's Education for Liberty*, in
Interchange, vol. 17, no. 3 (1986) pp. 68–71. Tarcov accomplishes for Locke
what Goerner and Roos accomplish for Aquinas (see Chapter 5 above). He
rehabilitates Locke by making his views perfectly compatible with
Straussian doctrine.

Dunn, John, *The Political Thought of John Locke* (Cambridge: Cambridge
University Press, 1969). See especially ch. 12 on the Straussian
interpretation of Locke.

Edmund, Michel-Pierre, 'Persecution et politique de la philosophie',
Libre, vol. 6 (1979) pp. 69–98.

Fortin, Ernest L., 'Gadamer on Strauss: An Interview', *Interpretation*, vol.
12, no. 1 (January 1984) pp. 1–13. Gadamer speaks of his life-long
relationship with Leo Strauss.

Friedrich, Karl J., 'Teacher of Evil', *New Leader*, vol. 42 (12 October 1959)
pp. 27–8. On Strauss's *Thoughts on Machiavelli*.

Gadamer, Hans-Georg, *Truth and Method* (New York: The Seabury Press,
1975); see esp. pp. 482–91, an account and criticism of Strauss's anti-
historicist method.

Germino, Dante, 'Second Thoughts on Leo Strauss's Machiavelli', *Journal
of Politics*, vol. 28 (1966) pp. 794–817.

Germino, Dante, 'The Revival of Political Theory', *Journal of Politics*, vol.
25 (August 1963) pp. 437–60. General discussion of Strauss and others.

Germino, Dante, 'Newfangled Aristotelianism', *New Oxford Review*, vol. 2 (March 1979) pp. 16–17, a review article of Harvey Mansfield, Jr, *The Spirit of Liberalism*, see below. Describes the effects of Strauss's teaching as a 'disguised hostility to the influence of revealed religion. . . . Christianity, especially, is not tough-minded or "manly" enough.' Newfangled Aristotelianism, or Straussianism is described as 'decidedly lacking in compassion for those who are not in the natural aristocracy as it defines the said community'.

Gilbert, Felix, review of *Thoughts on Machiavelli*, in *Yale Review*, vol. 48 (1959) pp. 466–9. Critical of Strauss's method.

Gildin, Hilail (ed.), *Political Philosophy: Six Essays by Leo Strauss* (Indianapolis, Ind.: Bobbs-Merrill, 1975). Recognizes in his introduction that Strauss is not merely an interpreter of the history of political philosophy.

Gourevitch, Victor, 'Philosophy and Politics: I', and 'Philosophy and Politics: II', *Review of Metaphysics*, vol. 22, no. 1 (September 1968) pp. 58–84 and vol. 22, no. 2 (December 1968) pp. 281–328 respectively. The most comprehensive and fair-minded study of the thought of Leo Strauss to date. Has some very interesting things to say about Strauss's understanding of love, or lack thereof.

Grant, George P., 'Tyranny and Wisdom: A Comment on the Controversy Between Leo Strauss and Alexander Kojève', *Social Research*, vol. 31 (1964) pp. 45–72, reprinted in his *Technology and Empire* (Toronto: House of Anansi, 1969). Grant is baffled by Strauss's hesitancy to speak on Christianity.

Gunnell, John, *Political Theory: Tradition and Interpretation* (Cambridge, Mass.: Winthrop Press, 1979) esp. pp. 36–40 and 72–6. Gunnell brings to light the fact that for Strauss, the study of the past is a very practical matter.

Gunnell, John, 'The Myth of the Tradition', *American Political Science Review*, vol. 72 (1978) pp. 122–34. Sees Strauss's work as part of a genre of writing that is shared by Hannah Arendt and Eric Voegelin. The *genre* uses the history of political thought to say something about the modern predicament.

Gunnell, John, 'Political Theory and Politics: The Case of Leo Strauss', *Political Theory*, vol. 13, no. 3 (August 1985) pp. 339–61. Finds a connection between Strauss and Nietzsche.

Gunnell, John, *Between Philosophy and Politics: The Alienation of Political Theory* (Amherst, Mass.: University of Massachusetts Press, 1986) esp. pp. 99–125.

Hallowell, John, review of Strauss's *Thoughts on Machiavelli*, in *Midwest Journal of Political Science*, vol. 3 (1959) pp. 300–3. Exceptionally favorable.

Hallowell, John, review of Strauss's *Natural Right and History*, in *American Political Science Review*, vol. 48 (1954) pp. 538–41. Recognizes that for Strauss 'the natural law doctrines of the Middle Ages appear to him to be a distortion of the classical tradition caused by the introduction of beliefs imported from revelation'. Disagrees that the reconciliation of reason and revelation is impossible.

Harbison, Warren, 'Irony and Deception', *Independent Journal of Philosophy*, vol. 2 (1978) pp. 89–94. Does not believe that Strauss had a teaching. He pleads Socratic ignorance on Strauss's behalf. I myself follow Strauss in regarding Socratic ignorance with a great deal of irony.

Harvard, William C., 'The Method and Results of Political Anthropology in America', *Archiv für Rechts-und-Sozialphilosophie*, vol. 47 (1961) pp. 395–415. Harvard is an admirer of Eric Voegelin and believes that the latter deals more profoundly and more precisely with problems of the good and revelation on which he believes Strauss is silent.

Himmelfarb, Milton, 'On Leo Strauss', *Commentary*, vol. 58, no. 2 (May 1974) pp. 60–6. One of the most insightful essays into the thought and character of Leo Strauss. Tackles the schism between Strauss the Jew and Strauss the philosopher, but is puzzled as to how it can be resolved. Fully cognizant of the esoteric nature of Strauss's writings.

Irwin, Terence, review of *Xenophon's Socrates*, in *Philosophical Review*, vol. 83 (1974) pp. 409–13. Finds the book 'almost valueless for anyone who wants to learn more about Socrates'. Strauss succeeds only in reminding us of how dull and tedious Xenophon is. Sees no coherent line of interpretation. This is not surprising for one unfamiliar with Strauss's work as a whole.

Jaffa, Harry V., *American Conservatism and the American Founding* (Durham, N.C.: Carolina Academic Press, 1984) esp. chs 8, 9 and 10. Includes Jaffa's exchange with Walter Berns.

Jaffa, Harry V., 'The Legacy of Leo Strauss', *Claremont Review*, vol. 3, no. 3 (Fall 1984) pp. 14–21. A critique of Thomas L. Pangle's 'Introduction' to Strauss's *Studies in Platonic Political Philosophy*. See also Pangle's response, 'The Platonism of Leo Strauss: A Reply to Harry Jaffa', in the same review, vol. 4, no. 1 (Spring 1985) pp. 18–20, and Jaffa's subsequent reply 'The Legacy of Leo Strauss Defended', in the same issue, pp. 20–4.

Jaffa, Harry V., 'Political Philosophy and Honor: The Leo Strauss Dissertation Award', in his *How to Think About the American Revolution* (Durham, N.C.: Carolina Academic Press, 1978) pp. 162–75. Makes some excellent points.

Jung, Hwa Jol, 'Strauss's Conception of Political Philosophy: A Critique', *Review of Politics*, vol. 29 (October 1967) pp. 492–517. A critique of Strauss's conception of political philosophy in the light of existential philosophy and phenomenology. Critical of Strauss for being an 'essentialist' and neglecting political action.

Jung, Hwa Jol, 'The Life-World, Historicity, and Truth: Reflections on Leo Strauss's Encounter with Heidegger and Husserl', *Journal of The British Society for Phenomenology*. vol. 9, no. 1 (1978) pp. 11–25.

Jung, Hwa Jol, 'Two Critics of Scientism: Leo Strauss and Edmund Husserl', *Independent Journal of Philosophy*, vol. 3 (1978) pp. 81–8.

Jung, Hwa Jol, 'A Post-Polemic', *American Political Science Review*, vol. 58 (June 1964) pp. 400–1. Argues that Strauss's interpretation of classical political philosophy is phenomenological: it shares Husserl and Heidegger's view that the task of philosophy is to understand the *Lebenswelt* or what Strauss calls the 'pre-scientific world'. This is the world of immediate experience, not the 'pre-historical world' that existed only prior to the development of philosophy and science.

Kendall, Willmoore, review of *Thoughts on Machiavelli*, in *Philosophical Review*, vol. 75, no. 2 (April 1966) pp. 247–54. Exceptionally favorable.

Kennington, Richard, 'Strauss's *Natural Right and History*, *Review of Metaphysics*, vol. 35 (1981) pp. 57–86. A very circuitous interpretation of *Natural Right and History* that attempts to use Strauss's method to interpret Strauss's own work.

Klein, Jacob, 'Memorial to Leo Strauss', in *St. John's Review* (formerly *The College*) vol. 25, no. 4 (January 1974). Also includes contributions by J. Winfree Smith, Ted A. Blanton and Laurence Berns. Klein tells us that Strauss was once an orthodox Jew but that he 'later changed his religious orientation radically, tying the question of god or gods to his political reasoning without letting his own life be dependent on any divinity or on any religious rites' (p. 2). He also describes Strauss as belonging to 'two worlds'. Smith points to Strauss's awareness of conflict between the Bible and Greek philosophy. Berns points to Strauss's insistence that there is no such thing as a Jewish philosophy, even though he was a Jew and a philosopher. Blanton tells us that Strauss spoke to different people in different ways, telling each what he believed they needed to hear (p. 3).

Lampert, Laurence, 'The Argument of Leo Strauss in *What Is Political Philosophy*,' *Modern Age*, vol. 22, no. 1 (Winter 1978) pp. 38–46. A very careful reading of Strauss's essay: an important work.

Le Fort, Claude, *Le travail de l'oeuvre Machiavel* (Paris: Gallimard, 1972) pp. 259–305. Claims that Strauss attributes to Machiavelli a nasty doctrine only to prepare the way for the acceptance of his own classical political ideas.

Lerner, Ralph, 'Leo Strauss', in *Encyclopedia Judaica*. Describes Strauss as one who has developed a 'systematic political philosophy in defense of classic natural law'.

Lowenthal, David, 'Leo Strauss's *Studies in Platonic Political Philosophy*', *Interpretation*, vol. 13, no. 3 (September 1985) pp. 297–320. Discussion of the Jaffa–Pangle debate. Sides with Pangle for the most part, but softens the implications of Pangle's position considerably.

Mansfield, Harvey C. J., 'Strauss's Machiavelli', *Political Theory*, vol. 3, no. 4 (November 1975) pp. 372–83. An exchange with J. G. A. Pocock.

McShea, Robert, 'Leo Strauss on Machiavelli', *Western Political Quarterly*, vol. 16 (1963) pp. 782–97. A fascinating piece of work. Very flirtatious in parts but very insightful in others. Points to apparent contradictions in Strauss's work and suspects that they betray an esoteric teaching. Aware of the extent of the antipathy between the classical and the biblical aspects of the Western tradition in the work of Leo Strauss.

Miller, Eugene F., 'Leo Strauss: The Recovery of Political Philosophy', in Anthony de Crespigny and Kenneth Minogue (eds), *Contemporary Political Philosophers* (New York & London: Dodd-Mead and Methuen, 1975). General. Explains the conflict between philosophy and society as having its source in the fact that philosophy is disposed to question opinion. Esoteric philosophy is therefore intended to conceal principles that might be offensive to established opinion. Although this is true, it is superficial and misses the mark.

Molnar, Thomas, review of *Studies in Platonic Political Philosophy*, in *The Modern Age*, vol. 29, no. 1 (Winter 1985) pp. 82–4.

Momigliano, Arnaldo, 'Ermeneutica e Pensiero Politico Classico in Leo Strauss', *Rivista Storica Italiana*, vol. 79 (1967) pp. 1164–72. Focuses on Strauss's hermeneutic, emphasizing its affinity with Jewish scholarship.

Neumann, Harry, review of Strauss's *Xenophon's Socratic Discourse*, in *Journal of the History of Philosophy*, vol. 9 (1971) pp. 239–43. The most penetrating review. Recognizes the contempt that Strauss harbors for gentlemen. Neumann asks some important questions: 'Does philosophy's exposure of the problematic origins of human nobility necessarily incite barbarism? . . . is Socratic striving for self-knowledge, a conscious or unconscious disguise for encouraging savagery?' Neumann does not answer these questions.

Neumann, Harry, review of Strauss's *Xenophon's Socrates*, in *Journal of the History of Philosophy*, vol. 12 (1974) pp. 252–6. Neumann is author of the most imaginative and at times the most insightful reviews of Strauss's books. He is the only writer influenced by Strauss who openly admits to being a 'nihilist' and equally influenced by Nietzsche. His writing is often oblique, but worth the effort.

Neumann, Harry, 'Civic Piety and Socratic Atheism: An Interpretation of Strauss's *Socrates and Aristophanes*', *Independent Journal of Philosophy*, vol. 2 (1978) pp. 33–7. See note 101 of Chapter 4 above.

Neumann, Harry, 'Socrates in Plato and Aristophanes', *American Journal of Philosophy*, vol. 90, no. 2 (1969) pp. 201–14. Oblique, but clearly influenced by Strauss. Believes that the Socratic universalism inherited by Western civilization in its Platonic–Christian form is the source of the illness of modernity.

Nicgorski, Walter, 'Leo Strauss and Liberal Education', *Interpretation*, vol. 13, no. 3 (May 1985) pp. 233–50. Discussion of Strauss's view of the ends of liberal education and the role played by the study of the Great Books.

Niemeyer, Gerhart, 'What is Political Knowledge?' *Review of Politics*, vol. 23 (January 1961) pp. 101–7. Niemeyer is critical of Strauss's vision of the classics for being 'closed' to the truths of revelation, and this, he argues, is inconsistent with the quest for truth itself. He is baffled by Strauss's views on 'virtue' in classical thought and by his criticism of modernity.

O'Brien, Michael J., review of Strauss's *Socrates and Aristophanes*, in *Phoenix*, vol. 21 (1967) pp. 231–2. A typical review of one who tries to make sense of one of Strauss's books independently of the others – is therefore perplexed.

Pangle, Thomas L., 'Introduction', in Strauss's *Studies in Platonic Political Philosophy*.

Pocock, J. G. A., 'Prophet and Inquisitor', *Political Theory*, vol. 3, no. 4 (November 1975) pp. 385–401. A response to Mansfield's article in the same issue.

Rooney, Miriam Theresa, review of Strauss's *Natural Right and History*, in

Catholic Historical Review, vol. 40 (1954–5) pp. 218–19. Believes Strauss to be a defender of natural law.

Rosen, Stanley, review of Strauss's *Xenophon's Socrates*, in *The Classical World*, vol. 66 (May 1973) pp. 470–1. Excellent review. Hints at the affinity that Strauss's Socrates has to Nietzsche.

Rothman, Stanley, 'The Revival of Classical Political Philosophy: A Critique', *American Political Science Review*, vol. 56, no. 2 (June 1962) pp. 341–52, followed by Joseph Cropsey, 'A Reply to Rothman', pp. 353–59. Rothman argues that Strauss's classic natural right is based on an outmoded and untenable cosmology and view of nature. He objects that the claim that what is natural is good is a tautology, otherwise it would make sense to ask why the natural is good. Rothman concludes by speculating on the reason for Strauss's appeal. He suggests that Strauss gives his disciples the hope that they can make the world better by coming into power as the philosopher kings of a new political order. Cropsey is particularly offended by the suggestion that a lust for power is at the root of Strauss's appeal. He emphasizes, following Strauss and contrary to popular belief, that Plato was a lover of democracy because it champions freedom and so allows the highest human type (i.e. the philosopher) to flourish.

Sabine, George H., review of Strauss's *Persecution and the Art of Writing*, in *Ethics*, vol. 63 (1952–3) pp. 220–2. Focuses on Strauss's method of interpretation. He finds the difference between the method and its results paradoxical. While the method is 'an invitation to perverse ingenuity', the results are 'not remarkably different' from what might have been said without it. See Strauss's reply to Sabine in *What Is Political Philosophy?*

Saunders, Trevor J., review of Strauss's *The Argument and the Action of Plato's Laws*, in *Political Theory*, vol. 4 (1976) pp. 239–42. Regards the book as a sorry sight. The poor assessment of the book is due to the fact that it is regarded by the reviewer as a conventional scholarly work on Plato's *Laws*. He is particularly critical of Strauss's interpretive method by which he believes 'Plato can be represented as saying practically anything'.

Schaar, John H., and Wolin, Sheldon S., review essay on Herbert J. Storing (ed.), *Essays on the Scientific Study of Politics*, in *American Political Science Review*, vol. 57 (March 1963) pp. 125–60. A criticism of Strauss and his students. Followed by replies from the authors of the collection including Leo Strauss.

Schaefer, David L. Jr, 'The Legacy of Leo Strauss: A Bibliographic Introduction', *Intercollegiate Review*, vol. 9, no. 3 (Summer 1974) pp. 139–48. An excellent introduction to Strauss.

Sokolowski, Robert, *The God of Faith and Reason: Foundations of Christian Theology* (Notre Dame, Ind.: University of Notre Dame Press, 1982) esp. pp. 155–63. Is fully aware of Strauss's antipathy to biblical religion, and to Christianity in particular. He delivers his message to Strauss and his followers using the words of Aquinas: 'But if there be anyone boasting of his knowledge, falsely so called, who wishes to say something against what we have written, let him not speak in corners, nor in the presence of boys who do not know how to judge about such difficult matters; but let him write against this treatise if he dares' (p. 163). See Walter Nicgorski's reply to Sokolowski in 'Strauss and Christianity: Reason, Politics and Christian Belief', *Claremont Review*, vol. 4, no. 2 (Summer 1985) pp. 18–21. Nicgorski argues that there is for Strauss only a 'tension' between the life of faith and the philosophical life, but there is no 'incompatibility' between them, especially with respect to politics and morality. The biblical tradition and the classical one share a common understanding of morality that regards 'modern' thought as an opponent (p. 21).

Steintrager, James, 'Political Philosophy, Political Theology and Morality', *Thomist*, vol. 32 (July 1968) pp. 307–32. Pays special attention to Strauss's silences (saying that they may be as significant as lengthy discussions). Attributes to Strauss riddles and elaborate methods of indirection. On the whole, a very enigmatic piece of work that attempts to defend Strauss against his Christian critics.

Stewart, Douglas J., review of Strauss's *Socrates and Aristophanes*, in *The Classical World*, vol. 60 (1966–7) pp. 119–20. A typical review of one of Strauss's books: dazzled by his insights and oppressed by the 'sludgy going' between these sparks of light. Completely baffled by Strauss's fascination with what is happening offstage!

Tarcov, Nathan, 'Philosophy and History: Tradition and Interpretation in the Work of Leo Strauss', *Polity*, vol. 16, no. 1 (Fall 1983) pp. 5–29. A response to Gunnell's 'Myth of the Tradition' above. He denies Gunnell's claim that Strauss does not write history of political theory as such, but puts myth in historical form to express his own views. Tarcov makes the important point that the ancients cannot strictly speaking provide us with solutions to modern problems. But he goes so far as to deny that Strauss sides with the ancients against the moderns. Believes that the crisis of the West rests in the latter's having lost confidence in its project but fails to see the extent to which Strauss regarded the project as ill-conceived from the beginning. Links the modern project closely with modern liberalism, therefore feels that Strauss must uphold the former if he is to uphold the latter. A very important essay even if it does not in my view successfully refute Gunnell's claims.

Ward, James F., 'Experience and Political Philosophy: Notes on Reading Leo Strauss', *Polity*, vol. 13, no. 4 (Summer 1981) pp. 668–87. Demystifies the idea of teleology by arguing that it refers simply to the diversity of things in the world of experience, their diverse tendencies and characteristics. In so far as man displays a tendency to ask certain questions, there must be permanent aspects of experience. This is the crux of Strauss's refutation of historicism. Emphasizes that Strauss is a 'zetetic' aware of permanent questions, but having no certain solutions. An important essay.

Warren, Scott, *The Emergence of Dialectical Theory: Philosophy and Political Inquiry* (Chicago, Ill., and London: University of Chicago Press, 1984) esp. pp. 15–27. Endorses Strauss's critique of value-free social science but finds his return to classical political philosophy disappointing.

Wilhelmsen, Frederick D., *Christianity and Political Philosophy* (Athens: The University of Georgia Press, 1978) ch. 8: 'Jaffa, the School of Strauss, and the Christian Tradition'. Paints the portrait of the 'Hellenized Jew'. See discussion in Chapter 3 above. See also Joseph J. Carpino's review of the book in *Interpretation*, vol. 8, nos. 2 & 3 (May 1980) pp. 204–22. Believes that there can be no such thing as Christian philosophy.

Yolton, J. W., 'Locke on the Law of Nature', *Philosophical Review*, vol. 67 (1958) pp. 477–98. One of the earliest and most devastating critiques of Strauss's methods of interpretation.

RELATED WORKS

Alvis, John, and West, Thomas G. (eds), *Shakespeare as Political Thinker* (Durham, N.C.: Carolina Academic Press, 1981).

Bloom, Allan, 'Interpretive Essay' in his translation of *The Republic of Plato* (New York: Basic Books, 1968).

Bloom, Allan, 'Introduction' to his translation of Jean-Jacques Rousseau's *Emile* (New York: Basic Books, 1979).

Bloom, Allan with Jaffa, Harry V. (eds), *Shakespeare's Politics* (Chicago, Ill.: University of Chicago Press, 1964).

Cropsey, Joseph, 'United States Policy and the Meaning of Modernity', in J. G. Gabbert (ed.), *American Foreign Policy and Revolutionary Change* (Washington State University Press, 1968).

Cropsey, Joseph, *Political Philosophy and the Issues of Politics* (Chicago, Ill.: University of Chicago Press, 1977).

Cropsey, Joseph (ed.), *Ancients and Moderns: Essays on the Tradition of Political Philosophy in Honor of Leo Strauss* (New York: Basic Books, 1964).

Dannhauser, Werner J., *Nietzsche's View of Socrates* (Ithaca, N.Y., and London: Cornell University Press, 1974).

Himilfarb, Milton, *The Jews of Modernity* (New York: Basic Books, 1973). Believes Strauss to be the greatest influence on the neo-conservatives.

Jaffa, Harry V., *Crisis of the House Divided: An Interpretation of the Issues in the Lincoln–Douglas Debates* (Chicago, Ill.: University of Chicago Press, 1959, 1982).

Jaffa, Harry V., *Thomism and Aristotelianism* (Westport, Conn.: Greenwood Press, 1952).

Kendall, Wilmoore, review of Cropsey (ed.), *Ancients and Moderns*, above. Believes that the diversity of topics and treatments in the collection undermines the idea that there is such a thing as a Straussian 'teaching' or 'position' about political things.

Kesler, Charles, 'Is Conservatism Un-American?', *National Review*. vol. 38, no. 5 (22 March 1985) pp. 28–37. Regards conservatives influenced by Leo Strauss to be anti-American because they are anti-modern (America and modernity being coeval with one another).

Maimonides, *Ethical Writings*, trans. Raymond L. Weiss with Charles E. Butterworth (New York: New York University Press, 1975). Maimonides describes how a 'disciple of wise men' should dress: becoming and clean, no stains or fatty spots or the like on his garments (p. 44). He should not wear 'exceeding light linen garments that they make in Egypt, nor shall his garments drag on the earth, as do the garments of the arrogant' (p. 45). He shall not 'go perfumed to the market place', and shall not go out alone at night. He should dress according to his means, but treat his wife better than his means. All these rules are meant to 'avoid suspicion' (p. 45).

Mansfield, Harvey C. Jr, *The Spirit of Liberalism* (Cambridge, Mass., and London: Harvard University Press, 1978).

Neumann, Harry, 'Plato's *Republic*: Utopia or Dystopia?', *The Modern Schoolman*, vol. 44 (1967) pp. 319–30.

Neumann, Harry, 'On the Platonism of More's *Utopia*', *Social Research*, vol. 33 (1966) pp. 495–512.

Pangle, Thomas L., 'Interpretive Essay', in his translation of *The Laws of Plato* (New York: Basic Books, 1980).

Pangle, Thomas L., 'The Roots of Contemporary Nihilism and its Political Consequences According to Nietzsche', *Review of Politics*, vol. 45, no. 1 (January 1983) pp. 45–70.

Pangle, Thomas L., 'Patriotism American Style', *National Review*, 29 November 1985. See also Harry V. Jaffa, 'Our Ancient Faith', a reply to Pangle in the same issue.

Scholem, Gershom G., *On the Kabbalah and Its Symbolism*, trans. Ralph Manhe (London: Routledge & Kegan Paul, 1965).

Scholem, Gershom G., *Jewish Gnosticism, Merkabah Mysticism, and Talmudic Tradition* (New York: The Jewish Theological Seminary of America, 1965)

Silver, Thomas B., and Schramm, Peter W. (eds), *Natural Right and Political Right: Essays in Honor of Harry V. Jaffa* (Durham, N.C.: Carolina Academic Press, 1984).

Storing, Herbert J., *What the Federalists Were For* (Chicago, Ill.: University of Chicago Press, 1981).

Storing, Herbert J. (ed.), *Essays on the Scientific Study of Politics* (New York and London: Holt, Rinehart & Winston, 1962).

Tarcov, Nathan, *Locke's Education for Liberty* (Chicago, Ill.: University of Chicago Press, 1984).

West, Thomas G., *Plato and Aristophanes: Four Texts on Socrates*, trans. T. G. West and G. S. West, with introduction by T. G. West (Ithaca, N.Y., and London: Cornell University Press, 1984).

West, Thomas G., *Plato's 'Apology of Socrates'* (Ithaca, N.Y.: Cornell University Press, 1979).

Index